# Restoring Nature

## Other Books of Interest from St. Augustine's Press

Maurice Ashley Agbaw-Ebai, *Light of Reason, Light of Faith:
Joseph Ratzinger and the German Enlightenment*

Fulvio Di Blasi, *God and the Natural Law:
A Rereading of Thomas Aquinas*

Fulvio Di Blasi, *From Aristotle to Thomas Aquinas:
Natural Law, Practical Knowledge, and the Person*

Christopher Kaczor, *The Gospel of Happiness:
How Secular Psychology Points to the Wisdom of Christian Practice*

Peter Kreeft, *A Socratic Introduction to Plato's Republic*

Gabriele Kuby, *The Abandoned Generation*

Peter Kreeft, *The Platonic Tradition*

Peter Kreeft, *The Philosophy of Jesus*

Marvin R. O'Connell, *Telling Stories that Matter: Memoirs and Essays*

Richard Peddicord, O.P., *The Sacred Monster of Thomism*

Josef Pieper, *Exercises in the Elements: Essays–Speeches–Notes*

Daniel J. Mahoney, *Recovering Politics, Civilization, and the Soul:
Essays on Pierre Manent and Roger Scruton*

Pierre Manent, *The Religion of Humanity: The Illusion of Our Times*

Joseph Bottum, *Spending the Winter*

Gene Fendt, *Camus' Plague: Myth for Our World*

Roger Scruton, *An Intelligent Person's Guide to Modern Culture*

Kenneth Weisbrode, *Real Influencers:
Fourteen Disappearing Acts that Left Fingerprints on History*

Anne Drury Hall, *Where the Muses Still Haunt: The Second Reading*

Allen Mendenhall, *Shouting Softly:
Lines on Law, Literature, and Culture*

Chilton Williamson, *The End of Liberalism*

Marion Montgomery, *With Walker Percy at the Tupperware Party*

# Restoring Nature
## Essays in Thomistic Philosophy and Theology

EDITED BY MICHAEL M. WADDELL

ST. AUGUSTINE'S PRESS
South Bend, Indiana

Copyright © 2023 by Michael M. Waddell

All rights reserved. No part of this book may be reproduced, stored in a retrieval system, or transmitted, in any form or by any means, electronic, mechanical, photocopying, recording, or otherwise, without the prior permission of
St. Augustine's Press.

Manufactured in the United States of America.

1 2 3 4 5 6  28 27 26 25 24 23

**Library of Congress Control Number: 2022951398**

Paperback ISBN: 978-1-58731-726-2

∞ The paper used in this publication meets the minimum requirements of the American National Standard for Information Sciences – Permanence of Paper for Printed Materials, ANSI Z39.48-1984.

St. Augustine's Press
www.staugustine.net

# Table of Contents

Editor's Introduction
Michael M. Waddell ........................................................................ 1

Foreword: A Once and Future Thomism
Ralph McInerny ............................................................................. 3

Art Perfects Nature
Benedict M. Ashley, O.P. ............................................................. 13

Prime Matter
A Thomistic Reply to Some Criticisms
Steven Baldner ............................................................................. 30

Philosophical Anthropology Facing Aquinas'
Concept of Human Nature
Angelo Campodonico ................................................................... 44

Creation and Evolution
William E. Carroll ........................................................................ 84

Nature as a Metaphysical Object
Lawrence Dewan, O.P. ............................................................... 120

What Nature? Whose Nature?
Reflecting on Some Recent Arguments in Natural Law Ethics
Fulvio Di Blasi ........................................................................... 158

Maritain on the Limits of the Empiriometric
Jude P. Dougherty ...................................................................... 194

Nature as the Basis of Moral Actions
Leo J. Elders, S.V.D. ........................................................................ 206

Human Nature, Poetic Narrative, and Moral Agency
Robert A. Gahl, Jr. ........................................................................... 239

The Order of Providence and the Sacrament of Order,
Paralleled in St. Thomas Aquinas
Anne Barbeau Gardiner .................................................................. 266

Nature as *Determinatio ad Unum*
The Case of Natural Virtue
Marie George ................................................................................... 283

Disclaimers in Aquinas's
*Commentary on the Nicomachean Ethics*?
A Reconsideration
Christopher Kaczor ......................................................................... 311

*Dignitatis Humanae*, Rights and Religious Liberty
Steven A. Long ................................................................................ 336

Is Usury a Sin against Nature?
Christopher Martin .......................................................................... 354

Distinguer pour Unir
Putnam vs. Aquinas on the Unity of Nature
John O'Callaghan ............................................................................ 369

Aquinas
Nature, Life and Teleology
Vittorio Possenti .............................................................................. 399

The Primary End of Marriage
Anthony Rizzi .................................................................................. 427

From Nature to God
The Physical Character of Saint Thomas Aquinas' First Way
Mario Enrique Sacchi ..................................................................... 438

Natural Theology in St. Thomas's Early Doctrine of Truth
Michael M. Waddell ....................................................................... 450

Intellectus Agens
Why Does Thomas Trust De Anima III.5?
Héctor Zagal .................................................................................. 475

## Editor's Introduction
### Michael M. Waddell

Once a cornerstone of magnificent philosophical and theological edifices, the concept of nature has been largely abandoned by modern thinkers. In these essays, a distinguished international group of philosophers and theologians seeks to reclaim nature—both by suggesting new ways in which the concept can help us to reflect on difficult questions and by reconsidering ways in which we have really been using it all along.

The volume contains extensive treatment of nature's much disputed role in ethics, as well as its importance for the philosophy of science, philosophical anthropology, metaphysics, the philosophy of art, theology and other areas. It had once occurred to me to organize the essays according to these various disciplines. However, many of the essays (like the concept of nature itself) run through multiple areas of reflection, and so they would have been devilishly difficult to classify. Since the reader will undoubtedly want to devour them all—from Ashley to Zagal—there seemed to be no need to force the essays into a Procrustean classificatory scheme.

One of the ironies of editing a volume on nature with submissions from an international group of authors is that one is immediately confronted with the fact that language and the canons of scholarly writing are largely conventional. Wishing to acknowledge legitimate differences of custom—and not wanting to delay publication of the volume—I have opted not to impose a monolithic style on the essays. Thus, the reader will find that different authors have employed different styles of citation, different abbreviations for titles of works, different manners of punctuation, and so forth. Indeed, the sensitive reader will occasionally notice

English prose being crafted with the lilt of an Italian, Spanish or Dutch mother tongue. So much the better to remind us of the universality of our project.

Before closing, it is my pleasure to thank several people who made the publication of this volume possible. Ralph McInerny conceived and was the driving force behind the University of Notre Dame's Thomistic Institutes (not to mention myriad other good works). The essays contained in this collection comprise the record of the last of those Institutes, which was held in the summer of 2001. This gathering was funded through the generosity of the Saint Gerard Foundation, the George Strake Foundation, and the Raih Family. Of course, there would be no published record of the Institutes but for the help of Bruce Fingerhut and St. Augustine's Press. Finally, Hans Arneson, Lenora Heckel, and Megan Johnson provided able editorial assistance for me in preparing the volume. I am deeply grateful to them all.

# Foreword: A Once and Future Thomism
## Ralph McInerny
## University of Notre Dame

At my age, one has two options. Knowingly to repeat oneself, or to do so unknowingly. In any case, repetition is if not the *mater studiorum*, the *mater somnii*. Tonight, my welcoming remarks will consciously echo things I have said before as our meetings begin. Doubtless, this is less inappropriate because this institute is a swan song so far as the Maritain Center's sponsorship is concerned. Perhaps the institute, or something like it, will be taken up by others elsewhere. Even if this is not done, it would not now be a tragedy, for reasons I shall develop.

## A Thomistic Renaissance?

Is a renaissance of Thomism already under way? Some years ago, when these Notre Dame summer institutes began, it is was with the hope that by bringing together senior, mature and young Catholic philosophers, the attractions of the thought of Thomas Aquinas would be clear and also show that there is a variety of ways in which one can carry on what Thomas began.

These meetings were already a tradition when *Fides et Ratio* appeared. This magnificent encyclical both provided an historical perspective on a perennial topic for Christian philosophers and reiterated the Church's judgment that in matters philosophical and theological, we can find no better master than Thomas Aquinas. The encyclical has galvanized philosophers and theologians. Now, in the new millennium, a *tour de monde* reveals many initiatives taking place around the globe that permit one to ask the question with which I began.

## Is a Renaissance of Thomism Already under Way?

The Pontifical Academy of Saint Thomas Aquinas has recently been reorganized and several meetings have been held which brought together Thomists from around the world. *Doctor Communis*, the Academy's publication, has taken on a new look.

The Dominicans at Fribourg have committed themselves to regaining the position of preeminence that was historically theirs. Our own Father Michael Sherwin, after a year teaching at Berkeley, will go to Fribourg as Professor of Moral Theology, successor to Father Pinckaers, who has graced this institute with his presence.

Father Fergus Kerr of Blackfriars, Oxford, is doing various things to increase the presences of Thomism at Oxford. Our own William Carroll will be teaching at Oxford over a three-year period. Lectures and conferences will continue.

In Germany, *Doctor Angelicus, An International Thomistic Jahrbuch*, is about to be launched by Rudolf Michael Schmitz and David Berger. Berger's recent book *Thomismus* has been described as Thomism of the strict observance.

In France, the *Revue thomiste* continues its tradition.

In the United States, *The Thomist* is once more what its title suggests, the premier locus for Thomistic philosophy and theology.

In Houston, at the University of St. Thomas, the Center for Thomistic Studies is getting a new lease on life.

In Buenos Aires, under the editorship of our own Mario Enrique Sacchi, *Sapienza* has become a polylingual leader in Thomistic studies.

The Roman Athenaeum, the Opus Dei university in Rome, which received status as a pontifical university while its rector was attending this conference, flourishes.

The Gregorianum has Kevin Flannery as dean of philosophy.

There are Hector Zagal and his associates at Universidad Panamericana in Mexico City.

Alejandro Llano of Pamplona was prevented from attending this year because of successful heart surgery a few weeks ago.

*Foreword: A Once and Future Thomism*

And at St. Andrews, the redoubtable John Haldane is a rallying point for those he calls Analytic Thomists.

One could go on. These are but a few straws in the wind. Participants from various countries could add to them. I cite these as signs of the times.

## A Twofold Task

It is not fanciful to say that Thomism has been in diaspora for a third of a century. From the time of *Aeterni Patris* until the opening of Vatican II, the wishes of Leo XIII for Christian Philosophy were realized in various ways. Journals, societies, and institutions were founded to implement the role that Thomas Aquinas was meant to have in the instruction of young Catholics, lay and clerical. The Thomistic Revival involved two efforts, ideally complementary, but possibly in conflict. Etienne Gilson, in a letter to Father Armand Mauer, written after the death of Jacques Maritain, said that he had at last become clear on the difference between Maritain and himself.

> The last book of Maritain is of decisive importance for a correct understanding of his thought. Its reading made me realize that I had never understood his true position. I was naïvely maintaining that one cannot consider oneself a Thomist without first ascertaining the authentic meaning of St. Thomas' doctrine, which only history can do; during all that time, he was considering himself a true disciple of St. Thomas because he was continuing his thought. To strive to rediscover the meaning of the doctrine as it has been in the mind of Thomas Aquinas was straight historicism. We have been talking at cross-purposes all the time.[1]

1  Étienne Gilson and Jacques Maritain, *Deux approches de l' être: Correspondance 1923-1971*. Ed. Gery Prouvost. Paris: Vrin, 1991. 275.

}5{

RESTORING NATURE

The aged Gilson was not content with stating this difference between himself and his old friend. He goes on to say of Maritain that "on all the points on which he prides himself on improving, completing Thomas Aquinas, my own feeling is that he is distorting the true thought of the Angelic Doctor."

Well, it has been said that wherever there are two Thomists gathered together, there are three opinions. Indeed, one was sometimes tempted to apply Johnson's dictum about the Irish to the followers of Thomas Aquinas: "They are an honest race. They never speak well of one another." I mention this not to rehearse the quarrels of the past, certainly not to endorse Gilson's judgment on Maritain, but to call attention to two indissoluble aspects of philosophizing and thus of philosophizing *ad mentem divi Thomae.*

A version of the opposition Gilson mentions often shows up in philosophy departments in the ancient quarrel about historical and doctrinal dissertations. There are imaginable colleagues for whom any prolonged attention to the historical setting of a text is regarded as a culpable departure from serious philosophizing. Such people are likely to lodge themselves in contemporary issues where, it is imagined, the historical has not yet had time to rear its head. But the proximate past can sometimes pose severer historical problems than the remote past, as witness the shelves that groan under books that give conflicting accounts of what Heidegger or Wittgenstein really meant. The only way to avoid the historical dimension of philosophizing is to adopt solipsism. But of course any attempt to define solipsism would immediately draw one into the great community of language and the history embedded in it. It has been said that the poet does not invent poetry, he adds to the sum total of poetry. What poetry is is a presupposition of his work. A sonnet, an epic, a triolet—these are forms he finds and does not invent. Of course, he may work variations on them. He may invent the Clerihew or the Pentalope. But always he will be guided by the poetry that preceded him. T. S. Eliot discusses this in "Tradition and the Individual Talent" and what he has to say applies, *mutatis mutandis,* to initiation into philosophy.

}6{

*Foreword: A Once and Future Thomism*

Doubtless, when it is a question of a Plato or Aristotle, an Anselm or an Aquinas, the accessibility of the past poses peculiar problems. Greek is a prerequisite in the one case, Latin in the other, and these languages are not in every way identical as found in Plato or Aristotle, in Anselm or Aquinas. The transmission of texts, the establishment of critical editions, the reconstruction of the historical setting in which the work was produced, its sources and influences—such efforts exfoliate luxuriantly from the original interest. So it was that classical philology and medieval studies came into being.

Given Gilson's scholarly work, given his role in the founding of the *Archives d'histoire doctrinale et littéraire du moyen âge*, given his role as the founder of the Pontifical Institute of Mediaeval Studies in Toronto, the great seedbed of medieval studies on this continent, it is not surprising that his emphasis falls where it does: "To rediscover the meaning of the doctrine as it has been in the mind of Thomas Aquinas." *Le thomisme*, in its many editions, and his works on Augustine, Scotus, and Bonaventure likewise exemplify this Gilsonian effort to enter into the mind of a medieval author. It annoys him that Maritain should regard the result of this as "pure historicism." But surely, when all is said and done, the most accurate statement of what a past thinker truly thought is an historical not a philosophical truth.

Gilson is not wholly fair to himself in this comparison with Maritain. No student of his works will have any difficulty discerning the apodictic voice of Gilson asserting what are meant to be philosophical truths. Often, he is as interested as Maritain in prolonging the thought of Thomas, showing its relevance for contemporary discussions, arguing. Significantly, he called his *Being and Some Philosophers* a work in dogmatic philosophy.

The philosophical task, and *a fortiori* the task of the fledgling Thomist, is twofold: to assimilate what has been done, and to continue the task oneself.

Immersion in the text is absolutely essential, the *sine qua non*. But the text got to us in ways we should understand: it was produced in an historical setting, knowledge of which is needed to grasp the meaning of the text, perhaps even the question it addresses.

There is of course room for, if not a division of labor, at least a division of emphasis, among Thomists. I should say that Gilson and Maritain differed more by the emphasis the former put on the historical and the latter put on the continuation of the philosophical task. My suggestion is that any and all philosophical work involves in various degrees and mixes both these elements. As the task of studying Thomas is taken up anew and pushed forward into this third millennium, there is no question of repeating the past or reviving its problematics.

## The Thomistic Revival Interrupted

As I have suggested, the revival of Thomism, begun by Leo XIII in 1879, after having gone through a number if distinct phases, seemed to come to an ignominious halt with Vatican II. This is simply historical fact and says nothing about the intent and content of conciliar documents. Call it a product of that false spirit of the Council; it is nonetheless true that many people appealed to the council as authority for jettisoning Thomas.

I am suggesting accordingly that the past third of a century has been more or less an interlude. *Fides et Ratio* can fairly be taken to be a charter to a revival of the Thomistic Revival—with any number of implicit warnings of dangers to be avoided.

Those who rejected Thomism in the post-conciliar period painted a dark picture of the Thomistic Revival, and that dark picture is often accepted as good money by those currently pursuing an interest in Thomas Aquinas. Horror stories have become set pieces of the retrospects of now aging rebels whose intellectual inventiveness was allegedly thwarted by handbooks and scholasticism and syllogisms.

One of the tasks that lies ahead, when those of us who were involved in it, if only as spear carriers, are no more, will be to acquire an accurate understanding of what the Thomistic Revival actually was. The letter of Gilson's I have quoted earlier indicates

*Foreword: A Once and Future Thomism*

how undisputed leaders of the revival had difficulty locating its nature. Among the ambitions, imperfectly realized, of the Jacques Maritain Center is to gather the materials that will be necessary for the history of the Thomistic Revival. We have invaluable Maritain papers and letters, but of course nothing that can compare with those to be found in Kolbsheim. We have the papers of Yves Simon. We have the papers of Charles DeKoninck (for the most part photocopies of the holdings of Laval University). A month ago, the sister of Joe Evans, my predecessor as director of the Maritain Center, gave us the letters Joe received from Maritain over a long stretch of years. These are particularly valuable for the history of the founding of the Center, as well as for the English translation of Maritain's works. Of course, there are archives in various places throughout the world that must play a role in that historical reconstruction.

## How Dead Was Thomism during the Last Third of a Century?

The 700th anniversary of the death of Saint Thomas was the occasion of many meetings, conferences and symposia, whose printed proceedings contain invaluable materials for the history of the revival. So too the centenary of the appearance of *Aeterni Patris* elicited similar reflections in meetings held around the world. These 1974 and 1979 commemorations make it clear that, while Thomism was to a great degree eclipsed, the eclipse was far from total. It was during those lean years that some of us were fated to live our scholarly lives, preserving some few fragments against our ruin, which may have interest now in what lies ahead. The *Bulletin thomiste* became the *Rassegna* and is now apparently in some limbo, or let us hope, purgatory. This record of what was done during the lean years suggests that Thomism can lay claim to Horace's remark *non omnis moriar*. During this post-conciliar period something notable happened to the study of Thomas, perhaps largely in English speaking countries. All but abandoned by Catholic institutions, Thomas was released into the public domain and, often under the aegis of medieval studies (a growth

}9{

industry during these years), Thomas Aquinas became the preferred object of study on secular campuses and by non-Catholic scholars. As the preface to the *Cambrdige History of Late Medieval Philosophy* shows, such scholars initially expressed contempt for the Catholic scholars who had preceded them; it was as if Thomas was to be rescued from the hands of the inept. That saucy attitude no longer lingers, and the achievements of what it would be unkind to call Protestant Poachers represent a spur and inspiration for future Thomistic study.

## Thomism is Not a Kind of Philosophy

It is my view, as I said last year in my opening remarks, that Thomism is not a *kind* of philosophy. If this is true, the choice of Thomas Aquinas as a mentor should not be compared with following Hegel or Plato or Husserl or Wittgenstein. Particularly in modern times, philosophies have been presented as unlike anything that has gone before and preferable to other possible approaches. Hence, the familiar locutions, "From a Kantian perspective . . . "; "Phenomenologically speaking . . . "; "After the linguistic turn . . . "; etc., etc. It seems almost like joining a club or, in happier cases, getting married, where one undertakes to eschew all others and cleave to one's spouse. Is Thomas presented to us by the Church as simply one among many possible masters?

Readers of *Aeterni Patris* are often surprised to find that Thomas is not even mentioned until the encyclical is half finished, and when he is, he is not mentioned exclusively, but as the strongest interest of a tradition that includes an army of others. This can be understood either as the claim that all Christian thinkers were lisping Thomists or that there is a pluralism within Christian philosophy. I will return to that.

It is the pluralism in the wider sense that must first be addressed. Is Thomism one kind of philosophy to be compared with other kinds and to be preferred by intrinsic reasons or for reasons of religious belief? The appeal by *Fides et Ratio* to the notion of an implicit philosophy, known by all, casts welcome light on this

*Foreword: A Once and Future Thomism*

point. Not only are there certain fundamental questions that every person sooner or later asks, there are answers to those questions which form a kind of patrimony of the race. In n. 4 of *Fides et Ratio*, the Holy Father provides a sketch of what he means by implicit philosophy. It is clearly composed of the principle or starting points of theoretical and practical thinking. Moreover, implicit philosophy is put forward as a means of appraising various philosophical systems. I take this to mean that some systems have been put forward that collide with implicit philosophy, and that this is *eo ipso* a negative appraisal of them. On this basis, Thomas takes pride of place precisely because his thought presumes and takes off from the contents of implicit philosophy. Only philosophizing that does so deserves the name philosophy. Thus, implicit philosophy is at once commodious and judgmental, excluding certain systems as fundamentally wrong-headed. But surely there can be philosophical variety among positions which nonetheless begin with and do not reject implicit philosophy. If one can thus argue that Thomism is not a kind of philosophy, then it is clear that any revival of Thomism should not be taken to be the adoption of a partisan or party stance. If Thomism is just a name for doing philosophy well, the Thomist is in principle interested in anything and everything—even in systems that receive a negative judgment with respect to their relation to implicit philosophy. No philosopher is wholly lacking in contributions to the quest for truth. Eclecticism? Far from it. One can learn from a philosopher even while rejecting the terms on which a given tenet was put forth. The human mind is made for truth. That, and the blessings of inconsistency, make any philosopher a possible source of philosophical truth.

## This Year's Institute

The first several times these summer institutes convened, there was no overriding theme. Participants were asked to speak on topics dictated by their present interests. The idea behind this was to make clear the variety of interests and approaches of those whose work is done under the inspiration of Thomas Aquinas. This seminar has always avoided being prescriptive, as if it aspired to define and direct the efforts of participants. If it is the case, as I think it is, that no one can foresee what the Thomism of the future will be like, it would be silly to seek to shape it. These institutes have hoped to encourage awareness of what others are doing and to provide an occasion for young persons to commingle with older. There is a kind of analogy with graduate studies. During those years, a student listens to a variety of professors and is however unconsciously developing an idea of what he himself hopes to be, an idea arrived at as much by the *via negationis* as the *via affirmationis* so far as the models before him go, for what can they contribute to the *via emenentiae* the tyro intends to trod? All the more so, these institutes were not meant to be occasions for the older scholar to tell the younger how to do it. In recent years, a theme has been chosen for our meetings: we had two institutes devoted to science and philosophy. We had an institute devoted to *Fides et Ratio*. The Proceedings of several institutes are or soon will be in print. It is my intention to publish this year's proceedings as well, and Michael Waddell has agreed to act as editor of that project.

# Art Perfects Nature
## Benedict M. Ashley, O.P.
## Aquinas Institute of Theology (Missouri)

### Creativity

Since the Enlightenment modern culture has been obsessed with the notion of "progress" and "novelty." The "new" is always also the "improved." "Evolutionary progress" is assumed to dominate world history. This attitude contrasts to ancient, medieval, and even Renaissance thought that generally assumed that conformity to antiquity and tradition were the best guarantees of the truth and quality of human productions. The scholars of those times quoted previous authors as authorities, while modern scholarship quotes them only to prove that the scholar has explored the past, found it wanting, and is ready now to improve on it.[1]

Hence for moderns "creativity" is exalted as the supreme value. In the process philosophy of Alfred North Whitehead "Creativity" is the first principle, superior even to that supreme actual occasion that is Whitehead's God.[2] Hence creation is not proper to God but is found in every quantum of reality. Only with the coming of so-called "post-modernity" has this infatuation with creativity come into question. For deconstructionists the interpretation of reality is without foundational principles but is an endless circular process of intertextuality, so that it becomes difficult

---

1    On the causes of this, see my *Theologies of the Body: Humanist and Christian*, 2n ed. (Boston: National Catholic Bioethics Center, 1996), pp. 51–100.

2    *Process and Reality* (New York: MacMillan/ Free Press, 1969, originally 1929), pp.25–26, pp. 36–39.

if at all possible to say that a thinker or artist is "original" since their productions are a mixture of sources that are always themselves such mixtures, etc., etc.[3]

A characteristic note of the thought of Aquinas is his opposition to the Neo-Platonic notion that creation is a power in which creatures participate. For him only God can create, because creation is to produce being *ex nihilo* and this is impossible for the power of any creature since creatures are by definition finite. This thesis does not deny, however, that God shares his power with his creatures. Indeed it is characteristic of Aquinas' understanding of God that God always does through secondary causes whatever is possible for them. In that sense the modern usage of the term "creativity" of creatures can be justified but it is, it seems to me, misleading.

## Nature

What place then does the "new" have in Aquinas' worldview? In Aristotle's astronomy change is perpetual but absolutely cyclical; yet it does not conform to the Neo-Platonic "myth of the Eternal Return" that Nietzche adopted, since, while the cycle repeats specifically, it does not repeat individuals.[4] Aquinas accepted this astronomy but only as an hypothesis that was excluded by the revealed doctrine of the origin of the universe at a finite time in the past. Yet for Aristotle more fundamental than the hypothesis of the eternity of the world was the truth that the sensible world exists only in change as *ens mobile*, becoming being. Thus, even if its existence is perpetual, it must also be teleological. The definition

3    For introduction to the leader of this philosophical movement, Jacques Derrida, see Christopher Norris, *Derrida* (Cambridge, MA: Harvard University Press, 1987), p.236.

4    The notion of any "eternal return" goes back at least to the Greek Neo-Platonist commentator on Aristotle, Simplicius. Since for Aristotle and Aquinas the principle of individuation is matter related to a quantity, the cycles of material change can never exactly repeated themselves.

of nature is "the principle of change and stability."[5] Thus the sensible, changeable, material world has a stability that is not absolute but is achieved through change. This stability, moreover, is only relative, since it is always subject to further change. Even Aristotle's hypothetically perpetual celestial bodies move teleologically in that their stability is a stability as movers that again and again return to the same point. Thus natural change results from natures that predetermine the result of change, and it is this that Aristotle understands as teleology in its most general sense. The universe is a stable system because the changes in it generally have a law-like character, that is, they are uniform and regular. *Natura est determinatum ad unum.*[6]

## Chance

Modern science, although it seems to reject "teleology," agrees that there are natural laws that are its primary business to discover. It rejects teleology only because it thinks that it implies purpose in nature, not simply law-like regularity; but this was not either Aristotle or Aquinas' understanding of teleology, since for them purposeful action is only one kind of teleological behavior, although the most evident.[7] It is remarkable, however, that in the advance

5   *S.Th.*, I, q. 29, a. 1, ad 4, quoting Aristotle, *Physics*, II, lect. 1, n.295. This definition is often cited as "the intrinsic principle of motion and rest," but this is as regards the simplest form of change. Since natural change is teleological, the goal of all change is stability, that is, relatively permanent existence.

6   *S. Th.*, I, q. 41, 2 c.

7   For Aristotle the final cause (*telos*) as such implies no "purpose" intrinsic to change, nor does it imply a vitalistic type of efficient cause, but only that an efficient cause is pre-determined to produce a regular stable effect. This, of course, is presupposed to the very notion of "natural law" in physics. Thus, to say that gravity tends to cause massive bodies uniformly to move toward each other according to definite natural law is to speak of their "teleology" in Aristotle's sense. See my articles in *The New Catholic Encyclopedia* on "Final Causality" (5:162–166) and "Teleology" (13:979–981).

of modern science explanations that are simply in terms of natural law are being more and more superseded. The modern theory of biological evolution is not in terms of a "law of evolution" leading to a uniform and therefore predictable result, as was the now outmoded conception of Teilhard de Chardin. It is primarily an historical theory that uses natural laws to understand a past scenario without making any claim to predict, except in a very general manner, in what direction this history will continue. At each point of the history of biological evolution the direction it took was only conditioned by natural laws but was ultimately determined by the chance interference of natural forces with each other.[8]

This predominance of historical chance over law determined nature—evident in modern biological evolution theories—has now spread to the whole cosmos with quantum theory. Quantum theory provides natural laws always but only probabilistic ones. This probabilism is not merely a matter of our ignorance but of the very nature of material things. Far from this discovery raising a difficulty for an Aristotelian view of material things, this follows necessarily from Aristotle's and Aquinas' view of sub-lunar matter—the only kind that we know actually exists.[9] For nineteenth century science "nature" was the substance they called matter, and natural laws were its properties that required it to behave in a mechanistically determined manner. But for Aristotle and Aquinas matter is only the potency of material things for change

---

8   Teilhard de Chardin accepted Henri Bergson's notion that evolution proceeds inevitably toward greater and more unified complexity, and calls this the "Omega Point." But as is evident from the debate between Richard Dawkins, *The Blind Watchmaker* (London: W. W. W. Norton 1985), and Michael J. Behe, *Darwin's Black Box* (New York: Free Press, 1996), Teilhard's concept of scientific evolution is obsolete.

9   Aristotle, followed by Aquinas, posited an essentially different type of matter for the celestial spheres that was subject only to change with respect to position but not with respect to the other categories that are the necessary properties of the bodies within the sphere of the moon.

*Art Perfects Nature*

and as such can never be wholly actualized by form; hence, at least for terrestrial matter, chance interference of one natural efficient cause with another is always possible, and natural laws hold only *in pluribus.*[10]

The Aristotelian celestial spheres, although they were free from friction, continued in motion only by the efficient activity of disembodied spirits. With the elimination of that hypothesis by Galileo's telescopic observation of the sunspots, science holds that the whole universe is subject to chance, and quantum theory locates this ultimately in every particle of material bodies. This entails the second law of thermodynamics, which states that in finite time the universe will arrive at an entropic equilibrium in which nothing but "quantum fluctuations" are possible. While, as Aquinas maintained, reason can never demonstrate that the time of the universe is finite,[11] current science does not see any way out of this ultimate entropic doom for the cosmos, even if there are a cycle of Big Crunches as well as Big Bangs. Thus quantum theory, even if it becomes a Grand Unified Theory or "Theory of Everything," will explain the history of the universe only in a very general manner.[12] Currently it is used to argue that the

---

10  *S.Th.,* I, q. 103.

11  *In Phys.,* VIII, lect. 2, nn. 2041–2058.

12  See Steven Weinberg, *Dreams of a Final Theory* (New York: Pantheon Books, 1992). He says, however, that "I do not mean to suggest that the final theory will be deduced from pure mathematics . . . . It seems to me that our best hope is to identify the final theory as one that is so rigid that it cannot be warped into some slightly different theory without introducing logical absurdities like infinite energies . . . . A final theory will be final in only one sense—it will bring to an end a certain sort of science, the ancient search for those principles that cannot be explained in terms of deeper principles" (pp. 17–18). An Aristotelian might say that we have such a final theory, namely, the four causes that are the principles of all material changes. These of course are utterly generic principles subject to specification, but that we will ever understand their specifications completely is doubtful. See also David Lindley, *The End of Physics: The Myth of a Unified Theory* (New York: Basic Books, 1993).

}17{

temperature of the universe after the Big Bang declined in a certain manner and some kind of aggregation of massive matter was inevitable, but this leaves many different possibilities and by no means predicts the inevitable emergence of life, let alone of intelligent life. The second law of thermodynamics permits the rise of complexity in small regions of the universe, but these will eventually disintegrate. The rate of entropic increase, however, is not definitely determined so there is no way to predict when ultimate cosmic equilibrium will take place.

## Freedom

Yet, although unpredictable by natural law, intelligent life—and with it free causality—has emerged in our universe. Some argue that there may be an infinite number of possible worlds, and that we intelligent, free beings exist in this world but not in others that have been or will be or exist now independent of this world. But this is to talk about what we do not and cannot know. For to talk about other worlds as "possible" is to talk about a free First Cause who makes them possible, and we could not know that God is free unless by analogy from our knowledge that we ourselves are free. Of course many have also argued that if we are free then there can be no God, since if there were a First Cause, it would take away our freedom. Aquinas, however, shows that since God's causality is only analogous to our causality, there is no contradiction in maintaining that God is the cause of our free actions, indeed of their very freedom. The divine causality is only analogous to our mode of causality and hence need not be coercive.[13] Thus we come to the conclusion that there are three modes of causality, nature, chance, and freedom.[14]

It is at the level of free causality that the teleology or predetermination of natural law and its negation by chance becomes purposeful. Intelligent beings can perceive the relation between

13  *S. Th.*, I-II, q. 10, a. 4.
14  *S. Th.*, I, q. 19, a. 6.

*Art Perfects Nature*

means and ends and hence can act purposefully. Aquinas, however, shows that this practical judgment of what means will serve to achieve a given end is generally not determinate. An end can be achieved by several alternative means, for each of which there are pro and con arguments, advantages and disadvantages, so that we are ultimately left free to choose among these alternatives.[15] Thus choice is not absolutely determined by knowledge, as Plato supposed, but by free will.[16] Hence, we require virtues that incline our wills to avoid wrong choices and to prefer good choices that conform best to our individual personalities and life situations. Thus "creativity" does enter into good human living.

## Prudence and Art

Aristotle and Aquinas distinguish between the theoretical sciences, whose conclusions are determined ultimately by the natures of things—and hence are essentially determinate—and the practical sciences, whose conclusions involve an element of freedom. The practical sciences are determined by the free choice of alternative means to given ends. Since some ends are fixed in human nature, this implies that some practical sciences are teleologically absolute, and free only with regard to the choice of means. This is the case with the ethical sciences, since human nature determines the needs that we must satisfy to attain happiness, and happiness itself is determined by our nature. On the contrary, some ends are a matter of free choice as possible instruments that we can intelligently produce for satisfying human needs in a better way than is possible simply by nature, and these pertain to "art" or technology. These arts, of course, should be subordinate to the ethically determined needs that they are designed to produce. Thus to use technology to produce effects that are harmful to human happiness as

15  *S. Th.*, I-II, q. 10, a. 2; II-II, q. 47, a. 15.
16  *S. Th.*, I-II, q. 59, a. 2. Aristotle, *Eth.*, VII, 2, 1145 b 23–1146a9; St. Thomas, *In. Eth.*, VII, lect 2, n. 1313.

}19{

determined by human nature is to abuse technology. Thus human free practical activity, whether it is ethical or technological, must always respect nature, and hence Aquinas' famous philosophical dictum that "art perfects nature." Analogously he also holds that "grace perfects nature" since grace is given to us by God to enable us to transcend the nature given us in creation without violating that lesser, but essential gift. If grace destroyed nature it would not be grace, since a gift that destroyed its recipient would not be a gift but violence.

## Self-Transcendence

Intelligent freedom is the specification of personhood, and its teleology is self-transcendence. First we transcend ourselves by the fact that we seek to know the world around us. "All humans desire to know," said Aristotle, who is, as Dante said, "the Master of Those Who Know." Our knowing is achieved through our senses and our intelligence. Our intelligence is dependent on the senses but connaturally is fitted to understand certain very general things about our material world directly and immediately. Most of what we know, however, must be acquired by reasoning from these connaturally evident first principles. We do not have, as Plato and Descartes thought, any innate ideas. Nor is there good evidence that what we know intellectually is determined by innate categories that constitute *a priori* conditions for knowledge, as Kant claimed.

Because our intellects are properties of a substance that is matter informed by soul, this soul must also be immaterial. Yet, as Aristotle showed,[17] though the human intelligence is finite in

---

17 "Illud quod primo cadit in apprehensione intellectus est ens; unde oportet quod cuicumque apprehenso per intellectum, intellectus attribuat hoc quod est ens" (*De Veritate*, q.21, a 4, ad 4). Thus human intelligence is open to all being although it may not have the power to achieve knowledge of particular beings, and must achieve some forms of knowledge indirectly by arguments from effects to cause.

## Art Perfects Nature

its powers, it is not *per se* limited to *a priori* categories. It is true that it is dependent for specifying information on the senses, and these have subjective limits. Yet even these limits are only negative. For example, we can see only six colors when in reality the spectrum is continuously varied. We do not, however, see any colors that are not in that spectrum. Our senses do not cause positive error.[18]

Moreover Kant's arguments to show that space and time are only the subjective conditions of sensation are inconclusive. Aristotle's whole argument in his *Physics* is to show that these and the other categories of natural science are not subjective but objective realities whose real existence is intellectually demonstrable from the data of sensation, primarily of touch. They are not imposed on phenomena but are inherent in sense phenomena and intelligible as such through the activity of our intelligence in distinguishing what is essential from what is non-essential in our changing world.

Since, however, reasoning from first principles is in a measure a free operation that can result in error, we need an art of logic or good reasoning. Logic is productive in the sense that technology is, and hence is only an "art" analogically since it deals not with real being but with purely mental beings, the relations between concepts. It is also only a theoretical science analogically since it does not deal with real being. Yet it certainly involves free choice, since I can will to make the effort to think logically or can impulsively rationalize with liability to error. Thus genuine "creativity" enters even into speculative thought, although its conclusions must ultimately be determined by the nature of things. Moreover, since our intellectual intuition depends on the adequacy of our observation and the perfection of the perceptual images that we form from observation, creativity is increased by the proper use of our internal senses or "imagination" in the general sense in which that term is used today.

This becomes especially apparent in what Aristotle developed

18  *Contra Gent.*, III, c. 107.

}21{

in his *Topics* as the art of dialectics. We need this logical art to eliminate false hypotheses and to arrive at better hypotheses that will either make possible highly probable theories or in the best cases advance intuition from the level of generic to more specific definitions of natural things. With Galileo this dialectical art made a critical advancement in two ways. First, it extended the Pythagorean discovery, used by the ancients and medievals only in a very limited way, that mathematical models are very useful in the dialectical explorations of natural science. Aquinas recognizes the validity of this *scientia mixta*. The great clarity and certitude of mathematics is thus put to the instrumental service of natural science in its arsenal of dialectical arguments, although its arguments can be strictly demonstrative only of negative conclusions. What is impossible mathematically is impossible physically, but mathematical models only approximate physical reality and different models can all apply. Second, following the example of Galileo's use of the telescope and of the balls rolling on an inclined plane to assist in the elimination of chance in observation, the art of instrumental observation and controlled experimentation became a much more useful dialectical instrument.

These additions to dialectic art, however, have not been without disadvantages. This growing separation between observation by our natural senses and the dialectical concepts intended to enhance it quickly lead modern science to abandon the foundations Aristotle has so carefully laid in his *Physics*. In its place science adopted the mechanism of Democritus that Aristotle had soundly refuted. When at the beginning of the last century Einstein showed the inadequacy of mechanism, new foundations were sought in Kantian apriorism. Today there is again much confused debate over the meaning of the most basic concepts of physics, such as "space," "time," "energy," "matter," "causality." Current physics is marvelously successful in predicting the observable results of its pragmatic use of its extremely artificial experiments, but is unable to give a physical interpretation of the significance of these measurements that is not filled with paradoxes. For example, physicists speak of "empty space" and at

*Art Perfects Nature*

the same time of the photons, gravitons, and neutrinos that fill it to the brim.[19]

Dialectical creativity, moreover, enters into speculative thought not only in the formation of scientific theories, but in a very different, yet analogous way in the fine arts. Aquinas shows that beauty is a relation of fit between the object known and the subjective condition of the knower. "A thing is received according to the condition of the receiver." Thus what is clear, specific, and illuminated to the sense of sight appears beautiful because its unity in diversity is immediately grasped by the eye. This makes possible an intellectual intuition of an object as "beautiful," as mathematicians declare of certain mathematical truths. Our connatural first principles are too vague and unspecific to be very beautiful, although they fit the intelligence; but as these become increasingly specified they become beautiful, and the conclusions of reasoning that specify them are thus also beautiful. There is, therefore, in all the sciences a degree of beauty.

This intellectual beauty is most manifest in the theoretical sciences, where truth can shine in its necessary clarity. Aristotle declares that "all humans desire to know" and that the goal of human life is the contemplation of divine things that are the causes and therefore the explanation of all things. It is in this contemplation that humans transcend themselves through a wisdom that makes them participants in the divine. Plato agreed, although he gave a less satisfactory account of how the weak human intelligence can hope for this wisdom.

The fine arts are arts that in one sense pertain to the practical and can be classified as technological, since they produce an objective work of art that is sensible. Yet their purpose is not ultimately practical but contemplative, since these works are not

---

19 On the paradoxical character of current physics see Lewis Wolpert, *The Unnatural Nature of Science* (Cambridge, MA: Harvard University Press, 1993) and David Lindley, *The End of Physics*, note 12 above.

useful except as objects of contemplation.[20] Surprisingly, therefore, they have a special relation to the art of logic, because it is logic that constructs mental relations between concepts that serve to promote intellectual intuition. Thus the fine arts produce real, sensible objects that serve the imagination in forming more specific concepts that serve contemplation. Thus the modern scientist is in a way a fine artist in making sensible as well as conceptual models that serve theory building. Science fiction has become not only an entertainment, but a way in which the non-scientists can appreciate the results of science and, I suspect, scientists themselves can enliven their theory building imaginations.

## Communication

Intelligent, free human persons transcend themselves not only by coming to know the material universe, but also by coming to understand that the material universe must be the effects of immaterial causes, ultimately of God, the First Immaterial Cause, but also of the human intelligence itself and very likely, or even certainly, of other created spiritual beings. Thus what it is best to know and contemplate are other persons in whom the material universe is included through knowledge. For human beings, at least, the acquiring of knowledge is, as Aristotle says, a social achievement. Each of us would be ignorant indeed without others to teach us and to share their knowledge with us. Moreover, as every teacher knows, we learn best when we teach others. Thus human nature is social and political not only at the level of

20 Aristotle in his *Poetics* and *Rhetoric* carefully distinguishes the aims of these two disciplines. On the history of this see Pierre Conway, O.P., and Benedict Ashley, O.P., *St.Thomas and the Liberal Arts* (Washington, DC: The Thomist Press, 1959). Aristotle indicates the contemplative character when he says, "Poetry is something more philosophic and of graver import than history, since its statements are of the nature rather of universals, whereas those of history are singulars" (*Poetics* c. 9, 1451b 5). Here "philosophical" means not practical but theoretical, contemplative knowledge.

*Art Perfects Nature*

practical life, but at the level of contemplation. While Aquinas rejects the Neo-Platonic view that the good necessarily diffuses itself, he strongly endorses the view that the good tends freely to communicate itself. This becomes the analogue by which best to understand the inner nature of God that is hidden from human reason, namely, that God is a Trinity of Persons. This free sharing of one's happiness is love in its fullest sense that surpasses mere *eros* or desire for one's own good. Thus the ultimate teleology of the intellectual free creature is the glory of God that is, as Von Balthasar has shown, the participation of all creatures in God's self-contemplation as infinite Beauty.

## The Modern Divorce of Art and Prudence from Nature

It would seem, therefore, that the modern obsession with creativity and the new is really an advance over the ancient obsession with the past. Unfortunately it also has a dark side, namely, that it has become a divorce of art and prudence from nature. I will not here enlarge on the neglect of the natural law basis of ethics and therefore of prudence, since that is a much discussed topic. Nor will I take up the question of ecology and environmentalism that concerns our culture's failure to respect the principle that art or technology should perfect nature not pollute or waste it. But I want to say something about the divorce of the fine arts from nature, because this is a much less recognized as a problem.

For Aristotle the fine arts are *mimesis*, the "imitation of nature," a notion that again seems at odds with modernity's insistence on creativity as a remaking of nature in which the natural is overcome.[21]

If we look to the history of art after the rise of Christianity we see that it first breathed a Christian meaning into the art of

21  While commentators on the *Poetics* differ in their explanations of *mimesis*, it is clear from the preceding note that Aristotle understood this as a representation of the essential (universal) nature of a subject and its actions as they manifest this essence.

}25{

paganism that was based on *mimesis*. Then under the combined influences of Jewish iconoclasm and Neo-Platonist dualism it developed the symbolic art of Byzantine icons that respected nature but saw in it only a symbol of the true spiritual world.[22] In the Middle Ages, however, the incarnational principle of grace perfecting nature began to emerge. In the Renaissance this was again combined with technologically advanced representation and the classical models in an idealizing art. With Protestant iconoclasm and the Enlightenment withdrawal from faith genre painting, landscape and other secular subjects came to dominate yet often retained at least a moral symbolism. Finally in the nineteenth century the spiritual meaning of art tended to fade away. It was first replaced by Realism that in a positivistic way simply represented the facts of life without any deeper meaning.[23]

As Realism advanced, it became Impressionism, in which the object evaporated into mere phenomena that, in order to distinguish itself from photography, became more and more subjective. Finally at the beginning of the twentieth century Modern Art appeared, in which representation of the object no longer governed the work of art but rather the subjectivity of the artist in Expressionism and the arbitrary rearrangement of objects in Cubism. This led to Abstract or Non-Objective art and ultimately to simple geometrical areas of color. A similar evolution took place in modernist literature. The dictum of Theodore Gautier that "the arts tend to the musical" is true in the sense that music has a formal beauty that, by its association with the dance and the wordless sounds of the singing voice that accompany the dance, is emotionally expressive.[24]

Thus, modern art criticism attacked representation and often settled for a meaningless formalism. As is evident in the work of

---

22  See Aiden Nichols, O.P., *The Art of God Incarnate: Theology and Image in Christian Tradition* (New York: Paulist Press, 1980), Chapter 5, "The vindication of the Icons," pp. 76–104.
23  See Lind Nochlin, *Realism* (New York: Penguin Books, 1971).
24  See my article, "The Significance of Non-Objective Art," *Proceedings of the American Catholic Philosophical Association*, 1965, 156–165.

*Art Perfects Nature*

perhaps the greatest of modernist painters, Picasso, who never succumbed to pure abstraction, what the modern art work really says is the assertion of the artist's absolute freedom in creativity. Picasso worked in many media and changed his styles many times in order to show that he could do anything he wanted.[25] Thus a limitless freedom and meaningless novelty came to dominate the art of the twentieth century.

In postmodernism this exaltation of novelty has collapsed in styles that are rhetorical rather than artistic in that their intent is to move the audience to political acts or at least to shock their complacency. Aristotle had insisted that the end of fine art is contemplation while persuasion to action pertains to the quite distinct art of rhetoric.[26]

The conclusion of this historical sketch is that fine art must return to its own purpose of contemplating the true as it is rendered beautiful, that is, accessible to our intuition through the senses. As we are learning that an abuse of technology leads to a destruction of the environment, the human body, and hence of the human community and the shared happiness of its members, so the abuse of the fine arts leads to a manipulation of paint and metal whose only meaning is the glorification of the novelty of the artist's imagination or enslavement to political agenda. There must be a return to *mimesis*.

*Mimesis*, or the "imitation of nature" that extends also to the imitation of human free action must not be thought of as simple photography or cinematic recording. It was that kind of "realism" that initiated the modern decline of the arts. What Aristotle intended by the word "imitation" was the perfecting of nature. This

25  See Brigette Leal et al., *The Ultimate Picasso* (New York: Abrams, 2000).

26  For Aristotle the art closing associated with the political is rhetoric, the art of persuasion to action, *Rhetoric* I, c. 1. It is paradoxical that critics attacked Soviet "realism" in art as mere propaganda lacking all artistic merit; yet, now that Communism, once the religion of bohemia, is dead, they praise art for its rhetorical promotion of political causes.

perfecting results from processes similar to the dialectic phase of the sciences, since it seeks to prepare for an intuition of the essential aspects of the world. The painter, for example, seeks to find the form of the object as it distinguishes the object from other objects. Sometimes the artist does this by caricaturing exaggeration, sometimes by an idealization, but what the artist seeks is the significant form freed from its meaningless, accidental features. This is especially evident in so-called "primitive" art such as that of Africa or Central America in which what the artist seeks to reveal is the awesome power of the gods.

While it is true, as the formalists emphasized, that good art always seeks out "formal"— that is, mathematical—relations, this is because mathematical relations, as in the models used by physicists, are the best analogates we have for significant non-mathematical relations. Thus, even a painting of Modrian that seems as purely non-objective as it is possible to produce actually has emotional symbolism.[27]

What I am arguing, therefore, is not that the modern art of the twentieth century was bad art, since much brilliant work was produced, but that its tendency has led to a dead end because it more and more separated itself from nature. Thus, like our technology that has failed to respect ecology, and our morality that has failed to respect the natural law—all in the name of creativity, that our goal is simply the "new" as if this is always the "improved"—art has ended in deconstruction of reality not its perfecting, in the chaos of chance rather than of true freedom.

## Making a Life

Human freedom best participates in God's true freedom when it is used to "create" the only reality that is entirely under human control, namely, the deliberate decisions that constitute a moral

27  For discussion on this issue as it was seen in the last part of the twentieth century see Dore Ashton, *A Reading of Modern Art*, rev. ed. (New York: Harper & Row, 1971).

*Art Perfects Nature*

or immoral human life and determine its final destiny. Freedom of choice is usually directed toward alternative means whose relation to some previously chosen end is intellectually understood. But a commitment first has to be made to this already chosen end, or *summum bonum*. That good is formally determined by human nature to be happiness and, according to Aristotle and Aquinas, consists in a hierarchical ordering of the goods required to satisfy the needs of human nature, physical, familial, social, and intellectual.[28] Our supreme need is to know and love God and for the sake of God to seek the common good of all creatures according to the order of our social relationships. Creaturely freedom reaches its climax, therefore, in a firm commitment to that true goal. On the contrary, a commitment to some illusory form of happiness, although free, entails eventual enslavement to vice and personal destruction. For angels, because of the clarity of their knowledge, this free choice of true or false happiness is final and everlasting. For us humans, with our weak intelligences, it can be wavering. True freedom is to make that right commitment as firm as possible and our choices of means to it as consistent as possible.[29] For us this is true freedom, true creativity, true perfecting of human nature and on it all other freedom, in science, in technology and in the fine arts depends.

28  On this see my article, "What is the End of the Human Person: The Vision of God and Integral Human Fulfillment," in *Moral Truth and Moral Tradition: Essays in Honour of Peter Geach and Elizabeth Anscombe*, ed. by Luke Gormally (Dublin and Portland, OR: Four Courts Press, 1994), pp. 68–96.

29  *S.Th.*, I, q. 64, a.2.

# Prime Matter:
## A Thomistic Reply to Some Criticisms
### Steven Baldner
### St. Francis Xavier University (Nova Scotia)

This last meeting of the Thomistic Institute is devoted to the topic of "nature." It is clear enough to Thomists that nature must be understood hylomorphically. This means, in part, that natural substances are composites of form and matter. Since there can only be one substantial form for any one substance, the composition of form and matter in a substance must mean that substantial form is united immediately to formless matter, that is, to prime matter. This prime matter is understood to be a principle, not a thing, to be real, but to be a pure potentiality of matter to accept any substantial form.

Furthermore, most Thomists, especially most of us here, would accept the claim that Aristotle's understanding of nature is fundamentally the same as Thomas'. Hence, criticisms of Aristotle's philosophy of nature are criticisms that bear equally on Thomas' philosophy of nature. Some of Aristotle's scholars have been very interested in the problem of matter, prime matter, and the elements.[1]

---

1   C.J.F. Williams, tr., *Aristotle's De generatione et corruptione* (Oxford: Clarendon Press, 1982); Mary Louise Gill, *Aristotle on Substance: The Paradox of Unity* (Princeton: Princeton University Press, 1989); Christopher Byrne, "Prime Matter and Actuality," *Journal of the History of Philosophy* 33 (1995) 197–224; "Matter and Aristotle's Material Cause," *Canadian Journal of Philosophy* 31 (2001) 85–111; in *Pacific Philosophical Quarterly* 76 (1995), Kit Fine, "The Problem of Mixture," 266–369; James Bogen, "Fire in the Belly: Aristotelian Elements, Organisms, and Chemical Compounds," 370–404; Alan Code, "Poten-

*Prime Matter: A Thomistic Reply to Some Criticisms*

And, some of these have brought very keen criticisms of the doctrine of prime matter. It is fitting, therefore, that a Thomist consider these criticisms as I propose to do in this short paper.

I have three scholars in mind—there are more critics than three—but these three give us a fair sense of the range of criticisms being made today. First, there is C.J.F. Williams, the translator of *De generatione et corruptione*, who argues that Aristotle does hold the traditional doctrine of prime matter, as Thomists have understood it, but that the position is simply incoherent.[2] Second, Mary Louise Gill has argued that in fact Aristotle does not even hold a doctrine of prime matter.[3] Third, my own colleague at St. Francis Xavier University, Christopher Byrne, has argued that Aristotle does indeed hold a consistent doctrine of prime matter but that this doctrine is not that of the traditional, Thomistic interpretation.[4]

Williams, to begin with, argues that the Aristotelian doctrine of substantial change, which Williams calls "generation *simpliciter*," is *intended* to be a different account from that of accidental change but turns out to be not different at all. Substantial change is defined by Williams thus: "one predicate in the category of substance ceases to hold of a thing and another comes to hold of it."[5] But this kind of analysis only makes sense if there is an *it* that is the same before and after the substantial change. And if the *it*—the subject—is the same before and after, then what we really have is accidental change, not substantial change. Aristotle, says Williams, attempts to explain how it is that prime matter both is and is not, by saying that it is not "in actuality" but is "in potentiality." "But this," says Williams, "is a mere juggling with words, and amounts to no more than a demand for a license to say contradictory things about identity and existence."

tiality in Aristotle's Science and Metaphysics," 405–418; and Richard Sharvy, "Aristotle on Mixtures," 439–457.

2  Williams, *Aristotle's De generatione*, pp. 216–219.
3  Gill, *Aristotle on Substance*, pp. 41–82.
4  Byrne, "Matter and Aristotle's Material Cause," pp. 85–111.
5  Williams, *Aristotle's De generatione*, p. 218.

The root of Aristotle's confusion is a confusion about actuality and potentiality. To say that prime matter is "pure potentiality" is to say that it is "nothing in actuality." But,

> what is actually nothing is nothing. If prime matter is nothing in actuality there is no such thing. What there is is a real confusion in Aristotle's thinking, a notion of prime matter which is internally incoherent and to which nothing therefore corresponds (even potentially).[6]

Williams, thus, finds the very idea of a real but pure potentiality to be nonsense. To him, although he does not quite put it in these terms, to be real is always to be actual. And for this reason the traditional doctrine of prime matter is incoherent.

So much for Williams. Gill and Byrne are defenders rather than critics of Aristotle, and each offers a rather compelling (although I think in the end incorrect) interpretation of Aristotle. Gill's argument, broadly, is that Aristotle sets forth two requirements for matter or for that which will serve as the material cause.[7] First, matter must be a τόδε τι, that is, it must be a particular individual or some definite, definable kind.[8] Second, the matter must be *separate*; that is, it must be distinct from form either in conceptual analysis or in being.[9] Since these are the two requirements for the underlying subject (the ὑποκείμενον), it is clear that prime matter as traditionally understood does not measure up. It is not separate, for prime matter can only be conceived by a kind of analogy, and it is clearly not a definite or definable kind. But if one were to insist that prime matter were separable and a definite kind, then another problem would arise. If prime matter is conceptually separate from form and is a definite *this* persisting through substantial change, then, in effect, we are no longer

6    Williams, *Aristotle's De generatione*, p. 219.
7    Gill, *Aristotle on Substance*, pp. 13–40.
8    Gill, *Aristotle on Substance*, pp. 31–34.
9    Gill, *Aristotle on Substance*, pp. 34–38.

*Prime Matter: A Thomistic Reply to Some Criticisms*

talking about substantial change. If prime matter is a definite *this*, then it has certain attributes before the substantial change, and these attributes are accidental to the *this*. After the substantial change, it has a new set of attributes, and these, too, are accidental. But to describe change in this way is to talk about accidental not substantial change. The traditional doctrine of prime matter is given to account for substantial change. Paradoxically, this traditional doctrine implies that all change is ultimately reduced to some sort of accidental change.[10]

This, by the way, is a criticism that is very close to that which was made by Williams. Like Williams, Gill finds the notion of a pure potentiality to be unacceptable, but unlike Williams, she does not find such a notion in Aristotle's text. Gill, however, as a defender of Aristotle, is left with the problem of explaining substantial change without the traditional doctrine of prime matter.

Gill's ingenious solution is to say that Aristotle never meant to advance a doctrine of prime matter in the first place. Aristotle did think that there is a basic instance of matter, an instance of pure, simple matter, but this instance is found in the four simple elements (earth, water, air, and fire). These elements, on Gill's interpretation of Aristotle, are not hylomorphically composed but are just simple instances of matter. They have certain active properties—in fact,

---

10  The following, says Gill, are the implications of the traditional view that prime matter is receptive of generation and destruction. "A subject is receptive of contrariety if it can survive an exchange of contrary properties; and if it survives such an exchange, the contrary properties belong to the subject accidentally. Thus a man is the subject of the contrariety musicality and non-musicality because he can have either property without ceasing to be the subject that he is: a man. Matter is supposed to be receptive of generation and destruction because it too can receive contrary properties; when one contrary replaces the other, something (e.g., air) perishes, and something else (e.g., water) comes to be. Yet, if this is Aristotle's view, then the production of water from air is not after all a generation but a mere alteration, because the transformation involves a replacement of properties accidental to the underlying material." Gill, *Aristotle on Substance*, pp. 61–62.

}33{

RESTORING NATURE

they really are nothing other than their active properties—and these active properties can be changed into one another and can become accidental characteristics of more complex substances. On Gill's account, therefore, the role of prime matter is taken over by the elements themselves, and the elements are reinterpreted to be simple instances of pure matter.[11] Further, it is the definable properties themselves of the four elements (hot/cold; wet/dry) that become the true substrate of substantial change.

Next is my colleague, Christopher Byrne. Like Gill, Byrne is a defender of Aristotle who offers an ingenious interpretation of Aristotle. For Byrne, the problem with the traditional interpretation of prime matter is that it leaves prime matter so impoverished that there is no role for prime matter to perform. He, therefore, proposes that Aristotle's prime matter be understood, not as pure potentiality in the traditional sense, but as a sort of Cartesian *res extensa*. Prime matter, on his view, is "physical stuff": it is extended, divisible, locatable in place, corporeal, individual, and so forth.[12] Matter in this sense, prime matter, is genuinely

---

11  "The four elements—earth, water, air, and fire—are the simple bodies, and each is identified as what it is by a pair of contraries. Aristotle says that the two contraries are yoked together, using this metaphor to indicate that the two contraries jointly define a particular element. Although the elements have two defining features, they are not composites, since they are not composed of simpler ingredients. They are pure matter, and as such, they can justly be called matter in the strictest (μάλιστα κυρίως) sense. The cosmic scale resembles the traditional scheme: crowned by pure form, the scale is rooted in pure matter. The pure matter, however, is the elements themselves. These simple materials come to be from and pass away into, one another, and they also serve as the ultimate ingredients out of which composite bodies are generated." Gill, *Aristotle on Substance*, p. 82.

12  "Contrary to the traditional doctrine of prime matter, I would argue that this ultimate substratum is not pure potentiality, but the matter of perceptible bodies, that is, the extended, divisible, movable stuff out of which all perceptible substances are made. This is the case because subtracting from a perceptible substance all of its particular

*Prime Matter: A Thomistic Reply to Some Criticisms*

common to all natural, physical things. It is, you might say, a nature that is common to all physical things.

He argues for this in several ways. (1) In order that physical interaction take place between the elements, there must be some nature in common among them.[13] Apart from such a common nature, the elements are nothing but their contrary qualities (hot/cold; wet/dry), but these contrary qualities cannot simply act upon one another. Something common, and something really possessing common properties, is required beyond the contrary qualities. This common nature is the substrate, which is prime matter. (2) Another argument has to do with the ubiquity of locomotion.[14] All natural, physical things are capable in some way of locomotion. Locomotion, however, necessarily requires location in place, bodily extension, divisibility of a corporeal body, individuality, and so forth. This common set of characteristics requires a common nature; there must be some real feature of the natural thing that is common to all locally movable beings. This common feature is, again, prime matter. (3) Third, Byrne argues that substantial change itself requires that there be a substrate persisting through the change.[15] This substrate is the material cause of generation and destruction, and it must have certain properties necessary to any physical interaction. But it cannot have these properties from the formal cause, because it is precisely the formal cause that is gained or lost during substantial change.

> qualitative and quantitative properties, in particular all of the properties that give it a particular, definite size or shape, does not mean that it ceases to be an extended body. All of these properties presuppose the existence of an extended body which they qualify or limit; ... the nature of prime matter is the nature of matter *tout court* because prime matter has whatever is left to matter when all of the particular properties are taken away that differentiate the various natural elements and perceptible substances." Byrne, "Prime Matter and Actuality," p. 213.

13  Byrne, "Matter and Aristotle's Material Cause," pp. 96–98.

14  Byrne, "Matter and Aristotle's Material Cause," pp. 98–100.

15  Byrne, "Matter and Aristotle's Material Cause," pp. 100–101.

Because the material cause persists through these processes [of generation and destruction], whereas the formal [cause] is gained or lost, the material cause cannot be what it is by virtue of the formal cause. Otherwise, a vicious circle is quickly generated in which the persisting material cause is made to be what it is by virtue of something that it is also in the process of gaining or losing. Rather, whatever acts as the material cause must be what it is independent of the formal cause.[16]

Or, again,

the substratum of generation and destruction retains throughout these processes the properties required to make something changeable and movable, and these properties cannot be given to the substratum by the formal cause because the latter is precisely what does not persist through these changes.[17]

(4) Finally, Byrne argues that in order for matter to be *receptive* of form, matter must have certain properties.[18] It must have certain properties to make it suitable for an external efficient cause to act upon it to bring out of its potentiality some new form.

The potentiality of the material cause, then, is not just a privative concept; it implies as well that the material cause already possess, in its own right, certain attributes that are required to produce a complete substance.[19]

16  Byrne, "Matter and Aristotle's Material Cause," p. 100.
17  Byrne, "Matter and Aristotle's Material Cause," p. 101.
18  Byrne, "Matter and Aristotle's Material Cause," pp. 101–103.
19  Byrne, "Matter and Aristotle's Material Cause," p. 102.

*Prime Matter: A Thomistic Reply to Some Criticisms*

In these ways, then, Byrne argues that prime matter must have identifiable properties—it must have some recognizable nature—if it is to perform the functions that it is supposed to perform.

Here, then, are three contemporary specialists in Aristotelian natural philosophy. One finds Aristotle's doctrine of prime matter to be incoherent, the second finds no doctrine at all of prime matter in Aristotle, and the third finds a prime matter in Aristotle that has the actual, formal properties of extension, mobility, and corporeality. A Thomist would have to say that these scholars have all gone wrong. But how? In all three of these positions there is at least one common theme: it is that the real is always reducible to the actual. These scholars all do recognize potentiality, but each one insists that the potential as such cannot be a principle of nature. Potentiality, for each one of them, must always be a function of some actual entity; it can never be a principle in itself. Hence, prime matter as a principle of pure potentiality can find no place in their analyses.

Why, then, do Thomists insist on this principle? The reason we recognize the principle of pure potentiality has to do with substantial, not accidental change, for if all changes were accidental there would be no need of prime matter. In every substantial change at least one new substance comes into existence and at least one substance ceases to exist. In this kind of change there are two and only two possibilities. Either there is a continuity of the newly existing substance with the preceding substance or there is not. By continuity, I mean that a substrate continues in existence from the previous to the subsequent substance. If there is no continuity, then we are saying that the new substance simply comes into existence out of nothing. If there is no continuity, the new substance would come into existence *after* the previous substance, but not *out of* the previous substance.[20] To say such,

---

20  Thomas insists that in substantial generation, as opposed to accidental change, the underlying matter of the change is precisely that *out of which (ex qua)* the generation occurs. See *De principiis naturae* in *Aquinas on Matter and Form and the Elements,* by Joseph Bobik (Notre Dame: University of Notre Dame Press, 1998) pp. 3–6.

}37{

however, is to contradict the dicta of the ancient natural philosophers and of common sense: *ex nihilo nihil fit* and *nihil redit in nihil*. Some philosophical positions, of course, are built upon the denial of these principles. I am thinking, for example, of process philosophy, according to which instants of reality cease to exist and are replaced by other instants of reality.[21] Process philosophers insist that the continuity we observe in change is but an illusion of our perception. One can argue about this, but for now I merely claim that the principles of common sense (that change is a continuous, not a discontinuous, reality) are behind my argument.

Now the question is, what is it that accounts for the continuity in substantial change? Here we are necessarily driven to some kind of hylomorphism. As Aristotle argues in book I of the *Physics*, all change, including substantial change, necessarily requires three principles, two contrary formal realities and one underlying substrate.[22] If change is real, it must be the loss of some reality and the gain of some reality—our two formal principles. But also if change is real, then there must be some underlying reality—our material principle. This, of course, is not a point of dispute with those who have argued against the traditional understanding of prime matter. Furthermore, the matter in question must be remote or basic rather than proximate or obvious. Matter can be considered in its more obvious manifestations, the flesh and blood of an animal, for instance, or we can look to more remote or more basic manifestations of matter.[23] Here, too, those who have disputed against the traditional view of prime matter recognize that the substrate is matter in the more basic or remote sense. Whatever is the substrate of substantial change, it is not

21  I have explained this elsewhere: Steven Baldner, "St. Thomas Aquinas and Charles Hartshorne on Change and Process" in *Philosophy and the God of Abraham: Essays in Memory of James A. Weisheipl, O.P.*, edited by R. James Long (Toronto: Pontifical Institute of Mediaeval Studies, 1991) pp. 19–29.
22  Aristotle, *Physics* 1.7 (198b30–191a23).
23  St. Thomas, *De principiis naturae* in Bobik, *Aquinas on Matter and Form and the Elements*, pp. 25–28.

*Prime Matter: A Thomistic Reply to Some Criticisms*

the obvious, secondary matter. The substrate is matter in some more basic sense.

Both the critics of the tradition and the defenders of it are, therefore, in agreement that matter in some basic sense is necessarily the substrate for substantial change. The question is, what do we mean by matter in this basic sense? Here we can go one of two ways. Either prime matter is something indeterminate, precisely that which is not form, and if so we have the traditional doctrine—the doctrine found by Williams to be incoherent. Or, prime matter is something determinate, and this is the course that Gill and Byrne have taken in interpreting Aristotle. Let us consider whether prime matter can possibly be determinate. If prime matter is determinate, then it must be determinate either as an accident or as a substance. Gill has chosen the first possibility and Byrne the second.

Gill's position, recall, is that the four Aristotelian elements serve in some way as the substrate, but it is not the elements themselves that survive in substantial change. It is the contrary properties (hot/cold; wet/dry) that survive; it is these contrary properties that serve as the true substrates of substantial change. When air, for example, is changed into water, the air is characterized by the properties of coldness and dryness. The water that is the result of the change is characterized by coldness and wetness. Coldness, then, is common to both the air and the water, and coldness itself—an accident—serves as the substrate of the substantial change.

But can an accident be the substrate of substantial change? Accidents are understood as dependent being; they are defined as that which inheres in another as in a subject.[24] If substantial change really is substantial, that is, if it is the end of the existence of one substance and the beginning of the existence of a new substance, and if accidents are dependent upon substances (and not *vice versa*), then accidents cannot serve as the substrate of substan-

24  St. Thomas, *De principiis naturae* in Bobik, *Aquinas on Matter and Form and the Elements*, pp. 1–5.

}39{

tial change. Accidents must always be accidents *of* something, but if there is nothing substantial in common during substantial change, then there is nothing of which accidents can be accidents. It is, I am trying to point out, just a misuse of the very meaning of accident to suppose, as Gill does, that accidents can serve as the substrate of substantial change.

If an accident cannot be the substrate of substantial change, then the other possibility is that something determinate but substantial can be the substrate. Here again, there are two possibilities. The determinate substantial substrate might be the four elements, or it might be something defined more generally. The notion that the substrate is the elements is a notion recognized by most commentators to be inconsistent with Aristotle's philosophy of nature. If we say that the elements are the underlying substrate, then we are really committed to a position that is reductionist and is a denial of substantial change. Clearly, if identifiable substances, such as the four elements (earth, water, air, and fire) are the substrates of substantial change, then substantial change is not really a substantial change, for the four elements then do not change. Such change would, of course, be merely accidental change: it would be the emergence of new properties out of the permanent underlying substance. As I say, this view is held by none of the interpreters of Aristotle. Everyone recognizes that Aristotle is trying to give us an explanation of a kind of change that is radically different from accidental change. This view, however, although it is clearly not Aristotelian, is an important erroneous view. Although it is squarely opposed to common experience, for the fact of substantial change is evident, it is the view that some interpreters of science feel that they are driven to adopt. Let me just note the fact that this reductionist position is not that of Aristotle or of common experience.

Christopher Byrne, however, takes up the second possibility. On his view, the underlying substrate can indeed be called prime matter, and prime matter is not identified with one of the four elements. It is something more basic, according to Byrne, and yet it has attributes such as extension, divisibility, mobility, location in

}40{

*Prime Matter: A Thomistic Reply to Some Criticisms*

place, and so forth. On this view, all substantial change requires a substrate that is extended, divisible, movable, and located in place. Prime matter is just this substrate.

Can a Thomist admit such a view? He cannot, if he insists that there can only be one substantial form for any one substance. If, however, one allows for a plurality of substantial forms, then something like Byrne's view would be plausible. By virtue of prime matter, substances would be extended, by virtue of the substantial form of an element or a compound, they would have physical properties, by virtue of vegetative form, they would have living properties, by virtue of an animal form, they would have sentient properties, and so forth. Any substance would be a series of nested substantial forms, each one specifying higher or lower properties. This is a plausible view, but Thomists have rejected it. Why?

The answer, I think, is that the empirical evidence for substantial unity is very strong.[25] The unity and coherence of specific kinds of substances is so definite and knowable, that it strongly suggests to the mind that there is a reason for this. Any natural substance is a unified and coherent whole precisely because some one principle specifies its unity and coherence. Any analysis of a substance will have to account for the fact that the substance is radically different from the substance or substances out of which it was made. This radical difference is, in every case of natural things, thoroughly pervasive of the whole substance. Salt, for example, is not really anything like sodium or chlorine, or a living plant or animal is not anything like its biochemical constituents. The specificity of each natural kind pervades each natural substance and must be accounted for in some way.

Now, of course, those who hold a plurality of substantial forms can give some account of substantial unity. They will say that the lower substantial forms are coordinated and united by

---

25 This is the point, I think, in *Summa theologiae* 1.76.3 where Thomas argues that there can only be one soul for a human being if a human being is to be *unum simpliciter*.

}41{

the ultimate, specific substantial form. So, for example, a dog might have a form of corporeity, a form of animality, and a form of dogness, but it is the form of dogness that pulls the whole together in a coherent way. If one says this, however, we want to know just what the lower forms, such as corporeity and animality, are really doing. If they are true substantial forms, then it would appear that there is something really animal that is specifically the same between a dog, say, and a cat. But, of course, we know that the animality of the dog is really very different from—only analogically the same as—the animality of a cat. So these lower substantial forms cannot be doing just what substantial forms are supposed to do, that is, they cannot be making something to be an actual substance. They do, however, identify certain properties that are present in a substance. But the properties in question are always *accidental* properties, and from the standpoint of the substantial form, these supposed lower substantial forms are merely short-hand ways of designating a whole range of accidental properties.[26] That the accidental properties are just specifically what they must be in order that the substance be the kind of substance it is is a fact that must be attributed to the unifying and specifying principle of the whole: the substantial form.

Concerning prime matter, if we say that prime matter is extended, the question is, how much? In the case of water, the prime matter would be extended so much, but when the water is substantially changed into air, then the extension of prime matter is greater. Why is this so? It is not because of prime matter, but because of substantial form. The form of air determines the greater extension of air, and the form of water determines the lesser extension of water. To maintain a plurality of substantial forms, one must then say that the form of corporeity (or of prime matter) determines extension as such but that the form of air or water determines the precise extension of the substance. The crucial point

26  The substantial form, says Thomas, gives being *simpliciter*; it does not merely specify accidental ways of being, although it does specify them also. *Summa theologiae* 1.76.4.

*Prime Matter: A Thomistic Reply to Some Criticisms*

to notice is that prime matter itself cannot determine any given extension; it must always be subordinate to the substantial form, which determines precise extension, and a whole range of other properties as well.

In the end, the position that there is a plurality of substantial forms must make the subordinate substantial forms bearers of very general properties. These general properties must be specifically determined by the substantial form. When we realize that there is no middle ground between the substantial and the accidental, then we also realize that these subordinate forms are really playing accidental roles. In the end, the doctrine of a plurality of substantial forms will reduce to something very much like the Thomistic doctrine. Byrne's position, then, however plausible, carries with it the limitations of any doctrine of a plurality of substantial forms.

To conclude, I don't think that there is any reason brought forth by the criticisms of Williams, Gill, or Byrne to make us abandon the traditional Thomistic and Aristotelian doctrine of prime matter. Williams, Gill, and Byrne have, however, drawn our attention to the difficulty of conceptualizing matter. It *is* very difficult to conceptualize a principle of pure potentiality, but it is even more difficult to explain nature without such a principle.

# Philosophical Anthropology Facing Aquinas' Concept of Human Nature
### Angelo Campodonico
### University of Genoa

## 1) Philosophical Anthropology and the Concept of Human Nature

Although nowadays the term "philosophical anthropology" is not very much used in the contemporary philosophical milieu and there are no chairs of this discipline in most philosophical faculties, except for the Catholic ones, I do believe that contemporary philosophers deal very often with topics which are deeply related to what we call "philosophical anthropology." Consider, for instance, the mind-body problem, the philosophy of intentionality and of human action, which is the necessary ground of ethical reflection, bioethics, problems concerning the different approaches to cultural anthropology, philosophy of politics and of interculturalism, searching for values shared by different cultures, and so on. Also the classical concept of human nature, which is deeply connected with the topic of philosophical anthropology, cannot be easily deleted. In fact it seems very difficult—if not impossible—to make comparisons between different cultures or to speak of human rights and duties without having, at least implicitly, a normative concept of human nature (in the classical or philosophical sense) and not only in the mere biological sense (which is the more often used in contemporary speech).

But how can Aquinas' concept of nature, and particularly of human nature, help us nowadays in facing the topics of Philosophical Anthropology? I will try to answer these questions,

*Philosophical Anthropology Facing Aquinas' Concept of Human Nature*

choosing only some of the main aspects of the problem. According to Thomas, nature is the substance or, rather, the form of those beings that have in themselves the principle of their action. Aristotle and Thomas do not have a static concept of nature. Nature is the principle of movement.[1] Nature has a dispositional character. Nature always tends towards unity (*ad unum*) when there are no obstacles. That means that where there is nature, there is also an end (*finis*), which means self-preservation and fulfilment. And where there is an end, there is also *ontological good*. As Lawrence Dewan holds:

> the vision of reality as a hierarchy of goodness is not a vision merely of moral goodness (which is goodness in the domain of free choice), but primarily a grasp of each sort of thing as intrinsically loveable, and of the many kinds of thing as possessing, this one more, this one less, what makes a thing worthy of actual existence.[2] Saying that a thing is 'worthy of actual existence' might lead one to judge that goodness is merely the approval expressed by the human being (or even a more exalted observer). The only cure for this 'subjectivist' conception of the situation is an understanding of the role of approval, i.e. of inclination or appetite or love, in the

1   Cf. *In V Met.*, l. V, n. 826: " . . . primo et proprie natura dicitur substantia, idest forma rerum habentium in se principium motus inquantum huiusmodi. Materia enim dicitur esse natura, quia est formae susceptibilis. Et generationes habent nomen naturae, quia sunt motus procedentes a forma, et iterum ad formas. Et idipsum, scilicet forma est principium motus rerum existentium secundum naturam, aut in actu, aut in potentia. Forma enim non semper facit motum in actu, sed quandoque in potentia tantum: sicut quando impeditur motus naturalis ab aliquo exteriori prohibente, vel etiam quando impeditur actio naturalis ex materiae defectu."

2   Cf. *ST*, I, 65, 1 *ad* 2, where Thomas replies to those who regard things as bad, unqualifiedly, simply because they are harmful in some way to humans.

schema of being. Goodness is what is approved of, yes, but it is not good because it is approved of; it is approved of because it is good.[3]

It seems very difficult nowadays to speak of something which is good in itself, only according to the ontological meaning of good. In fact we often hold that it would be a good thing to preserve things which have no utility for us or for mankind in general, just because they exist.

We can acknowledge a hierarchy of beings and natures in the world looking at the perfection of their actions (the more or less immanent or intimate character of their actions).[4] According to Aquinas,

> one takes seriously the particular natures of things, and primarily substances, as they reveal a hierarchy of perfection: elements, vegetative life, animal life, human life: all so many modes of substance. Furthermore, one takes seriously causal hierarchy: the need that beings have for higher beings: the priority of act over potency.[5]

## 2) The Meaning of Human Nature

Human nature is basically the very ground of every development of man. *Natural* in man is everything that is in us, that we find in ourselves (although we can never know it in a complete way), but we cannot choose and change. In other terms: natural is what is

3 Lawrence Dewan, "Wisdom as Foundational Ethical Theory in Thomas Aquinas" in William Sweet (ed.), *The Bases of Ethical Theory*, Marquette University Press, Milwaukee 2001, p. 47. This is true as regards the creature's approval of the goodness of things. God's love of a thing is prior to the thing's being and goodness. Cf. *ST*, I, 20, 2.
4 Cf. *CG*, IV, 11: "Quanto natura est altior, tanto emanans ex ea est intimior."
5 Lawrence Dewan, "Wisdom as Foundational Ethical Theory in Thomas Aquinas," p. 42.

*Philosophical Anthropology Facing Aquinas' Concept of Human Nature*

created in ourselves by God. Nature is creature ("natura est creatura"). Nature is the very ground of everything we can choose, which is free (first meaning) or the development of what is natural in the first sense, which is chosen by us, but according to human nature, in a way coherent with the nature of man (second meaning). Thomas holds:

> As Boethius says (*De duabus nat.*) and the Philosopher also (*Metaph.*V, 4) the word 'nature' is used in a manifold sense. For sometimes it stands for the intrinsic principle in movable things. In this sense nature is either matter or the material form, as stated in *Phys.* II, 1. In another sense nature stands for any substance or even for any being. And in this sense, *that is said to be natural to a thing which befits it in respect of its substance.* And this is that which of itself is in a thing. Now all things that do not of themselves belong to the thing in which they are, are reduced to something which belongs of itself to that thing, as to their principle. Wherefore taking nature in this sense, it is necessary that the principle of whatever belongs to a thing, be a natural principle. 1) This is evident in regard to the intellect: for the principles of intellectual knowledge are naturally known. In like manner the principle of voluntary movements must be something naturally willed. Now this is good in general, to which the will tends naturally, as does each power to its object; and again it is the last end, which stands in the same relation to things appetible, as the first principles of demonstration to things intelligible: 2) and speaking generally, it is all those things *which belong to the willer according to his nature.* For it is not only things pertaining to the will that the will desires, but also other things that are appropriate to the other powers; such as the knowledge of truth, which befits the intellect; and to be and to live and other like things which regard the natural well-being; all of

RESTORING NATURE

which are included in the object of the will, as so many particular goods.[6]

Therefore we can call *natural* in general (second meaning) also what concerns human fulfilment, what is moral (in according with reason and with *moral* or *natural* law).

Acts are called human insofar as they proceed from a deliberated will. Such acts already presuppose, and are ultimately brought about by certain merely natural operations of intellect and will, which is to say, operations that are not free or not rooted in a man's own mastery of his acts. Even the free will of the pure spirits, as finite and created beings, presupposes natural operations of intellect and will. With respect to these spirits, Aquinas uses a familiar phrase: "magis aguntur quam agunt; nihil enim habet dominium suae naturae." He holds:

> All natural things in the world are moved to act by something else except the First Agent, Who acts in such a manner that He is in no way moved to act by another; and in Whom nature and will are the same. So there is nothing unfitting in an angel being moved to act in so far as such natural inclination is implanted in him by the Author of his nature. Yet he is not so moved to act that he does not act himself, because he has free will.[7]

That is true in the case of man too.

6   Lawrence Dewan, "Wisdom as Foundational Ethical Theory in Thomas Aquinas," p. 35. The numbers in the quotation of Thomas are mine.
7   *ST*, I, 60, 1 ad 2: " . . . omnia quae sunt in toto mundo, aguntur ab aliquo, praeter primum agens, quod ita agit quod nullo modo ab alio agitur: in quo est idem natura et voluntas. Et ideo non est inconveniens si angelus agatur, inquantum inclinatio naturalis est sibi indita ab auctore suae naturae. Non tamen sic agitur quod non agat; cum habeat liberam voluntatem."

*Philosophical Anthropology Facing Aquinas' Concept of Human Nature*

In order to understand what is *natural* in man (in the first and main sense), we have to consider some polarities that we find in Aquinas' thought, in particular: nature-culture, nature-election or nature-freedom, and natural-supernatural. The second term of these polarities is the end of the first term. We cannot know human nature (in the philosophical sense) in a complete way without knowing also the second term. This means that the concept of human nature is also a dynamic one. In modern thought the oblivion of these main polarities, provoked by the scientific revolution, determines a new concept of nature—and also of human nature—a closed, essentialistic and individualistic one (nature conceived only as self-preservation, *conservatio sui*) as in Hobbes and Spinoza.[8] But the oblivion of the finalism of nature during the modern age is at the very root of the oblivion of the concept of nature itself in contemporary age. Therefore in contemporary culture there is often a deep gap between man and nature and between human nature and human freedom. On the one hand there are philosophies of nature (in the biological sense) without freedom and culture and, on the other hand, there are philosophies of freedom and of culture without nature. On the one hand ethical value is grounded in nature (non human nature), on the other hand only in freedom (human freedom). This is the case with existentialism.

According to Aquinas, human nature is a deep unity of body and soul as the form of the body. He often stresses this unity, particularly when he deals with the incarnation of Christ.[9] This unity, as well as what is rooted in this unity, is *natural*. But how can we know human nature? Not immediately (in a rationalistic or essentialistic way), but in a mediated way, reflecting on the specific

8    Cf. Robert Spaemann, *Die Frage Wozu*, Piper, München 1981, p.105–110. According to Thomas, by nature, we love our own specific being, our own specific self, more than our individual self; and all the more do we love the universal good which is God more than all else.

9    Cf. *ST*, III, quaestiones 2–6.

}49{

objects of our acts, on our human acts and then on our faculties.[10] In fact we are always acting beings. Furthermore *we can know other beings better than ourselves*. In contemporary terms, we might say with Paul Ricoeur that man knows his nature better and better by acting intentionally and interpreting his acts and his works.[11] Reflecting on our own acts, we can also grasp the meaning of the acts of other people and we can better understand our own acts. In particular, we can understand the meaning of human acts, because the peculiar human language is shared by every man (see the beginning of the *Thomas's Commentary on Aristotle's Politics*[12]). Therefore we can understand the main role of hermeneutics in philosophical anthropology.

## 3) Self-actualization and Virtue as a "Second Nature"

If in order to know human nature in a complete way it is necessary to reflect (by theoretical reason) on human acts, it is also necessary to develop all the main human experiences (thanks

10 Cf. *De ver*. X, 8: "Quantum igitur ad actualem cognitionem, qua aliquis considerat se in actu animam habere, sic dico, quod anima cognoscitur per actus suos. In hoc enim aliquis percipit se animam habere, et vivere, et esse, quod percipit se sentire et intelligere, et alia huismodi opera vitae exercere."

11 We find this topic in many works of Ricoeur. Among them, see Paul Ricoeur, *Oneself as Another*, University of Chicago Press, Chicago 1994.

12 Cf. *In I Politicorum*, l. I: "Est autem differentia inter sermonem et simplicem vocem. Nam vox est signum tristitiae et delectationis, et per consequens aliarum passionum, ut irae et timoris, quae omnes ordinantur ad delectationem et tristitiam, ut in II *Ethicorum* dicitur . . . . Sed loquutio humana significat quid est utile et quid nocivum. Ex quo sequitur quod significet iustum et iniustum. Consistit enim iustitia et iniustitia ex hoc quod aliqui adaequentur vel non adaequentur in rebus utilibus et nocivis. Et ideo loquutio est propria hominibus; quia hoc est proprium eis in comparatione ad alia animalia, quod habeant cognitionem boni et mali, iusti et iniusti, et aliorum huiusmodi, quae sermone significari possunt."

*Philosophical Anthropology Facing Aquinas' Concept of Human Nature*

also to the practical use of reason) and to become capable of reflecting on them. That means reflecting on theoretical experience, practical experience (art and ethics), aesthetic and artistic experience and, particularly, religious experience, which has a synthetic role since it is at the very top of both theoretical and practical use of reason.[13] To develop our human experience means—I believe—in classical and Thomistic terms, to develop those habits called "virtues," which are somehow natural (a second nature):

> By vital operations are meant those whose principles are within the operator, and in virtue of which the operator produces such operations of itself. It happens that there exist in men not merely such natural principles of certain operations as are their natural powers, but something over and above these, such as habits inclining them like a second nature to particular kinds of operations, so that the operations become sources of pleasure."[14]

In another article of the *Summa theologiae* Thomas holds in a synthetic way: "There is in every man a natural inclination to act according to reason: and this is to act according to virtue."[15]

On the deep relationship between speculative and ethical virtues Aquinas affirms:

13  See, for instance, the main role of invocation in religious experience.
14  *ST*, I, 18, 2 ad 2: "Contingit autem aliquorum operum inesse hominibus non solum principia naturalia, ut sunt potentiae naturales; sed etiam quaedam superaddita, ut sunt habitus inclinantes ad quaedam operationum genera quasi per modum naturae, et facientes illas operationes esse delectabiles."
15  *ST*, I-II, 94, 3: " . . . cum anima naturalis sit propria forma hominis, naturalis inclinatio inest cuilibet homini ad hoc quod agat secundum rationem. Et hoc est agere secundum virtutem. Unde secundum hoc, omnes actus virtutum sunt de lege naturali: dictat enim hoc naturaliter unicuique propria ratio, ut virtuose agat."

}51{

RESTORING NATURE

Since then the habits of the speculative intellect do not perfect the appetitive part, nor affect it in any way, but only the intellective part; they may indeed be called virtues in so far as they confer aptness for a good work, viz. the consideration of truth (since this is the good work of the intellect): yet they are not called virtues in the second way, as though conferring the right use of a power or habit. For if a man possess a habit of speculative science, it does not follow that he is inclined to make use of it, but he is made able to consider the truth in those matters of which he has scientific knowledge: that he make use of the knowledge which he has, is due to the motion of his will. Consequently a virtue which perfects the will, as charity or justice, confers the right use of these speculative habits. And in this way too there can be merit in the acts of these habits, if they be done out of charity.[16]

We can learn by experience, facing reality and developing virtues, because our practical reason is never deeply separated from theoretical reason (as often happens in modern and contemporary thought). Reason—also practical reason, which is directed towards undertaking particular actions here and now—knows things and natures as they really are thanks to theoretical reason. Therefore we can always learn from reality. In fact there is always *one reason*. I believe that we do not use the term "experience" in this sense, perhaps because very often we have an empiricist and subjective concept of experience. If we refuse this meaning, we can hold that "becoming virtuous" means "learning by experience." The virtuous man is an experienced man.

In Anthony Lisska's words:

16  *ST*, I-II, 57, 1, 2: "Cum igitur habitus intellectuales speculativi non perficiant partem appetitivam, nec aliquo modo ipsam respiciant, sed solam intellectivam; possunt quidem dici virtutes inquantum

}52{

*Philosophical Anthropology Facing Aquinas' Concept of Human Nature*

Choosing values in human beings is effective in achieving self-actualization only if the person is open to the experiences going on within the organism. The awareness of self-actualization is very important, and the awareness is related to the *openness to experiences necessary for functioning well as human beings*. Persons who are becoming more open in their "experiencing" share an organismic commonality of value directions. Rogers's research indicates that maturing humans exhibit what he calls a 'surprising commonality.'" In addition, Rogers argues that this commonality is not due to the influences of any one particular culture. His empirical evidence suggests a cross-cultural basis for this commonality. Rogers writes that 'this commonality of value directions is due to the fact that we all belong to the same species.'[17]

We can get to know human nature by reflecting on everyday experience. Still nowadays we know man also as a scientific object (an object of physics, biology, psychology, cultural anthropology, etc.). Of course Thomas did not know modern science, but his concept of abstraction leaves room for different approaches to the same subject. The main problem of philosophical anthropology in the last decades, and the very root of this old and new discipline, has been

---

faciunt facultatem bonae operationis, quae est consideratio veri (hoc enim est bonum opus intellectus): non tamen dicuntur virtutes secundo modo, quasi facientes bene uti potentia seu habitu. Ex hoc enim quod aliquis habet habitum scientiae speculativae, non inclinatur ad utendum, sed fit potens speculari verum in his quorum habet scientiam; sed quod utatur scientia habita, hoc et movente voluntate. Et ideo virtus quae perficit voluntatem, ut caritas vel iustitia. Facit etiam bene uti huiusmodi speculativis habitibus. Et secundum hoc etiam, in actibus horum habituum potest esse meritum, si ex caritate fiant . . ."

17 Anthony J. Lisska, *Aquinas's Theory of Natural Law. An Analytic Reconstruction*, Clarendon press, Oxford 1996, p. 220.

}53{

the problem of considering together the basic reflection approach and the scientific approach. That is why philosophical anthropology as well as the philosophy of nature are in some ways quite static, but in others in continuous development. It is apparent also that scientific discoveries become part of everyday experience in man. I think that the reflection approach comes first from a methodological point of view: not only can we understand scientific concepts thanks only to pre-scientific concepts, but we may even accept truths on human nature that science cannot confirm. In particular: the Aristotelian concept of form as the principle of order is still very important when we have to deal with macroscopic entities such as man and his actions.[18] This concept enables us to connect the reflection approach to the scientific approach. If we do not make use of the concept of form in philosophical anthropology, the only alternative is to conceive the human being and his actions in a materialistic way as a casual sum of particles and events. And this happens in contemporary thought as well as in pre-Aristotelian philosophy.[19]

## 4) Nature and the First Principles

Now let us look more precisely at what is the meaning of *natural* in man according to Thomas. In *Summa theologiae* he writes:

> It should be said that the nature of man can mean either that which is proper to man, and the all sins, insofar as they are against reason, are also against nature . . . Or it can mean that which is common to man and the other animals, and the certain special sins are said to be against nature, as is against the union of male and female, which is natural to all animals, that two

18  See H. Jonas, *The Phenomenon of Life. Toward a Philosophical Biology*, Harper & Row, New York 1966.

19  Cf. E. Runggaldier, *Was sind Handlungen? Eine philosophische Auseinandersetzung mit der Naturalismus*, Kohlhammer GmbH, Stuttgart, Berlin, Köln 1996.

*Philosophical Anthropology Facing Aquinas' Concept of Human Nature*

men should seek sexual union, which especially is called a vice against nature.[20]

It is noteworthy that from this point of view the biological tendencies of man (vegetative, sensitive etc), which are also common to every being and, particularly, to other animals are *natural*. These inclinations can be guided by reason. But natural is also what in our world is proper only to man, since he is a "rational animal," the first principles of reason and will:

> in man, nature can be taken in two ways. First inasmuch as intellect and reason is the principal part of man's nature, since in respect thereof he has his own specific nature. And in this sense, those pleasures may be called natural to man, which are derived from things pertaining to man in respect of his reason: for instance, it is natural to man to take pleasure in contemplating the truth and in doing works of virtue. Secondly, nature in man may be taken as contrasted with reason, and as denoting that which is common to man and other animals, especially the part of man which does not obey reason. And in this sense, that which pertains to the preservation of the body, either as regards the individual, as food, drink, sleep and the like, or as regards the species, as sexual intercourse, are said to afford man natural pleasure. Under each kind of pleasure, we find some that 'are not natural' speaking absolutely, and yet connatural in some respect. For it happens in an individual that some one

20  *ST*, I-II, 94, 3 ad 2: " . . . natura hominis potest dici vel illa quae est propria homini: et secundum hoc, omnia peccata, inquantum sunt contra rationem, sunt etiam contra naturam . . . Vel illa quae est communis homini et aliis animalibus: et secundum hoc, quaedam specialia peccata dicuntur esse contra naturam; sicut contra commixtionem maris et feminae quae est naturalis omnibus animalibus, est concubitus masculorum, quod specialiter dicitur vitium contra naturam."

of the natural principles of the species is corrupted, so that something which is contrary to the specific nature, becomes accidentally natural to this individual: thus it is natural to this hot water to give heat. Consequently it happens that something which is not natural to man, either in regard to reason, or in regard to the preservation of the body; from some ailment, thus to a man suffering from fever, sweet things seem bitter, and vice versa; or from an evil temperament, thus some take pleasure in eating earth and coals and the like; or on the part of the soul, thus from custom some take pleasure in cannibalism or in the unnatural intercourse of man and beast, or other such things, which are not in accord with human nature.[21]

21  *ST*, I-II, 31, 7: "Utrum aliqua delectatio sit non naturalis. Sed contra: Phil. dicit in VII *Ethic.*, quod quaedam delectationes sunt 'aegritudinales et contra naturam': dicendum quod naturale dicitur quod est secundum naturam, ut dicitur in II *Physic.* Natura autem in homine dupliciter sumi potest. Uno modo prout intellectus et ratio est potissime hominis natura, quia secundum eam homo in specie constituitur. Et secundum hoc, naturales delectationes hominis dici possunt quae sunt in eo quod convenit homini secundum rationem: sicut delectari in contemplatione veritatis, et in actibus virtutum, est naturale homini. Alio modo potest sumi natura in homine secundum quod condividitur rationi: id scilicet quod est commune homini et aliis, praecipue quod rationi non obedit. Secundum utrasque autem delectationes, contingit aliquas esse innaturales, simpliciter loquendo, sed connaturales secundum quid. Contingit enim in aliquo individuo corrumpi aliquod principiorum naturalium speciei; et sic id quod est contra naturam speciei, fieri per accidens naturale huic individuo . . . Ita igitur contingit quod id quod est contra naturam hominis, vel quantum ad rationem, vel quantum ad corporis conservationem, fiat huic homini connaturale, propter aliquam corruptionem naturae in eo existentem . . . vel etiam ex parte animae, sicut propter consuetudinem aliqui delectantur in comedendo homines, vel in coitu bestiarum aut masculorum, aut aliorum huiusmodi, quae non sunt secundum naturam humanam." Cf. also *CG*, III, 122, particularly 5.

*Philosophical Anthropology Facing Aquinas' Concept of Human Nature*

Here Aquinas holds that there may be corruption of human nature *in the individual man*. But what seems natural according to the individual man might not be natural according to the human species. That is very important nowadays in facing problems of interculturalism, sexual ethics, etc. I want to stress that if the nature, value, meaning and dignity of every human being as such is not really acknowledged, people search out a substitute of equality in dignity: everything becomes interchangeable. Therefore it becomes very difficult to speak of the corruption of nature in the individual man or of natural defects in the individual man.

Both first principles of theoretical and practical reason are *natural*. Sometimes Thomas calls the first principles of reason which are grounded on the *apprehensio* of being and of good (i.e., the principle of contradiction, the principle according to which the whole is larger than its parts, the first ethical principle, etc.) *ratio ut natura*, while the developments, which are grounded on those principles, are called *ratio ut ratio*.[22] More frequently he speaks of *"voluntas ut natura"* (the necessary openness of our will to the infinity of being and of goodness, which is the ground of every choice), while *"voluntas ut ratio"* means those choices (*electio*).[23] Also on the will (*voluntas*), connected with the knowledge of the infinity of being, is grounded the human desire of infinity, the *"desiderium naturale videndi Dei."*

According to Thomas, the peculiar role of man in the cosmos

22 Among these first principles of reason there is a hierarchical order. The principle of contradiction is the ground of the other principles (e.g., the principle according to which the whole is larger than its parts); the first principle of practical reason is the ground of the other practical principles.
23 Cf. *De ver.*, 22, 5: "Natura autem et voluntas hoc modo ordinata sunt ut etiam ipsa voluntas quaedam natura sit, quia omne quod in rebus invenitur natura quaedam dicitur. Et ideo in voluntate oportet inveniri non solum id quod voluntatis est, sed etiam quod naturae est. Hoc autem est cuiuslibet naturae creatae ut a Deo sit ordinata in bonum naturaliter appetens illud, unde et voluntati ipsi inest naturalis quidam appetitus boni sibi convenientis."

is grounded in his intellect, which is open towards the whole of being thanks to the first principles of theoretical reason:

> it is evident that all the parts are ordered to the perfection of the whole: for the whole is not because (*propter*) of the parts, but the parts are because of the whole. But intellectual natures have a greater affinity with the whole than do the other natures: for each intellectual substance is somehow all [beings] (*unaquaeque intellectualis substantia est quodammodo omnia*), inasmuch as it is inclusive (*comprehensiva*) of the whole of being (*totius entis*) by its intellect: whereas any other substance has only a particular participation in being (*entis*). Suitably, then, the others are provided for by God because of [or for the sake of] the intellectual substances.[24]

Furthermore Thomas holds that the closest resemblance to God in creatures comes through intellectuality:

> it is evident that the likeness of the species is approached in function of the ultimate difference. Now, some things are assimilated to God, firstly and most commonly, inasmuch as they are; but secondly, inasmuch as they live; but thirdly, inasmuch as they wisely consider or understand (*sapiunt vel intelligunt*) . . . Thus,

24  *CG*, 3, 112: "Manifestum est partes omnes ordinari ad perfectionem totius: non enim est totum propter partes, sed partes propter totum sunt. Naturae autem intellectuales maiorem habent affinitatem ad totum quam aliae naturae: nam unaquaeque intellectualis substantia est quodammodo omnia, inquantum totius entis comprehensiva est suo intellectu: quaelibet autem alia substantia particularem solam entis participationem habet. Convenienter igitur alia propter substantias intellectuales providentur a Deo." This reminds us of the point made in *ST*, I-II, 2, 6, that the intellectual part of the soul *infinitely* surpasses the corporeal good.

*Philosophical Anthropology Facing Aquinas' Concept of Human Nature*

therefore, it is evident that only intellectual creatures, properly speaking, are in the image of God.[25]

## 5) Natural law

One of the most interesting places where Thomas deals with nature in man is the famous passage of *Summa theologiae* connected with the topic of the first principles of practical reason:

> Just as being is the first thing grasped simply speaking, so the good is the first thing grasped by practical reason which is ordered to action, for every agent acts for the sake of an end, which has the character of good. Therefore, the first principle of practical reason is grounded in the notion of good: the good is that which all things desire. This, then, is the first precept of the law: good should be done and pursued and evil avoided. All other precepts of the law of nature are grounded in this one, such that all those things that are to be done or avoided pertain to precepts of natural law which practical reason naturally grasps as human goods. Because good has the note of end and evil has the contrary note, reason naturally grasps as goods all those things to which man has a natural inclination, and consequently as to be pursued in action, and the contrary of these are grasped as evil to be avoided. Therefore there is an order of the precepts of the law of nature that follows the order of the natural inclinations. For there is in man

---

25  *ST*, I, 93, 2: "Manifestum est autem quod similitudo speciei attenditur secundum ultimam differentiam. Assimilantur autem aliqua Deo, primo quidem, et maxime communiter, inquantum sunt; secundo vero, inquantum vivunt; tertio vero, inquantum sapiunt vel intelligunt . . . Sic ergo patet quod solae intellectuales creaturae, proprie loquendo, sunt ad imaginem Dei."

RESTORING NATURE

a first inclination to a good of the nature he shares with all substances insofar as each substance seeks the preservation of the existence it has according to its own nature; and following this inclination the things by which the life of man is preserved and in the contrary prevented pertain to natural law. Second, there is in man an inclination to more special things, according to the nature he shares with other animals. Following on this, those things that nature teaches all animals are said to be of natural law, such as the joining of male and female, and the raising of young, and the like. In a third way there is an inclination to know the truth about God and to live in society. Accordingly those things which look to this inclination pertain to natural law, for example, that a man should avoid ignorance, that he should not offend others with whom he must live, and other such things which are relevant to this.[26]

---

26 *ST*, I-II, 94, 2: "In his autem quae in apprehensione omnium cadunt, quidam ordo invenitur. Nam illud quod primo cadit in apprehensione est ens, cuius intellectus includitur in omnibus quaecumque quis apprehendit. Et ideo primum principium indemonstrabile est quod 'non est simul affirmare et negare', quod fundatur supra rationem entis et non entis: et super hoc principio omnia alia fundantur, ut dicitur in IV *Metaphys*. Sicut autem ens est primum quod cadit in apprehensione simpliciter, ita bonum est primum quod cadit in apprehensione practicae rationis, quae ordinatur ad opus: omne enim agens agit propter finem, qui habet rationem boni. Et ideo primum principium in ratione practica est quod fundatur supra rationem boni, quae est , 'Bonum est quod omnia appetunt'. Hoc est ergo primum praeceptum legis, quod bonum est faciendum et prosequendum, et malum vitandum. Et super hoc fundantur omnia alia praecepta legis naturae: ut scilicet omnia illa facienda vel vitanda pertineant ad praecepta legis naturae, quae ratio practica naturaliter apprehendit esse bona humana. Quia vero bonum habet rationem finis, malum autem rationem contrarii, inde est quod omnia illa ad quae homo habet naturalem inclinationem, ratio naturaliter apprehendit ut bona, et per consequens ut opere prose-

*Philosophical Anthropology Facing Aquinas' Concept of Human Nature*

It is noteworthy that in this famous article, Thomas does not start from a static or essentialistic concept of nature or from the will of God, from which to deduce the precepts of natural law, but from our everyday experience, the experience of every man living and facing reality in time. This man is a united whole of body and soul, inclinations and reason, practical and theoretical reason. Theoretical reason knows inclinations and the different degrees of the hierarchy of beings. Practical reason interprets natural inclinations and makes norms out of them here and now: "bonum est faciendum." That is possible because both inclinations and practical reason *have an end*. Both are *good* in the ontological sense. Ethical goodness is grounded on ontological goodness. Reason itself, as we have seen before, is natural (that means: has an end which is truth, or action in the case of practical reason), although transcending material beings. It is also noteworthy that, according to Thomas, man, although he cannot know his own essence (*natura*) in a complete way, can find out, looking at his acts in his nature, what is also proper to other things

> quenda, et contraria eorum ut mala et vitanda. Secundum igitur ordinem inclinationum naturalium, est ordo praeceptorum legis naturae. Inest enim primo inclinatio homini ad bonum secundum naturam in qua communicat cum omnibus substantiis: prout scilicet quaelibet substantia appetit conservationem sui esse secundum suam naturam. Et secundum hanc inclinationem, pertinent ad legem naturalem ea per quae vita hominis conservatur, et contrarium impeditur. Secundo inest homini inclinatio ad aliqua magis specialia, secundum naturam in qua communicat cum ceteris animalibus. Et secundum hoc, dicuntur ea esse de lege naturali quae natura omnia animalia docuit, ut est coniunctio maris et feminae, et educatio liberorum, et similia. Tertio modo inest homini inclinatio ad bonum secundum naturam rationis, quae est sibi propria: sicut homo habet naturalem inclinationem ad hoc quod veritatem cognoscat de Deo, et ad hoc quod societate vivat, et secundum hoc, ad legem naturalem pertinent ea quae ad huiusmodi inclinationem spectant: utpote quod homo ignorantiam vitet, quod alios non offendat cum quibus debat conversari, et cetera huiusmodi quae ad hoc spectant."

RESTORING NATURE

around him, the inclination towards self-preservation and the inclination towards the joining of male and female and the raising of the young. The natural ethics of Thomas is, therefore, not strictly anthropocentric (this is good nowadays, because many philosophers fight against anthropocentrism), although there is no ethics in our world without human reason.

Anthony Lisska attempts to explicate the developmental or self-actualization moral theory by the following nine principles:

1) A dispositional property is developmental in character;
2) The natural bent of a dispositional property is towards the completion of the developmental process;
3) The well-being of a human person is determined by the harmonious completion of the dispositional properties, which determine the content of a human essence;
4) The end—i.e. well-being is, by definition, a good;
5) There are as many goods as there are ends;
6) The concept of good is incommensurable; this follows from (5) above;
7) The hindering of any developing process frustrates that process;
8) To frustrate a natural process in a human being denies the possibility of attaining human well-being;
9) The source and foundation of the concept of morality is a fully functioning human person.[27]

In this concept of natural law,

> there is no fact/value dichotomy because the 'value'—in this case, the 'end' of the natural process—is the result of the normal development of the 'fact'—in this case, the dispositional property. There is no radical bifurcation between fact and value, because the value, i.e., the good, is nothing more than the development of

27  Anthony Lisska, *Aquinas' Theory of Natural Law*, p. 103.

}62{

the process structured by the nature of the set of dispositions. It follows, therefore, that a value is not derived from a fact through the process of 'adding' the value to the fact.[28]

Furthermore,

in so far as an immoral action in Aquinas's moral theory is what it is because it strikes against the developmental properties of a human person, it prevents that person from reaching a state of 'functioning well' or 'flourishing'. This denial serves at least an analogous function to what 'engaging in a contradiction' does for Kant. Therefore, using Kantian ethical categories, Aquinas is not offering a hypothetical imperative for moral obligation, as so many of his critics has suggested.[29]

Among the three kinds of inclinations and precepts there is a hierarchical order, from the first to the third. Thomas holds:

even granted that the end of reason and will were the conservation of human existence, it could not be said that the end of man is a bodily good. To be a man involves soul and body, and although the existence of body depends on soul, the existence of the human soul does not depend on body, as was shown earlier; the body is for the sake of the soul, as matter is for the sake of form, and instruments for the sake of the agent in order that he may act through them. Hence all goods of the body are ordered to goods of the soul as to their end.[30]

28  Anthony Lisska, *Aquinas' Theory of Natural Law*, p. 199.
29  Anthony Lisska, *Aquinas' Theory of Natural Law*, p. 204.
30  *ST*, I-II, 2, 5: "Manifestum est autem quod ordinatur ad aliquid sicut ad finem: non enim homo est summum bonum. Unde impossibile

Although the highest inclinations and precepts are more perfect than the lowest and therefore we might die for our children (second precept) or for the sake of freedom and of religious faith (third precept), the lowest inclinations and precepts are normally the necessary ground in order to cultivate the highest inclinations. In fact they are stronger and more common.[31] We do not preserve our nature, looking only or first of all at our individual self-preservation, although we must look also at our preservation. It is easier for us to preserve our lives or to love our children than to cultivate friendship or religion. Furthermore we normally cannot cultivate friendship and religion without searching for the preservation of our lives and of our human species. I would like to stress that comparisons among different cultures are possible on the basis of these inclinations and goods, which are common to every man, but, in fact, may be interpreted and ordered in different ways.

From the ethical point of view

> it is perfectly possible for a philosopher to say, for instance, that the precepts corresponding to the inclinations to worship God are higher than all others, that the precepts corresponding to the inclinations to preserve life, are next in order, etc., without saying or suggesting in any way that the various levels might be played off

est quod ultimus finis rationis et voluntatis humanae sit conservatio humani esse. Secundo, quia, dato quod finis rationis et voluntatis humanae esset conservatio humani esse, non tamen posset dici quod finis hominis esset aliquod corporis bonum. Esse enim hominis consistit in anima et corpore: et quamvis esse corporis dependeat ab anima, esse tamen humanae animae non dependet a corpore . . . ipsumque corpus est propter animam, sicut materia propter formam, et instrumenta propter motorem, ut per eas suas actiones exerceat. Unde omnia bona corporis ordinantur ad bona animae, sicut ad finem." Cf. Ralph McInerny, *Aquinas on Human Action. A Theory of Practice*, CUA, Washington 1992, p. 121–124.

31  This point is very much stressed by Nicolai Hartmann in many works.

against each other, since, for one thing, precepts are not goods, but rather human artifacts aimed at preserving goods and, secondly, things put into an order do not count one against the other, as if a higher one contained more of that which a lower one contained . . . It may very well be that there are real reasons (i.e., reasons pertaining to the way things stand in the world) why a certain order is posited; but the ordering is not something found in the world: it is something we do. And this is enough to exclude most consequentialists theories, for they usually involve a confusion of two distinct procedures: counting and ordering.[32]

In fact the main problem of ethics concerns the *integrity* of its approach.[33] When practical reason does not consider in an integral way every dimension of reality and therefore every precept, the human act cannot be good.[34] According to the phrase of Dyonisius,

32  Kevin L. Flannery S.J., *Acts Amid Precepts. The Aristotelian Logical Structure of Thomas Aquinas's Moral Theory*, CUA, Washington 2001, p. 107.
33  Flannery, *Acts Amid Precepts. The Aristotelian Logical Structure of Thomas Aquinas's Moral Theory*, p. 217: "If we wish to evaluate the morality of a particular act, we cannot look just at it, nor even can we just take into consideration the act and the goods at which it aims; we must, rather, understand where in the structure of practical reason it fits. It is true that the goods that constitute the basis, and in a certain sense, the principles of practical reason are enormously important, especially when one considers the system as a whole: they define the system in such a way that an attack on one of them is necessarily an attack on practical reason itself. But also important are the concrete cultural contexts within which we pursue these goods and avoid that which is incompatible with their pursuit, for it is in that context that the order (the 'lawlikeness') of practical reason is found."
34  Cf. Angelo Campodonico, "Experience of Reality, Integrity and God" in John O'Callaghan (ed.), *Science, Philosophy and Theology*, St. Augustine's Press, South Bend, IN 2002: "When our knowledge

often quoted by Thomas, "the good comes about from the integral cause, but evil from single defects." To sum up: integrity allows

concerns accidental and individual things (and that is the case of human actions and endeavours), hermeneutics is a substitute for science. If we want to grasp the true meaning of something, we have to gather many aspects of that subject, considering them as a whole and possibly from the point of view of the whole. For instance: Aquinas suggests in his ethics that I must look at the aim of my action, at its matter and its circumstances, if I want to know what I must do now: ' . . . malum contingit ex singularibus defectibus, bonum vero ex tota et integra causa'. What I am saying is that in this and similar cases we must ask: Is something missing? Is this the only point of view on that subject? Can I look at this problem from a wider point of view? This is actually the method of hermeneutics that in ethics needs also moral integrity of man (practical truth).

To sum up, science and hermeneutics share a common criterion: they are always based on a perfection or integrity pattern. From this point of view the classical Aristotelian science pattern is the basis of empirical science pattern and of hermeneutics' pattern too. But that pattern is not necessarily a priori: it develops, as I hold, through experience of reality and its order." See also Angelo Campodonico, "Bonum ex integra causa" in Timothy L. Smith (ed.), *Aquinas's Sources. The Notre Dame Symposium*, St. Augustine's Press, South Bend, IN 2002: "According to Thomas, when he is acting, the good man must consider together the wholeness and integrity (*integritas*) of himself with its ontological order and the wholeness and integrity of the situation where he is acting with its ontological order. To be a moral man means to answer here and now with the wholeness (integrity) of ourselves to the wholeness (integrity) of being.

This development and sometimes conversion (change) from the inside of the aristotelian anthropology and ethics, thanks to the neo platonic tradition, takes place because there is also a previous strong influence of the Bible on Aquinas' thought. In particular: like Augustine and Dionysius, Aquinas reads the platonic topic of the unity as ontological good, from a Christian point of view. Unity is good, as the unity of the experience of man is good, according to the Gospel's phrase that Augustine often quotes: 'For what is a man profited, if he shall gain the whole world, and lose his own soul? Or what shall a man give in exchange for his soul?'. See *ST.* I-II, 73, 1, 3: ' . . . dicendum quod amor Dei est congregativus, inquantum affectus a

us also to stress together, in the field of ethics, the instances of contemporary phenomenology (the ethics of value) and of the Kantian and neo-Kantian ethics of law (the topic of responsibility and of ecstatic love), but without their risks (still natural law, according to Thomas, has an ontological ground—his ethics is not a formal one). It stresses as well the neo-Aristotelian ethics centered on the tendency toward ends and the fulfillment of man (ethics of virtue) and on the role of others (communitarianism). I believe that all these aspects that we find together in the thought of Aquinas are still very important for contemporary ethics:

> Pursuing the good that is the object of any one precept is always a good thing, provided another good (protected

multis ducit in unum: et ideo virtutes, quae ex amore Dei causantur connexionem habent. Sed amor sui disgregat affectum hominis in diversa, prout homo scilicet se amat appetendo sibi bona temporalia, quae sunt varia et diversa; et ideo vitia et peccata, quae causantur ex amore Dei non sunt connexa'. Here connection means integrity (among virtues). The love of God is the very root of the connection of ethical virtues among them. Evil and the vices are the opposite of ethical integrity.

The Platonic tradition, particularly Dionysius and Proclus, allows Thomas to give a more ontological, aesthetic and also ethical value to Aristotelian ethics, which seems to be a more empirical and eudaimonistic one, reading it from a Christian point of view. This topic is important also from the point of view of contemporary philosophy. Nowadays the topic of integrity in anthropology and in ethics seems to be very important in the first place for the great role played by hermeneutics in considering the characters and the circumstances of the ethical action; in the second place, because, in a period of a crisis of ethics, it shows the criteria useful to value one ethics in comparison with another one. Which attitude considers every aspect of the action, which misses any aspect? Which attitude considers coherently every value? These are very important questions. In the third place, the topic of integrity connects also ethics and aesthetics (*integritas* is a basic character of beauty), allowing to read in the moral action a beauty, which has appeal. This character has been missed by modern and kantian ethics."

by another precept or by other precepts) is not harmed. The crucial question becomes, then, not whether one precept has more value than another, but whether a good is being attacked. If going to Church means for some reason directly taking a life, then one ought not go to Church. If preserving a life means directly harming the truth, then one ought not to preserve the life—the presupposition being, of course, that one is not directly taking the life. The crucial question in such cases is, obviously, When is a person directly attacking a good?[35]

## 6) The Main Precepts of Natural Law

What seems to be good, but with different values of goodness in our moral experience of natural law, on the theoretical and metaphysical ground looks actuated in different ways by the act of existing. Since on the ground of our ethical experience of reality goodness contemplates different degrees of good, the act of existing contemplates different degrees of actualization. As Kevin Flannery holds:

> The order presumably recognized by all as existing in the theoretical reason exists also in practical reason. This is an order that takes in also the most basic inclinations, uniting them with the most fundamental practical principle, FPPR. It is possible, thus, for Thomas to affirm that natural law contains many precepts. This is not to countenance chaos within the realm of precepts but to recognize that natural law is a complex but ordered whole.[36]

---

35 Kevin L. Flannery S.J., *Acts Amid Precepts. The Aristotelian Logical Structure of Thomas Aquinas's Moral Theory*, p. 108.

36 Kevin L. Flannery S.J., *Acts Amid Precepts. The Aristotelian Logical Structure of Thomas Aquinas's Moral Theory*, p. 48. In fact we must consider together not only the goods pertaining to the different precepts, but also the goods which pertain to a single precept.

*Philosophical Anthropology Facing Aquinas' Concept of Human Nature*

Let us now examine briefly each precept. In fact they cannot be considered separately. There is a kind of movement not only from the first to the third, but also from the third to the first, since man is a *rational* animal and his reason informs every inclination.

The principle of self-preservation implies that it is *natural* not only to preserve our own existence, but not to seek another nature (that means that it is *natural* to assent to our nature). Self-preservation is not contrary to our desire of fulfilling our nature. In fact: only in seeking our own fulfilment do we really preserve our nature. Therefore, on the one hand, there is not an isolated inclination towards individual self-preservation, as we have seen when dealing with the concept of nature during the modern age. Furthermore, self-preservation means first of all to preserve our human species and particularly to love God as He is the very source of our being:

> where one is the whole cause of the existence and goodness of the other, that one is naturally more loved than self; because, as we said above, each part naturally loves the whole more than itself: and each individual naturally loves the good of the species more than its own individual good. Now God is not only the good of one species, but is absolutely the universal good; hence everything in its own way naturally loves God more than itself.[37]

And in the same article:

---

37  *ST*, I, 60, 5 ad 1: " ... in illis quorum unum est tota ratio existendi et bonitatis alii, magis diligitur naturaliter tale alterum quam ipsum ... quod unaquaeque pars diligit naturaliter totum plus quam se. Et quodlibet singulare naturaliter diligit plus bonum suae speciei, quam bonum suum singulare. Deus autem non solum est bonum unius speciei, sed est ipsum universale bonum simpliciter. Unde unumquodque suo modo naturaliter diligit Deum plus quam seipsum."

## Restoring Nature

> Nature's operation is self-centered not merely as to certain particular details, but much more as to what is common; for everything is inclined to preserve not merely its individuality, but likewise its species. And much more has everything a natural inclination towards what is absolutely the universal good.[38]

By nature we love our own specific being, our own specific self, more than our individual self (this topic concerns also the second precept); and all the more do we love the universal good which is God more than all else. On the other hand, we must underline that

> although it is true that seeking, for instance, the good of personal survival can be understood as a way of seeking happiness or *eudaimonia* or even God, seeking personal survival has full intelligibility on its own. To adapt and apply an observation of Aristotle's, a person striving for personal survival and told of some distinct and higher good supposedly involved in his striving, might well ask of what use it might be in explaining what he is doing.[39]

According to the principle of self-preservation, we cannot claim to leave our condition as finite creatures by becoming angels or God through our own efforts (as the devil tried to do):

> Without doubt the angel sinned by seeking to be as God. But this can be understood in two ways: first, by

---

38  *ST.* I, 60, 5 ad 3: "...natura reflectitur in seipsam non solum quantum ad id quod est singulare, sed multo magis quantum ad commune: inclinatur enim unumquodque ad conservandum non solum suum individuum, sed etiam suam speciem. Et multo magis habet naturalem inclinationem unumquodque in id quod est bonum universale simpliciter."

39  Kevin L. Flannery S.J., *Acts Amid Precepts. The Aristotelian Logical Structure of Thomas Aquinas's Moral Theory*, p. 28.

equality; secondly, by likeness. He could not seek to be as God in the first way; because by natural knowledge he knew that this was impossible: and there was no habit preceding his first sinful act, nor any passion fettering his mind, so as to lead him to choose what was impossible by failing in some particular, *as sometimes happens in ourselves.* And even supposing it were possible, *it would be against the natural desire; because there exists in everything the natural desire of preserving its own nature; which would not be preserved were it to be changed in another nature. Consequently, no creature of a lower order can ever covet the grade of a higher nature; just as an ass does not desire to be a horse: for were it to be so upraised, it would cease to be itself. But herein the imagination plays us false; for one is liable to think that, because a man seeks to occupy a higher grade as to accidentals, which can increase without the destruction of the subject, he can also seek a higher grade of nature, to which he could not attain without ceasing to exist.*[40]

40  Cf. *ST*, I, 63, 3: "Respondeo dicendum quod angelus, absque omni dubio, peccavit appetendo esse ut deus. Sed hoc potest intelligi dupliciter: uno modo per aequiparantiam; alio modo per similitudinem; primo quidem modo non potuit appetere esse ut Deus; quia scivit hoc esse impossibile naturali cognitione; nec primum actum peccandi in primo praecessit vel habitus vel passio ligans cognoscitivam ipsius virtutem, ut in particulari deficiens eligere impossibile, sicut in nobis interdum accidit. Et tamen, dato quod esset possibile, hoc esset contra naturale desiderium. Inest enim unicuique naturale desiderium ad conservandum suum esse: quod non conservaretur, si transmutaretur in alteram naturam. Unde nulla res quae est in inferiori gradu naturae potest appetere superioris naturae gradum, sicut asinus non appetit esse equum: quae si transferretur in gradum superioris naturae, iam ipsum non esset. Sed in hoc imaginatio decipitur: quia enim homo appetit esse in altiori gradu quantum ad aliqua accidentalia, quae possunt crescere absque corruptione subiecti, aestimatur quod possit appetere altiorem gradum naturae, in quem pervenire non posset nisi esse desineret."

RESTORING NATURE

Therefore we can only desire God to help us in fulfilling our nature. This is the topic of the "naturale desiderium videndi Dei" and of the gift of Grace.[41]

The second precept is connected to the inclination to the joining of male and female and the raising of young. More precisely we might speak in general of dispositions or inclinations towards sensory apprehensions. That means to have sensory experiences and to care for offspring. In the other animals procreation is a substitute of individual immortality, because there is only immortality of the species and not of the single individual. But we too, as animals, though rational, are responsible for future generations (as Hans Jonas stresses in his *The Principle Responsibility*[42]).

The third inclination is connected in fact with many precepts, particularly with dispositions or inclinations toward rational cognitivity. That means to understand (rational curiosity) and to live together in social communities. To cultivate reason means to cultivate culture (in its wide sense), society (the relationship with other human beings) and, particularly, religion (the relationship with God, whose existence can be known by *natural* reason, at least implicitly). Also very important nowadays, as always, is the topic of others (intersubjectivity). Thomas deals with this topic when he deals with the specific characters of human language, the desire of honour,[43] friendship, politics, religion, etc. Contrary to Aristotle, according to Thomas friendship is possible also between man and God (the topic of charity).

It seems very interesting to make comparisons between the third inclination (the third precept of natural law) and the topic of the hierarchical order of being:

> When the thing in which there is good is nobler than
> the soul itself, in which is the idea understood, by com-

41 Cf. *ST*, I-II, 5, 5 ad 2.
42 See Hans Jonas, *The Imperative of Responsibility*, University of Chicago Press, Chicago 1985.
43 Cf. *ST*, I-II, 2, 2, 3.

}72{

*Philosophical Anthropology Facing Aquinas' Concept of Human Nature*

parison with such a thing, the will is higher than the intellect. But when the thing which is good is less noble than the soul, then even in comparison with that thing the intellect is higher than the will. Wherefore the love of God is better than the knowledge of God; but, on the contrary, the knowledge of corporeal things is better than the love thereof. Absolutely, however, the intellect is nobler than the will.[44]

We can hold that we are able to love God, but also other human beings and, particularly, ourselves more than we know them.[45]

Very often in Aquinas' works it is apparent that the topic of the "other" is implicit. For instance, when Thomas holds that an act is moral only when both the *interior* act and the *exterior* act are right, according to the phrase *"bonum ex integra causa"* (in contemporary terms we may speak of a mix of *internalism* and *externalism* in his ethics), we might ask: how can we know that an exterior act is a good one? I believe that Thomas implicitly thinks that others can know the morality of our exterior acts as well as

44  *ST*, I, 82, 3: "Quando igitur res in qua est bonum, est nobilior ipsa anima, in qua est ratio intellecta; per comparationem ad talem rem, voluntas est altior intellectu. Quando vero res in qua est bonum, est infra animam; tunc etiam per comparationem ad talem rem, intellectus est altior voluntate. Unde melior est amor Dei quam cognitio: e contrario autem melior est cognitio rerum corporalium quam amor. Simpliciter tamen intellectus est nobilior quam voluntas."

45  Some contemporary philosophers stress this point. See Harry Frankfurt, *The Importance of What We Care About*, CUP, Cambridge 1988, p. 133: "As conscious beings, we exist only in response to other things, and we cannot know ourselves at all without knowing them. Moreover, there is nothing in theory, and certainly nothing in experience, to support the extraordinary judgement that it is the truth about himself that is the easiest for a person to know. Facts about ourselves are not peculiarly solid and resistant to skeptical dissolution. Our natures are, indeed, elusively insubstantial—notoriously less stable and less inherent than the natures of other things. And insofar as this is the case, sincerity itself is bullshit."

those virtues that are the sources of those acts better than we do. This is why they can advise us. We might say that the others are somehow "in ourselves." To sum up: I think that very often in Thomas' works the topic of intersubjectivity, which is very important nowadays, is only implicit, and that is not strange. Nowadays we talk very much about the "community," because we are not very often communitarians. However, community was very important in everyday life during the Middle ages. Still the relationship with other people is *natural* and we always need that.

To sum up: we are beings, we are living beings, we are intelligent beings. Therefore we need to develop ourselves, facing the challenges of reality, i.e., of other beings, of living beings and intelligent beings, and with the whole of ourselves, reason and passion, body and soul. This is the meaning of human experience as self-actualization.

## 7) The Basic Natural Experiences at the Very Root of Our Desire for Happiness and Fulfilment

According to Platonic thought, the source of the acts of reason and will is the contemplation of eternal truths. Aristotle does not agree with Plato's concept of eternal truths. As in Aristotle, so in Thomas only some natural acts, deeply connected with the first principles, which have in themselves their own end (the *praxis teleia* or *actio immanens*) such as living, being happy, contemplating the truth, living friendship and love (although some of these seldom occur in our lives), are paradigmatic for every other kind of acts which have their ends outside themselves (the *kinesis* or *actio transitiva*). This is the case of *art* (technology in contemporary terms). Thomas holds:

> when nothing else is produced in addition to the activity of the potency, the actuality then exists in the agent as its perfection and does not pass over into something external in order to perfect it; for example, the act of seeing is in the one seeing as his perfection, and the act

}74{

*Philosophical Anthropology Facing Aquinas' Concept of Human Nature*

of speculating is in the one speculating, and life is in the soul (if we understand by life vital activity). Hence it has been shown that happiness also consists in an activity of the kind which exists in the one acting, and not of the kind which passes over into something external; for happiness is a good of the one who is happy, namely his perfect life. Hence, just as life is in one who lives, in a similar fashion, happiness is in one who is happy. Thus it is evident that happiness does not consist either in building or in any activity of the kind which passes over into something external, but it consists in understanding and willing.[46]

Those natural acts, having their end in themselves, are somehow circular. Only those perfect and fulfilled kinds of acts are at the very root of our natural desire for happiness and of hope. We can speak in contemporary terms of *basic human experiences*. Prominent among those acts is the act of living, because we are always living, but also being angry or committing sin and making mistakes. From the biological point of view we do not live *more or less*, but we *live* (as long as we live). And when we live there is always, within ourselves, an order, an *actio immanens*, a goodness (in an ontological sense, because there is an inclination of our body towards preservation and fulfilment) and an in-

---

46 *In IX Met.*, VIII, 1865: " . . . quando non est aliquod opus operatum praeter actionem potentiae, tunc actio existit in agente ut perfectio eius, et non transit in aliquod exterius perficiendum; sicut visio est in vidente ut perfectio eius, et speculatio in speculante, et vita in anima, ut per vitam intelligamus opera vitae. Unde manifestum est quod etiam felicitas in tali operatione consistit, quae est in operante, non quae transit in rem exteriorem, cum felicitas sit bonum felicis, et perfectio eius. Est enim aliqua vita felicis, scilicet vita perfecta eius. Unde sicut vita est in vivente, ita felicitas in felice. Et sic patet quod felicitas non consistit nec in aedificando, nec in aliqua huiusmodi actione, quae in exterius transeat, sed in intelligendo et volendo." Cf. Aristotle, *Met.* IX, VIII, 790.

tegrity (*integritas*), which means unity of the parts of a whole among themselves.[47] It may be that we do not pay explicit attention to them, but still those natural acts are implicitly the very source of our desire for happiness. Of course, we have to note that in us life is not only biological life, but is also intellectual and moral life (in an analogous way): *intelligere est vivere*. This is the Aristotelian difference between *zen* and *bionai*. These kinds of life always presuppose biological life. The intentional and transcendental character of our knowledge both preserves and deeply changes from within our biological life.

> we note that we do not speak merely of 'intellect' when the time comes to make the comparison, but of 'intellectual nature'. It is as if we are to view the intellect as a new dimension of natural being, expanding the meaning of 'tendency', 'inclination', 'order towards the good'. Thus, we see reality as shot through with tendency towards the good, but those beings which have intellect or mind have *inclination* in its most perfect realization, as *beings which experience the appeal of goodness as such.*[48]

As happens in our biological life, as well as in our intellectual life and in our conduct (or ethical life), in facing reality, we always have to come back to our first principles, theoretical and practical, as if in a circular movement. We cannot abandon those first principles and go on without them. The ground of *ratio* as

47  Cf. *ST*, I, 18, 2: "Vitae nomen sumitur ex quodam exterius apparenti circa rem, quod est movere seipsum: non tamen est impositum hoc nomen ad hoc significandum, sed ad significandam substantiam cui convenit secundum suam naturam movere se ipsam, vel agere se quocumque modo ad operationem. Et secundum hoc, vivere nihil aliud est quam esse in tali natura: et vita significat hoc ipsum, sed in abstracto . . ."

48  Lawrence Dewan, "Wisdom as Foundational Ethical Theory in Thomas Aquinas," p. 54.

*Philosophical Anthropology Facing Aquinas' Concept of Human Nature*

*discursus* (from *currere*—to run) is *intellectus principiorum*, the apprehension of the first principles of theoretical reason, just as the ground of our own ethical choices is the apprehension of the first principles of natural law. The insight of the first principles of knowledge (*prima principia indemonstrabilia per se nota*) is paradigmatic, because even when we make mistakes in our reasoning and in our conduct, our first principles can grasp always and immediately the true and the good. Therefore, although we may not understand the truth and make mistakes, we can always have a new start in our search for truth and moral good. It is noteworthy that Thomas also calls the first natural principles (theoretical and practical) *habitus* (*prima principia quorum est habitus, habitus principiorum*), because we can always use them, since they are in potency in ourselves.[49] Particularly in our relationships with other people, in friendship (*amor amicitiae*) and in love (particularly in the contemplation—love of Christ) we can have experience of happiness, of the top level of life. That is why we always remember some happy periods of our life. To sum up: recovering human nature means recovering a fresh start in our lives and that is always possible thanks to the *natural* first principles and to some *natural* acts. Aquinas makes an interesting comparison between the "fresh start" of the first principles and the newness (*novitas essendi*) of God's creation, and between creation and the gift of Grace.[50] Perhaps, from this point of view, we

49  Cf. Luca Tuninetti, *"Per se notum." Die logische Beschaffenheit des Selbstverständlichen im Denken des Thomas von Aquin*, Brill, Leiden 1996.
50  Cf. *De pot.*, III, 1 ad 6: "Sicut vero intelligere principia, quod est concludendi principium, non est ex aliquo ex quo concludatur, ita creatio, quae est omnis motus principium, non est ex aliquo"; *De pot.*, III, 8 ad 3: " . . . gratia, cum non sit forma subsistens, nec esse nec fieri ei proprie per se competit: unde non proprie creatur per modum illum quo substantiae per se subsistentes creantur. Infusio tamen gratiae accedit ad rationem creationis in quantum gratia non habet causam in subiecto, nec efficientem, nec talem materiam in qua sit hoc modo in potentia, quod per agens naturale educi possit in actum, sicut est de aliis formis naturalibus."

RESTORING NATURE

can also make an analogous comparison between the "fresh start" of natural first principles and the "fresh start" produced in man by God's forgiveness.

## 8) Nature and History

Let us consider another important aspect of the problem of human nature. Human beings, who have a nature, always face events of which they cannot have foreknowledge and which seem not to have an order and a nature. We may speak of chance or luck. Chance nowadays has an ambiguous meaning. On the one hand it deals with the chaotic universe of the ideology of evolutionism and nihilism (there is a deep relationship between them), according to which "in principle there was Chance." Although— I suppose—we cannot logically deduce from evolutionism the negation of human nature (in the classical sense), it is a fact that people often use this argument. But, on the other hand, chance is also very important in our lives, particularly nowadays, because we are always looking for something new, for something exceptional for our lives. This is apparent if we consider some slang expressions of ordinary language. From this point of view the study of everyday language is very interesting.[51]

I believe that we are always by nature looking for something new. But why? Because we are naturally open to the whole of being, but we find in our world only finite beings. Some of them ("others") are open to the whole of being, but still they too are finite and contingent beings. Only what appears new, really new (we might say *cum novitate essendi*), as grounded in the newness of the act of being, can fulfill our natural desire for happiness and truth. Therefore also chance and luck are very important in our lives.[52]

51  Cf. Dom Cupitt, *The New Religion of Life in Everyday Speech*, SCM Press, London 1999.
52  Cf. *CG*, III, 74 *passim*: "Quod divina providentia non excludit fortunam et casum. In his enim quae in minori parte accidunt, dicitur esse fortuna et casus. Si autem non provenirent aliqua ut in minori

*Philosophical Anthropology Facing Aquinas' Concept of Human Nature*

But this kind of newness always requires nature and necessity as its ground. Thomas holds that we can know that there is chance, because we know—at least implicitly—that there is nature, order and necessity in ourselves and in the world in general.[53] According to Aquinas, if it is true that we must speak of chance from the point of view of secondary causes (and of man)—the autonomous role of secondary causes is very much stressed by him—from God's point of view there is no chance at all.[54]

> parte, omnia ex necessitate acciderent: nam ea quae sunt contingentia ut in pluribus, in hoc solo a necessariis differunt, quod possunt in minori parte deficere. Esset autem contra rationem providentiae divinae si omnia ex necessitate contingerent . . . Esset etiam contra perfectionem universi si nulla res corruptibilis esset, nec aliqua virtus deficere potens . . . Multitudo et diversitas causarum ex ordine divinae providentiae et dispositionis procedit. Supposita autem causarum diversitate oportet unam alteri quandoque concurrere per quam impediatur, vel iuvetur, ad suum effectum producendum. Ex concursu autem duarum vel plurium causarum contingit aliquid casualiter evenire, dum finis non intentus ex concursu alicuius causae provenit. Non est igitur divinae providentiae contrarium quod sint aliqua fortuita et casualia in rebus . . . Nullius autem causae naturalis intentio se extendit ultra virtutem eius: esset enim frustra. Oportet ergo quod intentio causae particularis non se extendat ad omnia quae contingere possunt. Ex hoc autem contingit aliquid casualiter vel fortuito, quod evenient aliqua praeter intentionem agentium. Ordo igitur divinae providentiae exigit quod sit casus et fortuna in rebus."

53  Cf. John Bowlin, *Contingency and Fortune in Aquinas*, CUP, Cambridge 1999, p. 130: "Indeed, despite contemporary assertions to the contrary, contingency cannot go all the way down. It couldn't. A creature that was not directed to some ends by natural necessity would not be a particular kind of thing with a particular sort of agency. Indeed, it would not be a creature. It would be chaos."

54  Cf. *ST*, I, 22, 4: "Et ideo quibusdam effectus praeparavit Deus causas necessarias ut necessario evenirent: quibusdam vero causas contingentes secundum conditionem proximarum causarum." Ad 3: " . . . modus contingentiae et necessitatis cadit sub provisione Dei, qui est universale provisor totius entis: non autem sub provisione aliquorum particularium provisorum."

RESTORING NATURE

In fact it is absurd to oppose to each other nature and chance or nature and history. This happens—maybe—because we often have too static and essentialistic a concept of nature and of God. But, as noticed before, in Thomas there is a *dispositional* or *dynamic* concept of nature. It is noteworthy that in Aquinas' thought we can find a deep and often implicit sense of history and of the role of secondary causality in nature and in history, although he does not discuss this topic extensively in an explicit way.[55] But the internal logic of his metaphysics of creation is deeply open to the newness (*novitas*) of historical events and therefore to chance. This is not strange for a philosopher who is also a great Christian theologian.[56]

55 On Aquinas' sense of history see his etymology of some words. Cf. *In I Sent.*, d. 23, q. 1, a. 1: " . . . secundum Boetium sumptum est nomen personae a personando, eo quod in tragoediis et comoediis recitatores sibi ponebant quamdam larvam ad repraesentandum illum cuius gesta narrabant decantando. Et inde est quod tractum est in usus ut quodlibet individuum hominis de quo potest talis narratio fieri, persona dicatur: et ex hoc etiam dicitur *prosopon* in graeco a pro quod est ante, et sopos quod est facies, quia huiusmodi larvas ante facies ponebant." Cf. Max Seckler, *Das Heil in der Geschichte. Geschichtstheologisches Denken bei Thomas von Aquin*, Kosel Verlag, Munich 1964.

56 See John Bowlin, *Contingency and Fortune in Aquinas*, p. 215–16: "He (Thomas) cannot revise his treatment of the virtues in the manner the Stoics suggest, effectively eliminating their exposure to luck, for this would not only ignore his confidence in unreconstructed Aristotelian virtue, it would also deny the reality and consequence of our fall from grace—that virtue and happiness are in fact exposed to misfortune in ways that can undo each. Nor can he simply rest content in his Aristotelian commitments and maintain that the virtues do well enough against fortune's challenges, for this would ignore the obvious—that virtue in Eden does far better. And of course it is this fact that gives him grounds to find fault with what he has, to yearn for something more, and to tempt Stoic revisions of his largely Aristotelian treatment of the moral virtues. His actual response, if we can call it that, resides between these two alternatives, and since hope is the mean between confidence and despair we should not be surprised to find Aquinas's reply in his treatment of the theological virtues."

*Philosophical Anthropology Facing Aquinas' Concept of Human Nature*

This means that the events of history, of contemporary history, help us, more and more, to discover human nature and natural law also by way of negation (in a dialectical way). If this is true, we ought to look with open eyes at the events of the times we live in, and not only at those of past times, because in this way we can get to know in greater depth human nature and natural law. Nature and history, nature and time are not against each other; they are complementary living polarities. I think that this is, in fact, Aquinas' concept of the relationship between nature and history.

Lastly, from the ethical and religious point of view, there is of course a deep gap between newness, as the continuing search for new things which as such cannot fulfill our desire (this is the sense of Augustine's *avaritia*), and the search for newness as the search for a meaning of everyday experience, thanks to the fact that beings participate in the infinity of God and therefore may acquire a symbolic meaning in our lives.

## Conclusion: Recovering Human Nature

Nowadays somebody holds: if there were a natural law, a unique human nature, there would be more uniformity in ideas about the right and the wrong, and in the customs and institutions which embody these concepts.

A threefold response to this objection might be suggested:

1) A consideration in Aquinas's meta-ethics of the particular and contingent nature of practical judgments using practical reason. Aquinas' concept of human nature is a dynamic and dispositional one, not an essentialistic and static one.
2) A consideration of the biological work determining a specific unity to human beings as members of a natural kind; there may be more unity than cultural anthropologists have been wont to admit;
3) A consideration of the psychological unity which appears in constant studies of human behaviour. Carl Rogers has

}81{

suggested similarities in his discussion of self-actualization theories of human development."[57]

In general: by facing different cultures, we can understand, though often with many efforts, the problems of others or, at least, that we have not understood those problems yet.[58]

> Relativists . . . tend to understate the amount of attunement, recognition and overlap that actually obtains across cultures, particularly in the areas of the grounding experiences. The Aristotelian, in developing her conceptions in a culturally sensitive way, should insist, as Aristotle himself does, upon the evidence of such attunement and recognition. Despite the evident differences in the specific cultural shaping of the grounding experiences, we do recognize the experiences of people in other cultures as similar to our own.[59]

But also this kind of comprehension always presupposes that we know something of their grounding experiences and of their nature.

To sum up: facing Aquinas' concept of human nature from the point of view of contemporary philosophical anthropology, although we need to make explicit some of the topics which in his

---

57 Anthony Lisska, *Aquinas's Theory of Natural Law. An Analytic Reconstruction*, p. 211.

58. Cf. Martha Nussbaum, "Non-Relative Virtues: An Aristotelian Approach" in *The Quality of Life*, M.C. Nussbaum and Amartya Sen (eds.), Clarendon Press, New York 1993, p. 242–269, in particular p. 260: "the relativist has, so far, show no reason why we could not . . . say that certain ways of conceptualizing death are more in keeping with the totality of our evidence and the totality of our wishes for flourishing life than others; that certain ways of experiencing appetitive desire are for similar reasons more promising than others."

59 Martha Nussbaum, "Non-Relative Virtues: An Aristotelian Approach," p. 261.

*Creation and Evolution*

thought are absent (particularly modern science and evolution) or sometimes only implicit (particularly the basic role of language, of intersubjectivity, of cultural diversity and of history), we must acknowledge that Aquinas' concept of human nature (particularly first principles and natural law) is still basic. In particular: freedom and morality are rooted in human nature. Furthermore, in Aquinas' "weltanschauung" there is a kind of methodical (not ontological) anthropocentrism (the concept of man as a microcosm) that might be recovered today, after the scientific revolution and the contemporary discovery of the "anthropic principle."[60] I think that human experience, the apex of the evolution of nature, in its *natural* openness to the totality of being and to other men (since they are *quodammodo omnia* as we are), is the living criterion of our approaching reality. But this does not mean subjectivism, thanks to intentionality (we can recognize other beings as different) and thanks to the fact that in man the main dimensions of reality are integrated at a higher level or sketched at a lower level.

I would very much like to thank Prof. Maria Vittoria Gianelli for having helped me in translating this paper.

---

60 Nowadays many physicists would recognize that that the precise co-ordination of the laws of physics shows a degree of order and hence of intelligibility, which affirms an underlying purpose in the universe. Some even go so far as to claim that the laws of nature are precisely the laws necessary to produce a universe that can sustain our own lives and the world that we know (*anthropic principle*).

# Creation and Evolution
## William E. Carroll
## Cornell College (Iowa)

One day a little boy in Chicago asked his mother where he came from. His mother, pleased to have the opportunity to discuss such an important matter with her son, began by offering an elementary account of human biology, even introducing some references to the theory of evolution. Lest she restrict her analysis to the realm of the purely physical, she spoke of God's role in the creation of each human soul, and ultimately of God as the source of all that is. After his mother had finished, her young son, looking somewhat bemused, said to her that he had wondered where he had come from, because his friend next door had said that he came from New York.

As this famous anecdote indicates, it is easy to be confused about different kinds of origins. The failure to keep such kinds distinct has led to considerable confusion in discourse concerning philosophical and theological implications of contemporary cosmology and evolutionary biology. Stories of origins go to the heart of every culture, and examinations of accounts of origins in biology, cosmology, and theology allow us to probe the relationship between science and religion. Investigations of the nature and origins of life concern various scientific, philosophical, and theological disciplines. Although any discussion of evolution and creation requires insights from each of these three areas, it is not always easy to keep these disciplines distinct: to know, for example, what is the appropriate competence of each field of inquiry. Nor is it always easy to remember that a truly adequate view of life and its origins requires the insights of all three. As

*Creation and Evolution*

Jacques Maritain observed, we must distinguish in order to unite.[1]

The debate in the United States about what ought to be taught in the schools reveals how discussions about creation and evolution can easily become obscured in broader political, social, and cultural contexts. Evolution and creation take on cultural connotations, serve as ideological markers, with the result that each comes to stand for a competing world-view. For some, to embrace evolution is to affirm an exclusively secular and atheistic view of reality, and evolution is accordingly either welcomed or rejected on such grounds. As Daniel Dennett would say,[2] Darwin's ideas are truly dangerous, especially for anyone who wishes to embrace a religious view of the world. Or, as the author of the entry on "evolution" in the fifteenth edition of *The New Encyclopedia Brittanica* put it: "Darwin did two things: he showed that evolution was a fact contradicting scriptural legends of creation and that its cause, natural selection, was automatic with no room for divine guidance or design."[3]

There are two fundamental pillars of evolutionary biology which are important for contemporary discussions of the relationship among biology, philosophy, and theology. The first is the claim of common ancestry: the view that all living things are historically and organically interconnected. Commentators describing the recent publication of a kind of rough draft of the total genetic constitution of the human species, its genome, have been quick to point out that, since human genes look much like those of fruit flies, worms, and even plants, we have further confirmation of common descent from "the same humble beginnings and that the connections are written in our genes."[4] To affirm a

1 *Distinguer pour unir, ou Les degrés du savoir* (Paris: de Brouwer, 1932).
2 *Darwin's Dangerous Idea: Evolution and the Meanings of Life* (New York: Simon & Schuster, 1995).
3 Gavin de Beer, "Evolution," *The New Encyclopedia Brittanica*, 15th edition (1973–74).
4 David Baltimore, writing in *The New York Times*, 25 June 2000, p. 17. Baltimore thinks that the discoveries of the human genome project

}85{

## Restoring Nature

fundamental continuity among living things challenges the notion that distinct species were created by God through special interventions in nature. Common descent challenges as well the theological view that human beings, created in the image and likeness of God, represent an ontological discontinuity with the rest of nature.[5] Specifically, it would seem that any notion of an immaterial human soul must be rejected if one is to accept the truths of contemporary biology.

More troublesome, so it seems, is the commitment to natural selection as the mechanism by which biological change has occurred.[6] As a result of chance variations at the genetic level,

"should be, but won't be, the end of creationism." Ernan McMullin, commenting on the contributions of molecular biology to the thesis of common ancestry, writes that a comparison of the DNA, as well as of the proteins which DNA encodes, among different types of organisms "shows that there are striking similarities in chemical composition among them. These similarities are just the kind that one would expect from the hypothesis of common ancestry . . ." The molecular-level differences among species give an indication of the relative order of branching among the species. "What is impressive here is the *coherence* of the results given by examining many different macromolecules in this light. Without common descent, this intricate network of resemblances would make no sense." McMullin does not think that evidence from molecular biology in some sense proves that there is a common ancestry; he claims that there is a remarkable "consilience" between this evidence and the hypothesis of common ancestry. "Evolution and Special Creation," *Zygon* 28:3 (September 1993), pp. 299–335, at pp. 317 and 319.

5 Jon Seger, an evolutionary biologist and geneticist, observed that the human genome project is "evolution laid out for all to see. There's nothing peculiar or distinctive about us." According to Nicholas Wade, editor of the special science section of *The New York Times* dedicated to the announcement of the successes of the human genome project, "[t]he conditions of human existence, the reach of human abilities, the purpose of life—at least in a biological sense—have boundaries that are engraved in the genome's gnomic text." *The New York Times*, 28 June 2000, pp. 21 and D1.

6 For a good recent book on the challenges of evolutionary biology to traditional theology, see John F. Haught, *God After Darwin: A Theo-*

*Creation and Evolution*

variations in organisms result in some being better adapted to their environment and, as a result, nature "selects" these better adapted organisms and eliminates competitors. It is through this process of natural selection that evolutionary biology explains the way in which we can account for the diversity of species in the world. Although there are debates among evolutionary theorists about the randomness and contingency at the basis of evolution, many biologists argue that *at the very least* biology itself does not reveal any fundamental order, purpose, or meaning in nature. For some the randomness of evolutionary change is conclusive evidence that there is no purpose whatsoever in nature. Richard Dawkins once remarked that "although atheism might have been logically tenable before Darwin, Darwin made it possible to be an intellectually fulfilled atheist."[7] On another occasion Dawkins wrote that the universe revealed by evolutionary thought "has precisely the properties we should expect if there is, at bottom, no design, no purpose, no evil and no good, nothing but blind, pitiless indifference."[8] Daniel Dennett writes in no less stark terms:

> Love it or hate it, phenomena like this [DNA] exhibit the heart of the power of the Darwinian idea. An impersonal, unreflective, robotic, mindless little scrap of molecular machinery is the ultimate basis of all agency, and hence meaning, and hence consciousness, in the universe.[9]

Sir Francis Crick, co-discoverer of the double-helix structure of the DNA molecule, writes at the beginning of *The Astonishing Hypothesis* (1994):

> *logy of Evolution* (Boulder, Colorado: Westview Press, 2000). Another good source on this subject is: Mariano Artigas, *Las fronteras del evolucionismo* (Madrid: Ediciones Palabra, 1991).
>
> 7   *The Blind Watchmaker* (New York: Norton, 1986), pp. 6–7.
> 8   *River Out of Eden* (New York: Harper Collins, 1995), pp. 132–3.
> 9   *Darwin's Dangerous Idea: Evolution and the Meanings of Life* (New York: Simon & Schuster, 1995), p. 203.

> The Astonishing Hypothesis is that 'You,' your joys and your sorrows, your memories and your ambitions, your sense of personal identity and your free will, are in fact no more than the behavior of a vast assembly of nerve cells and their associated molecules.

Despite some oversimplifications in this brief summary, it ought to be clear that the contemporary natural sciences, and in particular biology, present challenges to traditional theological and philosophical notions of nature, human nature, and God.[10] Too often, however, these perceived challenges are the result of fundamental confusions. As we shall see, those scientists like Dawkins and Dennett fail to distinguish between the order of biological explanation and the order of philosophical explanation. They do not recognize that creation is first of all a category of metaphysical reflection and that, furthermore, the materialism which they embrace is a position in natural philosophy not required by the evidence of biology itself. Similarly, many of the critics of the general conclusions of evolutionary biology, as we shall see, also confuse the order of biological explanation and the order of philosophical explanation. Defenders of "special

---

10   A distinguished evolutionary biologist, Ernst Mayr, in summarizing recently the importance of Darwin's influence on modern thought, sees a fundamental incompatibility between Darwinian biology and traditional theology and philosophy: "Darwinism rejects all supernatural phenomena and causation. The theory of evolution by natural selection explains the adaptedness and diversity of the world solely materialistically . . . . Darwinism refutes typology [essentialism] . . . . Darwin's theory of natural selection made any invocation of teleology unnecessary . . . . Of all of Darwin's proposals, the one his contemporaries found most difficult to accept was the theory of common descent applied to Man. For theologians and philosophers alike, Man was a creature above and apart from other living beings." Ernst Mayr, "Darwin's Influence on Modern Thought," *Scientific American* (July 2000), pp. 79–83, at pp. 81–2. See, also, Mayr, *One Long Argument: Charles Darwin and the Genesis of Modern Evolutionary Thought* (Cambridge, MA: Harvard University Press, 1993).

*Creation and Evolution*

creation" and of "irreducible complexities" in nature think that divine agency will show up in such gaps of nature. But "gaps" of nature are the provenance of the specialized empirical sciences. Divine agency, rather, ought to be seen in the fundamental teleology of all natural things, in the need for a First Mover, and in the complete dependence of all things on God as the source of their existence. It is natural philosophy, a more general science of nature than the specialized empirical sciences, which examines the first two topics; and it is metaphysics which proves that all that is comes from God as cause.

I think that we can find important parallels between the reactions to Aristotelian science in mediaeval Islam, Judaism, and Christianity and the reactions to Darwinian and Neo-Darwinian theories of evolution in the modern and contemporary world. By re-visiting the mediaeval discussion of creation and the natural sciences, especially as found in the thought of Thomas Aquinas, we may be able to resolve a good deal of confusion concerning the relationship between creation and evolution. Obviously, the contemporary natural sciences are in crucial ways quite different from their Aristotelian predecessors. Aquinas and others in the Middle Ages would have found strange indeed Darwinian arguments of common descent by natural selection. Nevertheless, I think that the understanding of creation forged by Aquinas and the *principles* he advanced for distinguishing between creation and the natural sciences remain true.

To understand how the thought of Aquinas is important for contemporary discourse on creation and evolution we need to return, however briefly, to the intellectual world of the Latin Middle Ages. Throughout the thirteenth century, brilliant scholars such as Albert the Great and Thomas Aquinas wrestled with the implications for Christian theology of the most advanced science of their day, namely, the works of Aristotle and his Muslim commentators, which had recently been translated into Latin. Following in the tradition of Avicenna, Averroes, and Maimonides, Aquinas developed an analysis of creation that remains, I think, one of the enduring accomplishments of Western culture. In emphasizing the contribution of Aquinas, I do not want, however, to deny the sophisticated analyses of his Muslim and Jewish predecessors, analyses which Aquinas often cited.[11]

## Thomas Aquinas' Understanding of Creation

It seemed to many of Aquinas' contemporaries that there was a fundamental incompatibility between the claim of ancient science that something cannot come from nothing and the affirmation of Christian faith that God produced everything from nothing. Furthermore, for the Greeks, since something must always come from something, there must always be something; the universe must be eternal.

The scientific works of Aristotle and several of his mediaeval commentators provided an arsenal of arguments which appear, at least, to be contrary to the truths of Christianity. In particular, how is one to reconcile the claim, found throughout Aristotle, that the world is eternal with the Christian affirmation of creation, a creation understood as meaning that the world is temporally finite, that is, has a temporal beginning of its existence? In 1215 the Fourth Lateran Council had solemnly proclaimed that God created all that is from nothing [*de nihil condidit*] and that this creation occurred *ab initio temporis*. In 1277 the Bishop of Paris, Étienne Tempier, issued a list of propositions condemned as heretical, among them the claim that the world is eternal. As chancellor of the University of Paris, the bishop was well aware of the debates about creation and the eternity of the world which raged through the thirteenth century.[12] The controversy was part of the wider

---

11   For an account of Aquinas' indebtedness to his Muslim and Jewish predecessors, see Steven E. Baldner and William E. Carroll, *Aquinas on Creation* (Toronto: Pontifical Institute of Mediaeval Studies Press, 1997), pp. 12–34.

12   See Luca Bianchi, *L'errore di Aristotele: La polemica contro l'eternità del mondo nel XIII secolo* (Firenze: La Nuova Italia Editrice, 1984); *Il Ve-*

*Creation and Evolution*

encounter between the heritage of classical antiquity and the doctrines of Christianity: an encounter between those claims to truth founded on reason and those founded on faith. If faith affirms that the world has a temporal beginning, can reason demonstrate this must be true? What can reason demonstrate about the fact of creation itself, as distinct from the question of a temporal beginning? Indeed, can one speak of creation as distinct from a temporally finite universe? These are some of the questions which thirteenth century Christian thinkers confronted as they wrestled with the heritage of Greek science. These questions are distant adumbrations of discourse in our own day about the meaning of creation in the context of the insights of evolutionary biology.

A master principle which informs Aquinas' analysis of creation is that the truths of science cannot contradict the truths of faith. God is the author of all truth and whatever reason discovers to be true about reality ought not to be challenged by an appeal to sacred texts.

On the specific questions of creation out of nothing and the eternity of the world, the key to Aquinas' analysis is the distinction he draws between creation and change. The natural sciences, whether Aristotelian or those of our own day, have as their subject the world of changing things: from subatomic particles to acorns to galaxies. Whenever there is a change there must be something that changes. The ancient Greeks are right: from nothing, nothing comes; that is, if the verb "to come" means to change. All change requires an underlying material reality.

Creation, on the other hand, is the radical causing of the whole existence of whatever exists. To cause completely something to exist is not to produce a change in something, is not to work on or with some existing material. If, in producing

*scovo e i Filosofi: La condanna parigiana del 1277 e l'evoluzione dell'aristotelismo scolastico* (Bergamo: Pierluigi Lubrina Editrice, 1990); and *Censure et liberté intellectuelle à l'université de Paris (XIIIe - XIVe siècles),* (Paris: Les Belles Lettres, 1999).

something new, an agent were to use something already existing, the agent would not be the *complete* cause of the new thing. But such complete causing is precisely what creation is. To build a house or paint a picture involves working with existing materials and either action is radically different from creation. To create is to cause existence, and all things are totally dependent upon a Creator for the very fact that they are. The Creator does not take nothing and make something out of nothing. Rather, any thing left entirely to itself, wholly separated from the cause of its existence, would be absolutely nothing. Creation is not some distant event; it is the complete causing of the existence of everything that is. Creation, thus, as Aquinas shows, is a subject for metaphysics and theology; it is not a subject for the natural sciences. Although Scripture reveals that God is Creator, for Aquinas, the fundamental understanding of creation is accessible to reason alone, in the discipline of metaphysics; it does not necessarily require faith. Aquinas thought that by starting from the recognition of the distinction between what things are, their essences, and that they are, their existence, one could reason conclusively to an absolutely first cause which causes the existence of everything that is.[13] Aquinas shows that there are two related senses of creation, one philosophical, the other theological. The philosophical sense discloses the metaphysical dependence of everything on God as cause. The theological sense of creation, although much richer, nevertheless incorporates all that philosophy teaches and adds as well that the universe is temporally finite.

Aquinas saw no contradiction in the notion of an eternal created universe. He thought that it was a matter of biblical revelation that the world is not eternal. He also thought that reason alone could not conclude whether the world had a temporal beginning. But even if the universe were not to have had a temporal beginning, it still would depend upon God for its very being, its existence. The root sense of creation does not concern temporal origination; rather

13 An account of Aquinas' first magisterial discussion of creation can be found in Baldner and Carroll, *Aquinas on Creation*.

*Creation and Evolution*

it affirms metaphysical dependence.[14] For Aquinas, there is no conflict between the doctrine of creation and any physical theory. Theories in the natural sciences account for change. Whether the changes described are cosmological or biological, unending or finite, they remain processes. Creation accounts for the existence of things, not for changes in things. An evolving universe, just like Aristotle's eternal universe, is still a created universe. No explanation of evolutionary change, no matter how radically random or contingent it claims to be, challenges the metaphysical account of creation, that is, of the dependence of the existence of all things upon God as cause. When some thinkers deny creation on the basis of theories of evolution, or reject evolution in defense of creation, they misunderstand creation or evolution, or both.

## Divine Agency and the Autonomy of Nature

For some in the Middle Ages any appeal to the autonomy of nature, that is, any appeal to the discovery of real causes in the natural order, seemed to challenge divine omnipotence. One reaction, made famous by some Muslim thinkers, known as the *kalam* theologians, was to protect God's power and sovereignty by denying that there are real causes in nature. Thus, they would say that when fire is burning a piece of paper it is really God who is the true agent of the burning; the fire is but an instrument. Accordingly, events that occur in the natural world are only occasions in which God acts.[15]

14  The *complete* dependence of the creature on the Creator means that there is a kind of priority of non-being to being in any creature, but this priority is not fundamentally temporal. It is, as Aquinas said, a priority according to nature, not according to time. Both Albert the Great and Bonaventure argued, contrary to the view of Aquinas, that to be created *necessarily* means to have being *after* non-being. Thus, unlike Aquinas, they inextricably linked creation with temporal origination. See Baldner and Carroll, *Aquinas on Creation*.
15  The best known representative of this position in Islam was al-Ghazali (1058–1111); see *The Incoherence of the Philosophers*, trans. by Mi-

RESTORING NATURE

There is another dimension to this argument about God's power and the existence of causes in nature. Averroes, for example, rejected the doctrine of creation out of nothing, because he thought that to affirm the kind of divine omnipotence which produces things out of nothing is to deny a regularity and predictability to the natural world. Thus, for Averroes, to defend the intelligibility of nature one must deny the doctrine of creation out of nothing.[16] Averroes' position seemed to Muslim theologians to be a direct threat to orthodox belief in God: for Averroes denies God's omnipotence in the name of the sciences of nature. This debate between *kalam* theologians and Averroes[17] anticipates, as we shall see, discussions in our own day about evolutionary biology and divine action in the world.

Contrary to the positions both of the *kalam* theologians and of their opponent, Averroes, Aquinas argues that a doctrine of creation out of nothing, which affirms the radical dependence of all being

chael E. Marmura (Provo, Utah: Brigham Young University Press, 1997). Maimonides (1135–1204), an ardent critic, describes the position of the *kalam* theologians in this way: "They [the theologians] assert that when a man moves a pen, it is not the man who moves it; for the motion occurring in the pen is an accident created by God in the pen. Similarly the motion of the hand, which we think of as moving the pen, is an accident created by God in the moving hand. Only God has instituted the habit that the motion of the hand is concomitant with the motion of the pen, without the hand exercising in any respect an influence on, or being causative in regard to, the motion of the pen." *The Guide of the Perplexed* I.73; trans. by S. Pines (Chicago: University of Chicago Press, 1963), p. 202.

16  Averroes (1126–1198) thought that if one were to maintain that what exists could come from what does not exist (i.e., creation out-of-nothing), then "anything whatever might proceed from anything whatever, and there would be no congruity between causes and effect..." *Tah~fut al-Tah~fut* 452, trans. Simon Van den Bergh (Cambridge: E.J. Gibb Memorial Trust, 1987), 1:273.

17  A good account of this debate in mediaeval Islam and Judaism can be found in: Herbert Davidson, *Proofs for Eternity, Creation, and the Existence of God in Medieval Islamic and Jewish Philosophy* (Oxford: Oxford University Press, 1987).

}94{

*Creation and Evolution*

upon God as its cause, is fully compatible with the discovery of causes in nature. God's omnipotence does not challenge the possibility of real causality for creatures, including that particular causality, free will, which is characteristic of human beings. Aquinas would reject any notion of divine withdrawal from the world so as to leave room, so to speak, for the actions of creatures. Aquinas does not think that God "allows" or "permits" creatures to behave the way they do.[18] Similarly, Aquinas would reject a process theology which denies God's immutability and His omnipotence (as well as His knowledge of the future) so that God would be said to be evolving or changing with the universe and everything in it.[19] For

18  Aquinas' view of divine causality raises the specter of the so-called "problem of evil." Aquinas is able to respond successfully to objections that his view of God's causality makes God the source of evil; an exposition of Aquinas' views on this matter are, however, well beyond the scope of this essay.

19  Aquinas' understanding of divine action and its relation to biological change would allow us to avoid various attempts to accommodate the contingency affirmed in some evolutionary theories by re-thinking divine omnipotence, omniscience, and God's a-temporality. Keith Ward, Regius Professor of Divinity at Oxford, is a good example of this latter approach. Ward thinks that the traditional attempt to make God the "efficient cause of all things, without compromising the simplicity and unchangeability which are characteristics of the Aristotelian picture of God" was "an heroic failure," since it "could not account for the contingency of the universe." This is so because "[t]hat which is wholly necessary can only produce that which is necessary. A contingent universe can only be accounted for if one makes free creativity a characteristic of the First Mover, which entails placing change and contingency within the First Mover itself." *Religion and Creation* (Oxford: Clarendon Press, 1996), p. 202. According to Ward, God's omniscience "is the capacity to know everything that becomes actual, *whenever* it does so . . . . The classical hypothesis [of a God who does not change] does not . . . seem compelling." (italics added, p. 188) In a sense, God must wait to know what is actual since there is an inherent contingency in nature itself, and, as actualities change so does God's knowledge. Ward's arguments are far more sophisticated than can be adequately set forth in a footnote, but for

# RESTORING NATURE

Aquinas such views fail to do justice either to God or to creation. Creatures are what they are (including those which are free), precisely because God is present to them as cause. Were God to withdraw, all that exists would cease to be. Creaturely freedom and the integrity of nature, in general, are guaranteed by God's creative causality. On the other hand, the occasionalism of *kalam* theologians (e.g., al-Ghazali) protected the God of revelation from being marginalized from nature and history, but at too high a price, the denial of real causes in nature. If we follow Aquinas' lead, we can see that there is no need to choose between a robust view of creation as the constant exercise of divine omnipotence and the explanatory domain of evolutionary biology.[20]

> the claim that the Thomistic view of divine agency and the world of change is a great success, rather than "an heroic failure," see William E. Carroll, "Aquinas and the Metaphysical Foundations of Science," *Sapientia* 54:1 (1999), pp. 69–91.
>
> 20 There is a temptation in some circles to examine genetic mutations in the light of the insights of quantum mechanics and to discuss divine action in the context of the ontological indeterminism associated with the quantum world. It was William Pollard, who, in 1958, wrote: "The phenomenon of gene mutation is the only one so far known in these sciences which produces gross macroscopic effects but seems to depend directly on changes in individual molecules which are in turn governed by the Heisenberg uncertainty principle." *Chance and Providence: God's Action in a World Governed by Scientific Law* (London: Faber and Faber, 1958), p. 56. Recent reflections on genetic mutation and divine action are part of the wider notion that quantum mechanics shows us that there is a kind of metaphysical space which allows for divine action which does not "interfere" with nature. Thus special divine action can be seen as the "providential determination of otherwise undetermined events . . . . God's action will take the form of realizing one of several potentials in the quantum system, not of manipulating sub-atomic particles as a quasi-physical force." In an excellent essay on this topic, Robert J. Russell adopts "the *theological* view that God's special action can be considered as objective and non-interventionist if the quantum events underlying genetic mutations are given an indeterminist interpretation philosophically. If it can be shown scientifically that quantum mechanics plays a role in

}96{

*Creation and Evolution*

Aquinas shows us how to distinguish between the being or existence of creatures and the operations they perform. God causes creatures to exist in such a way that they are the real causes of their own operations. For Aquinas, God is at work in every operation of nature, but the autonomy of nature is not an indication of some reduction in God's power or activity; rather, it is an indication of His goodness. It is important to recognize that divine causality and creaturely causality function at fundamentally different levels. In the *Summa contra Gentiles*, Aquinas remarks that

> the same effect is not attributed to a natural cause and to divine power in such a way that it is partly done by God, and partly by the natural agent; rather, it is wholly done by both, according to a different way, just as the same effect is wholly attributed to the instrument and also wholly to the principal agent.[21]

It is not the case of partial or co-causes with each contributing a separate element to produce the effect. God, as Creator, transcends[22]

genetic mutations, then by extension it can be claimed theologically that God's action in genetic mutations is a form of objectively special, non-interventionist divine action. Moreover, since genetics plays a key role in biological evolution, we can argue by inference that God's action plays a key role in biological evolution . . . ." Russell, thus, presents a sophisticated form of theistic evolution. Robert J. Russell, "Special Providence and Genetic Mutation: A New Defense of Theistic Evolution," in *Evolutionary and Molecular Biology: Scientific Perspectives on Divine Action*, edited by Robert J. Russell, William R. Stoeger, and Francisco J. Ayala, pp. 191–223, at p. 213 and p. 206, italics in original (Vatican City: Vatican Observatory Publications, 1998).

21 *Summa contra Gentiles* III 70.8.

22 For a discussion of the sense of divine transcendence as used by Aquinas and how it differs from the modern conception of transcendence (as *contrasted* with immanence), see Kathryn Tanner, *God and Creation in Christian Theology: Tyranny or Empowerment?* (Oxford: Basil Blackwell, 1988); and William Placher, *The Domestication of Transcendence* (Louisville, KY: Westminster Press, 1996).

the order of created causes in such a way that He is their enabling origin. Yet the "same God who transcends the created order is also intimately and immanently present within that order as upholding all causes in their causing, including the human will." For Aquinas

> the differing metaphysical levels of primary and secondary causation require us to say that any created effect comes totally and immediately from God as the transcendent primary cause and totally and immediately from the creature as secondary cause.[23]

## Creation and Genesis

Some defenders as well as critics of evolution, as we shall see later, think that belief in the Genesis account of creation is incompatible with evolutionary biology. Aquinas, however, did not think that

---

23 Brian J. Shanley, O.P., "Divine Causation and Human Freedom in Aquinas," *American Catholic Philosophical Quarterly* 72:1 (1998), pp. 100 and 108. Shanley argues that no real explanation of exactly *how* God's causality functions is possible, since God transcends the mundane world of causation. Recently, Michael Miller has argued that Bernard Lonergan, following in the tradition of Aquinas, provides a more philosophically satisfying account of divine causation without sacrificing divine transcendence: in "Transcendence and Divine Causality," *American Catholic Philosophical Quarterly* 73:4 (Autumn 1999), pp. 537–554. David Burrell observes that the "terms 'primary' and 'secondary' [causality] come into play when we are faced with the situation where one thing is by virtue of the other. So each can properly be said to be a cause, yet what makes one secondary is the intrinsic dependence on the one which is primary. This stipulation clearly distinguishes a secondary cause from an instrument, which is *not* a cause in its own right: it is not the hammer which drives the nails but the carpenter using it." Burrell, *Freedom and Causation in Three Traditions* (Notre Dame, IN: University of Notre Dame Press, 1993), p. 97. See also William E. Carroll, "Aquinas and the Metaphysical Foundations of Science," *Sapientia* 54:1 (1999), pp. 69–91.

*Creation and Evolution*

the Book of Genesis presented any difficulties for the natural sciences, for the Bible is not a textbook in the sciences. What is essential to Christian faith, according to Aquinas is the "fact of creation," not the manner or mode of the formation of the world. In commenting on different views concerning whether all things were created simultaneously and as distinct species, Aquinas remarks:

> There are some things that are by their very nature the substance of faith, as to say of God that He is three and one ... about which it is forbidden to think otherwise. ... There are other things that relate to the faith only incidentally ... and, with respect to these, Christian authors have different opinions, interpreting the Sacred Scripture in various ways. Thus with respect to the origin of the world, there is one point that is of the substance of faith, *viz.*, to know that it began by creation .... But the manner and the order according to which creation took place concerns the faith only incidentally.

Aquinas notes that although the interpretation regarding successive creation, or what we might call "episodic creation," is "more common, and seems superficially to be more in accord with the letter," still that of simultaneous creation is "more conformed to reason and better adapted to preserve Sacred Scripture from the mockery of infidels."[24]

Aquinas' firm adherence to the truth of Scripture without falling into the trap of literalistic readings of the text offers valuable correction for exegesis of the Bible which concludes that one must choose between the literal interpretation of the Bible and modern science. For Aquinas, the literal meaning of the Bible is what God, its ultimate author, intends the words to mean. The

---

24  Thus Aquinas concludes, "this last opinion [Augustine's] has my preference;" yet he adds that he will undertake to defend both positions. *In II Sent.*, dist. 12, q. 3, a. 1.

RESTORING NATURE

literal sense of the text includes metaphors, similes, and other figures of speech useful to accommodate the truth of the Bible to the understanding of its readers. For example, when one reads in the Bible that God stretches out His hand, one ought not to think that God has a hand. The literal meaning of such passages concerns God's power, not His anatomy. Nor ought one to think that the six days at the beginning of Genesis literally refer to God's acting in time, for God's creative act is instantaneous and eternal.[25]

Aquinas, following the lead of Augustine, thinks that the natural sciences serve as a kind of veto in biblical interpretation. Augustine observed that when examining questions of natural phenomena that seemed to be discussed in the Bible, one should defer to the authority of the sciences, when available, to show what the text cannot mean. In examining, for example whether the light spoken of in the opening of Genesis (before the creation of the Sun and the Moon) is physical light, Augustine says that if

---

25 Throughout his commentary on Genesis, Aquinas adheres to the following principle: there is a distinction between primary and secondary material in the Bible. When writing about the codifying of articles of faith in a credal statement, Aquinas responds to the objection that "all things contained in Holy Scripture are matters faith" and because of their multitude "cannot be reduced to a certain number." "[O]f things to be believed some of them belong to faith, whereas others are purely subsidiary, for, as happens in any branch of knowledge, some matters are its essential interest, while it touches on others only to make the first matters clear. Now because faith is chiefly about the things we hope to see in heaven, 'for faith is the substance of things hoped for,' [Hebrews xi.1] it follows that those things which order us directly to eternal life essentially belong to faith; such as the three Persons of almighty God, the mystery of Christ's incarnation, and other like truths . . . . Some things, however, are proposed in Holy Scripture, not as being the main matters of faith, but to bring them out; for instance, that Abraham had two sons, that a dead man came to life at the touch of Elisha's bones, and other like matters narrated in Scripture to disclose God's majesty or Christ's incarnation." [ST II-II, q. 1, a. 6. ad 1]

}100{

*Creation and Evolution*

physicists show us that there cannot be physical light without a luminous source then we know that this particular passage does not refer to physical light.[26] The Bible cannot authentically be understood as affirming as true what the natural sciences teach us is false.

## Creation and Evolution in the Contemporary World

If we look at the way in which the relationship between creation and evolution is presented today we often see creation identified with the view that the great diversity of living things is the result of specific divine interventions; that God, for example, produced in a direct way, without intermediaries, the different kinds of minerals, plants, and animals that exist. If this were true, then the record of the past, regardless of its age, would reveal fundamental discontinuities: discontinuities which could only be accounted for by an appeal to direct divine action *in* the world. Arguments in support of this view are advanced on the basis of evidence adduced from both Scripture and science.[27]

To insist that creation *must* mean that God has periodically produced new and distinct forms of life is to confuse the fact of creation with what Aquinas would call the manner or mode of formation of beings in the world. Such an insistence has its source in a literalistic reading of Genesis, which Aquinas would reject. Proponents of "episodic creation" also appeal to a variety of arguments based on science to support their claims. Thus, we have the argument that evolutionary continuity is scientifically impossible because, for example, the fossil record fails to support Darwin's idea of the gradual development of new forms of life and that, accordingly, we must recognize the sudden appearance of new kinds of life. Another claim is that the only kind of genetic transforma-

---

26 Augustine, *On the Literal Meaning of Genesis* I:38–39.
27 For an excellent analysis of this view, see Howard Van Till, "The Creation: Intelligently Designed or Optimally Equipped?" *Theology Today* 55:3 (October 1998), pp.344–364.

}101{

tion that can be demonstrated shows us variation within kinds—what is called microevolution—but not macroevolution, that is, from one kind to another. There are also appeals to the second law of thermodynamics to argue that it is not possible for more complex forms of life to develop from less complex forms, since the principle of entropy would be violated.[28] One of the more sophisticated defenses of what has been called "special creation" can be found in the work of Alvin Plantinga,[29] who thinks that to argue that God created man, as well as the many kinds of plants and animals, separately and by special acts, is more probable than the thesis of common ancestry. Plantinga takes the famous example of the development of the mammalian eye, points to the extraordinary complexity of it and of the whole visual system, and concludes: "That it [the evolution of the eye in Darwinian terms] is *possible* is clear; that it *happened* is doubtful; that it is *certain*, however, is ridiculous."[30] Plantinga's real opponents are people such as Dawkins and Dennett who argue that the grand evolutionary synthesis necessarily implies a commitment to a naturalism which excludes God.[31] For Plantinga, creation, understood in the Christian sense, must mean special or episodic creation.

28  Van Till, p. 350.
29  Alvin Plantinga, "When Faith and Reason Clash: Evolution and the Bible," *Christian Scholar's Review* 21 (1991), pp. 8–32; "Evolution, Neutrality, and Antecedent Probability: A Reply to McMullin and Van Till," *Christian Scholar's Review* 21 (1991), pp. 80–109.
30  Plantinga, "When Faith and Reason Clash . . ." (italics in the original), p. 26.
31  One well-known critic of evolutionary thought, Philip Johnson, rejects attempts to accommodate evolution and belief in the Creator: "I think that most theistic evolutionists accept as scientific the claim that natural selection performed the creating, but would like to reject the accompanying metaphysical doctrine that the scientific understanding of evolution excludes design and purpose. The problem with this way of dividing things is that the metaphysical statement is no mere embellishment but the essential foundation of the claim." *Darwin on Trial*, 2nd edition (Downers Grove, IL: Intervarsity Press, 1993), p. 168.

*Creation and Evolution*

Perhaps the best known of the scientific arguments against the master narrative of evolution is the work of the biochemist, Michael Behe, who argues that there are specific life forms (e.g., the cell) and biotic subsystems which are, in his terms, "irreducibily complex," and which could not possibly be brought about by means of natural selection.[32] Irreducibly complex systems and life forms disclose "intelligent design" and lead us, ineluctably, to the existence of a designer.

The theological arguments based on Behe's work are similar to arguments for creation based on Big Bang cosmology. Traditionally, the Big Bang has been seen as a singularity at which the laws of physics break down. Physics cannot explain the primal Big Bang; thus we seem to have strong evidence, if not actual proof, for a Creator.[33] Philosophers such as William Lane Craig have argued that contemporary Big Bang cosmology confirms the doctrine of creation out-of-nothing since it shows that the universe is temporally finite.[34] It does not seem, however, that the singularity affirmed in modern cosmology encompasses the *absolute* beginning of the universe. As we have seen, Aquinas does not think that the sciences themselves can conclude whether or not the universe is temporally finite. Obviously, as Aquinas was aware, if we were to know that there is an absolute beginning to the universe we would know

---

32  Michael Behe, *Darwin's Black Box: The Biochemical Challenge to Evolution* (New York: The Free Press, 1996).

33  In the 1950s and 1960s, Soviet cosmologists were prohibited from teaching Big Bang cosmology; it was termed "theistic science."

34  Among William Lane Craig's many works in defense of this position one should examine the book he co-authored with Quentin Smith, *Theism, Atheism, and Big Bang Cosmology* (Oxford: Oxford University Press, 1993). Robert J. Russell claims that, whereas Big Bang cosmology does not confirm creation out of nothing, the notion of t=0 in that cosmology remains relevant for the doctrine of creation. Robert J. Russell, "T=0: Is it Theologically Significant?" in *Religion and Science: History, Method, and Dialogue*, edited by W. Mark Richardson and Wesley J. Wildman, pp. 201–224 (New York: Routledge, 1996).

}103{

that the universe is created out of nothing and that God exists.[35] Of course, what some cosmologists have termed an inexplicable singularity, recent theorists have sought to make explicable. Alexander Vilenkin has developed an explanation of the Big Bang itself in terms of "quantum tunneling from nothing." Stephen Hawking argues that an understanding of quantum gravity will enable us to do away with the notion of a singularity altogether, and he concludes that without an initial singularity there is nothing for a Creator to do. Hawking identifies creation with a temporal beginning of the universe. Thus, he thinks that by denying such a beginning he denies creation. But Big Bang cosmology, even with recent variations, neither supports nor detracts from the doctrine of creation, since cosmology studies change and creation is not a change. The Big Bang is not a primal event before which there is absolutely nothing.[36]

Behe's "irreducible complexities" are biological "singularities." In the hands of defenders, the existence of such "singularities" is strong, if not conclusive, evidence for an agent outside the regular course of nature. Most biologists respond to

35 Although Aquinas does not think that one can use reason alone to conclude that the universe is temporally finite and thus know, *on this basis*, that it is created out of nothing, he does think, as we have seen, that in the discipline of metaphysics one can know that the universe is created. Remember the distinction Aquinas draws between creation understood philosophically, as dependence in the order of being, and creation known through faith, which does affirm an absolute temporal beginning.

36 The fact that the natural sciences, including cosmology, study change excludes an absolute beginning of the universe from their purview, since such a beginning could not be a change. Any change presupposes some reality which is there to change. For a detailed discussion of the relationship between Big Bang cosmology and creation, see: William E. Carroll, "Thomas Aquinas and Big Bang Cosmology," *Sapientia* 53:1 (1998), pp. 73–95; "Big Bang Cosmology, Quantum Tunneling from Nothing, and Creation," *Laval théologique et philosophique* 44 (1988), pp. 59–75.

*Creation and Evolution*

Behe's claims of irreducible complexity by distinguishing between our not being able *to explain* the origin of complex structures like the cell in terms of evolutionary biology and Behe's conclusion that *in principle* no such explanation is possible and that, therefore, we must admit the role of an intelligent designer. They might very well accept the former—the epistemological claim—but they would reject the latter—the ontological claim. As several commentators have observed, those who argue for "irreducible complexity" and then move to claims about intelligent design represent a contemporary version of what has been called the "god of the gaps." This is the view that the natural order *itself* and the changes in it require an appeal to a divine agent operating within the world as a *supplement* to other agents and causes in the world. Seventeenth century "physico-theologians" such as Robert Boyle were exponents of this type of argument from design. In the same tradition, early in the eighteenth century, William Whewell, defender of the geological theory of catastrophism, argued that a uniformitarian explanation of change in terms of natural causes could not explain the diversity of species in the world. "We see in the transition from an earth peopled by one set of animals to the same earth swarming with entirely new forms of organic life," he wrote, "a distinct manifestation of creative power, *transcending the known laws of nature*: and, it appears to us, that geology [i.e., catastrophism] has thus lighted a new lamp along the path of natural theology."[37] In an important sense, if we have belief in God depend on the existence of

> gaps in the explanatory chain . . . [we ultimately] pit religion *against* science . . . . It is also to make evolution and creation seem like exclusive concepts. Creation [in

37  W. Whewell, "Lyell: *Principles of Geology*," *British Critic* 9 (1831), p. 194. Cited in Ernan McMullin, "Introduction: Evolution and Creation," *Evolution and Creation*, edited by Ernan McMullin (Notre Dame, IN: University of Notre Dame Press, 1985), p. 35. Italics added.

such a view] is portrayed as a series of interventions in natural process, and evolutionary natural process is held to be in principle insufficient to bring about major features of the world. A theory of evolution thus necessarily appears as a threat to the foundations of religious belief.[38]

It seems to me that if we recognize that there are sciences of nature, then such gaps can only be epistemological difficulties to be overcome. If nature is intelligible in terms of causes discoverable in it, we cannot think that changes in nature require special divine agency. The "god" in the "god of the gaps" is more powerful than any other agent in nature, but such a god is not the God of orthodox Christianity, Islam, and Judaism. Such a god can easily become a disappearing god as gaps in our scientific knowledge close.[39]

The "god of the gaps" or the intelligent designer of Behe's analysis is not the Creator; at least this god is not the Creator described by Aquinas. Nor is the argument from design to the existence of a Designer really the same as Aquinas' argument for the existence of God from order and purpose in nature. According to Aquinas, natural things disclose an *intrinsic* intelligibility and directedness in their behavior, which require that God be the source. Finality and purpose, keys to an argument for the existence of God, have their foundation in nature as a principle in things. Eight hundred years before Aquinas, Augustine makes a crucial distinction between God's causal activity and what in our own day has come to be called "intelligent design."

It is one thing to build and to govern creatures from *within* and from the summit of the whole causal nexus— and only God, the Creator, does this; it is another thing

38  McMullin, ibid.
39  This, in part, is the theme of Michael J. Buckley in *At the Origins of Modern Atheism* (New Haven, CT: Yale University Press, 1987).

*Creation and Evolution*

to apply *externally* forces and capacities bestowed by Him in order to bring forth at such and such a time, or in such and such a shape, what has been created. For all things were created at the beginning, being primordially woven into the texture of the world; but they await the proper opportunity for their existence.[40]

An important fear that informs the concerns of many believers is that theories of evolution, cosmic and biological, "transfer the agency of creative action from God" to the material world itself, and that this transferral is a rejection of the religious doctrine of creation.[41] The theological concern is that to recognize the complete competence of the natural sciences to explain the changes that occur in the world, without any appeal to specific interventions by God, "is essentially equivalent to . . . [denying] divine action of any sort in this world."[42] We have already seen how

40 *De trinitate* III.9. Also: "All the normal course of nature is subject to its own natural laws. According to these all living creatures have their determinate inclinations . . . and also the elements of non-living material things have their determinate qualities and forces, in virtue of which they function as they do and develop as they do . . . . From these primordial principles everything that comes about emerges in its own time and in the due course of events." Augustine, *De genesi ad litteram* IX.17. Howard Van Till has written a great deal on the relationship between patristic discussions of creation and the contemporary debate about evolution and creation, and he argues that Augustine and others recognize a "functional integrity" to nature: that the universe was brought into being in a less than fully formed state, "but gifted with the capacities to transform itself, in conformity with God's will, from unformed matter into a truly marvelous array of physical structures and life forms." Howard Van Till, "Basil, Augustine, and the Doctrine of Creation's Functional Integrity," *The Canadian Catholic Review* 17:3 (July 1999), p. 35. This article originally appeared in *Science and Christian Belief* 8:1 (April 1996), pp. 21–38.

41 Howard Van Till, "Basil, Augustine, and the Doctrine of Creation's Functional Integrity," *The Canadian Catholic Review* 17:3 (July 1999), p. 24.

42 Ibid., p. 28.

Aquinas responded to very similar fears in the Middle Ages. Aristotelian science seemed to threaten the sovereignty and omnipotence of God. But remember that Aquinas recognized that a world in which the natural processes are explicable in their own terms does not challenge the role of the Creator. One need not choose between a natural world understandable in terms of causes within it and an omnipotent Creator constantly causing this world to be. Aquinas thinks that a world of necessary connections between causes and effects, connections which he thinks are the hallmarks of its intelligibility, does not mean that the world is not dependent upon God.[43] Necessity in nature is not a rival to the fundamentally different kind of necessity attributed to God.[44]

Those like Richard Dawkins and Daniel Dennett, who argue for a denial of creation on the basis of evolutionary biology, see the incompatibility between evolution and divine action in fundamentally the same way as theistic opponents of evolution.[45] They fail to distinguish between the claims of the empirical sciences and conclusions in natural philosophy and metaphysics. That is, they assume that the natural sciences

43 The Aristotelian idea of scientific knowledge requires the discovery of such a causal nexus. Contemporary theories of science often eschew an appeal to the discovery of such necessary connections in nature. Furthermore, the "intelligibility" of the world is frequently seen exclusively in terms of mathematical formalism rather than in the intrinsic principles found in nature and in the relations among things, where Aquinas would locate it.

44 Aquinas distinguishes between necessary things which have a cause of their necessity and God who is necessary in Himself. See *Summa contra Gentiles* II, 55; *Summa theologiae* I, q. 22, a. 4; Baldner and Carroll, *Aquinas on Creation*, pp. 28–29; and Carroll, "Aquinas and the Metaphysical Foundations of Science," *op. cit.*, p. 79, n. 38.

45 We have already seen Alvin Plantinga's argument that creation must mean "special creation," and, in note 31, I quoted Philip Johnson's rejection of theistic evolution because he thought it was an oxymoron.

}108{

*Creation and Evolution*

*require* a materialist understanding of all of reality.[46] Furthermore, they mistakenly conclude that arguments for creation are essentially arguments from design in nature, and, thus, the creation which Dawkins and Dennett deny is really not the fundamental notion of creation set forth by thinkers such as Thomas Aquinas. We can see some of these misunderstandings in the following quotation from the Harvard geneticist, Richard Lewontin:

> [When science speaks to members of the general public] the problem is to get them to reject irrational and supernatural explanations of the world, the demons that exist only in their imaginations, and to accept a social intellectual apparatus, *Science*, as the only begetter of truth .... We take the side of science in spite of the patent absurdity of some of its constructs, in spite of its failure to fulfill many of its extravagant promises of health and life, in spite of the tolerance of the scientific community for unsubstantiated just-so stories, because we have a prior commitment, a commitment to materialism. It is not that the methods and institutions of science somehow compel us to accept a material explanation of the phenomenal world, but, on the contrary, that we are forced by our *a priori* adherence to material causes to create an apparatus of investigation and a set of concepts that produce material explanations, no matter how counter-intuitive, no matter how mystifying to the uninitiated. Moreover, that

46  Although many authors writing on the relationship among philosophy, theology, and the natural sciences recognize the philosophical and theological shortcomings (and errors) in analyses like those of Dawkins and Dennett, I think that a Thomistic approach is the best way to have a constructive engagement among these disciplines.

materialism is absolute, for we cannot allow a Divine Foot in the door.[47]

The reference to science as "the only begetter of truth" follows logically from the philosophical commitment to materialism. Even Francisco Ayala, a distinguished biologist familiar with theological arguments, writes the following:

> [I]t was Darwin's greatest achievement to show that the directive organization of living beings can be explained as the result of a natural process, natural selection, without any need to resort to a creator or other external agent . . . . Darwin's theory encountered opposition in religious circles, not so much because he proposed the evolutionary origin of living things (which had been proposed many times before, even by Christian theologians), but because his mechanism, natural selection, excluded God as accounting for the obvious design of organisms . . . . This is the conceptual revolution that Darwin completed—that everything in nature, including the origin of living organisms, can be explained by material processes governed by natural laws. This is nothing if not a fundamental vision that has forever changed how mankind perceives itself and its place in the universe.[48]

To refer to "a creator or *other* external agent" or to be concerned about not letting "a Divine Foot in the door" mistakenly locates creation on the same metaphysical level as agency in this

47 Richard Lewontin's review of Carl Sagan's *The Demon-Haunted World: Science as a Candle in the Dark*, in the *New York Review of Books* (January 9, 1997).
48 Francisco J. Ayala, "Darwin's Revolution," in *Creative Evolution?!* edited by John H. Campbell and J. William Schopf (Boston: Jones & Bartlett, 1994), pp.4–5. See his recent "Arguing for Evolution," in *Science Teacher* 67: 2 (February, 2000), pp. 30–32.

*Creation and Evolution*

world, and makes divine causality a competitor with other forms of causality. In such a scenario, the more we attribute causality to nature, the more we must reduce the causality attributed to God—or vice versa. As I have argued, Aquinas helps us to see the error in this kind of opposition.

## Human Nature and the Creation of the Soul: A Preliminary Approach

Can "everything in nature," as Ayala says, "be explained in terms of material processes?" Surely not everything *about* nature can be explained in terms of material processes. As we have seen, that everything is created—that is, completely dependent upon God as cause of existence—is a truth *about* nature which cannot be explained by material causality. Aquinas would say that the natural sciences are fully competent to account for the changes that occur in the natural world, but this does not mean that "everything *in* nature" can be explained in terms of material causes. Before we can judge whether all things in nature can be explained by material causes we must know what the things in nature are which need to be explained. To know what the natural world is like we need both the empirical sciences *and* a philosophy of nature.

Throughout this essay I have sought to make a clear distinction between creation and change: to argue, that is, that creation is a concept in metaphysics and theology, not in the natural sciences. But I would argue, in addition, that the natural sciences alone, without, that is, a philosophy of nature, cannot provide an adequate account of the natural order itself. Furthermore, an exclusively material explanation of nature, that is, an explanation which relies *only* on the discovery of constituent parts, does not describe nature as it really is. A thorough refutation of materialism is not within the scope of this essay; it would involve a recognition that any whole, whether it be a chemical compound or a living organism, is more than the sum of its material parts. The whole exists and behaves in ways different from the existence and

}111{

behavior of its constituent parts. Water, for example, exhibits properties not found in either oxygen or hydrogen. We cannot account for the "more" of the whole in terms of the sum of the material parts. At the very least, we should recognize, as Richard Lewontin did in the passage quoted above, that to claim that *only* materialist explanations of reality are acceptable is a philosophical assumption not required by the "methods and institutions of science."

When Aquinas remarks that the sciences of nature are fully competent to account for the world of physical reality he includes in the category of "sciences of nature" what we would call philosophy of nature. This is a more general science of nature than is proper to any one of the empirical sciences. Thus, a philosophy of nature, as distinct from the metaphysical study of creation, discusses questions such as what is change; what is time; whether bodies are composed of matter and form; is a materialist account of nature, or a dualist, or some other account true? The debate about randomness and chance in biological processes and whether there is purpose or finality discoverable in nature are also topics to be examined in natural philosophy.[49]

49 The debate about contingency in evolutionary processes and the implications of such contingency for notions of purpose, meaning, and finality in nature occurs in the domain of natural philosophy, and is, as I have suggested, quite separate from the topic of creation and evolution. Perhaps the most famous representative of theistic evolution is Pierre Teilhard de Chardin, who claimed that evolutionary change reveals a steady "complexification" as part of "a grand orthogenesis of everything living toward a higher degree of immanent spontaneity." *The Phenomenon of Man* (New York: Harper, 1965), p. 151. He was so convinced of the progressive directionality of evolution that he thought its goal was an Omega Point in which consciousness will be fully realized and would provide an ultimate explanation for the entire course of evolution. With greater circumspection, Christian DeDuve, has argued that the kind of progressive development revealed in the history of evolution follows almost inevitably given the right environment. The universe, as he says, is

*Creation and Evolution*

A good example of the kind of analysis needed, which brings a sophisticated philosophical reflection to the discoveries of the empirical sciences, is William Stoeger's discussion of chance and purpose in biology. Stoeger points out that the natural sciences discover an order and directedness *inherent* in physical reality: "in the laws, regularities, and evolving conditions as they function together to constitute the processes and relationships which emerge at each stage of cosmic history." These laws and conditions are more than a pattern of regularities that we observe; "that pattern must have some sufficient cause in nature itself." Although

"pregnant with life." "In this organic cloud, which pervades the universe, life is almost bound to arise, in a molecular form not very different from its form on Earth, wherever physical conditions are similar to those that prevailed on our planet some four billion years ago. This conclusion seems to me inescapable. Those who claim that life is a highly improbable event, possibly unique, have not looked closely enough at the chemical realities underlying the origin of life. Life is either a reproducible, almost commonplace manifestation of matter, given certain conditions, or a miracle. Too many steps are involved to allow for something in between." *Vital Dust* (New York: Basic Books, 1995), p. 292. De Duve, a Nobel laureate in biochemistry, is particularly concerned to refute the views of Stephen J. Gould, who rejects any appeals to "trends" or directionality in the course of evolutionary history. Commenting on the appearance of the human species, Gould writes that if we were to "replay the tape a million times from a Burgess beginning . . . I doubt that anything like *Homo sapiens* would ever evolve again." Gould describes man as a "tiny twig on an improbable branch of a contingent limb on a fortunate tree." *Wonderful Life* (Cambridge, MA: Harvard University Press, 1989), pp. 289, 291. Ernan McMullin provides an excellent account of the dispute in contemporary biological theory about purpose and randomness in: "Cosmic Purpose and the Contingency of Human Evolution," *Theology Today* 55:3 (October 1998), pp. 389–414. For the same issue in a wider context, see Mariano Artigas, *The Mind of the Universe: Understanding Science and Religion* (Philadelphia: Templeton Foundation Press, 2000) and Ian Barbour, *When Science Meets Religion: Enemies, Strangers, or Partners?* (San Francisco: Harper, 2000).

}113{

RESTORING NATURE

chance events are frequent and important in biological evolution, rendering its actual course indeterminate or unpredictable in exact outcome from any particular stage, these events and their short—and long-term effects—whether they be of point mutations at the level of molecular DNA, or the impact of a meteorite—are always within a context of regularities, constraints, and possibilities.

Thus, to refer to such events as "pure chance" or "to assert blithely that evolution proceeds by purely chance events is much less than a precise description of this source of unpredictability in biological evolution." To speak of regularities in nature, or of there being laws of nature, means that there are processes oriented towards certain general ends. "If there were no end-directed or end-seeking behavior in physical reality, there would be no regularities, functions, or structures about which we could formulate laws of nature." Furthermore, even though the contemporary natural sciences often seek to discover efficient causes without reference to purposes (final causes),

any ordering of efficient causes and their effects implicitly acknowledges and presupposes that the efficient causes and the processes which embody them are directed towards the realization of certain specific types of ends. Efficient causes always have certain specifiable *effects*.[50]

50 Stoeger also raises the theological question of the relationship between chance events and God's action in the world. He correctly observes that the fundamental issue here is the problem of temporality and divine action, a topic discussed above in this essay. William R. Stoeger, "The Immanent Directionality of the Evolutionary Process, and its Relationship to Teleology," in *Evolutionary and Molecular Biology: Scientific Perspectives on Divine Action*, edited by Robert J. Russell, William R. Stoeger, and Francisco Ayala, pp. 163–190, at pp. 169, 172, 179–180, and 187.

}114{

*Creation and Evolution*

It ought to be clear that to recognize, as Aquinas does, that reason alone is sufficient to describe the various processes that occur *in* nature does not mean that current theories of evolution do in fact provide a fully adequate scientific account of the origin and development of life. If we were to seek a complete analysis of biology in light of Thomistic natural philosophy there would be many questions which would have to be raised: not the least of which would be the arguments Aquinas advances for the existence of the human soul and the fundamental ontological distinction between human beings and the rest of nature.[51] Aquinas thinks that the human soul, given that its proper function is not that of any bodily organ, must be both immaterial and therefore specially created by God. Such an application of his doctrine of

---

51  Recently, Pope John Paul II, after noting that evolution was "more than a hypothesis," referred to the need to reject, as "incompatible with the truth about man," those philosophical interpretations of contemporary biology which see "the mind as emerging from the forces of living matter, or as a mere epiphenomenon of this matter." The Pope asked rhetorically whether the "ontological discontinuity" which separates man from the rest of nature does not "run counter to that physical continuity which seems to be the main thread of research into evolution in the fields of physics and chemistry." He answered his own question: "The sciences of observation describe and measure the multiple manifestations of life with increasing precision and correlate them with the time line. The moment of transition to the spiritual cannot be the object of this kind of observation, which nevertheless can discover at the experimental level a series of very valuable signs indicating what is specific to the human being. But the experience of metaphysical knowledge, of self-awareness and self-reflection, of moral conscience, freedom, or again, of aesthetic and religious experience, falls within the competence of philosophical analysis and reflection, while theology brings out its ultimate meaning according to the Creator's plan." John Paul II, "Message to the Pontifical Academy of Sciences," (22 October 1996), reprinted in a special edition of *The Quarterly Review of Biology* 72:4 (December 1997), pp. 381–283, at p. 383. This edition of the review also contains commentary on the Pope's message by Michael Ruse, Richard Dawkins, and others.

RESTORING NATURE

creation to the human soul depends on his arguments about the existence and nature of the soul, arguments which he advances in natural philosophy. Any understanding of the human person as the composite of body and soul which is consistent with evolutionary biology requires an understanding of the doctrine of creation and the compatibility of divine agency and natural causes. Hence the importance of the analysis of creation I have been offering for the particular discussion of human nature and contemporary biology. It is not my purpose here to examine Aquinas' conception of human nature and, in particular, how he defends the view that man is composed of body and soul. Let me just note, however, that Aquinas is not a dualist; he does not think that the body is one entity and the soul another. A human being is one thing, understood in terms of the unity of two principles, one material, the other spiritual. Aquinas' analysis of the human soul is an integral part of his explanation of living things, which is itself part of his even broader understanding of the distinction between form and matter, the co-principles of all physical reality.[52]

A rejection of Aquinas' specific claims about the human soul would not in any way challenge the truth of his analysis of creation. Nor does Aquinas' analysis of creation and its compatibility with contemporary evolutionary thought require us to accept or reject any evolutionary theory. Analyses of evolutionary theory occur in the disciplines of biology and natural philosophy. It is important to remember the point I made at the beginning of this essay, that we must recognize the appropriate competence of each of the various disciplines which investigate the nature and origins

52  That the rational soul is the informing principle of each human being follows from Aquinas' view that each individual substance, inanimate and animate, must have an informing principle, and that the differences among informing principles are correlative to the differences among existing substances. For a discussion of this question, see Roger Pouivet, "Aristotle and Aquinas on Soul," unpublished paper presented at the Institute of Thomistic Studies, Jacques Maritain Center, University of Notre Dame, 14–21 July 2000.

}116{

*Creation and Evolution*

of life. Throughout I have sought to show the value of Aquinas' thought for distinguishing creation from evolution. Whatever exists is caused to be by God; this is a conclusion in metaphysics; whether human souls are among the things that exist is a question to be answered in natural philosophy; whether living things have evolved by natural selection is the subject of evolutionary biology.

## Conclusion

We should remember, however, that evolutionary biology's commitment to common descent by natural selection is essentially an explanation of origin and development; it is a historical account. Several years ago Carl Friedrich von Weizsäcker wrote: "For philosophers, the most important discovery of modern science has been the history of Nature."[53] However much we recognize the value of this insight, we need to guard against the genetic fallacy: that is, making judgments about what things are exclusively on the basis of how things have come to be. There is also the danger of historicism—an embrace of flux and change as the *only* constants—which denies essences, natures (and species), and according to which the *only* explanatory principle is historical development. However necessary evolutionary biology is for understanding nature, it is not a substitute for the complete study of *what* things are and *how* they behave. These are questions which engage not only the empirical sciences but also the philosophy of nature. What things are and how they function involve discussions in terms of matter and form, potentiality and actuality, substance and accident, the nature of change, etc. It would be wrong to say that there is nothing in the natural order which cannot be accounted for by causes which the empirical sciences discover since the human soul exists in the natural order. The discovery of the existence of the human soul takes place in the

53  Forward to Bernd-Olaf Küppers, *Der Ursprung biologischer Information* (Munich: R. Piper and Co., 1986); *Information and the Origin of Life*, trans. by Paul Wooley (Cambridge, MA: MIT Press, 1990), p. xi.

}117{

realm of the philosophy of nature, not in that of the empirical sciences.[54] Thus we must recognize that any evolutionary theory remains an incomplete scientific account of living things. At the very least the question of the completeness or incompleteness of evolutionary theories as accounts of living things is a philosophical question, not resolvable by the empirical sciences themselves.

Although we do not have to appeal to divine action *in* the natural world to account for what the empirical sciences discover, it does not follow that a materialist account of reality is true. As we have seen, materialism is a philosophical position; it is not a conclusion of the empirical sciences. We must not confuse the order of explanation in the empirical sciences with the orders of explanation in natural philosophy and in metaphysics.

Thomas Aquinas as biblical exegete, metaphysician, and philosopher of nature offers us a rich array of insights for contemporary discourse on the relationship among sacred texts, the natural sciences, and philosophy. He can help us to avoid the whirlpool of a reductionist materialism as well as the stumbling block of biblical literalism. His principles continue to serve as an

---

54 However much we recognize that the existence of the human soul is a topic in natural philosophy, we need to remember that natural philosophy must always be grounded in the discoveries of the empirical sciences. Contemporary biologists need not concern themselves with what it is that makes the living body just the sort of body that it is. The answer to this question in natural philosophy is the soul. Biologists may very well be content to say that living beings are what they are and do what they do because they have the sort of bodies they have; they may feel no need to ask the further philosophical question of why the living body is just such a body. The philosophical answer to that question is the soul, the substantial form of the living being, and nothing about the biological sciences requires the gratuitous philosophical reductionism which denies or ignores the existence of the soul. If one accepts the reductionism and materialism of authors such as Dawkins and Dennett, there would be no justification in reality for treating living things differently from non-living things, nor for making distinctions in the treatment of different living things.

*Creation and Evolution*

anchor of intelligibility in a sea of confusing claims. Rather than excluding Darwin from the curriculum, the schools should add Aquinas.

An earlier version of this essay appeared as "Creation, Evolution, and Thomas Aquinas," in *Revue des Questions Scientifiques* 171.4 (2000), 319–347.

# Nature as a Metaphysical Object
### Lawrence Dewan, O.P.
## Dominican College of Philosophy and Theology
### (Ontario)

## General Considerations

A paper on nature as a metaphysical object[1] is, as we shall see, a paper on essence.[2] Is there anything more to say about

---

1   By "a metaphysical object" I mean what is a proper target of attention of the science of metaphysics; thus, in *ST* 1.11.3.*ad* 2, Thomas, speaking of the "one" which is interchangeable with "a being," calls it "*quoddam metaphysicum*," in contrast to the "one" which is the principle of number; this latter, he says, is "*de genere mathematicorum*." In *CM* 5.5 (808), he carefully explains how "*natura*," as said of all substance, pertains to first philosophy, just as does "substance," taken in all its universality.

At the outset of his *Commentary on the Nicomachean Ethics* Thomas lists among the orders with which reason has to do, the order of *natural* things. He says:

> There is a certain order which reason does not make, but only considers: such as is the order of natural things [*ordo rerum naturalium*]. [*In Eth.* 1.1 (#1).]

And he goes on to list the diverse sciences which relate to the various orders mentioned. As regards the order of natural things, he says:

> ... to natural philosophy it pertains to consider the order of things which human reason considers but does not make: we are taking "natural philosophy" as including within it also metaphysics [*ita quod sub naturali philosophia comprehendamus et metaphysicam*]. [*In Eth.* 1.1 (#2).]

2   *ST* 1.60.1 (ed. Ottawa, 362b5–7):

## Nature as a Metaphysical Object

essence? Essence had a difficult time in the 20th century, when the insistence was decidedly on existence. It might be wise to begin with a reminder of essence's right to "equal time." Since there are actually metaphysicians "out there" who think of essence as a mere limit on actual existence, or as a metaphysical item only needed to make possible the existence of creatures, beings other than the supreme being,[3] perhaps the best

> ... nature is prior to intellect, for the nature of each thing is its essence.

3.  In his book *Introduction à la philosophie chrétienne* (Paris: Vrin, 1960), looking for the basis for the possibility of having beings other than God himself, Étienne Gilson tells us:

> The difficulties to be surmounted are particularly serious in a theology like this one, where the first Cause TRANSCENDS THE ORDER OF ESSENCE. Indeed, it is a matter of understanding how essences can emanate from the being in which no distinctive essence is added to the *esse* to form a composition with it? This way of posing the question should, besides, suffice to allow us to see in what direction the answer must be sought. IF ONE LOCATED GOD IN THE ORDER OF ESSENCE, EVEN AT ITS SUMMIT, it would become extremely difficult, not to say impossible, to find outside of God a place for the world of creatures ... But we begin here with the notion of a God ENTIRELY TRANSCENDING THE ORDER OF ESSENCES, which includes the totality of creatures, whence one can infer that no problem of addition or subtraction will arise as between him and the being he creates. [170–171; my italics and caps; the question mark is Gilson's]

And towards the end of the meditation, he tells us:

> THE PROPERTY OF ESSENCE [LE PROPRE DE L'ESSENCE], finite mode of participating in being, is to render possible the existence of a *natura rerum* which is neither nothing nor God. [198; my italics and small caps]

Thus, it is clear that the word "essence," for Gilson, means properly a finite participation in being.

Of course, one can say that God transcends the entire order of being, as including both essence and existence; but that is obviously

}121{

## Restoring Nature

recommendation of essence we can provide is its status in the case of God. Suffice to say, then, that while in God the subsisting thing, the essence, and the act of being are one simple identical item, nevertheless that simple item verifies what is proper to each: inasmuch as God is not in another, he is a subsisting thing; inasmuch as he has whatness, he is an essence; and inasmuch as he is, actually, he is the act of being.[4] Indeed, what we call "essence" in creatures exists by priority in God,

> not what Gilson had in mind; cf. Thomas, *Expositio libri Peryermenias* 1.14 (ed. Leonine, t. 1*1, Rome/Paris, 1989: Commissio Leonina/Vrin, lines 438–442):
>
>> ... the divine will is to be understood as standing outside the order of beings [*ut extra ordinem entium existens*], as a cause pouring forth being in its entirety [*totum ens*] and all its differences. Now, the possible and the necessary are differences of being ...
>
> In another late text, *ST* 3.75.4 (2943a18–19), we have:
>
>> ... his [i.e. God's] action extends to the entire NATURE of being [*ad totam naturam entis*] ...
>
> This is in the context of the discussion of the change involved in the sacrament of the Eucharist. In the ad 3, there, God is called the author of *ens*, and the nature is also termed "*entitas*," "entity."
>
> 4  In *SCG* 4.11 (ed. Pera #3472–3473), we read:
>
>> ... those things which in creatures are divided are unqualifiedly one in God: thus, for example, in the creature essence and being [*esse*] are other; and in some [creatures] that which subsists in its own essence is also other than its essence or nature: for this man is neither his own humanity nor his being [*esse*]; but God is his essence and his being.
>>
>> And though these in God are one in the truest way, nevertheless in God there is WHATEVER PERTAINS TO THE INTELLIGIBLE ROLE [*ratio*] of the subsisting thing, or of the essence, or of the being [*esse*]; for it belongs to him not to be in another, inasmuch as he is subsisting; to be a what [*esse quid*], inasmuch as he is essence; and being in act [*esse in actu*], by reason of being itself [*ipsius esse*].

}122{

*Nature as a Metaphysical Object*

and exists there in a higher way: essence is most truly essence in God.[5]

The word "nature" has many meanings. Aristotle presented a whole series of meanings of *"phusis"* in *Metaph*. 5.[6] Boethius also had occasion to leave us a set of meanings of *"natura,"* the most relevant Latin term.[7] Thomas Aquinas recounted several times the findings of these authors, sometimes offering personal reflections on them.[8]

Aristotle begins with the generation or birth of living things as a meaning; in Thomas's Latin, *"natura"* in that meaning is equated with *"nativitas."*[9] Aristotle subsequently moves to the principles, within things, of such an event, and to the principle of a thing's other changes or movements.[10] The word is extended in

---

5. Cf. *De ente et essentia* c. 1 (ed. Leonine, lines 53–63. My italics.):

> But because *"ens"* is said absolutely and primarily of substances, and posteriorly and in a somewhat qualified sense of accidents, thus it is that *essentia* also properly and truly is in substances, but in accidents it is in a certain measure and in a qualified sense. But of substances, some are simple and some are composite, and in both there is *essentia*; but in the simple *in a truer and more noble degree* [*ueriori et nobiliori modo*], inasmuch as they also have more noble *esse*; for they are the *cause* of those which are composite, at least [this is true of] the first simple substance which is God.

6   Aristotle, *Metaphysics* 5.4 (1014b16–1015a19).

7   Boethius, *Contra Eutychen et Nestorium*, c. 1. Cf. *The Theological Tractates*, with an English translation by H. F. Stewart and E.K. Rand, London and New York, 1918 [reprint 1926]: Heinemann and Putnam [Loeb Classics].

8   E.g., *ST* 1.29.1.*ad* 4; also 3.2.1.

9   Thomas, *CM* 5.5 (808).

10  Here we have the meaning which will be given primacy in both the *Metaphysics* and the *Physics*. In *Physics* 2.1 (192b21–23), nature is a cause or principle of being moved and of being at rest, being within firstly and by virtue of itself and not by accompaniment. This is primarily the substantial form, secondarily the matter (193b3–8). In the *Metaphysics*, it is ultimately the form [*ousia*, which Thomas, *CM* 5.5 (826), interprets as *form* here] of things having a principle of move-

use even to the *essence* of changeable things. Lastly, by what Aristotle describes as a *"metaphor,"* the word is applied to ALL *ousia*.[11] It is with this last "metaphorical" use of the word that I will be concerned. Lest the word "metaphor" lead one to think of this use as negligible, let us recall Thomas's treatment of the word "light" [*lux*]. Is it said properly or metaphorically[12] as applied to spiritual things? Well, if you consider the word as regards its first imposition, it is indeed metaphorically applied to spiritual things; however, if you consider its subsequent history in the mouths of speakers [*"secundum usum loquentium"*], it is said properly as applied to spiritual things.[13] I would say that the same is true of the use of "nature" as applied to the essence of all beings.

Aristotle is, of course, reporting on actual Greek usage. One has an impressive use of *"phusis"* placed by Plato on the lips of the youthful Socrates in the dialogue *Parmenides*. Socrates speaks of the Forms of things as "patterns fixed in nature" [*paradeigmata hestanai en té phusei*], where "nature" clearly means the realm of the unchangeable, i.e. true being.[14] In fact, the relation of this area of vocabulary to the expression of being is striking. Thus, the English word "be" is cognate with the Greek *"phusis,"* and stems from the Sanskrit *"bhu,"* meaning "to become," i.e. to arrive at the terminus of generation.[15]

Again, Plato, in the *Cratylus*, writes :

ment within themselves as themselves (1015a13–15). The importance of the notion of substance for this conception cannot be too strongly underlined; selfhood, or a primary "within," depends on the notion of substance, since among the modes of unity, identity or selfhood is the mode proper to substance as substance; cf. *CM* 4.2 (561) and 10.4 (2002–2005).

11 Aristotle, *Metaph*. 5.4 (1015a11–13); cf. Thomas, *CM* 5.5 (823).

12 For Thomas's explanation of the difference between things said metaphorically and things said properly, cf. *ST* 1.13.3.*ad* 1 and *ad* 3.

13 *ST* 1.67.1.

14 Plato, *Parmenides* 132D.

15 Cf. *Concise Oxford Dictionary*, London, 1964 [fifth edition]: Oxford University Press, concerning "be."

*Nature as a Metaphysical Object*

> [*Socrates*] . . . [things] must be supposed to have their own proper and permanent essence [*ousian*]; they are not in relation to us, or influenced by us, fluctuating according to our fancy, but they are independent, and maintain to their own essence the relation prescribed by nature [*héper pephuken*].[16]

And:

> [*Socrates*] Are not actions a class of being [*ti eidos tôn ontôn*]? . . . Then the actions also are done according to their proper nature [*kata tén autôn phusin*], and not according to our opinion of them?[17]

Clearly, in this metaphysical discussion, what a thing is "as to nature" is contrasted with the mere being in human opinion.

My aim, then, in this paper, is to consider to some extent Thomas's use of this notion of nature as an object found universally, but analogically. What texts come to mind? Their great variety is already suggested by the variety of topics proposed by speakers for this week's proceedings. Certainly, texts include those on natural intellectual knowledge; on natural love in intellectual creatures; on nature and will in God; on the distinction between natural being and intentional being; on such a question as "is death natural?," etc. The point is to see what special task this notion of "nature" as applied universally performs. Why is it needed? Obviously, I can only hope to stimulate interest in so wide a topic.

But what is a "metaphysical outlook"? We might begin to answer that by recalling Aristotle's characterization of the science which seeks the first causes as the science of being as being. As Thomas reads him, Aristotle tells us that a cause must be the cause of some *nature*, and that the highest cause must be *the cause*

16  Plato, *Cratylus* 386d-e [trans. Benjamin Jowett].
17  *Cratylus* 387a.

}125{

## RESTORING NATURE

*of the nature of being.*[18] Thus, to engage in metaphysics, one must grasp the beings themselves which we experience as exhibiting the sort of unity we mean by "a nature."[19] It will not be a specific

18  As Thomas, *CM* 4.1 (533), on Aristotle at 1003a26–32, paraphrases: Every principle is the essential principle and cause of some *nature*. But we seek the *first* principles and the *highest* causes ... therefore, *they* are the essential cause of some *nature*. But of no other nature than that of *being* ... [Italics mine]

In *ST* 1.45.5.*ad* 1 (288b35–38), Thomas qualifies his use of the term *"natura"* for the field of reality as falling under the cause of being as such:

... sicut hic homo participat humanam naturam, ita quodcumque ens creatum participat, UT ITA DIXERIM, NATURAM ESSENDI; quia solus Deus est suum esse ... [ ... as this man participates human nature, so also each created being whatsoever participates, *if I may so speak*, the nature of being, because God alone is his own being ... ]

19  I will cite an early text along these lines, *Commentary on the* SENTENCES 2.1.1.1 (ed. Mandonnet, pp. 12–13), part of the prehistory of the Fourth Way (*ST* 1.2.3); Thomas is aiming to show that there must be one and only one unqualifiedly first principle:

This is apparent ... from the very nature of things [*ex ipsa rerum natura*]. For there is found in all things the nature of entity [*natura entitatis*], in some [as] more noble [*magis nobilis*], and in some less [*minus*]; in such fashion, nevertheless, that the natures of the very things themselves are not that very being itself [*hoc ipsum esse*] which they have: otherwise being [*esse*] would be [part] of the notion of every quiddity whatsoever, which is false, since the quiddity of anything whatsoever can be understood even when one is not understanding concerning it *that it is.* Therefore, it is necessary that they have being [*esse*] from another, and it is necessary to come to something whose nature is its very being [*cujus natura est ipsum suum esse*]; otherwise one would proceed to infinity; and this is that which gives being [*esse*] to all; nor can it be anything else but one, since THE NATURE OF ENTITY [NATURA ENTITATIS] IS OF ONE INTELLIGIBILITY [UNIUS RATIONIS] IN ALL, ACCORDING TO ANALOGY [SECUNDUM ANALOGIAM]: for

}126{

## Nature as a Metaphysical Object

nature or a generic nature. It will, nevertheless, have a unity which can well be described as "natural."[20]

In order to so view reality, we do not start with the "biggest picture." We start with the relevant sort of unity, but exhibited more locally. Thus, in his *Commentary on Aristotle's Metaphysics* (*CM*) 4, Thomas explains the Aristotelian conception of the unity of the field of metaphysics by means of a presentation of being in four modes or measures. In presenting four "modes of being," Thomas begins with the weakest, the least, and moves towards the strongest. The four are (1) negations and privations, (2) generations and corruptions and movements, (3) inhering accidents, and (4) substances. Here is his presentation:

> unity in the caused requires unity in the proper [*per se*] cause. This is the route taken by Avicenna in his *Metaphysics* 8.

> Here, then, the unity of the first principle is concluded to from the unity of the hierarchy of acts of being, a unity described as the "nature of entity."

20 We might recall *ST* 1–2.10.1.*ad* 3, concerning whether the human will is moved towards anything naturally. The objector argues that nature is determined to something one, but that the will relates to opposites; thus, it has no natural movement. Thomas replies:

> It is to be said that to a nature something one always corresponds, [but] something proportionate to the nature. For to the generic nature [*naturae . . . in genere*] there corresponds something generically one [*unum in genere*]; and to the specific nature there corresponds something specifically one; while to the individuated nature there corresponds one individual something. Therefore, since the will is a certain immaterial power, just as is the intellect, there corresponds to it naturally some one common thing, viz. the good; just as to the intellect there corresponds some one common thing, viz. the true, or that-which-is [*ens*], or the what-it-is [*quod quid est*]. Still, under the good, taken universally [*sub bono . . . communi*], many particular goods are contained, to none of which is the will determined.

> The point of the reply is that there is a *unity* proper to the altogether universal intelligibles.

One should know that the aforementioned [by Aristotle] modes of being [*modi essendi*] can be reduced to four. For one of them, which is the weakest, "is" only *in the mind*, namely *negation* and *privation*; we say they "are" in the mind, because the mind treats them as though they were some sort of beings, when it affirms or negates something in their regard. (The difference between negation and privation will be explained later.)

Another mode is close to the first as regards weakness, according to which *generation* and *corruption* and *movement* are called "beings." The reason [they are weak] is that they have, mixed in, something of negation and privation. Thus, it is said in [Aristotle's] *Physics*, bk. 3, that movement is *imperfect* actuality.

Now, in third place those items are called ["beings"] that have no admixture of not-being, and yet still have weak being, because they "are," not *by themselves*, but *in another*, the way *qualities*, *quantities*, and *properties* of substances "are."

But it is the fourth kind which is the most perfect, namely that which has being *in nature* [*esse in natura*] [i.e. not merely in the mind], and without an admixture of privation, and has *solid* and *firm* being, as *existing by virtue of itself*, the way *substances* "are."

And to this, as to what is first and principal, all the others are referred back. Thus, qualities and quantities are said to "be," inasmuch as they have "being-*in*" substances; movements and generations [are said to "be"] inasmuch as they *tend* towards substance, or to one of the others [i.e. quality or quantity]; and privations and negations [are said to "be"], inasmuch as they *remove* something pertaining to the other three modes.[21]

---

21  *CM* 4.1 (Cathala #540–543). We note the use here of "being in *nature*," as contrasted with being in the mind.

}128{

*Nature as a Metaphysical Object*

It is this kind of "sizing up" of what we immediately experience which constitutes the metaphysical outlook.[22]

Thomas obviously considers that reality is constituted with a unity along the lines suggested by this fourfold presentation. Thus, in other texts we see that *substances themselves* are presented to us in modes or levels or intensities of being. Thus, in *Summa Theologiae* (*ST*) 1.12.4, on whether any created intellect can by its own *natural* powers see the divine essence, Thomas establishes the premise that:

> ... the knowing [performed] by any knower is in keeping with the mode of its [the knower's] *nature*.

And he continues:

> Therefore, if the mode of being of any known thing exceeds *the mode of the nature* of the knower, necessarily the knowledge of that thing is beyond the *nature* of that knower.

And we are then presented with the hierarchy:

> Now, there are many modes of being.
>
> Some things are, whose NATURE does not have being save in this individual matter; and of this mode are all corporeal things.
>
> But some things are, whose NATURES are subsistent by themselves, not in some matter; which nevertheless are not their own being, but are [things] having being: and

22 This is an approach mainly in terms of being as divided by the categories, though the inclusion of change shows that being as divided by act and potency is also in play; change is "imperfect actuality" [*actus imperfectus*]. Thomas teaches that the approach in terms of act and potency is wider than that in terms of the categories; the latter is about perfect being, while the form includes even the imperfect: CM 5.9 (889).

RESTORING NATURE

of this mode are incorporeal substances, which we call "angels."

Of God alone the proper mode of being is that he be his own being subsisting.[23]

Clearly, this is a vision which has to be built up, and we see many signs of the process of building in various places. However, one thing is especially clear: that in the presentation of the hierarchy as a hierarchy of being as being, the importance of cognition, and particularly *intellectual cognition*, as constituting a principle of division, is most evident. The reason for this is the ineluctable role of ontology in the explanation of cognition. Aristotle's *mot* that the soul, through sense and intellect, is in a way all things suggests that there is a difference from the viewpoint of being itself, as between the thing which has intellect and the thing which does not. Thus, Thomas, in explaining why the rational creature is a subject of divine providence in a special way, says:

> It is evident that all parts are ordered towards the perfection of the whole: for the whole is not for the sake of the parts, but the parts are for the sake of the whole. But intellectual natures [*naturae intellectuales*] have a greater affinity with the whole than [do] other natures [*aliae naturae*]: for each intellectual substance is in a way all things, inasmuch as through its intellect it is inclusive

23  *ST* 1.12.4 (64b13–23). In this article, we seem to have the use of the word "nature" very much in the sense of "essence as ordered towards operation." One might even say that the act of being of the thing is being viewed as a quasi-*movement* caused by the essence. Cf. *ST* 1–2.10.1.*ad* 1, where the act of being [*esse*] is called "*motus proprius naturae*" (unless "*motus*" there should read "*modus*"?). Cf. also *ST* 1.42.1.*ad* 1, where the form or nature is seen as having two effects, the act of being and the operation. Thus, the notion of magnitude of perfection is applied even to the divine nature. For a remarkable presentation of the ontological hierarchy of substances, cf. *SCG* 3.20 (especially paras. 1–4), on how things imitate the divine goodness.

}130{

*Nature as a Metaphysical Object*

of being in its entirety [*totius entis comprehensiva est*]; whereas any other substance has a merely particular participation in being [*particularem solam entis participationem habet*]. Thus, fittingly, the others are provided for by God for the sake of the intellectual substances.[24]

Both levels of substance have being, but one has it in a more complete and so meaningful way. Accordingly, it occurs to me that a consideration of the presentation of this mode of nature will serve to stimulate interest in nature as a metaphysical object.

Among the various presentations by Thomas of the meanings of the word "*natura*," the foregoing texts put me in mind of one which contains an especially illuminating specification. In the *De ente et essentia* (*EE*), commenting on the use of "nature" to mean the *essence* of a thing, Thomas says:

> [Essence] by another name is also called "nature," taking "nature" according to the first way of those four which Boethius presents in the book *On the Two Natures*: according as every item which can be grasped by intellect in any way is called a "nature": for a thing is intelligible only through its definition and essence; and thus also the Philosopher says in *Metaphysics* 5 that every substance[25] is a nature. Nevertheless, the word "nature" taken in this way seems to signify the essence of the thing according as it has *an order towards the proper operation of the thing*, since no thing is bereft of a proper operation.[26]

24  *SCG* 3.112 (2860).
25  Here, "substance" is translating Aristotle's "*ousia*," and clearly means essence; cf. on the variety of meanings of the Latin "*substantia*," Thomas, *De potentia* 9.1.
26  *EE* c. 1, lines 36–49:

> Hoc etiam alio nomine natura dicitur, accipiendo naturam secundum primum modum illorum quatuor quod Boetius in libro De duabus naturis assignat: secundum scilicet quod

}131{

# Restoring Nature

It is this conception of essence as ordered to the thing's proper operation[27] which will be the key to my approach here today.

We should reflect on the idea of a proper operation, and, indeed, on the conception of operation. Obviously, it pertains to the move from a consideration of "nature" as naming the proper principles of physical things, as presented in Aristotle's *Physics* 2.1, to what is meant by "nature" as said of every essence. The Aristotelian definition in *Phys.* 2 speaks of a principle of *movement* or *change*. As Boethius says in this connection: "every body has

> natura dicitur omne illud quod intellectu quoquo modo capi potest, non enim res est intelligibilis nisi per diffinitionem et essentiam suam; et sic etiam Philosophus dicit in V Methaphisice quod omnis substantia est natura. Tamen nomen NATURE hoc modo sumpte uidetur significare ESSENTIAM REI *SECUNDUM QUOD HABET ORDINEM AD PROPRIAM OPERATIONEM REI*, CUM NULLA RES PROPRIA OPERATIONE DESTITUATUR.

Thus, here Thomas relates this general usage of "nature" to the first meaning proposed by Boethius:

> Natura est earum rerum quae, cum sint, quoquomodo intellectu capi possunt. [*De persona et duabus naturis* c. 1 (PL 64, 1431 B)]

(This is not the meaning from Boethius used in other presentations of "nature" as bearing upon essence, and notably not the meaning used in presenting Boethius in *CM* 5.)

The statement that no thing is without its proper operation is presented in *DV* 19.1 *sed contra* 1 as coming from St. John Damascene's *De fide orthodoxa* 2.23. Cf. Saint John Damascene, *De fide orthodoxa*, Versions of Burgundio and Cerbanus, edited by Eligius M. Buytaert, O.F.M., St. Bonaventure, N.Y., 1955: Franciscan Institute, cap. 37, pp. 142–143:

> . . . Operatio enim est naturalis uniuscuiusque substantiae virtus et motus. Et rursus, operatio est naturalis omnis substantiae innatus motus . . . Impossibile enim substantiam expertem esse naturali operatione. [lines 1–10, in part]

27  Cf. *ST* 1.42.3.*ad* 4:

*Nature as a Metaphysical Object*

its proper *movement*."[28] Thomas, I might add, relates the doctrine that "nothing is without its proper *operation*" to St. John Damascene.[29] Now, consider the following argument from an objector to the view that life pertains to God:

> Some things are said to "live," inasmuch as they move themselves . . . But to be moved does not befit God. Therefore, neither does "to live."

Thomas answers:

> . . . "natura" quodammodo importat rationem principii, non autem "essentia" . . .

28 The work of Boethius to which Thomas regularly refers as *"Liber de duabus naturis"* is usually presented under the title *Contra Eutychen et Nestorium*. It can be found in Boethius, *The Theological Tractates*, with an English translation by H. F. Stewart and E.K. Rand, London and New York, 1918 [reprint 1926]: Heinemann and Putnam [Loeb Classics]. Boethius, in his chapter 1, presents the meanings of the term *"natura."* He begins with the widest meaning and only comes in the end to the meaning given in Aristotle's *Physics* 2. We read:

> Quod si naturae nomen relictis incorporeis substantiis ad corporales usque contrahitur, ut corporeae tantum substantiae naturam habere uideantur, sicut Aristoteles ceterique et eiusmodi et multimodae philosophiae sectatores putant, definiemus eam, ut hi etiam qui naturam non nisi in corporibus esse posuerunt. Est autem eius definitio hoc modo: **"natura est motus principium per se non per accidens."** Quod "motus principium" dixi hoc est, quoniam **corpus omne habet proprium motum**, ut ignis sursum, terra deorsum. Item quod "per se principium motus" naturam esse proposui et non "per accidens," tale est, quoniam lectum quoque ligneum deorsum ferri necesse est, sed non [?] deorsum per accidens fertur. Idcirco enim quia lignum est, quod est terra, pondere et grauitate deducitur. Non enim quia lectus est, deorsum cadit, sed quia terra est, id est quia terrae contigit, ut lectus esset; unde fit ut lignum naturaliter esse dicamus, lectum uero artificialiter.

29 Cf. above, note 26.

}133{

## RESTORING NATURE

. . . as is said in *Metaph*. 9, action is twofold: one which goes forth into external matter, as to heat and to cut; the other, which remains within the agent, as to understand, to sense, and to will. The difference between the two is as follows: that the first [sort of] action is not the perfection of the agent which brings the movement about, but rather [is the perfection] of the very thing moved; whereas the second [sort of] action is the perfection of the agent. Hence, because movement is the act of the moveable thing, the second [sort of] act, inasmuch as it is the act of the one performing the operation, is called its "movement," on the basis of this likeness, that just as movement is the act of the moveable, so this sort of action is the act of the agent: though, admittedly, movement is the act of the imperfect, i.e. of that which exists in potency, whereas this sort of action is the act of the perfect, i.e. of that which exists in act, as is said in *De anima* 3. Therefore, in this mode in which understanding is a movement, that which understands itself is said to move itself. And in this way also, Plato held that God moves himself, not in the way that movement is the act of the imperfect.[30]

This sort of extension of the vocabulary of "movement" to operation in general helps to explain the movement of thought from "nature" in the *Phys*. 2 sense to "nature" in the sense of essence as ordered towards its proper operation. Thomas, commenting on the text of Aristotle's *De anima* 3 referred to above, stresses the difference between sensation and physical motion [*a motu physico*, line 32]; sensation, along with intellection and volition, is *properly* called an "operation."[31]

30  *ST* 1.18.3.*obj*. 1 and *ad* 1.
31  *In De anima* 3.6 [Leonine lines 8–36], commenting on *De anima* 3.7 (431a6).

}134{

*Nature as a Metaphysical Object*

The term "act," also, is used for both movement and operation, as is clear from the above. Movement is the act of a thing in potency, whereas operation is the act of a thing in act.[32] Indeed, Thomas will, in a metaphysical context, use the vocabulary of "operation" and "action" for the movement or change proper to the physical thing. Thus, we read:

> ... the bodies of those things whose being is in [the domain of] change imitate incorruptible bodies in this respect, that they always act; thus, for example, fire, which just in virtue of itself always heats, and earth, which just in virtue of itself always performs its proper and natural operations. And this indeed is the case because they have movement and their own proper operation just in virtue of themselves, and within them, inasmuch as their forms are the principles of such movements and actions.[33]

We must also recall the doctrine of the *importance* for a thing of its proper operation. We remember the text:

32  For the three modes of act, viz. form, operation, and imperfect act (which includes the movement of the mobile thing), cf. Aristotle, *Metaph.* 9.6 (1048b6–17) as commented upon by Thomas at *CM* 9.5 (1828–1831). For the origin of the vocabulary of "act" for the discussion of being, as coming from the vocabulary of movement, cf. Aristotle, *Metaph.* 9.3 (1047a30–b2) as commented upon in *CM* 9.3 (1805–1806).
33  *CM* 9.9 (1880), paraphrasing Aristotle, *Metaph.* 9.8 (1050b28–30). The Latin of the cited passage runs:

> ... corpora eorum, quorum esse est in transmutatione, imitantur corpora incorruptibilia in eo, quod semper agunt; sicut ignis, qui secundum se semper calefacit, et terra quae secundum se semper facit operationes proprias et naturales. Et hoc ideo est, quia habent motum et operationem suam propriam secundum se, et in eis, inquantum scilicet formae eorum sunt principia talium motuum et actionum.

}135{

RESTORING NATURE

... it is evident that operation is the ultimate act of the one performing the operation: hence, it is called "second act" by the Philosopher in *De anima* 2 [412a23]: for the thing having form can be merely potentially operating, as for example, the scientist is potentially considering. And thus it is that in other things "each thing is said to be for the sake of its operation," as is said in *De caelo* 2 [286a8].[34]

An especially good general picture of the nature and its order towards both being and operation is provided in the *ST* discussion

34  *ST* 1–2.3.2 (ed. Ottawa, 727b28–36):

Manifestum est autem quod operatio est ultimus actus operantis; unde et actus secundus a Philosopho nominatur, in II *De anima*; nam habens formam potest esse in potentia operans, sicut sciens est in potentia considerans. Et inde est quod in aliis rebus "res unaquaeque dicitur esse propter suam operationem," ut dicitur in II *De caelo*.

In his *In Aristotelis* DE CAELO ET MUNDO *expositio* 2.4 (334 [5]), Thomas says:

... [Aristotle here says] that each thing which has a proper operation is for the sake of its operation [*propter suam operationem*]: for anything whatsoever has appetite for its own perfection, as for its goal [*suum finem*]; and the operation is the ultimate perfection of the thing (or at least the product of the operation, in those things in which there is some product besides the operation, as is said in *Ethics* 1 [1094a3–7]); for it is said in *De anima* 2 [412a23] that form is first act, while operation is second act, as the perfection and the end of the one operating. And this is true both in corporeal things and in spiritual things, for example in the habits of the soul; and both in natural things and in artificial things.

But [Aristotle] says "which has a work" because of those things which are against nature, as are monstrosities; they do not have any work, taken precisely as such, but rather they have a deficiency as regards the operative power, as is evident in the case of those which are born lame or blind: for lameness is not an end intended by nature, for the sake of which it brings about the birth of the lame animal; but rather this happens aside from the intention of nature, from the deficiency of the natural principles.

}136{

*Nature as a Metaphysical Object*

of the Trinity; speaking of the *equality of magnitude* which obtains among the three Persons in God, Thomas says:

The *magnitude* of God is nothing else but THE PERFECTION OF HIS VERY NATURE.[35]

In the question's first article, an objector is introduced to argue that there can be no equality in God because there is no quantity. And to this, Thomas provides the following reply:

> . . . quantity is twofold. One is called "quantity of mass" or "dimensive quantity," which is found in corporeal things only, and so has no place in the Divine Persons. But the other is "quantity of power" [*quantitas virtutis*], which is caught sight of in connection with the *perfection* of some NATURE OR FORM. It is this [latter] quantity which is signified when something is said to be "more" or "less" warm, inasmuch as it is more *perfect* or less *perfect* as regards such a quality.[36] Such quantity of power [*quantitas virtualis*] is seen first of all at its root, that is, in the very perfection of the FORM OR NATURE, and thus one speaks of "spiritual greatness" [*magnitudo spiritualis*], as one speaks of heat as "great" because of its intensity and perfection. And thus Augustine says in *De trin.* 6, that "in those things which are 'great', not by reason of their mass, that is 'greater' which is '*better*'"; for the more *perfect* is what one calls "better."
>
> Secondly, however, quantity of power [*quantitas virtualis*] is seen in the EFFECTS of form. And the first effect of form is *being*, for every thing has being in accordance with its form. The second effect is *operation*, for every agent acts by virtue [*per*] of its form. Thus, quantity of power is seen as regards being and as regards operation;

35  *ST* 1.42.4 (268a24–25).
36  Here, the text says: "*in tali caliditate*," i.e. "in such warmth," but I am conjecturing "*in tali qualitate*," i.e., "in such a quality."

as regards being, inasmuch as those things which are of a more perfect nature have a greater duration; and as regards operation, inasmuch as those things which are of a more perfect nature, are more powerful as regards action . . . [37]

While we see these considerations applied, in the above quotation, to any *particular* nature, thus making being [*esse*] the effect of the nature, ultimately Thomas regularly takes the case of what is most *formal* of all, namely *being* itself.[38] Thus, he will speak of God, presented as being itself, subsisting by itself, as possessed of the entire *perfection* of being. We see this in a text such as the following:

. . . God is being itself, subsisting by itself [*ipsum esse per se subsistens*]: hence it is necessary that the total perfection of being [*totam perfectionem essendi*] be contained in him. For it is evident that if something warm does not have the total perfection of the warm, this is because warmth is not participated in according to its perfect character [*perfectam rationem*]; but if warmth were subsisting by itself, there could not be lacking to it anything of the power of warmth. Hence, since God is being subsisting, nothing of the perfection of being can be lacking to him. But the perfections of all things pertain to the perfection of being: for it is according to this that some [particular] things are called "perfect," viz. that they have being in some measure [*aliquo modo esse habent*]. Hence, it follows that the perfection of no thing is lacking to God.[39]

This text, showing what I would call the "Fourth Way" viewpoint, is absolutely typical of Thomas's metaphysical overview,

37   *ST* 1.42.1.*ad* 1.
38   *ST* 1.7.1 (37a43–44), and 1.4.1.*ad* 3.
39   *ST* 1.4.2.

}138{

*Nature as a Metaphysical Object*

for the whole of his career. It is a vision wherein being itself is considered as a nature.[40]

## More Particularly: The Nature of the Human Soul

The presentation of the human soul in *ST* 1.75–89 affords us the opportunity to watch Thomas contemplate a nature precisely as a nature. In the prologue to q. 75, in the midst of the treatise on the divine work of distinction,[41] we arrive at the consideration of the human being, a composite of spiritual and corporeal substance. However, after dividing the presentation into consideration of [1] the nature of man and [2] the production of man, it is immediately noted that it belongs to the theologian to consider the nature of man as regards man's *soul*. The body enters into the discussion only as regards its relation to the soul. Thus, qq. 75–89 are on *the essence of the human soul*. Thomas finds in pseudo-Dionysius's *On the Celestial Hierarchy* the approach he requires for this study, a three-step approach suitable to the study of spiritual substances, in terms of essence, power, and operation.[42] Philosophically, this is clearly an exercise in metaphysics.[43]

40 Cf. above, nn. 18 and 19; also *ST* 1.14.6 (97b43–51):

> ... the proper *nature* of each thing has solidity [*consistit*] inasmuch as it participates the divine perfection in some measure. But God would not perfectly know himself if he did not know in whatever measure his perfection is participable by others; nor would he know THE VERY NATURE OF BEING [*ipsam naturam essendi*] if he did not know all the modes of being.

41 Cf. *ST* 1.44.prologue (qq. 47–102 are on the divine work of distinguishing created things, one from another); 1.48.prologue (qq. 50–102 are on the distinguishing of the spiritual and the corporeal creature).

42 *ST* 1.75.prologue; and cf. 1.77.1.*sed contra*.

43 Notice the discussion of the limits of physics relative to metaphysics, as found in *CP* 2.4 (Maggiolo ed., #175 [10]), concerning Aristotle at 2.2 (194b13–15). We read:

> Hence, the consideration of the physicist which is concerning forms extends right up to the rational soul. But how it is with

}139{

RESTORING NATURE

Thomas has considerable confidence in the quality of his knowledge of the human soul. In discussing the limitations of our knowledge of God and angels, he raises the question whether our intellect through knowledge of material things can come to understand the immaterial substances. An objector argues in favour of such understanding:

> The human soul is in the genus of immaterial substances. But it can be understood by us through its act, by which it understands material things. Therefore, also other immaterial substances can be understood by us through their effects on material things.

Thomas, however, replies:

> . . . the human soul understands itself through its own act of understanding, which is its proper act, perfectly demonstrating ITS POWER AND ITS NATURE. But neither through this, nor through other things which are found in material things, can THE POWER AND NATURE of the immaterial substances be perfectly known; because such [effects] do not adequately measure up to their powers.[44]

> forms totally separate from matter, and what they are, or even how it is with this form, i.e., the rational soul, according as it is separable and able to exist without the body, and what it is as separable in virtue of its essence: to determine all this pertains to primary philosophy. Cf. *ST* 1.76.1.*ad* 1.

44  *ST* 1.88.2.obj. 3 and *ad* 3. The Latin of the reply reads:

> . . . anima humana intelligit seipsam per suum intelligere, quod est actus proprius eius, perfecte demonstrans virtutem eius et naturam. Sed neque per hoc neque per alia quae in rebus materialibus inveniuntur, perfecte cognosci potest immaterialium substantiarum virtus et natura; quia huiusmodi non adaequant earum virtutes.

*Nature as a Metaphysical Object*

While qq. 75–89 are rich in materials relevant to our topic, q. 77, located between the discussion of the essence of the soul in itself and the discussion of the operation of understanding, is an ideal focal-point for seeing the essence ordered towards operation, i.e., the *nature*. The first issue is the very distinction between essence and power. As Thomas himself points out, not everyone sees the need to make this distinction.[45] The single article here depends on a three-step presentation already given in treating of the angels, viz. 1.54.1–3. Thomas there begins by distinguishing between the substance of the angel (and of any creature) and its act of understanding (or any operation); he next shows the necessity to distinguish between the angel's act of being and its act of understanding (indeed, between any creaturely act of being and any operation); and lastly he argues that the essence of the angel (or of any creature) cannot be identified with its operative power.

Of these three articles, the most important and enlightening is the second, distinguishing between the act of being and the act of understanding. Thomas recalls the distinction between actions which remain in the agent, such as to sense, to understand, and to will, and actions which project forth and influence something else, such as to heat and to cut. The problem is not here with these latter, since they are not easily confused with the substance or the act of being of the agent. However, "I think" and "I am" might be confused, and so the basis of distinction is the object of the operation: to understand and to will have an infinite object, viz. all things, whereas the creaturely act of being is finite.[46]

As I said, 1.77.1 is based on 1.54.1–3, and concludes that in no creature can there be identity between essence and operative power. 1.77.2 presents the rationale for the multiplicity of powers of the human soul. The point is that the multiplicity of powers pertains to the place of man and human soul in the hierarchy of reality. Man belongs in the upper echelon of reality inasmuch as he can attain to "the universal and perfect good," i.e., to beatitude.

45  *ST* 1.77.1 (463b6).
46  *ST* 1.54.2.

However, among things so endowed, he is at the lowest level, and so needs many kinds of operation to do so.

1.77.3 explains how one distinguishes one operative power from another, i.e., on the basis of the objects of the operation. One notes here how important it is that the distinctions are rather evident in the realm of the external senses, thus providing a model for the discussion of the more immaterial powers.

With 1.77.4 we come to what more directly concerns us at present. Is there an *order* among the powers of the human soul? Without this vision of order, we would have little conception of the unity of the source, i.e., of the soul as a nature. That this is so is brought out in 1.77.6, where the first objection against the powers flowing from the essence of the soul is the simplicity of the soul versus the multiplicity of powers:

> From one simple item diverse items do not proceed. But the essence of the soul is one and simple. Since, therefore, the powers of the soul are many and diverse, they cannot proceed from its essence.

And Thomas replies:

> It is to be said that from one simple item many can *naturally* proceed in some *order*. And, again, because of the multiplicity of recipients. Thus, therefore, from the one essence of the soul many and diverse powers proceed, for one reason, because of the *order* of the powers, for another, because of the diversity of corporeal organs.[47]

This means that, in order to have a decent conception of the order of the essence towards the powers and operations, i.e., of the essence as a nature, one must consider the order of the powers, already presented in a. 4.

We might note in a. 4, first of all, the sort of thing we have in

47  *ST* 1.77.6.*ad* 1.

*Nature as a Metaphysical Object*

the *sed contra*, recalling that Aristotle had compared the powers of the soul to the sequence of geometrical figures. The idea that one must proceed from one to many by virtue of an order is linked to the *coherence* of the procession, its *per se* character. Obviously one can associate a merely chaotic variety of accidental entities with a substance, but they are not *per se* associates if they do not have something to do with the very *unity* of the substance.[48] Thus, Thomas begins precisely on this point:

> It is to be said that since the soul is one, while the powers are many, and it is by some order that there is procession from something one to a multiplicity, it is necessary that there be order among the powers of the soul.

48   Cf. 1.76.4.*ad* 3:

> . . . in matter there are considered diverse grades of perfection, viz. being, living, sensing, understanding. But always the following supervening one is more perfect that the previous one. Therefore, the form which gives merely the first grade of perfection to matter is most imperfect; but the form which gives the first and the second and the third, and so on, is most perfect; and nevertheless, it is immediately [united] to the matter.

And cf. also *ST* 1.76.5.*ad* 3:

> It is to be said that the parts of the animal, as the eye, the hand, the flesh, and the bone, and such, are not in a species; but rather [it is] the whole [which is in a species]; and so it cannot be said, properly speaking, that they are of diverse species, but rather that they are of diverse dispositions. And this suits THE INTELLECTIVE SOUL, WHICH THOUGH IT IS ONE AS TO ITS ESSENCE, NEVERTHELESS BECAUSE OF ITS OWN PERFECTION IS MANY AS TO POWER; and therefore for the sake of the diverse operations it requires diverse dispositions in the parts of the body to which it is united. And for this reason we see that the diversity of parts is greater in the perfect animals than in the imperfect, and in these latter than in plants.

He then specifies:

> Now, a threefold order is seen among them. Two of them are considered as to the dependence of one power on another; the third is taken from the order of [their] objects.
>
> But the dependence of one power on another can be taken in two ways: in one way, according to the order of NATURE,[49] inasmuch as the more perfect are prior to the less perfect; in the other way, according to the order of generation and time, inasmuch as from the imperfect one comes to the perfect.
>
> Therefore, according to the first order of powers, the intellective powers are prior to the sensitive powers: hence, they direct them and dominate them. And, similarly, in this order the sensitive powers are prior to the powers of the nutritive soul.
>
> But according to the second order, the converse is the case. For the nutritive powers of the soul are prior, on the pathway of generation, to the sensitive powers: hence, they prepare the body for the actions of the latter [powers]. And it is similar for the sensitive powers relative to the intellective powers.
>
> But as regards the third order, some sensitive powers are ordered among themselves, viz., sight, hearing, and smell. For the visible is naturally prior, because it is common to superior and inferior bodies. And audible sound is brought about in air, which is naturally prior to the mixture of the elements, which odor follows upon.

Notice here the following objection and reply. The second objector says:

---

49  On the natural order in being, cf. *CM* 5.13 (950–953), concerning Aristotle, *Metaph.* 5.11 (1019a2–14).

*Nature as a Metaphysical Object*

> ... The powers of the soul relate to their objects and to the soul itself. But based on the soul there is no order among them, because the soul is one. Similarly also, based on the objects, which are diverse and altogether disparate, as is clear in the case of color and sound. Therefore, there is no order among the powers of the soul.

Thomas replies:

> It is to be said that this order of the powers of the soul has its base in the soul, which according to a certain order stands related to the diverse acts, even though it is one as to its essence; and also, as based on the objects; and also as based on the acts, as was said.[50]

The third reply here notes that in the case of the first two sorts of order, the *operation* of one power depends on the *operation* of another.

Obviously, here in 1.77.4 we are close to the vision of human unity itself, inasmuch as we see this order in the multiplicity.

1.77.5 asks whether all the powers are in the soul as in a subject. Here we have the distinction between the intellect and will, on the one hand, viz., the powers which have no corporeal organ, and all the other powers which do have an organ. The latter have as their subject the composite of soul and body, the former the soul alone. However, it is noted already, all the powers have the soul as their principle[51]

It is aa. 6 and 7 of q. 77 which most concern us here. Do the

---

50  *ST* 1.77.4.*ad* 2.

51  This doctrine will affect the reply in the last article of q. 77, viz. a. 8, as to whether the powers remain in the soul when it is separated from the body. Only the intellect and will remain actually, though the others remain as in their source [*virtute*]. Notice *ST* 1.77.8.*ad* 2: the powers having the composite as subject are not natural properties of the soul alone, but are properties of the composite.

powers *flow* from the essence of the soul? Does one power *flow* from another? If we are to see the essence of the soul as a nature, i.e., as ordered towards its proper operation, this doctrine is central.

In a. 6, the *sed contra* sends us to Aristotle's *Metaphysics* 7, stating that the subject is introduced into the very definition of the proper accident.[52] The idea is that the powers of the soul are its natural properties, and thus are caused by the soul.

The body of the article could not be more metaphysical. It consists mainly in a distinction between the role of the substantial form and that of the accidental form (where the accidental form is a proper accident of the substance). It begins:

> It is to be said that the substantial form and the accidental form partly agree and partly differ. They agree in this, that each is act, and in function of each something is in some measure in act.
>
> But they differ in two respects. Firstly, because the substantial form brings about being, unqualifiedly, and its subject is a being in potency only. The accidental form, on the other hand, does not bring about being, unqualifiedly; but rather, being such, or so much, or in some relation; for its subject is a being in act. Hence, it is clear that actuality [*actualitas*] is found by priority in the substantial form rather than in its subject; and because what is first is cause in every order, the substantial form causes being in act in its subject. But, conversely, actuality is found by priority in the subject of the accidental form rather than in the accidental form; hence, the actuality of the accidental form is caused by the actuality of the subject. And this takes place in such a way that the subject, inasmuch as it is in potency, is receptive of

52 The footnote in the Ottawa ed. sends us to *Metaph.* 7.4 (1029b30), but I would suggest 7.4 and 5 (1030a17–1031a14); cf. *CM* 7.4.

}146{

*Nature as a Metaphysical Object*

the accidental form; while inasmuch as it is in act, it is productive of it. And I say this regarding the proper and essential [*per se*] accident; for relative to the extraneous accident, the subject is merely receptive; an extrinsic agent is productive of such an accident.

But, secondly, the substantial and accidental forms differ, because since the less principal is for the sake of the more principal, matter is for the sake of the substantial form; but, conversely, the accidental form is for the sake of the completion of the subject.

All this is said subsequent to a. 5, in which we saw that some powers, viz., the intellect and the will, have the soul itself as their subject. Thus, Thomas now briefly makes his point:

But it is evident from things already said [1.77.5] that the subject of the powers of the soul is either the soul alone, which can be the subject of an accident inasmuch as it has something of potentiality, as was said above [1.77.1.*ad* 6; 1.75.5.*ad* 4]; or else the composite. But the composite is in act through the soul. Hence, it is manifest that all the powers of the soul, whether their subject is the soul alone or the composite, flow from the essence of the soul as from a principle; because it was just said that the accident is caused by the subject according as it is in act, and is received in it inasmuch as it is in potency.

This concludes the body of the article. The basic idea is that the substantial form as such is the source of actuality for the accidental forms.

The doctrine of the powers flowing from the essence of the soul is thus based on the priority as to actuality of the subject of the accidental form over the accidental form itself; which in turn is based on the priority of substance and hence substantial form

RESTORING NATURE

over accident. It is the fundamental doctrine of being which is in play.[53]

Let us move quickly on to a. 7, on the flow of one power from another. The body of the article begins:

> It is to be said that in those things which proceed in a *natural* order from something one, just as the first is the cause of all, so also that which is closer to the first is in some measure [*quodammodo*] the cause of those which are more remote.
>
> But it has been shown above [1.77.4] that among the powers of the soul there is manifold order. And so one power of the soul proceeds from the essence of the soul through the mediation of another. [470a19–27]

53 On the ontology of substance and accident, cf. *SCG* 4.14 (par. "*Quamvis autem in Deo* . . ."):

> . . . in us relations have dependent being [*esse*], because their being is other than the being of the substance: hence, they have a mode of being proper [to them] in function of their own proper character [*rationem*], just as is the case with the other accidents. Indeed, because all accidents are certain forms added to the substance, and caused by the principles of the substance, it is necessary that their being be added on, over the being of the substance, and depending on it [the being of the substance]; and the being of each of them is prior or posterior inasmuch as the accidental form, as regards its proper character, is closer to substance or more perfect. For which reason, a relation really added to the substance has the last and most imperfect being: last, because not only does it presuppose the being of the substance, but also the being of other accidents from which the relation is caused: as, for example, one in quantity causes equality, and one in quality likeness; but most imperfect, because the proper character of relation consists in the fact that it is towards another: hence, its proper being, which it adds to the substance, depends not only on the being of the substance, but also on the being of something external.

}148{

*Nature as a Metaphysical Object*

Having made this general point, Thomas now looks at the situation more closely. We read:

> But because the essence of the soul compares to the powers both [1] as active and final principle and also [2] as receptive principle, either separately by itself or together with the body; and the agent and the end is more perfect, whereas the receptive principle, as such, is less perfect; the consequence is that the powers of the soul which are prior according to the order of perfection and of nature are the principles of the others in the mode of end and active principle: for we see that sense is for the sake of intellect, not the converse; moreover, sense is a lesser [*deficiens*] participation in intellect; hence, according to natural origin it is in some measure [*quodammodo*] from intellect, as the imperfect from the perfect.
>
> But in function of the pathway [*viam*] of the receptive principle, conversely, the imperfect powers have the role of principles with respect to the others; just as the *soul*, inasmuch as it has the sensitive power, is considered as a subject and a sort of material with respect to the intellect; and for that reason, the more imperfect powers are prior on the pathway of generation: for animal is generated prior to man.[54]

The comparison with the soul, as having a conception in terms of the sequence of types of soul, is to be noted here. The nobility of the soul is seen in its being the single principle of the variety of powers.[55]

This is the entire body of the article. My point is, as always, that the order of causal flow of the powers pertains to the doctrine of the unity of source, and so to the vision of the essence of the soul as a nature, a nature with a certain proper perfection.

54  *ST* 1.77.7.
55  Cf. *ST* 1.76.3 (454b28–56).

}149{

Before concluding, I wish to add a few points which complete the picture. Thomas takes on the complex task of presenting the essence of the soul as source of all the powers of *man*. I will focus for the moment on the soul as source and subject of the two spiritual powers, the intellect and the will. In terms of what we have seen, it is clear that one of these powers flows from the other, and in fact, the will flows from the intellect, the less perfect from the more perfect. This is the significance of the articles in which Thomas makes the comparison of the one power to the other, e.g., *ST* 1.82.3. We might note one objection and reply in that context, one which harmonizes very much with what we have seen. The objector, arguing for the greater nobility of the will, says:

> Natural things are found to proceed from the imperfect to the perfect. And this also is apparent among the powers of the soul: the process is from sense to intellect, which is more noble. But the natural process is from the act of the intellect to the act of the will. Therefore, the will is a more perfect and more noble power than the intellect.

To which Thomas replies:

> It is to be said that that which is prior as to generation and time is more imperfect: because in one and the same thing potency temporally precedes act and imperfection perfection. But that which is prior, unqualifiedly, and as regards the order of *nature*, is more perfect: for thus act is prior to potency. And it is in this way that intellect is prior to will, as the motive principle [*motivum*] to the mobile item, and as the active to the passive: for the understood good moves the will.[56]

---

56   *ST* 1.82.3.*ad* 2.

}150{

*Nature as a Metaphysical Object*

We note that the sequence here is not temporal, but rather one of the imperfect following upon the perfect. The act of the will which follows upon that of the intellect can very well be *simultaneous* with that of the intellect.[57]

We should note how Thomas conceives of the "flow" of powers from the essence of the soul, and of one power from another. In 1.77.6.*ad* 3, the objector argues:

> ... "Emanation" names a sort of movement. But nothing is moved by itself, as is proved in *Physics*, book 7 [241b24], save perhaps by reason of a part: as an animal is said to be moved by itself, because one of its parts is the mover and another is the moved. Nor, also, is the soul moved, as is proved in *De anima* 1 [408a34]. Therefore, it is not the case that the soul causes in itself its own powers.

That is, this whole idea of the *flow* of the powers, which have their *seat in* the essence, from the essence *itself*, doesn't make sense: one identical thing would be both mover and moved. And Thomas replies:

> It is to be said that the emanation of the proper accidents from the subject is not by virtue of any change [*transmutationem*]; but rather by a natural following forth [*naturalem resultationem*]: the way in which from one item another naturally [*naturaliter*] results: as, for example, color from light.[58]

Here, the idea is that light and color are given together in one same instant, but that color is able to affect the transparent medium (e.g., the air around the colored body) only with the aid

---

57  Cf. e.g. *DV* 29.8 [Leonine lines 212–ff.].
58  *ST*1.77.6.*ad* 3; this is explicitly applied to the flow of one power from another in 1.77.7.*ad* 1.

}151{

of light (color being a participation of light by the body limiting the transparent medium).[59]

One would have eventually to discuss the outmoded character of this example. I had at first thought that our best examples of what Thomas means are such sequences as arm and hand, or eye and socket muscles. We find in things a natural order of forms, without which a thing which is one would be incomplete. However, that is more a case of final causality than of productive causality. We might better resort to something more intellectual. When one already knows the major premise and one comes to see the minor in its role as minor, at the same moment one sees the conclusion. The conclusion is an effect of the premise, a natural sequel.[60]

We see something of the importance of the doctrine of emanation of powers from soul and power from power when, speaking later of how the intellect knows the act of the will and the will itself, Thomas first of all faces an objector who argues that since

59 Cf. *In De anima* 2.14 (Leonine lines 342–387, especially lines 373–380 as follows):

> . . . it is to be said that the power of color in acting is imperfect, as compared to the power of light: for color is nothing else but a light in some measure obscured by being mixed with the opaque body; hence it does not have the power to render the medium in that disposition by which it is rendered receptive of color; which pure light can do.

60 Cf. *De substantiis separatis*, c. 9 [Leonine lines 180–234] (Lescoe tr., p. 63): what is brought into being by change must have being *after* not being, whereas in the mode of production which is by simple emanation or influence the effect or result can be understood as always having being. Thomas sees the sort of thing he has in mind best exemplified for us humans, not in corporeal causes and effects, but rather in "intellectual things which are at a greater remove from motion." Thus, he points out that the truth of the principles is the cause of the truth which is in the conclusions, which conclusions are always true; he introduces Aristotle on necessary things which have a cause of their necessity: *Metaph.* 5.6 (1015b9) and *Phys.* 8.3 (252a32–b6).

}152{

*Nature as a Metaphysical Object*

the intellect is an entirely different power than the will, the act of the will is not in the intellect and so is not known by the intellect. Thomas replies:

> . . . the argument would work if the will and the intellect, just as they are diverse powers, so also they differed as to subject: for thus what is in the will would be absent from the intellect. Now, however, since both are rooted in the one substance of the soul, and one of them is in some measure [*quodammodo*] the principle of the other, the consequence is that what is in the will is also in some measure in the intellect.[61]

So also, explaining what Augustine meant by saying that the affections of the soul are known through certain "*notiones*," Thomas says:

> . . . the affections of the soul are not in the intellect merely through likeness, as bodies are; nor through presence as in a subject, as [in the case of] the arts; but rather as the result [or: sequel] in the principle [*sicut principiatum in principio*] in which one has the notion [*notio*] of the result . . . [62]

Lastly, we should note a problem: if the power cannot be identical with the essence of the soul because, it would seem, of the very nobility of the object of the power (at least in the case of intellect and will), how can the essence itself still be seen as the source of the power? Can the greater come from the lesser? A manifestation of this problem is seen in the particular case of the agent intellect. Thomas teaches that the agent intellect is a power

---

61  *ST* 1.87.4.*ad* 1. On the natural sequence: substance, intellect, will, cf. my paper, "The Real Distinction between Intellect and Will," *Angelicum* 57 (1980), 557–593.

62  *ST* 1.87.4.*ad* 3.

}153{

RESTORING NATURE

of the human soul. The argument for this point in the *ST* is not simple. Thomas first teaches that there must be, above the human intellect, a higher intellect on which it depends, and from which it obtains the power [*virtus*] to understand. That this is a power within the soul itself, participated from the higher mind, Thomas concludes both on general principles and in view of our own actual experience.

However, one of the objections runs:

> If the agent intellect is something belonging to the soul, it must be some *power* . . . . But every power flows from the essence of the soul. Therefore, it would follow that the agent intellect would proceed from the essence of the soul. And thus it would not be in the soul by participation from some higher intellect; which is unacceptable. Therefore . . .

Thomas answers:

> . . . since the essence of the soul is immaterial, created by the supreme intellect, nothing stands in the way of the power which is participated from the supreme intellect, [the power] by which it abstracts from matter, proceeding from its essence, just as the other powers.[63]

We see that, for an adequate conception of the essence of the soul as a nature, i.e., as ordered to operation, and in particular to the intellectual operation, it must be seen as itself flowing from the divine creative cause.

This falls in with the picture we were given in 1.77.6: the property relates to the essence both as in potency relative to the essence and as act relative to the essence. As act relative to the essence's potency, it indicates the need for something above the essence of the soul. This is in accord with the need for completion

63   *ST* 1.79.4.*ad* 5.

}154{

*Nature as a Metaphysical Object*

which the soul (and every creature) has. It is to this situation Thomas refers when explaining later how supernatural grace can be a quality of the soul. A most important ontological remark is found in the reply to an objection. Substance, it is objected, is nobler than quality, and grace is nobler than the nature of the soul. Thus, it cannot be its quality. Thomas replies:

> It is to be said that every substance either is the very *nature* of the thing of which it is the substance, or else is a part of the nature (in which way the matter or the substantial form is called "substance"). And because grace is above human nature, it cannot be that it is the substance or the substantial form: rather, it is an accidental form of the soul itself. For that which is in God substantially is brought to be accidentally in the soul participating the divine goodness: as is clear in the case of *science*. Therefore, in accord with that, because the soul imperfectly participates the divine goodness, the very participation in the divine goodness which is grace has being in a more imperfect mode in the soul than [the mode of being by which] the soul subsists in itself. Nevertheless, it is more noble than the nature of the soul, inasmuch as it is an expression or participation of the divine goodness, though not as to the mode of being [*non autem quantum ad modum essendi*].[64]

This is true even of a natural virtue such as theoretical science, which is a participation in beatitude.[65] The mode of being is accidental, but the sort of participation in the divine goodness is so noble that it cannot be substantial in creatures.

To complete this picture of the divine agent above the human soul, let us look now at *ST* 2–2.2.3. It asks whether believing something beyond natural reason is necessary for salvation. It

64   *ST* 1–2.110.2.*ad* 2.
65   *ST* 1–2.66.3.*ad*.1.

# RESTORING NATURE

uses the vision of the natural cosmic hierarchy as a basis for a conception of the relation of the human mind to God. We read:

> In all ordered *natures* it is found that two things concur for the perfection of the lower *nature*: one which is according to its proper movement; the other which is according to the movement of the *superior nature.*
>
> For example, water, according to its proper movement is moved towards the center [of the universe], but according to the movement of the moon it is moved about the center as regard flowing and flowing back; similarly, also, the spheres of the planets are moved by their proper movements from west to east, but by the movement of the first sphere from east to west.
>
> Now, only the created rational nature has *immediate* order to God. Because the other creatures do not attain to anything universal, but only to something particular, participating the divine goodness either as to being only, as inanimate things, or also in living and knowing singulars, as plants and animals; but the rational nature, inasmuch as it knows the universal intelligibility of being and the good [*universalem boni et entis rationem*], has an *immediate* order to the universal principle of being [*ad universale essendi principium*].
>
> Therefore, the perfection of the rational creature does not consist merely in that which befits it according to its own nature, but in that also which is attributed to it from some supernatural participation of divine goodness. Hence, earlier it was said that the ultimate beatitude of man consists in some supernatural vision of God.[66]

Thomas goes on to explain the role of faith in the attainment of this beatitude. My primary point in citing this text is not the general

66   *ST* 2–2.2.3 [1415b41–1416a25].

}156{

*Nature as a Metaphysical Object*

doctrine of hierarchy of natures, where the examples are in obvious need of updating; nor am I concerned for the moment with the need for faith; rather, I underline the view of the rational *nature* as such, as *immediately* under the divine influence.[67]

There should be no hesitation in seeing here a metaphysical conception of nature. Thus, Thomas speaks of the divine nature as the "higher nature":

> It is to be said that because the nature of man depends on a higher nature, natural knowledge does not suffice for his perfection, but some supernatural [knowledge] is required . . . [68]

## Conclusion:

My aim today has been to recall how all-embracing and important is the conception of nature as essence ordered towards operation. After indicating the presence of this notion in the very conception of metaphysics as a science, I have focused on a particularly prominent case, the essence of the human soul as exhibiting such an order.

---

67 This was also seen in the fact that the human soul can only come into existence by being itself created, unlike other substantial forms (*ST* 1.90.1–3); and in the fact that it is God who, as supreme in the order of immateriality, is the source of the intellective power (*ST* 1.105.3).

68 *ST* 2–2.2.3.*ad* 1.

# What Nature? Whose Nature? Reflecting on Some Recent Arguments in Natural Law Ethics[1]

### Fulvio Di Blasi
### Jacques Maritain Center
### (University of Notre Dame)

What kind of nature is the foundation of morality? What does the adjective "natural" mean when it is followed by law? Everyone working on Aristotle and Aquinas usually agrees that nature is the measure of what is good, and that evil is somehow against nature. But the meaning and the ethical relevance of nature among contemporary Thomistic authors seem sometimes so far away from their classical roots that one can easily wonder if the alleged link between nature and morality is today no more than a slogan.

I think the concept of nature, as used in ethics by John Finnis, Germain Grisez, Joseph Boyle, William May, Robert George, and their followers, on the one hand, and by Martin Rhonheimer, on the other, is closer to modern philosophy than to Aquinas's realism, at least under two main respects: (1) the tendency of making ideas in themselves, rather than material reality, the first object of philosophical reflection; and (2) the tendency of focusing on the

---

1    This article was written for the 2001 Thomistic Institute sponsored by the Jacques Maritain Center, University of Notre Dame. I thank Ralph McInerny for inviting me. I thank also Stephen Brock for his useful comments and Jeffrey Langan and Timothy Smith for their help in correcting my English.

agent's subjectivity rather than on an objective (ethical) order. These tendencies are respectively the objects of my "What Nature" and "Whose Nature" provocative questions.

In this paper, I want to focus on the way in which these authors tend to approach specific ethical issues. There is a consistency between metaphysical views and ethical methodology. And I would like to show that some relevant mistakes they make in applied ethics depend on their peculiar and non-classical way of looking at nature. For my present purposes, it is very important to show how the tendencies I mentioned can become a real methodological background. Consequently, my general strategy will be the following: first, through my "What Nature" and "Whose Nature" questions, I will sketch the two tendencies and the way in which they affect ethical methodology; second, I will analyse in more detail, in the light of those tendencies, some arguments that the above-mentioned scholars propose with respect to contraception and sodomitical acts; finally, I will sketch Aquinas's approach to nature as the basis of morality.

Another premise is *de rigueur*. Finnis, Grisez, Rhonheimer, etc., are effectively defending the Church's ethical teaching against strong modern and contemporary objections (esp. those rooted in proportionalism and analytical philosophy), and are widely rediscovering the treasures of classical philosophy and theology. They are making a tremendous contribution that I greatly appreciate and do not want to deny. I simply believe that they became a little entangled in the same philosophical background of the arguments they criticize, and that this background prevents a more refined understanding of the authentic Thomistic tradition of thought.

Moreover, those scholars' theories are very different from one another in many respects, and also very refined and nuanced. Especially in the case of Rhonheimer—who, unlike the others, does not belong to Grisez's school—the generalizations involved in this article risk being unfair. I have to stress forcefully, therefore, that the point of this article is not to give full justice to anybody's specific viewpoint but to underline common philosophical

RESTORING NATURE

tendencies. I apologize for grouping together very different and rich authors but, if I am wrong, it must be at the level of the general interpretation of current philosophical tendencies, and not at the secondary level of the peculiar traits of someone's thoughts or of one or more specific points or arguments.

## 1. What Nature?

My "What-Question" is concerned with the tendency of focusing on a sort of world of values in itself as if it were something different from (and morally prior to) the real, *material*, world. "Nature" as the ground of ethics becomes the "nature of practical reason." And understanding (or studying) nature becomes equal to understanding the values which exist and act in our practical reason. This is a sort of immanentistic point of view which creates the problem of connecting the realm of values (ideas) with the realm of facts: the same problem created by Decartes's dualism between *res extensa* and *res cogitans* (or between body and spirit).[2] The values are grasped by practical reason, not due to an understanding of the intrinsic meaning of material reality, but independently of it. And they (the values) are then supposed, so to speak, to colonize material reality giving it ethical *order* and meaning. The logical problem is not anymore the "is-ought" but the "ought-is."

This tendency is pretty clear, e.g., in the opposition outlined by Rhonheimer between nature (natural order) and reason (moral order), as well as in his doctrine of "the measuring function of the reason"—which tends to present human reason as a *non-measured measure* of morality.[3] With respect to the concept of nature, it is easy

2    Of course, this is not to say that there is not explicit concern in the authors I have in mind (especially in Rhonheimer) to avoid dualism. I just think that dualism remains as an unintended outcome of their philosophies.

3    M. Rhonheimer, *Natural Law and Practical Reason. A Thomist View of Moral Autonomy* [1987] (Fordham: New York 2000), pp. 15–6, 307 ff; *La Prospettiva della Morale. Fondamenti dell'Etica Filosofica* (Armando Editore: Roma 1994), pp. 127–8; "Sulla Fondazione di Norme Morali

*What Nature? Whose Nature?*

to detect, at this level of Rhonheimer's discourse, an ambiguous terminology. He speaks, e.g., of (a) a "nature" that does not contain the final moral orientation; and (b) a "practical reason" that, consequently, "creates,"[4] is the "measure of morality,"[5] "establishes the hierarchy"[6] and "constitutes the difference between good and evil."[7] Or, again, of (a) "natural inclinations" which do not contain in themselves the "ordering to the right end,"[8] and (b) a "moral goodness," or "order of operative perfection (morality)," that goes "beyond the nature," "beyond the principles of the *essentia*," "beyond the order of nature."[9] Natural law is, for Rhonheimer, nothing more than the law of the practical reason. And "natural" refers consequently to the "nature of practical reason."

With regard to Finnis, Grisez, *et al.*, the tendency I am referring to was already strongly criticized in terms of excessive separation between theoretical and practical reason, or—in the empiricist vocabulary—between facts (of nature) and values.[10]

a Partire dalla Natura," *Rivista di Filosofia Neo-Scolastica* 4 (1997), pp. 521–23. To avoid misunderstandings: I am not neglecting that Rhonheimer says explicitly that eternal law measures human reason. However, his view seems epistemologically much closer to a kind of Augustinian direct illumination by God than to a Thomistic (realistic) account of the way in which our intellect knows (and is measured by) the world God created. I think it is essential, in order to understand Aquinas' view, to focus on the existence of the eternal law in the creatures as in the measured subjects: this existence gives our intellect a way to grasp, analogically and intentionally, the content of eternal law.

4  M. Rhonheimer, *Natural Law and Practical Reason*, p. 69.
5  Ibid., p. 37; see, also, pp. 40–2.
6  Ibid., p. 312.
7  Ibid., p. 311.
8  Ibid., p. 249.
9  Ibid., pp. 20–1.
10  See, e.g., R. McInerny, "The Principles of Natural Law," *The American Journal of Jurisprudence* 25 (1980); and the reply by J. Finnis and G. Grisez, "The Basic Principles of Natural Law: A Reply to Ralph McInerny," *The American Journal of Jurisprudence* 26 (1981). See also

This way of thinking is typical of the world of analytic philosophy and, insofar as it underlines a complete autonomy of practical reason at the level of the human value-knowledge, it can be properly called Kantian. Henry Veatch explained very well both the flaws of the "trascendental turn" in analytical philosophy and the reasonableness of a value-teleological reading of (the facts of) nature.[11] And Yves Simon had already warned that the tendency of talking about values instead of natural laws is a dangerous outcome of immanentistic philosophy.[12]

## 2. Aquinas's Realism

In this regard, I would like to note that, on the basis of Aquinas's own gnosiology, we have to distinguish between three kinds of objects of human intellectual knowledge: (1) the ideas in themselves (*species intelligibiles*: object of second intention); (2) the bodily reality itself (*quidditas rei materialis*: proper object of first intention); and (3) the *ens in universali* (common object).[13]

The first, says Aquinas, is not "the very object" because the *species intelligibilis* is only "the form by which our intellect understands": it is "the likeness [in us] of the thing understood [*similitudo*

R.A. Gahl, Jr., *Practical Reasoning in the Foundation of Natural Law according to Grisez, Finnis, and Boyle* (Athenaeum Romanum Sanctae Crucis: Rome 1994).

11  H.B. Veatch, *Human Rights: Fact or Fancy?* (Louisiana State University Press: Baton Rouge, La. 1985). See also A.J. Lisska, *Aquinas's Theory of Natural Law: An Analytic Reconstruction* (Clarendon Press: Oxford 1996).

12  Y. Simon, *The Tradition of Natural Law. A Philosopher's Reflections* (Fordham University Press: New York 1965), pp. 50–1.

13  See, esp., Aquinas, *ST*, I, q. 85, a. 2; *De Veritate*, q. 1, a. 1 c. I will not explain here the meaning of the common object but let me refer, for all the topics of this section, to my *Dio e la Legge Naturale. Una Rilettura di Tommaso d'Aquino* (ETS: Pisa 1999), pp. 103–16, 143 (forthcoming in English: *God and the Natural Law: A Rereading of Thomas Aquinas*, St. Augustine Press, South Bend).

*rei intellectae*]."[14] The ideas are what actually exist in the intellect as they are abstracted from the particular, material things; but they are not what we actually think of, *id quod actu intelligitur*. The first and proper object of our thinking is rather the material thing itself—the "*res*"—insofar as it is intrinsically intelligible: it is the "*quidditas, sive natura in materia corporali existens*"—"*De ratione autem hujus naturae est, quod in aliquo individuo existat*"—through which our intellect "rises to a certain knowledge of things invisible."[15] The ideas (*species intelligibiles*) are instead "the means" by which our intellect knows, thinks of, the reality.

It is only in a second phase that we can think of our own thinking (reflect), i.e., think of the ideas we use to know reality:

> *Sed quia intellectus supra seipsum reflectitur, secundum eandem reflexionem intelligit et suum intelligere, et speciem qua intelligit. Et sic species intellectiva secundario est id quod intelligitur. Sed id quod intelligitur primo, est res cuius species intelligibilis est similitudo.*[16]

The ideas are therefore objects of "second intention": they are the natures of the things *as known by us* (with all the limitations that this intentional relationship involves). But the "proper and first intention object" is the bodily reality itself: what we primarily think of, and know, in the constant, bodily, existential contact with reality.

Now, even in the light of this too brief sketch, it should be evident that the values, at the level of our reflective intellectual (practical) experience, are *species intelligibiles*: a "second intention object." As such they are not what we actually know and think of. Our "first intention," is rather for the value of friendship "as it materially exists in our best friend Francesco." Gnosiologically, our idea of friendship is an abstraction from the real, material, friends we have: it is a *logical* entity. And this means, in turn, that, in order to understand ethics,

14  *ST*, I, q. 85, a. 2 c.
15  *ST*, I, q. 84, a. 7 c.
16  *ST*, I, q. 85, a. 2.

we do not have to focus first on our own thinking of values but on the teleological (ordered) material reality in which the values are *inscribed* (e.g., on the real friendship-relation between Francesco and me), and from which they are then *abstracted* by original insights of our reason. This also corresponds to the trascendental concept of "good" as a relation between *ens* and will: the will does not "create" anything but "goes towards" the being known by the intellect. The consequences of this gnosiology for ethical discourse are significant. We can think, for example, of the difference between trying to understand marriage: (a) by abstractly focusing on a kind of "value of marriage in itself"; or (b) by focusing on the value of marriage as the intrinsic teleological meaning inscribed in the two (bodily) sexes as they exist, interact, etc.

## 3. Whose Nature?

The "whose-question" relates to a kind of reduction of morality to the intentionality of the agent, losing sight of the objective ground to be found in a reality existing *outside* and *independently* from the agent's experience of values.[17] The Finnis-Grisez ethical methodology comes down to an analysis of the agent's intentionality towards the abstract (basic) values in themselves. "Immoral," according to this view, is simply "going intentionally against one (or more) basic values." And the evil of immoral actions seems equal to contradicting our own practical reason (our intentionality towards the values): as if every sin were *just* a sin against practical reason itself. This tendency looks very much like Abelard's ethics according to which the external action does not add anything to the moral good or evil: what is morally important is only the consent of the will.[18]

---

17  It goes without saying that I keep talking about *tendencies*, not about explicit and systematic elements. But tendencies that I see as connected with (and due to) a general philosophical background.

18  P. Abelard, *Ethics* [*Scito te Ipsum*], 25, 30, 35, 48 in P. Abelard, *Ethical Writings*, trans. P.V. Spade (Hackett: Indianapolis, IN 1995).

*What Nature? Whose Nature?*

An example of this is Rhonheimer's suggestion (actually, timid and ambiguous because vaguely contradicted in other parts of his book) that "when someone kills an innocent person, the *moral* evil is not in the death of the innocent but in the injustice of the murderer's will, in the deformation of his will."[19] To get an idea of the ethical paradox involved in this view, let us imagine an "ideal moral world" in which every punishment was objectively measured, not according to the damage caused to the victims, but according to the degree of the aggressor's

19 M. Rhonheimer, *Natural Law and Practical Reason*, pp. 328, 334, 396–7, 402. Grisez, Finnis, May and Boyle make a similar mistake: see, section 5, point f. I do not want of course to say that "the injustice of the murderer's will" is not a moral evil but, rather, that it is so because of the objective injustice/immorality of the death of the innocent. In the order of justice (which is neither *a-moral* nor *pre-moral*) the right (the *ius*) "besides its relation to the agent, is set up by its relation to others." Consequently, "a thing is said to be just, as having the rectitude of justice, when it is the term of an act of justice, without taking into account the way in which it is done by the agent" (*ST*, II-II, q. 57, a. 1 c). This means that, morally speaking, what matters is that the innocent does not die and, only secondarily, that nobody wants to kill him.

But what is the *objective* difference between an innocent dying out of a murder and an innocent dying out of a natural cause (earthquake, etc.)? It is not just "the murderer's will?" The answer is no! The difference is that, according to justice, no innocent is supposed to be killed by other human beings. Every innocent can claim a right to live from other human beings, but not from either God or every kind of natural event. This is the moral precept; and this is the moral order established by God. The term 'right' makes (proper) sense only in the context of the relationships human beings have towards each other. And this means, in turn, that also the term 'innocent,' in the context of formulating the intrinsically evil action "killing the innocent," makes sense only in that same context. So, nobody is innocent with respect either to God or to natural events. The death of the *innocent* (i.e., the death of he who has been unjustly killed by his fellows human beings) is an objective damage to the order established by God because, according to that order, the innocent had a *right* to live.

}165{

bad intention towards the values grasped by his practical reason.[20] Another clear example (to which I will come back later) is Finnis's, Grisez's and Boyle's suggestion that contraception and "deliberate homicide" belong to the same kind of evil action (contra-life): as if the death of an existing person were just a marginal circumstance with respect to the *genus* of the action which must be determined *only by the agent's intentionality*.

These unpretentious examples should be enough to show the point of my question: Whose nature is the basis of ethics? "My" nature (the nature of my intentionality towards the values grasped by my practical reason) or a nature transcending me and that my intentionality should respect in order to be good?

## 4. Why is the Good "Good?"

From the reductivist "value-centered" approach, several difficulties flow into ethical theory.[21] Think, for example, of the distinction between objective and subjective responsibility, or of the concept of not-guilty-ignorance (both relativizing the importance of the agent's intentionality in itself). But the main problem is perhaps that, without connecting the values to the material structure of reality (the *bonum* to the *ens*), the same way of outlining values, and of analyzing the agent's intentionality,

---

20  Usually, in criminal law, once the guilt is ascertained, the better or worse agent's intentionality can lower or increase the punishment. But the relevant punishment to be lowered or increased is the one provided for by the law according to the objective damage caused by the crime to the common good. It goes without saying that the objective damage suffered by the victim is what the legislator should primarily look at in order to prudentially evaluate the damage to the common good.

21  For detailed criticisms see F. Di Blasi, "I Valori Fondamentali nella Teoria Neoclassica della Legge Naturale," *Rivista Internazionale di Filosofia del Diritto* 2 (1999); "Legge Naturale e Volontà di Dio: Finnis, Grisez, Suárez e la Teoria Convenzionale," *Iustitia*, 3 (2000).

# What Nature? Whose Nature?

will be necessarily vague, not well determined, and *intuitive*. "Intuitionism" is actually a very good criticism of this immanentistic approach.[22]

Moreover, an existential doubt would dominate our lives: "Why are the values good?" If the values are good only because they are originally grasped as such by our practical reason, no other proof can be given for the "real" bounty of ethics than the existence in us of those original insights. The only possible salvation would be a sort of post-modern (Cartesian) external recourse to faith such as: it is impossible that God is misleading me in my insights as to what is good. I think that there is something like that in Grisez: for example, in his *hypotheses* of (and not analogical path to) the existence of God and His freedom and *benevolence*; in his way of describing the value of religion[23]; in his *belief* that there is ultimately a connection between

22  In my "I Valori Fondamentali nella Teoria Neoclassica della Legge Naturale" I show, e.g., that the descriptions of the basic values offered by Finnis, Grisez, and Boyle over the years not only tend to change a lot and to become more and more vague, but are also too shortly and simply sketched (no more than two or three pages each time)—sometimes with clear contradictions, as in J. Finnis, *Natural Law and Natural Rights* (Clarendon Press: Oxford 1980), where "play" is, at the same time, a basic, incommensurable value in chapter IV and a kind of friendship (another incommensurable value) in chapter VI. Another, and more recent, example is the identification of marriage as another basic (irreducible, incommensurable) human good: G. Grisez, *The Way of the Lord Jesus: Living a Christian Life* (Vol. II, Franciscan Press: Quincy 1993); J. Finnis, *Aquinas: Moral, Political, and Legal Theory* (Oxford University Press: New York 1998). Now, the reader familiar with these writings cannot avoid raising the question: "How can marriage be incommensurable with, and irreducible to, at least the values of friendship and life?" If the act, e.g., of 'taking care of my children' can be described at the same time as an act of friendship, an act of love for my family, and an act of love for (human) life, the incommensurable values as described by Finnis and Grisez cannot account for the intentionality of that action.

23  See, G. Grisez, "Natural Law, God, Religion, and Human Fulfilment," *The American Journal of Jurisprudence*.

}167{

integral human fulfillment and human nature, etc. Moral bounty does not appear as written in the material world, which does not speak properly and directly of God: this is another way of creating a separation between ethics and metaphysics, a separation between natural finality and values, and between Creation (its intelligibility: the law as it exists in the measured subject) and God (the rational Legislator). Why should the basic human goods be *intelligible*—as Grisez likes to repeat—if not because they correspond to human nature? Here G.E. Moore's "open-question argument" would be appropriate: human values are always open to the question "Why?" A question to which "Nature" is the only possible answer; the only thing needed is a sound and viable (not factualistic) concept of nature.

It should go without saying that I am not questioning that the notion of good is *first* in the order of practical reason; that it is grounded on a kind of original insight; and that, properly speaking, there is no deduction of ethics from metaphysics. I am questioning, rather, that the original insight is not grounded on our metaphysical knowledge of nature, and that this metaphysical understanding is not morally relevant. An example of what I mean perhaps comes from *Contra Gentiles*, book III, chapter 141: *On the diversity and order of punishments*. In this chapter we read that "external goods are subordinated to internal goods, and body to soul," and that "external and bodily goods are goods for man to the extent that they contribute to the good of reason, but to the extent that they hinder the rational good they turn into evils for man." From this we get a clear *moral* idea that we should have "a greater fear" of spiritual punishments than of "bodily ones," and that "it will not be a punishment for a virtuous man if he be deprived of external goods as an aid to virtue." This moral insight, as such, cannot be deduced but still it is grounded on a theoretical understanding of what is higher and lower (subordinated) in human nature. The *theoretical* "why" is precisely the final *moral* answer people look for.

}168{

*What Nature? Whose Nature?*

## 5. Contraception and the Contra-Life Argument

It is well known that Finnis, Grisez, Boyle and May proposed an argument against contraception centered on an alleged *necessary* contra-life intention involved in every choice to use a contraceptive. Whatever further purpose one might have, they say, that choice's "relevant immediate intention . . . is that the prospective new life not begin."[24] Now, I have a great esteem for them, both as scholars and as persons, but I have to say that, at the scientific level, I find their argument interesting above all because of the great number of inconsistencies and "against-common-sense" theses it entails. I think that scholars so brilliant as they are cannot lose sight of so many obvious points unless it is due to a deep misunderstanding at a very general philosophical level.

Very briefly:

a) They think that contraception is essentially immoral because it necessarily involves a contra-life intention that they describe in the following surprising way: people who contracept "find the prospect [of a possible baby] repugnant"; and their will is properly characterized, with respect to the baby, in terms of "practical hatred."[25]

b) They think that the definition of contraception does not involve any intention to enjoy sexual pleasure or engaging in sex.[26]

c) Consequently, they state that "the morality of contraception" does not belong to "sexual ethics."[27]

24 G. Grisez, J. Boyle, J. Finnis, W.E. May, "Every Marital Act Ought to be Open to New Life: Toward a Clearer Understanding," *The Thomist* 52 (1988), p. 370. The best criticism I know of their argument is J. Smith, *Humanae Vitae: A Generation Later* (The Catholic University of America Press: Washington, D.C. 1991), pp. 105–6, 340–70; but there is also a short criticism in M. Rhonheimer, *Etica della Procreazione* (Mursia: Roma 2000), pp. 37–40.

25 "Every Marital Act Ought to be Open to New Life," p. 373.

26 Ibid., p. 370. "Contraception," they write, "is only contingently related to marital intercourse. For the definition of contraception neither includes nor entails that one who does it engages in sexual intercourse, much less marital intercourse."

27 Ibid., p. 371.

RESTORING NATURE

d) And since people who contracept only *"usually . . .* are interested in sexual intercourse,"[28] they say that "a dictator," "who would engage in no sexual behavior whatsoever, and might not will any such behavior," but "who wanted to control population," "might contracept by having a fertility-reducing additive put in the public water supply."[29]

e) Since "contraception must be defined by its [contra-life] intention"[30] they think it is "similar to deliberate homicide."[31]

f) And, to make the way they are focusing on *intentionality* clear, they say that "although the goodness of the life which is destroyed provides the reason why deliberate killing is wrong, the moral evil of killing primarily is in the killer's heart"; and they add, as an example of the same point, that "a man can commit adultery without ever touching a woman"[32] (as if the sixth commandment were exactly the same as the ninth).

g) Since contraception is always wrong because using contraceptives necessarily involves a contra-life intention, and since they agree that "women who are victims of rape" are "morally justified" in using contraceptives (of course, not abortive), they try to show that these women somehow choose to use contraceptives without a real intent to avoid conceptions. These women, they say, do it out of "a defense of the woman's ovum . . . against the rapist's sperm" but *without ever projecting and rejecting the baby.*"[33] [It goes without saying that if this break between contraceptives and the agent's intentionality is possible their whole (contra-life-intention) argument fails, because it would be possible to choose to use a contraceptive without having a contra-life intention.]

28  Ibid., p. 373 [Italics mine].
29  Ibid., pp. 369–70. It goes without saying that the dictator's action should better be described as 'violence' against his citizens's freedom and bodily integrity.
30  Ibid., p. 371.
31  Ibid., p. 372.
32  Ibid., pp. 372–3.
33  Ibid., p. 390 [Italics is mine].

*What Nature? Whose Nature?*

h) They also say that, even if it is possible for people who contracept to have the same good reasons of people who practice natural family planning, (1) contraception is wrong because of the contralife choice "to impede the baby's coming to be," while (2) NFP is good because "it is a choice *not to do something* . . . with the *acceptance as side effects* of both the baby's not-coming-to-be and the bad consequences of his or her not-coming-to-be."[34] [Here, it seems that not only does the mere difference between action and omission change the nature of the relevant human action, but it also seems that there is a certain confusion on the relevant difference between end, means and side effects. The end of NFP's abstension is basically the same as contraception's positive acts: avoiding—right now—having a baby. They are both, under this respect, a means to this end. How can it (the end) become an unintended side effect? And why only in the case of NFP?]

## 6. The Tendency against Philosophical Realism

My purpose now is not to dwell at length on all of Grisez, Finnis, May and Boyle's arguments on contraception. I am concerned here only with the philosophical tendency underlying their discussion. And I think the above sketch is enough to state my point. What are the fathers of the "contra-life argument" looking at? It is not difficult to see that they are looking only at a value in itself and at our intentionality towards it. And they try the impossible: connecting *value* (which does not come from facts) with a factual state of affairs, i.e., connecting the contra-value intentionality with the mere *fact* of using contraceptives. It was probably while moving into a sort of ideal (Platonic) value-world that they lost sight of (material) reality and common sense: making a muddle between contraception and NFP, and between the fifth and the sixth commandments, justice and chastity, etc.

To a more *realist* eye, what is obvious about contraception is exactly the conjugal act and its nature (with the meanings

34  Ibid., pp. 401–2.

}171{

inscribed in it). When we talk about contraception as a moral issue, we do not talk either about factual instruments as such or about violence (as in the dictator's case). We talk rather about people who: (a) want to engage in complete sexual actions (this is the relevant *end*); (b) for whatever reasons (good or bad) do not now want to have a(nother) baby; (c) do not want to wait; and (d) decide to engage in sex doing something to impede a possible procreation (this is the contraceptive *means*).[35] Beyond this description there is no moral question about contraception. That is why the (moral) definition of contraception includes the intention to have sex, and why contraception is—not a sexual act in itself, of course,[36] but—an obvious sin against the sixth commandment, and it belongs to sexual ethics and to the virtue of chastity.

"Women who are victims of rape" do not have any intention to perform the conjugal act: that is why they do not commit the contraceptive intrinsically evil act. And people who use NFP do not choose to perform the conjugal act at the cost of positively modifying its nature (which includes its rhythms). The *bonum delectabile* (pleasure) does not prevail on the *bonum honestum*. That is why "abstension" is a different moral act than contraception: because it involves a different moral intentionality—not towards the end of not having a baby, of course, but—towards the objective meaning of the conjugal act (i.e., respect *vs*. denial). It is, more or less, like abstaining from food when the only possibility to keep eating would require one to vomit, or to do something else in order to stop the digestion process. These two choices (abstaining *vs*. vomiting) do have different moral intentionalities towards the objective meaning of eating (again: respect *vs*. denial).

---

35  This is how Paul VI defines contraception: "Every action which, either in anticipation of the conjugal act, or in its accomplishment, or in the development of its natural consequences, proposes, whether as an end or as a means, to render procreation impossible" (*Humanae Vitae*, 14).

36  This is another confusing point of "Every Marital Act Ought to be Open to New Life" (see, esp., pp. 369 and 371).

*What Nature? Whose Nature?*

Am I sketching a sort of perverted faculty argument? Not at all. The conjugal act is something very special: this is an undeniable *moral fact* and a starting point for the ethicist. The moral importance of the conjugal act must not be deduced but explained. It is so important that we do not have any perfect marriage without it. The conjugal act is the only place in which the two ends of marriage (union and procreation) *bodily* coexist: in which union is procreation and procreation is union. Now, for a *philosophical realism*, this fact has a tremendous importance.

Philosophical realism means that all our knowledge comes from our five (external) senses, from the material reality we experience. There is no dualism between body and spirit. If material reality does not speak to us of spiritual things, we simply do not know any spiritual thing (soul, values or God). If our knowledge of marriage, chastity, family, responsible parenthood, etc., does not come from material reality, it is simply false. But it is true as far as those concepts (marriage, family, etc.) are "means" by which our (theoretical and practical) intellect knows the *material* reality of the human being's existence as male and female. The existing (factual) reality of sex is what comes first. And our certainty in sexual ethics depends on how much it speaks clearly to us.

This is why the conjugal act is so important. It is, at the same time, the summit of sexual reality and the clearest element of it. It is what all our sexual attraction is aiming at (the analogy with the other animals is very helpful here). It makes undoubtably clear the final meaning of the person's sexual identity, but also that sexual union is not an end in itself. The summit of human bodily union is a pro*creative* moment looking beyond the couple. That is why everybody spontaneously connects the reality of sex with marriage and family. The point is that we know what marriage is—and we are certain about its two ends, about the evil of contraception, etc.— because the conjugal act is what it is, and not the other way around. Conjugal union (marriage) is the *theoretical* meaning of the existence of the twofold human being, and the conjugal act is the seat of that meaning.

RESTORING NATURE

I do not want now to develop a detailed argument against contraception. My only concern is to say that sexual ethics, far from committing itself to showing that the immorality of contraception does not depend on the conjugal act's *nature*, should rather deepen the understanding of its nature and explain why it is so *important*.

## 7. The Argument from Abstinence

I think Rhonheimer's explanation of the immorality of contraception is more reasonable and refined than Grisez's, Finnis's, Boyle's and May's, and I am sympathetic to it. He explicitly criticizes the contra-life argument and he rightly underlines, for example, the ambiguity of talking about natural and artificial methods, the deep unity existing between unitive and procreative meanings of conjugal love, the need for a deep understanding of the agents' intentionality towards that love, etc. However, Rhonheimer's basic methodology is harmed by the dualism he sees between nature and reason, or between bodily facts and rational values. In this respect, his approach to ethical issues is similar to Finnis's, Grisez's, etc.; and for this reason his own argument against contraception cannot in the end reach the desired conclusion. Let me state very clearly once again that I am not saying that Rhonheimer's specific ethical arguments are similar to Finnis's, Grisez's etc., but only his general approach to ethics.

The basic point governing his ethical methodology is that "the measure and rule" of morality cannot be found in the order of nature—that is, in the "natural inclination," or "sexual drive,"[37] or "biological laws," or "biological-procreative openness"[38]—but in the reason itself.[39] Consequently, in dealing with specific moral issues, he tends to shift the focus from what he sees as the *mere biological facts* of human nature to the *general rational values* of the

37  M. Rhonheimer, *Natural Law and Practical Reason*, p. 122.
38  Ibid., p. 114.
39  Ibid., p. 111.

}174{

*What Nature? Whose Nature?*

practical reason, as if these values were somehow coming *from the outside* to inform human (factual) biological nature. This methodological step is dominated by the distinction/opposition between nature and reason that I already mentioned. And it requires exactly the same further (but logically impossible) step we have already seen in the contra-life argument, and which consists in the attempt to create a *necessary connection* between the rational *values* and the mere *factual states of affairs*: a connection of such a kind that you cannot achieve the former if not through the latter.

## The Principle of Inseparability

In his most accurate and detailed study on the immorality of contraception,[40] Rhonheimer's argument takes explicitly three main steps: (1) explaining the anthropological meaning of "the principle of inseparability" and defining the object of the conjugal act (this is, he says, the "corner-stone of the argument"); (2) explaining the meaning of "procreative responsibility" in the context of a virtue-ethics; and (3) explaining the difference between contraceptive sex and periodic continence (this is "the heart of the argument").[41]

The first step contains remarkable passages on the substantial bodily-spiritual unity of the human person[42] and on the marital union as the truth of human sexuality.[43] The principle of inseparability means that it is impossible to separate *intentionally* the two meanings of the conjugal act (unitive and procreative) without destroying both of them. This is because the procreative meaning essentially belongs to the same marital loving union (the inseparability of the two meanings is willed by God).[44] Rhonheimer distinguishes very carefully between *mere biological*

---

40  M. Rhonheimer, *Etica della Procreazione* (Mursia: Roma 2000). See also "Contraception, Sexual Behavior, and Natural Law: Philosophical Foundation of the Norm of 'Humanae Vitae,'" *The Linacre Quarterly* 56/2 (1989).

41  See, M. Rhonheimer, *Etica della Procreazione*, p. 45.

42  Ibid., pp. 46–9.

43  Ibid., p. 60.

44  Ibid., pp. 52–8.

}175{

RESTORING NATURE

functions and *intentional* meanings. The "meanings" belong to the essence of the conjugal act as a human action. So, even biologically infertile acts can still be intentionally ordered by the couple to procreation; without this intentionality even the unitive meaning would be destroyed.[45]

This distinction surprises me. If the "meanings" belong to the action as "intentionally chosen," what Rhonheimer himself recognizes would become impossible: i.e., the possibility of a reciprocal self-giving by the spouses in the conjugal act independent of the intention to procreate.[46] Another thing that surprises me is the distinction between "the traditional doctrine of the two ends of marriage" and the doctrine of "two meanings of the conjugal act." Rhonheimer thinks that the former is not concerned with intentionality but only with the description of marriage as "a special type *of social reality.*" If it were not so, the (primary) procreative end would make instrumental the (secondary) loving union.[47] Now, my difficulty with this approach is not only that, following the same trend of reasoning, the same love of God would make the other people (loved ultimately for God's sake) mere instruments; but above all that, in the history of canon law, the traditional doctrine of the ends of marriage is associated precisely with the understanding of the necessary intentionality the agents should have in order to contract a valid marriage. The "traditional doctrine" has always belonged to an ethical context.

Finally, Rhonheimer defines the (intentional) object of the "conjugal act" as a "bodily loving union" which essentially includes the procreative meaning.[48] But he hastens to add that, up to this point, there is nothing in his argument that can support the thesis of the immorality of contraception. We still do not know, he says, why the bond between the two meanings should be respected even at the level of every single conjugal act. To

45  Ibid., p. 55.
46  Ibid., p. 58.
47  Ibid., pp. 60–2.
48  Ibid., p. 59.

}176{

## What Nature? Whose Nature?

answer this question we need another argument showing that contraception is intrinsically opposed to "procreative responsibility."[49]

### The Argument from Abstinence

It should be spontaneous now to ask: "Why this need for another argument?" If the procreative meaning belongs essentially to the conjugal act, it necessarily follows that not even *one* conjugal act can be performed without respecting it. That is why here I can interpret Rhonheimer only as shifting his focus from the material nature of the conjugal act to an abstract, general, meaning of human love in itself.[50] Only if the procreative meaning belongs primarily to the *conjugal love* do we still need the link with every single conjugal act. Moreover, from my point of view, Rhonheimer's new focus is another sign of his tendency of not looking for moral answers by means of an interpretation of nature.

So, Rhonheimer's proper argument against contraception begins with "procreative responsibility" (or "responsible parenthood")[51] as an integral part of "the virtue of chastity." I like to call it "*argument from abstinence*" because its methodological hinge seems to be *the positive need for abstinence* in order to live chastity and responsible parenthood.[52] And, apologizing for the oversimplification of a nuanced and rich analysis, I would summarize the argument in the following three points:

(1) Procreative responsibility (or responsible parenthood)—defined as "the making use of, and compliance with, a natural striving, in the framework of an *ordinatio rationis*"[53]—requires the exercise of the virtue of chastity; or, better, it is part of this virtue.

---

49 Ibid., pp. 64–5.
50 Ibid., pp. 70–1: here this shift appears clearly.
51 The difference between these two concepts is not very clear: see, e.g., ibid., pp. 66–8.
52 Ibid., p. 107: "La contraccezione è un provvedimento che rende *superflui* la responsabilità procreativa del compimento di atti sessuali e la virtù corrispondente della *temperantia*."
53 *Natural Law and Practical Reason*, p. 112; *Etica della Procreazione*, p. 68.

(2) Chastity—"the virtue that establishes and preserves the order and measure of human sexuality"[54]—requires marital abstinence.

(3) Marital abstinence—"the governing of the natural inclination through reason and will"[55]; the *"mastery over the sexual drive itself"*[56]; "bodily act of procreative responsibility"[57]—cannot be exercised in contraceptive acts.

### Abstinence from What?

In *Natural Law and Practical Reason* the positive need for abstinence was much clearer. However, Rhonheimer's view does not seem substantially different in *Etica della Procreazione*, where the focus is always on the recurrent statement that in contraceptive acts spouses do not need to modify their sexual behavior according to procreative responsibility (or the governance of reason).[58] In any case, it is evident that Rhonheimer's argument works (tautologically) as far as abstinence is defined either as required from procreative responsibility or as required from the virtue of chastity. The obvious question is: why should "governance," "mastery," or "procreative responsibility" necessarily require the *negative act* of abstinence?

I agree, of course, that chastity requires abstinence, but only accidentally: when the values inscribed in human sexuality cannot be realized by engaging here, now, and in this particular way, in a sexual activity. The reason for abstinence is the *factual*, material, way in which human sexuality exists. And this factual existence is the only starting point for answering the question: "Abstinence from what?" We must abstain from homosexual actions, e.g., because they deny the male and female sexual identity and its unitive and procreative meaning; we must abstain from

---

54  *Natural Law and Practical Reason*, p. 112; *Etica della Procreazione*, pp. 67, 69.
55  *Natural Law and Practical Reason*, p. 114.
56  Ibid., p. 122.
57  *Etica della Procreazione*, pp. 72–3.
58  See, ibid., pp. 75–77, 107.

*What Nature? Whose Nature?*

sodomy because it denies the objective unitive and procreative meaning of genital organs; we must abstain from contraception because it denies the objective unitive and procreative meaning of the conjugal act; etc. If we do not *abstain*, in all these cases, we go against the love of God (who made the natural order in this way) and we lose a contemplative, self-giving, moral disposition towards reality, instrumentalizing it in view of our own pleasure.

It seems to me that Rhonheimer's argument cannot answer the question "Abstinence from what?" precisely because it loses sight of the *nature* of the conjugal act.[59] It cannot clarify why contraception should be an intrinsically evil act, why it cannot be done even as an exception. In other words, it cannot cover the distance between the general need for abstinence and every single action. As a matter of fact, we can easily imagine a couple that live in a better way with chastity and abstinence than many others and use contraception only once in a while. And we can compare it with another imaginary couple that have never been abstinent at all and already have fifteen kids. If abstinence is the key of sexual morality, why do we not talk about intrinsically evil actions in this last case? Actually, it seems that Rhonheimer tends to refer to people who use contraceptives as people who cannot control their sexual impulses and are not able to modify their sexual behavior according to a reasonable plan.[60] It goes without saying that in plenty of cases this is not true at all.

Rhonheimer's argument tends to reverse the terms of the question about abstinence, going, in this way, against common sense. Abstinence is not a positive requirement: we do not have to live looking for ways to abstain. Rather, it is always a negative, even if very frequent, requirement: that is to say, we have to

---

59  Actually, in his second-step attempt to connect value and fact he sometimes timidly suggests that the relevant facts are not *just facts* (see., e.g., ibid., p. 120; *Etica della Procreazione*, p. 77). But this little welcomed inconsistency is not enough to cancel the break between values and nature due to his without-*ordinatio-ad-debitum*-order-of-nature premise.

60  M. Rhonheimer, *Etica della Procreazione*, pp. 75–7.

RESTORING NATURE

abstain every time our looking for pleasure denies, or puts in danger, the meaning of our sexual identity (the *bonum honestum*).

### *The Starting Point*

It is obvious, in a sense, that the starting point of an against-contraception argument cannot be responsible parenthood—or procreative responsibility—in itself, because the point of responsible parenthood is to understand if it is good or not to have a child right now; and this is a very prudential question. On the other hand, the point of contraception is that, whatever is objectively good with regard to children, you cannot voluntarily engage in complete sexual intercourse using contraception. Refusing contraception does not essentially involve actualizing a responsible-parenthood intentionality. Let us put it this way: if a married couple has a *non-contraceptive* conjugal act in the context of a *totally irresponsible* attitude towards children, we still do not talk about intrinsically evil actions; but we do if the couple uses contraceptives in the context of a perfectly good reason to delay the pregnancy. In both cases the intrinsically good/evil question does not depend on responsible parenthood.

The starting point cannot even be the twofold meaning of the conjugal *love* in itself. And the obvious reason is that there are thousands of morally good ways to instantiate conjugal love, and *all of them, except one*, are allowed even when the couple does not want to have a child. The *required abstinence* is only for the conjugal act: of course, there should be something in its *nature* explaining the precise reason for the immorality of contraception.

## 8. "Value of Marriage" and "Acts of the Reproductive Type"

In their "Marriage and the Liberal Imagination"[61] Robert George and Gerard Bradley criticize Stephen Macedo's thesis that

---

61  I quote from the reprinted version in R.P. George, *In Defense of Natural Law* (Oxford University Press: Oxford 1999), pp. 139–60.

}180{

*What Nature? Whose Nature?*

"whatever values can possibly be realized in the acts of genital union of sterile spouses can equally be realized by those spouses—or similarly committed couples, whether of the same sex or opposite sexes—in oral or anal sex acts."[62] Macedo claims that the point of sex in an infertile marriage, since it is not reproduction, should necessarily be the same as, e.g., in the case of loving gay couples. George and Bradley, consequently, think that a sound criticism of Macedo's view implies, first of all, refusing the traditional doctrine of reproduction as the primary end of marriage;[63] and, second, focusing on the value of marriage in itself.

Their argument involves two basic steps. (1) On the one hand, they maintain that sex is morally right only when it aims at the "intrinsic good of marriage itself"; otherwise, it "damages personal (and interpersonal) integrity by reducing persons' bodies to the status of means to extrinsic ends."[64] (2) On the other hand, they explain that "sodomy is intrinsically not-marital" because marriage, "considered as a two-in-one-flesh communion of persons," "is consummated and actualized by acts of the reproductive type."[65]

Now, what surprises me most in this strategy is that it would have been much easier to say that "primary end" does not mean "unique end," and that what is immoral is "to pervert" the primary end, not "to enjoy" the secondary. There is nothing wrong, e.g., in eating icecream just because we like it; even if it did not contain any nutrition. But it would be immoral to eat 35 ice cream

---

62 Ibid., pp. 139–40. Macedo's article they are referring to is: "Homosexuality and the Conservative Mind," *Georgetown Law Journal* 84 (1995).

63 George-Bradley, "Marriage and the Liberal Imagination," p. 141: "St. Augustine, among others, seems to have treated marriage as a purely instrumental good whose primary value has to do with procreation and the nurturing of new human beings."

64 Ibid., p. 147.

65 To my current purpose (i.e., underlining their general philosophical tendency) it is not relevant if either George or Bradley changed their relevant explanation after the article I am quoting from.

cones using special drugs to impede the digestion process to satiate us. Pleasure is not wrong as far as it does not deny the natural order. And enjoying sex is good as far as nothing is done which denies either its reproductive or its unitive meaning. The only way to understand why sodomitical acts deny the meaning of marriage is to focus on the perversion they imply with respect to the way sexual identity and the genital organs are made. This perversion is evident to everyone who is willing to look sincerely at the *facts* of the natural order; to them St. Paul's simple warning is enough:

> For this cause God has given them up to shameful lusts; for their women have exchanged the natural use for that which is against nature, and in like manner the men also, having abandoned the natural use of the woman, have burned in their lusts one towards another, men with men doing shameless things and receiving in themselves the fitting recompense of their perversity. (Rm 1: 26–7)

However, George and Bradley are unwilling (a) to focus on the evident facts of nature, and then, (b) to explain their meaning with respect to the human being as a whole (union between body and spirit; sexual identity as part of personal identity; relationship between pleasure and good; love of God and self-giving; etc.). No, they choose to go the other way around by (a) focusing on a value of marriage that, in itself, does not depend on reproduction, and then (b) by trying to connect it with a supposedly extrinsic—factual—state of affairs, which is the reproductive character of the conjugal act. I will show now that their attempt does not work.

### Reproduction and the Definition of Marriage

First of all, the definition of marriage they offer makes sense only if procreation *is* the primary end of marriage. And the reason is easy to see. They define marriage as a "two-in-one-flesh communion of persons that is consummated and actualized by sexual acts of the

*What Nature? Whose Nature?*

reproductive type."[66] But how can the objective character of marriage's *proper acts* be either secundary or extrinsic to the good of marriage? This is a logical point. If (a) reproduction is what intrinsically defines the acts of the reproductive type as the *specific* kind of acts they are, i.e., those acts objectively ordered to reproduction; and (b) if these *specific* acts as such are what consummates and actualizes the good of marriage (defining it as the *specific* communion of persons it is); it follows (c) that procreation, far from being extrinsic or secondary, is exactly the *defining trait* of marriage as a *specific* communion of persons.

### Intentionality and Technical Necessity

But here they could protest that I am missing their point, i.e., that to commit a "sexual act of the reproductive type" does not mean necessarily to tend intentionally to the end of reproduction. And, actually, they assert quite clearly that "spouses have a reason to mate quite irrespective of whether their marriage will, or even can, be productive."[67]

Now, given their definition, this sounds really strange: we have acts of the reproductive type (a) actualizing marriage but (b) committed without any relevance, in the agents's intentionality, for procreation (i.e., for their objective meaning). In this case, the term "act," as used in the phrase "acts of the reproductive type," should logically refer, not to *human actions*—which, according to their theory, must always be defined by the agent's intentionality, as *what is chosen*—but to some factual bodies-joining mechanism. And if so, if the defining character of the relevant acts does not have any intrinsic value in the very process of committing them, the link between these acts and the good of marriage does not have anything to do with values but is rather a kind of *technical necessity*. It is like saying: "As a matter of *fact*, you cannot actualize the good of marriage other than by engaging yourself in that material situation." Such technical necessity should be explained accurately. If it were true, we could not anymore exclude as immoral

66  George-Bradley, "Marriage and the Liberal Imagination," p. 139.
67  Ibid., p. 147.

}183{

the sexual acts committed by someone who, after a succesful sex-change operation, was able to mate according to the "acts of the reproductive type."

## Naturalistic Fallacy

But we must go further. Making the "acts of the reproductive type" the core of the definition of marriage would imply—according to the interpretation of the is-ought question that George and Bradley share with Grisez and Finnis—committing a naturalistic fallacy, trying to confer an absolute value to a *factual* state of affairs. Or, in other words, trying to create a *necessary* link between the value of marriage, on the one hand, and the biological function (reproduction) of some *material* acts, on the other. George and Bradley would commit the very logical mistake that all the new-classical theorists object to in the so-called conventional natural law theory.

The problem here is not, of course, to consider whether or not *reproduction* is a part of the value of marriage,[68] because, even in this case, we could pursue reproduction (and marriage as well) also outside of the acts of the reproductive type (e.g., through the in-vitro-fertilization): the problem is in attempting to create a *necessary* connection between a general rational value (not coming from nature), on the one hand, and a particular factual situation, on the other.

## Narrow Starting-Point and Wrong Conclusion

But even if we agree on the existence of a kind of necessary link between marriage and "sexual acts of the reproductive type," would it mean that no other act could actualize the good of marriage, and that every other kind of act would be immoral? Actually, what is more stunning in the proposed definition of marriage is that it appears extremely narrow, and that it cannot work as it is meant to work.

---

68 As George does, together with Patrick Lee, in "What Sex Can Be: Self-Alienation, Illusion or One-Flesh Union," in R.P. George, *In Defense of Natural Law* (Oxford University Press: Oxford 1999), pp. 161–83.

*What Nature? Whose Nature?*

Let us recall George and Bradley's strategy. They basically want to find a criterion to judge the morality and immorality of sexual acts. And they find exactly the following: only *marital* acts are morally good. Of course, the necessary further step is defining *what is marital*. And the answer is: "sexual acts of the reproductive type"! So, when sexual acts are not "of the reproductive type" we are able to argue that they are *non marital* and, therefore, *immoral*. Now, this argument proves too much, trying to use (in a mere material way) the most unitive sexual act as the only criterion of morality in marriage.

There are plenty of ways (more or less sexual) to actualize the good of marriage, from giving a kiss and living together, to choosing the house, the appropriate school for the kids, etc. That is why, e.g., the spouses can live a wonderful marriage even when, because of an accident, they could no longer have complete sexual intercourse. But if we agree that the "sexual acts of the reproductive type" are (maybe the most important but) not the only possible *marital acts*, and that there are a number of other sexual acts (kissing, embracing, caressing, etc.) not intrinsically evil, the original strategy to condemn sodomy appears definitely frustrated, and the proposed definition of marriage inadequate.

And this is actually where all the problems lie. George and Bradley's starting point is inadequate, not only because the "conjugal act" is not the only "marital act," but also because it is not just a "sexual act of the reproductive type." The conjugal act is rather an act with a twofold meaning—unitive and procreative—in which the unitive meaning exists in, and is qualified by, the natural reproductive structure of human sexuality. Without knowing this natural structure we would not know even what marital unity really means.

Paradoxically, while trying to criticize the primacy of procreation, George and Bradley make it the only defining trait of the conjugal act. That is why an unintended but necessary consequence of their description is that spouses cannot engage in sexual intercourse without tending to the reproductive end.

## 9. Sketching Aquinas's Approach to Nature as the Basis of Morality

In chapter 129 of the third book of the *Summa Contra Gentiles* Aquinas tries to show "that things prescribed by divine [revealed] law are right, not only because they are put forth by law, but also because they are in accord with nature [*secundum naturam*]."[69] Generally speaking, in the part of the *Contra Gentiles* in which he deals with the different kinds of moral precepts it is clear: (1) that *agere secundum rationem* is equal to *agere secundum ordinem naturalem*; and (2) that understanding the order of nature requires understanding: (a) its natural ends or goods; (b) the natural measures according to which those ends should be pursued; and (c) the natural hierarchy existing between the several ends. Aquinas's description of the natural order is, accordingly, much richer than the perverted faculty argument suggests.

To begin with, let us see how the term *ordo naturalis* appears in chapter 129:

> Indeed, as a result of the precepts of divine law, man's mind is subordinated to God, and all other things that are in man's power are ordered under reason. Now, the natural order requires [*naturalis ordo requirit*] that lower things be subject to higher things. Therefore, the things prescribed by divine law are naturally right in themselves [*naturaliter recta*].

The meaning of this passage is quite clear. The divine revealed law contains a moral hierarchy. Therefore, what the divine law

---

69 Aquinas, *Summa Contra Gentiles*, III, ch. 129. In this section I focus on the *Contra Gentiles*, not because I think it is the best place to look, but only because, due to a specific study I have recently done, it is easier (faster) for me to collect and comment on appropriate quotations from this text. Anyway, from my reading of Aquinas, I maintain that there are no relevant changes in his other works as to the subjects I am dealing with.

}186{

*What Nature? Whose Nature?*

prescribes is *etiam secundum naturam* precisely because the natural order possesses the same moral hierarchy. But let us continue:

> Again, according to the natural order [*secundum naturalem ordinem*], the body of man is for the sake of his soul and the lower powers of the soul are for the sake of reason, just as in other things matter is for the sake of form and instruments are for the sake of the principal agent. But, because of one thing being ordered to another, it ought to furnish help to that other, and not offer it any hindrance. So, it is naturally right [*naturaliter rectum*] for the body and the lower powers of the soul to be so managed by man that thereby his activity of reason, and his good, are least hindered and are, instead, helped. But, if it happens otherwise, the result will naturally be sinful. Therefore, drinking bouts and feastings, and inordinate sexual activities through which rational activity is hindered, and domination by the passions which do not permit free judgment of reason— these are naturally evil things [*sunt naturaliter mala*].

In this passage, both the existence of an intelligible hierarchy in the natural order and the grounding of the moral conclusion upon the understanding of the natural order are unquestionable. But the natural order contains also *the measure* according to which we should use the "lower things":

> Furthermore, we showed above that man has this natural endowment, he may use lower things for the needs of his life. Now, there is a definite measure [*mensura determinata*] according to which the use of the aforesaid things is proper to human life, and if this measure is set aside the result is harmful to man, as is evident in the immoderate eating of food. Therefore, there are some human acts that are naturally fitting [*naturaliter convenientes*] and others that are naturally unfitting [*naturaliter inconvenientes*].

}187{

In chapter 129, the natural inclinations of the order of nature include also the inclination to God.[70] And this is consistent with the meaning of the entire chapter because (a) the divine law requires the love of God as the ultimate end, and (b) it should be, also under this respect, *secundum naturam*.

> Besides, those acts by which he inclines towards his natural end [*finem naturalem*] are naturally appropriate to an agent, but those that have the contrary effect are naturally inappropriate to the agent. Now, we showed above that man is naturally ordered to God as his end [*homo naturaliter ordinatur in Deum sicut in finem*]. Therefore, the things by which man is brought to the knowledge and love of God are naturally right, but whatever things have the contrary effect are naturally evil for man.

Finally, the chapter will conclude:

> Therefore, it is clear that good and evil in human activities [*bonum et malum in humanis actibus*] are based not only on the prescription of law, but also on the natural order [*non solum sunt secundum legis positionem, sed secundum naturalem ordinem*].

In the light of this sketch of Aquinas's approach, the following statement that we find in Rhonheimer's book is surprising:

> If we begin this way, and say that "nature" is the norm of morality—as *mensura* (measure) or *regula* (rule) . . .

---

70  For the relationship between 'inclination to God' and 'natural law' in the *Summa Theologiae*, let me refer to my "Natural Law as Inclination to God," in J. Goyette, M.S. Latkovic, and R. Myers (eds.), *St. Thomas Aquinas and the Natural Law Tradition*, Catholic University of America Press: Washington, D.C., forthcoming.

## What Nature? Whose Nature?

we have disoriented ourselves in gaining access to the texts of St. Thomas, in which one searches in vain for a statement that nature is the measure of what is good.[71]

Or also the claim that "the assumption that practical judgments are ultimately grounded in theoretical judgments about the 'order of nature'" was "not at all" Thomas's viewpoint.[72] As a matter of fact, there is no doubt that in the passages just cited "nature" is *methodologically investigated* as the "norm" and "measure" of what is good, and that practical judgments are ultimately grounded in theoretical judgments about the order of nature.

There is a very interesting passage in the *Contra Gentiles* relating the *ordo naturalis* with the *agere secundum rationem*. Let us read it.

> Just as the exercise of sexual capacities is without sin, provided it be carried on with reason [*si secundum rationem fiat*], so also in the case of the use of food. Now, any action is performed in accord with reason [*secundum rationem*] when it is ordered in keeping with what befits its proper end [*quando ordinatur secundum quod congruit debito fini*]. But the proper end of taking food is the preservation of the body by nutrition. So, whatever food can contribute to this end may be taken without sin. Therefore, the taking of food is not in itself a sin.[73]

It goes without saying that in this passage Aquinas leaves the natural hierarchy out of consideration. The actual question is only about the intrinsic goodness of eating (or having sexual relations). But still the use of the term *secundum rationem* is clarifying. *Secundum rationem* is whatever "befits its proper end." Therefore, if an

71  M. Rhonheimer, *Natural Law and Practical Reason*, p. 8.
72  See, ibid., p. 555.
73  Aquinas, *Summa Contra Gentiles*, III, ch. 127.

}189{

RESTORING NATURE

action is conformed to a natural inclination's proper end it is, in itself, *secundum rationem* and not evil—it could become evil (not *secundum rationem*) only under the hierarchical point of view: if, here and now, it goes against the proper end of a higher natural inclination. This natural-hierarchy-conformity character of the moral action is stressed in another passage of the *Contra Gentiles*:

> But sin does occur in our act of appetition, because, since our nature [*natura nostra*] is composed of the spiritual and the corporeal there are several goods for us. Our good in regard to understanding is indeed different from what it is according to sensation, or even according to the body. Now, there is a certain order [*ordo quidam est*] of these various things that are man's goods, based on the fact that what is less primary is subordinated to what is more primary. Hence, a sin occurs in our will when, failing to observe this order [*tali ordine non servato*], we desire what is only relatively good for us [*secundum quid*], in opposition to what is absolutely good [*simpliciter*].[74]

I think it should be clear enough that, for Aquinas, we act *secundum rationem* when we (try to) respect the order of nature in all the intelligible aspects as we know them. But before ending this section, I would like to quote a long passage in order to give a clear example of Aquinas's manner of proceeding in ethics by way of reading the (*facts* of the) natural order. I think that many misinterpretations of his ethics come today, not from misreading specific points, but from a general inability to adopt either his own point of view on nature or, what is the same, his ethical methodology. The passage I have in mind involves an argument against the particular case of fornication in which the agents do not take any precautions to avoid a possible pregnancy (Aquinas methodologically distinguishes this case from the other in which the fornicators use

74  Ibid., ch. 108.

}190{

*What Nature? Whose Nature?*

contraception).[75] Going slowly through Aquinas's words, the reader will appreciate his style and his way of looking at reality. And I am sure that it will turn out to be evident *in what sense* there is no difference, in Aquinas's ethics, between the *facts* of nature and the values grasped by our practical reason.

> Likewise, it must also be contrary to the good for man if the semen be emitted under conditions such that generation could result but the proper upbringing would be prevented. We should take into consideration the fact that, among some animals where the female is able to take care of the upbringing of offspring, male and female do not remain together for any time after the act of generation. This is obviously the case with dogs. But in the case of animals of which the female is not able to provide for the upbringing of offspring, the male and female do stay together after the act of generation as long as is necessary for the upbringing and instruction of the offspring. Examples are found among certain species of birds whose young are not able to seek out food for themselves immediately after hatching. In fact, since a bird does not nourish its young with milk, made available by nature as it were, as occurs in the case of quadrupeds, but the bird must look elsewhere for food for its young, and since besides this it must protect them by sitting on them, the female is not able to do this by herself. So, as a result of divine providence, there is naturally implanted in the male of these animals a tendency to remain with the female in order to bring up the young. Now, it is abundantly evident that the female in the human species is not at all able to take care of the upbringing of offspring by herself, since the needs of human life demand many things which cannot

75 I explained in detail Aquinas' twofold case against fornication in my *God and the Natural Law.*

RESTORING NATURE

be provided by one person alone. Therefore, it is appropriate to human nature [*est igitur conveniens secundum naturam humanam*] that a man remain together with a woman after the generative act, and not leave her immediately to have such relations with another woman, as is the practice with fornicators.

Nor, indeed, is the fact that a woman may be able by means of her own wealth to care for the child by herself an obstacle to this argument. For natural rectitude in human acts [*rectitudo naturalis in humanis actibus*] is not dependent on things accidentally possible in the case of one individual, but, rather, on those conditions which accompany the entire species [*secundum ea quae totam speciem consequuntur*].

Again, we must consider that in the human species offspring require not only nourishment for the body, as in the case of other animals, but also education for the soul. For other animals naturally possess their own kinds of prudence whereby they are enabled to take care of themselves. But a man lives by reason, which he must develop by lengthy, temporal experience so that he may achieve prudence. Hence, children must be instructed by parents who are already experienced people. Nor are they able to receive such instruction as soon as they are born, but after a long time, and especially after they have reached the age of discretion. Moreover, a long time is needed for this instruction. Then, too, because of the impulsion of the passions, through which prudent judgment is vitiated, they require not merely instruction but correction. Now, a woman alone is not adequate to this task; rather, this demands the work of husband, in whom reason is more developed for giving instruction and strength is more available for giving punishment. Therefore, in the human species, it is not enough, as in the case of birds, to devote a small amount of time to bringing up

*What Nature? Whose Nature?*

offspring, for a long period of life is required. Hence, since among all animals it is necessary for male and female to remain together as long as the work of the father is needed by the offspring, it is natural to the human being [*naturale est homini*] for the man to establish a lasting association with a designated woman, over no short period of time. Now, we call this society matrimony. Therefore, matrimony is natural for man [*matrimonium homini naturale*], and promiscuous performance of the sexual act, outside matrimony, is contrary to man's good [*contra hominis bonum*]. For this reason, it must be a sin.[76]

Aquinas, of course, is not undertaking here an explanation of the indissolubility of marriage. Not even he wants to analyse all the possible reasons why matrimony is natural for man. He is just focusing on those aspects of the natural order that seem to him enough to conclude that there is a need for "a lasting association," and that "promiscuous performance of the sexual act, outside matrimony, is contrary to man's good." If we do not pay too much attention to his *cultural* idea of men and women, and if we add to his picture our much deeper knowledge and sensitivity about the importance of both father and mother for the child's life in all its aspects—if we, in other words, focus on the rationale of the argument in itself—we will have a good idea of Aquinas's reasonable way of understanding ethics by reading the natural order.

76  Aquinas, *Summa Contra Gentiles*, III, ch. 122.

}193{

# Maritain on the Limits of the Empiriometric
## Jude P. Dougherty
## The Catholic University of America

At the end of the 19th century, the European philosophical turf was shared by two factions, both coalitions, those of an idealistic strain, largely Hegelians, on one side, and those of a materialist or skeptical bent, indebted to British empiricism and the *Critiques* of Kant, on the other. Long eclipsed was the metaphysics of Aristotle and the Schoolmen.

Henri Bergson, in an attempt to confront the mechanistic and deterministic philosophies of his day, philosophies often presented by their advocates as the rational foundation of modern science, developed a metaphysics of being critical of both Hegel and the empiricists. One of his most promising disciples was the young Jacques Maritain, who had turned to Bergson, then lecturing at the Collège de France because of a similar discontent with the prevailing intellectual milieu. Maritain, although initially attracted to the philosophy of Bergson, soon became critical of his mentor because in his judgment Bergson's metaphysics remained linked to and dependent upon the science of phenomena it hoped to replace. Never achieving metaphysics in the Aristotelian sense of the term,[1] it remained in Maritain's judgment a process philosophy, not a philosophy of being. Maritain's subsequent reading of Aristotle led him, under the influence of Ernest Psichari, to Thomas Aquinas. He was to say later that he was already a Thomist before he read a word of St. Thomas.

Maritain was not alone in the search for a way out of the prevailing philosophical climate. In reaction to German idealism, which itself was framed as a reaction to Kant's *Critiques*, new and

}194{

*Maritain on the Limits of the Empiriometric*

critical realisms were beginning to emerge on both sides of the Atlantic. Hegel, initially embraced as an antidote to empiricism, was abandoned when it became clear that Hegelians were hard pressed to account for the march of new scientific techniques which were leading to remarkable discoveries in the natural sciences. Above all, Maritain was confronted with August Comte's positivism. Schooled in the British empiricism of the day, Comte not only ruled out metaphysics but ruled out theoretical physics as well, and both for the same reason, a denial of the efficacy of causal reasoning. According to Comte, physics errs, as does metaphysics, when it postulates abstract entities as explanatory causes. The success of 19th and 20th century theoretical physics had yet to undermine positivism as a philosophy of science. Quite apart from its speculative implication, Comte recognized the social implications of the empiricism emanating from the British Isles, implications which led directly to a secular humanism which he codified in his "religion of humanity."

Generally accorded the title "Father of Positivism," Comte is also regarded as one of the progenitors of sociology. Although Comte's interests led him away from the philosophy of science per se and into the field of sociology, the term he coined came to be used in the wider sense of a philosophy of knowledge which limited knowledge to sensory experience. Hence Maritain's attempt to counter the "brutal empiricism and nominalist pseudo-rationalism" by showing that knowledge is not limited to the descriptive sciences, that ancient truths about nature, human nature and cognitive ability remained viable and, indeed, vital to humanity. Maritain was later to press the point in a work published under the title *Ransoming the Time*.[2]

Reflections on the nature and capacity of human knowledge

1   Jacques Maritain, *Redeeming the Time* (London: Geoffrey Bles, 1943), p. 47.

2   Jacques Maritain, *Ransoming the Time* (New York, Scribner's Sons, 1941); also published in England as *Redeeming the Time* (London, Geoffrey Bles, 1943).

}195{

date to the pre-Socratics. Plato's discussion of science and the claims to knowledge by the Greeks, as Maritain recognized, will forever remain a starting point for the philosophy of science. It was Plato who bequeathed to Western philosophy the insight that all science is of the universal. Aristotle concurred, but he found the universal not in some realm of archetypes but in the nature common to members of the species. Aristotle taught that by a process of abstraction we come to know the essence, quiddity, or nature of a thing, prescinding from its accidental features which it may or may not have while remaining the thing that it is. Such is the object of science, the nature of an entity, the structure of a process, its properties and potentialities. Yet to have scientific knowledge is not simply to know what is, not simply to have uncovered a law of nature. For Aristotle, to have scientific knowledge is to know the entity, process, or property in the light of its cause or causes. Presupposed by Aristotle are two principles, the principle of causality and the principle of substance, both principles rejected by the British empiricists.

The positivism which Maritain confronted denies at once the intelligibility of nature and the power of intellect to grasp "the more" that is given in the sense report. Maritain offers an elaborate defense of the first principles of thought and being in his *Existence and the Existent*, affirming that there is more in the sense report than the senses themselves are formally able to appreciate.[3] John Locke, in denying the reality of substance, reduces what we call substances to "constellations of events" or sense reports. According to Locke, we use terms which imply substances, but this usage is merely a shorthand way of pointing to something without repeating at length the properties we associate with that something or constellation. Ockham revisited.

David Hume's account of causality similarly limits knowledge to a simple sense report. We experience succession, Hume tells us,

3    Jacques Maritain, *Existence and the Existent*, trans. by L. Galantière and G. Phelan from Court Traité de l'existence et de l'existent (New York, Pantheon Books, 1948).

*Maritain on the Limits of the Empiriometric*

not causality. "Cause" is the name we give to the antecedent, contiguous in place, continuous in time, and habitually associated with the consequent which we designate "effect."

If there are no natures or substances independent of the mind's creating them, if there is no causality, the enterprise of metaphysics collapses. For after all, metaphysics is based on the assumption that the realm of being is greater or wider in designation than the being reported by the senses. If the material order reported by the senses is all there is, then the most general science of reality is natural philosophy or the philosophy of nature. If there is an immaterial order of being as well as the material world of sense, then the most general science or reality is the philosophy of being, also known as metaphysics or ontology. One can conclude to or reach the immaterial order only by a process of reasoning. Such reasoning has led mankind through the ages to affirm the existence of God, to posit an immaterial component of human knowing and a spiritual or immaterial soul.

It is to be noted that the same sort of reasoning that leads one to affirm the existence of God also leads one to affirm the existence of the submicroscopic. As Comte himself recognized, causal reasoning is common to both natural theology and theoretical physics. The efficacy of causal reasoning is dramatically seen in those sciences where the postulated entities of one generation become the encountered ones of another. It can be shown that limiting knowledge to the sense report has implications not only for the natural sciences but for law, the social sciences, and theology as well. On a strict positivist account, science, in effect, is reduced to description and prediction, the social sciences are denied their object, "human nature," and of course natural theology is denied its object since there is no way to reason to the existence of God.

Maritain first takes his task in developing a philosophy of science to be the defense of the first principles of thought and being. Put simply, things exist apart from a knowing mind (intelligibility); things are what they are (identity); a thing cannot be and not be at the same time and in the same respect (non-contradiction); a thing is either intelligible in terms of itself or in terms of another

}197{

(efficient causality or sufficient reason); every agent acts on account of a preconceived end, or, put another way, being in act is intelligible (final causality). These principles are so fundamental that there are none prior to them by which they may be demonstrated. They are the principles upon which all demonstration depends, principles which though they cannot be demonstrated can be defended. Maritain's entire philosophy of science may be regarded as their defense against Locke, Hume, and certain misleading misinterpretations of relativity theory and quantum mechanics.

He next focuses his attention on the abstracting intellect and the degrees of abstraction which make possible the various sciences from physics to metaphysics. In these discussions he displays his indebtedness to Aristotle and Aquinas as well as to the Thomistic interpreters Cajetan and John of St. Thomas.

Quite apart from his subscription to an Aristotelian-Thomistic theory of knowledge, Maritain was aware that the British empiricists as well as Comte failed to pay much attention to actual practice in the sciences. Maritain begins a chapter of a major work, *The Degrees of Knowledge*, entitled "Philosophy and Experimental Science," by quoting Émile Meyerson, "True science, the only one that we know, is in no way, and in none of its parts in accord with the positivist scheme."[4] The empiricists notwithstanding, reasoning on a causal basis from the observed to the unobserved is in common practice in the natural sciences. The existence of bacteria was inferred long before the microscope displayed their reality. In physics and chemistry molecular structures were similarly inferred long before electron microscopes and particle accelerators graphically confirmed their reality. It is not misleading to say that in physics causal explanation is taken for granted. The encountered is routinely explained by the

---

4   Jacques Maritain, "Philosophy and Experimental Science," in *The Degrees of Knowledge (Les Degrès Du Savoir)* trans. from the 4th French ed. by Gerald Phelan (New York: Scribner's, 1959), p. 21. The English-language translation employed is the one cited here.

*Maritain on the Limits of the Empiriometric*

nonencountered. No one who looks at the course of nineteenth and twentieth century theoretical physics can affirm that science is simply description and prediction.

Maritain had not only studied biology in Heidelberg but was conversant with the work of Max Planck, Albert Einstein, Louis de Broglie, Schrödinger, and Werner Heisenberg, to name only a few. He attached particular importance to quantum mechanics and relativity theory because they call into question the validity of certain common-sense conceptions of space and time.

Scientific knowledge, Maritain writes, is knowledge, in which, under the compulsion of evidence, the mind points out the reasons why things are the way they are and not otherwise.[5] Science deals with things, but not the flux of the singular. It lays hold of what things are by means of a process of abstraction, discovering their intelligible nature—a universal nature, not the contingent of the singular. "The contingencies of the singular escape science. The necessities of the universal are the proper objects of its grasp."[6] He continues, "The *universality* of the object of knowledge is the condition of its necessity, the very condition of perfect knowledge or science."[7] The sciences of explanation "set before the mind intelligibles freed from the concrete existence that cloaks them . . . essences delivered from existence in time."[8]

Maritain can quote Aristotle and Aquinas in support of his position. This is the first stage of his attempt to show that metaphysics, indeed science, is possible by pointing to the mind's ability to abstract from the singular to capture the universal or intelligible, common nature of many, to see the many as a class. This abstractive power enables us to identify "laws of nature" and is the basis of all taxonomy. Maritain, again following Thomas, calls this the first degree of abstraction. The second degree is mathematical abstraction, the kind of abstraction involved when

5    Ibid., p. 23.
6    Ibid., p. 27.
7    Ibid.
8    Ibid., p. 33.

RESTORING NATURE

the mind not only leaves behind the singular but also the defining characteristics of a class to focus only on the entity as a unit or as something possessing extension or a certain configuration. Thus, arithmetic and geometry and their derivative sciences come into being. We can speak of "five" or "six," leaving behind the fact that we may be talking about bells, books, or candles. Similarly, we can talk about the properties of circles, spheres, cones, and straight lines even though none exists as such in reality. Obviously there are circular, spherical, and conical objects in reality, but none is a perfect exemplar of the idealized abstraction.

Maritain discusses at length the so-called intermediate sciences, the physico-mathematical sciences. "Physico-mathematical science," he writes,

> is not formally a physical science. Although it is physical as regards the matter in which it verifies its judgments, and although it is oriented towards physical reality and physical causes as the terminus of its investigations, physico-mathematical science does not, however, aim to grasp the inner ontological nature itself.[9]

Beware of abstractions, he cautions.

Discussing the nature of quantity, extension, and number, he notes,

> The enormous progress made by modern mathematics has rendered more indispensable than ever before the philosophical study of the first principles of mathematical science, which alone can provide a rational account of the true nature of mathematical abstraction and the mental objects which it considers, the properties and mutual relationships of the continuous and discontinuous, the real meaning of *surds* and *transfinite numbers*, the infinitesimal, *non-Euclidian space*, etc. and finally the valid-

9    Ibid., p. 61.

*Maritain on the Limits of the Empiriometric*

ity of mathematical transcripts of physical reality, and of such hypotheses, for example, as the theory of relativity.[10]

It is at the third degree of abstraction that the object of metaphysics is attained. At that level the intellect prescinds from every feature, physical and quantitative, to focus on what the whole of reality has in common, namely, being. At this level

the mind can consider objects abstracted from and purified of *all* matter. In this case it considers in things only their very being with which they are saturated, being as such and its laws. These are objects of thought which not only can be *conceived* without matter, but which can even exist without it.[11]

Returning to his discussion of natural science, there are two possible ways, he says, of interpreting the conceptions of modern physics. "The one transports them literally, just as they are, on the philosophical plane, and thereby throws the mind into a zone of metaphysical confusion. The other discerns their spirit and their noetic value in an effort to determine their proper import."[12]

One may ask, is real space Euclidean or non-Euclidean? Is the space postulated by the Einsteinian theory of gravitation real or not? The student of modern physics, Maritain responds, must beware of equivocations. The world "real" has not the same meaning for the philosopher, for the mathematician, and for the physicist. For the mathematician, a space is "real" when it is capable of mathematical existence, that is to say, when it implies no internal contradiction and duly corresponds to the mathematical notion of space, that is, duly constitutes a system of objects of thought verifying the axioms of geometry.[13]

10   Ibid., p. 164.
11   Ibid., p. 36.
12   Ibid., p. 171.
13   Ibid., pp. 165–67.

## RESTORING NATURE

For the physicist, space is real when the geometry to which it corresponds permits the construction of a physico-mathematical universe in which all our pointer-readings are "explained" and which at the same time symbolizes physical phenomena in a coherent and complete fashion. For a long time Euclidean space sufficed for the interpretations of physics, but today to interpret the measurements it gathers from nature within which geometry and physics are as far as possible amalgamated, it is necessary to have recourse to spherical and elliptical spaces. For us, it is a question of knowing what is real space in the philosophical sense of the word, that is, what is "real" as opposed to an "entity of reason."

Euclidean, Riemannian, and other geometrical entities are "translatable" from one system to another, and all these geometries are equally "true," but they cannot be equally real in the philosophical sense of the word. Mathematical intelligibility by itself alone tells us nothing. The straight line of an elliptical plane and the figure which corresponds to it in a Euclidean model are not different expressions of the same thing.

> They are intrinsically different entities, belonging to intrinsically different worlds, and from one of these worlds to the other they correspond analogically. To affirm the reality of one space is not to affirm at the same time the reality of all the others, but their unreality.[14]

Nor will the verification of our senses and of our measuring instruments tell us anything about their reality since with them we quit the mathematical order for the physical order. The mathematical model may serve as a "nucleus of condensation," a model which enables us to correct and interpret the ensemble of measurements taken.

Euclidean space is directly constructible in intuition. Others of necessity are referable to the Euclidean notion of space for their intelligibility. All attempts that have been made to obtain an in-

14   Ibid., p.167.

}202{

*Maritain on the Limits of the Empiriometric*

tuitive representation of non-Euclidean geometries, by Einstein, for example, show that these geometries can be rendered imaginable only by reduction to Euclidean geometry. "The model of the thermic universe invented by Poincaré, in which we would be born with the geometry of Lobatchevsky, and that sequence of very simplified sensations that Jean Ncod has thought up and which would give a fictitious subject the idea of the most diverse geometries, confirm by a sort of counter-proof this privilege of Euclidean space."[15] In sum, non-Euclidean geometries presuppose notions of Euclidean geometry. They offer analogical concepts with Euclidean concepts providing the primary analogate. In spite of the use that astronomy makes of them, non-Euclidean space is a being of reason. "It is Euclidean space which appears to the philosopher to be an *ens geometricum reale*."[16] This real geometric space is finite; that is to say, actually existing space is co-extensive with the amplitude of the world. Infinite geometric space is a being of reason.

Speaking of the atom presented by the "new physics," Maritain says that physicists tend to form a pure abstract mathematical equivalent of a given atomic structure, which thereby becomes unrepresentable to the imagination and at the same time becomes divested of any ontological meaning.

> The equivalent tends to become a more and more fictitious and more and more perfect symbol of the real nature, unknown in itself, of that existing something as other to which determinately corresponds the name atom. Thus, it knows this nature more and more profoundly, yet more and more enigmatically, and metaphorically, to put it bluntly, in the measure that it constructs the myth—a being in reason founded *in re* — which takes its place.[17]

15  Ibid., p. 168.
16  Ibid., p. 169.
17  Ibid., p. 173.

Maritain then turns to the epistemological conditions and characteristics of a philosophy of nature which undergirds empiriological knowledge in general. He quotes Sir Arthur Eddington, who writes that the physicist of today knows "'that our knowledge of objects treated in physics consists solely in readings of pointer and other indicators' and who knows likewise that 'this schedule of pointer readings' is attached to some unknown background.'"[18]

Like Eddington, Maritain is insistent that a mathematical reading of sensible phenomena cannot speak the last word about the physical real. Physico-mathematical knowledge is not to be mistaken for an undergirding philosophical account of nature. We cannot ask a physico-mathematical approach to give an ontological explanation of the sensible real, let alone an account of human thought and volition. True, the human mind inevitably tends toward a mechanistic philosophy and endeavors to explain everything in terms of extension and movement. "It was bound inevitably," Maritain writes, "to endeavor to make ontological reality intelligible in terms of extension and movement."[19] A Cartesian legacy resurfacing, Maritain might say.

Given that the natural sciences aim at giving a mathematical interpretation of sensible nature, it is easy to conclude, as do many of our contemporaries, that science is capable of explaining the whole ontological reality by extension and movement. But it has yet to do so! "Well, if science cannot do so right away, it will be able later on," is a common refrain when asked for the evidence. The spiritual dimension of man remains elusive, yet the twenty-first century disciples of Hume remain confident that the genome project will eventually disclose all.

Maritain's life work can be read as a rebuttal of contemporary claims that complex organic forms and the spiritual component of human nature are the result of material forces combining with random mutations, the result of necessity and chance, with no

18  Ibid., pp. 173–74.
19  Ibid., p. 42.

*Maritain on the Limits of the Empiriometric*

creative intelligence behind them. Cultural shifts, if not an outright hedonism, obviously flow from this line of reasoning.

To follow Maritain's every line of argument would require a volume in itself. Throughout his long career and extensive publication he has defended a realism which is not satisfied with a purely empirical or phenomenal account of what is. In the latter half of the twentieth century that realism has gained notable adherents. To mention only two: William A. Wallace, principally in his *Modeling of Nature*,[20] has carried the Aristotelian-Thomistic analysis into yet another generation; and Rom Harré, in the *Principles of Scientific Thinking*, has shown the necessity of recognizing a nature or structure beyond the empirically given, one that is responsible for measurable traits and is conceptually present to the mind by means of an iconic or sentential model.[21] While Harré remains a materialist, he is not satisfied with the reduction of science to description and prediction, which he believes fails to recognize its explanatory character. Others outside the Aristotelian tradition have come to the similar conclusion regarding the nature of scientific inquiry. Yet the recognition of an immaterial order, attainable through reasoned enquiry, is far from accepted in today's academic climate, and for the reasons Maritain gives, the failure to acknowledge, put simply, that more is given in the sense report of reality than the senses are able to appreciate.

20  William A. Wallace, *The Modeling of Nature: Philosophy of Science and Philosophy of Nature in Synthesis* (Washington, DC: The Catholic University of America Press, 1996).

21  Rom Harré, *Principles of Scientific Explanation* (Chicago: University of Chicago Press, 1970).

# Nature as the Basis of Moral Actions
Leo J. Elders, S.V.D.
## Institute of Philosophy "Rolduc"
## (The Netherlands)

Traditionally many philosophers and theologians have seen a narrow connection between our human nature and the morality of our actions in this sense that actions performed against the natural structure, properties or inclinations of our human nature, and even against the nature of things in the world around us, were seen as sinful, while those in agreement with nature were considered morally good. As we shall see, the issue is far from easy and has given rise to fierce dispute especially among students of law and theologians. Moreover, the present day spiritual climate exercised a noticeable influence on the thought of several moral theologians turning them away from the traditional doctrine. As John Paul II writes, interest in empirical observation, technical progress and certain forms of liberalism have led people to see an opposition between freedom and nature.[1] Freedom is contrasted with man's physical and biological nature, which man should make subservient to his needs and wishes. In this view, our human nature is no more than a substratum of our actions to be left behind or at least to be transformed. We hardly have a definite nature, but must continuously make ourselves. However, three centuries of moral philosophy according to the liberal and individualistic point of view have not succeeded in giving a coherent account of the basis of morality. A renewed study, in the light of contemporary thought, of this not quite novel issue may perhaps be helpful to clarify some of its aspects.

1    This position is the central argument of Veritatis splendor.

*Nature as the Basis of Moral Actions*

In the following I propose to consider successively: (1) the idea of nature in the past and present; (2) nature and the natural law; (3) Aquinas on applying the natural law arguments and some dissenting views; (4) arguments against recourse to nature; (5) some conclusions.

## I. A Concise History of the Concept of Nature

When examining the history of the concept of nature, we see that the Ionian philosophers used the term «nature» to denote the proper nature of things, their behavior and especially the material out of which they are made. Furthermore, they also used the word to denote coming-into-being, that is, the generation of things with a particular nature. In this way «nature» came to mean the continuous process of coming into being and perishing as well as the result reached in change, sc. the things which have a particular nature. Finally, to the Pre-Socratics the term also meant the whole of reality, just as we speak of "nature" as the order of things imbued with reason. The first philosophical treatises were entitled *On nature*.

In the second half of the fifth century B.C, the term began to be used to denote *human* nature. Philosophers now spoke of an opposition between "nature" and "law." Those living in Greece in this age of enlightenment were reluctant to let themselves be bound by rules or custom and preferred to give free rein to their natural urges.[2] Plato criticized this line of arguing defended by the Sophists. He also rejected determinism. Design and art are at work in the world and this requires a mind. Moreover the nature of the different species of things depends in each of them on an idea.[3]

According to Aristotle nature is the essence of the things which have in themselves a principle of movement. For this reason nature is related to activity and movement. As against Plato Aristotle

2    Cf. F. Heinimann, *Nomos and Physis. Herkunft und Bedeutung einer Antithese im griechischen Denken des 5. Jahrhunderts*, Basel 1945; M. Pohlenz, "Nomos and Physis," in *Hermes*, 1953, 418–438.
3    See D. Manusperger, *Physis bei Platon,*, Berlin 1969.

}207{

RESTORING NATURE

returned to the ancient tradition of the Pre-Socratics with regard to the original meaning of the term. However, he did accept the best of Plato's insights: *physis* is in the first place the form which gives things their intelligibility. As a matter of fact Aristotle ascribed to nature the attributes which Plato assigned to the soul, sc. regularity and purposiveness.[4] He distinguishes nature from chance and artefacts. His account is placed in the context of causality: where do things come from and how is process in nature possible? The answer is: "owing to the nature of these things." Nature is not an outside cause, but the principle of movement and rest in things themselves. It is the essence or substance of those things which have the origin of change within themselves. Among the Presocratics the tendency had prevailed to reduce nature to matter, but Aristotle considers the form as its main constituent. The nature of the elements is the principle of their movements.[5] But he also uses the term *physis* in the sense of the whole of physical reality and the teleological order of the universe.

In the monism of the Stoa nature is a combination of matter, force and mind. The force, active in the universe, imposes form on matter. Zeno considered this principle the same as the *physis*, which is tied to and identified with fire. It accomplished the tasks Plato had assigned to the World Soul and is comparable to the artist who shapes material objects. Therefore, it is man's duty to live consistently with nature. Nature is the same as the Logos which is the innermost core of reality and man's intellect is part of it. For this reason Chrysippus could explain Zeno's *dictum* to act consistently as meaning that one must act in conformity with nature ὁμολογουμένως ζῆν τῇ φύσει. Marcus Aurelius invites his readers to "follow straight your path, guided by your own nature and the universal Power."[6] In a remarkable passage Cicero writes that neither the laws of the various nations or the decrees

4    Cf. *Physics*, II, ch. 1; *Metaphysics* V, ch. 4.
5    In *In Iib. Phys.*, l. 1, n. 145, Thomas explains that "principle" means both the formal and material as well as the efficient cause.
6    *Meditations*, V.

}208{

*Nature as the Basis of Moral Actions*

of governments nor the sentences of judges and the opinion of the majority determine what is right, if not based on the norm of nature (*naturae norma*), which is the only criterion to allow us to distinguish what is good and honest from what is bad and illicit.[7] According to Cicero, nature as a norm is present in our mind and we know this norm spontaneously.[8]

In the Neo-Platonism of Plotinus, on the other hand, a new view is proposed: nature is a hypostasis, a mediated manifestation of the One, derived from Soul, sc. a soul of lower rank, placed between the World Soul and material things. Its function is to direct cosmic process.

The early Christian authors were influenced by Stoicism and its impressive moral doctrine of a life in harmony with nature and reason. Despite the fact that they borrowed heavily from the Stoa, their moral teaching was profoundly religious and based on the Old and the New Testament. When writing about daily life, nourishment, clothes and make-up, Clement of Alexandria strongly insists on the lessons nature teaches us: all ostentatious luxury must be avoided, and we should follow nature. In his *Paidagogos* II, 1, 4 ff. he insists that we should use such things as our body, food, sexual faculties and material possessions according to their nature, that is, according to what they are meant to be for man. As to human sexual life Clement states the principle that one should never force our faculties to something contrary to their natural purpose.[9] He and the Fathers explicitly condemn the attempt to render nature, which God has made, sterile.

---

7   *De legibus*, I, xvi, 43: "Quodsi populorum iussis, si principum decretis, si sententiis iudicum iura constituerentur, ius esset latrocinari, ius adulterare, ius testamenta falsa supponere si haec suffragiis aut scitis multitudinis probarentur ... Atqui nos legem bonam a mala nulla alia nisi naturae norma dividere possumus, nec simul ius et inuria natura diiudicatur, sed omnino omnia honesta et turpia."

8   *Pro Milone*, 4, 11: "Est igitur haec ... non scripta sed nata lex, quam non didicimus, accepimus, legimus, verum ex natura ipsa arripuimus."

9   *Paidagogos*, II, 10, 95.

RESTORING NATURE

The moral theology of Origen is profoundly biblical. In his Fifth Homily on the *Book of Joshua* he insists on the place of Christ in the life of Christians: even the commandments of natural law must be understood in the light of Christ; they come to us from God. Another early Christian author for whom "nature" was a key concept in our moral life is Tertullian. Whatever nature teaches us has also been transmitted to us by God, and he writes: "Listen to nature . . . she is our teacher."[10] Nature has received the its rules from God. Obeying nature is obeying God. Speaking about luxury, Tertullian goes so far as to say that God finds no pleasure in what he did not make himself, such as gaudy colors of vestments. The use people make of certain things often has not much to do with their origin in God.[11] He even writes that what comes to us from nature is the work of God, but what is a human product is the work of the devil.[12] A similar argument is used by St. Cyprian in his condemnation of the exaggerated luxury in the Carthago of his days. God has made things quite simple, and for that reason women should not change the color of their hair and the outward aspect of their ears or skin, but leave them in the state in which they received them.[13] Michel Spanneut sees a strong Stoic influence in this exhortation to preserve the simplicity of nature.[14]

However, the Fathers of the Golden Age go much beyond this position and point out that sanctity makes us lead a life above nature.[15] As a matter of fact, they insist a great deal on a life according to the demands of the Gospel, and frequently refer to biblical texts.

---

10 *De testimonio animae,*V, 1–2.: "Magistra natura, anima discipula est. Quidquid aut illa edocuit aut ista perdidicit. A Deo traditum est, magistro scilicet ipsius magistrae . . . Senti illam, quae ut sentias efficit."

11 *De cuktu feminarum,* I., 8, 2. Cf. M. Spanneut, *Tertullien et les premiers moralistes chrétiens,* Gembloux / Paris 1969.

12 *Op. cit.,,* II, 5, 4: "Quod nascitur opus Dei est. Ergo quod infingitur, diaboli negotium est."

13 *De habitu virginum,* 11.

14 *Le stoïcisme des Pêres de l'Église,* 257–266.

15 St. Gregory of Nyssa, *Vita sanctæ Macrinæ,* I, 5:

}210{

*Nature as the Basis of Moral Actions*

Nevertheless the theme of nature as a source of moral knowledge remains present. In his treatise *On Providence*, VIII S. John Chrysostome writes that having shaped man, God placed an inborn law in him which is as a pilot to guide him and which is above our reasoning. Abel and Cain knew this law without ever having studied. Unfortunately most people neglect these lessons nature dispenses. Therefore, God opened another road to teach man. Nature is not changed by grace, but our will and our insight are.[16] In his homilies on the *Letter to the Romans*, c. 6,[17] St. John Chrysostom insists on this inborn, god-given knowledge of one's moral obligations, but he does not develop a systematic theory of the contents of natural law.

The value of St. Ambrose's moral teachings is sometimes downgraded by some authors who argue that he borrowed heavily from Philo, Cicero and Plotinus. To this we say that, although the terms he uses are indeed the same as those used by his non-Christian predecessors, Ambrose gives a wholly new meaning to their sentences. We have to do with a process of substitution—a Christian content replaces pagan ideas—not of a synthesis of Christian and pagan thought.[18] Given his familiarity with Cicero, it is remarkable that he does not make more of the latter's stand in favor of natural law. For him, a basic pagan doctrine, such as taking revenge, must give way before the Gospel, which prohibits it. We find an occasional reference to nature as a source of moral law, for instance, where he writes that nature has established a right to property common to all.[19]

Passing now to St. Augustine we notice that the Bishop of Hippo Regius holds that, comparable to the intellectual illumination of the human mind by God, there is also a moral illumina-

16  *V Catech. Bapt*, 11 (Wenger).
17  *Homil. 6.*
18  Cf. G. Madec, *Saint Ambroise et la philosophie,* Paris 1974, p. 175: "Ambroise semble avoir été doué d'une aptitude extra-ordinaire et déconcertante à vider les formules de leur substance, pour se les approprier dans le sens qui lui convenait ou qu'il estimait vrai. Or, il s'agit là d'un processus de substitution et non pas de synthèse."
19  *De officiis ministrorum*, I 28.

}211{

tion: man receives from God moral insight, his conscience, which is a participation in the eternal law of God.[20] In several texts Augustine mentions this law. God, our Creator, wrote with his own hand a law in our hearts: what we do not want that one does to us, we should not do to others.[21] In order to see this divine law, man only has to turn to his innermost.[22] However, the overall impression we get when studying the works of the great Doctor is that moral teachings have been absorbed into the doctrine of the faith.[23] His moral theology is drawn from Holy Scripture.[24] It is very difficult to grasp without divine grace the full extent of the precepts God placed in our heart.[25] One could say that the doctrine of natural law, as apparent to man, is somewhat pushed to the background by Augustine. Nevertheless, with regard to certain questions Augustine resorts to a careful examination by reason and argument.[26] The goal to be attained in human life is happiness, better, beatitude, which is the authentic accomplishment of our nature.

Although St. Augustine uses "nature" in its ordinary meaning, sc. the essential nature of things (in this sense even God is a

20  See E. Gilson, *Introduction à l'étude de saint Augustin,* p. 167; cf. *Contra Faustum manich.* XXII, 27.
21  *Enarr. in Ps. 51,* 1; *Enarr. in Ps. 118,* 25, 4; *Enarr. in Ps. 145,* 5: "Consilium sibi ex luce Dei dat ipsa anima per rationalem mentem, unde concipit consilium fixum in aeternitate auctoris sui . . . Legit ibi quiddam tremendum, laudandum, amandum, desiderandum et appetendum."
22  *De libero arbitrio* II, 16, 41: " . . . et in te ipsum redeas atque intelligas te id quod attingis sensibus corporis, probare aut improbare non posse, nisi apud te habeas quasdam pulchritudinis leges, ad quas referas quaeque pulchra sentis exterius."
23  Cf. Th. Deman, *Le traitement scientifique de la morale chrétienne selon saint Augustin,* Montréal 1957, p. 21.
24  *De bono viduitatis,* 1, 2: "Quid ego amplius te doceam quam id quod apud Apostolum legimus? Sancta enim Scriptura nostrae doctrinae regulam figit."
25  *De spiritu et littera,* XXVII, 47.
26  *Op. cit.,* 15, 19.

## Nature as the Basis of Moral Actions

nature[27]), when he is using the term, his point of view is decidedly historical and theological. He sees human nature against the background of man's relation to God. Human nature is man's being such as God created Adam: " . . . nature as it has been created originally without defect is properly called human nature."[28] Man's nature has been corrupted by the Fall, a position not shared by Aquinas.[29] The reduction of nature to God's will is so prominent in Augustine that he even argues that miracles are not against nature, because of the fact that "God's will is the nature of all things."[30] In conformity with this position, Augustine stressed that we should devoutly use the resemblance natural things, such as physical bodies and animals, possess to signify a higher reality. He introduced the expression "the Book of Nature" which, he writes, is a source of knowledge of a higher reality, as the Bible is in its own way.[31] In the Middle Ages the expression "the Book of Nature" was frequently used.

In the Christian Platonism of Dionysius the sensible world manifests the divine mysteries.[32] According to Peter Damian we can draw examples for our moral life from the nature of the entire animal world which, as he thinks, is just one sacred allegory.[33] But references to natural law are scarce in his works. Peter Abelard, as one might expect, stresses over and against the Augustinian tradition man's reason as being able to formulate the basic laws

---

27  *De trinitate*, XV, c. 1: "Deus est natura, scilicet non creata sed creatrix."

28  *Retract.*, I, 10, 3: "Naturam qualis sine vitio primitus condta erat, - ipsa enim vere et proprie natura hominis dicitur."

29  Cf. I-II 85, 1: "Primum bonum naturae nec tollitur nec diminuitur per peccatum."

30  *De civ. Dei*, XXI, 8, 2: " . . . cum voluntas tanti utique Conditoris conditae rei cuiusque natura sit."

31  See *De Genesi ad litt.*: *PL* 32, 219; *Enarr. in Ps.* 45, 7.

32  *De divinis nominibus*, 700 C. Cf. also Isidore of Sevilla, *De natura rerum*, See Tullio Gregory, *L'idea d natura nella filosofia medievale*, Firenze 1964.

33  *De bonop religiosi status*: *PL* 145, 785.

RESTORING NATURE

of human life. Justice is derived from the natural law, which is prior to the Gospel, both in time as by its nature.[34] According to Peter Lombard, the true sense of the concept of nature is "that state of rectitude in which we have been created, and that manifests itself as a spark of reason—the *synderesis*—and the movement of the will toward the good." This nature, which before the Fall was shining in all its splendor, now shows itself only as a spark, as what is left in us of human nature.[35] In conclusion we could say that at the end of the 12th century most theologians consider human nature as a source of moral doctrine, inasmuch as reason distinguishes what is right and what is wrong. God has written a norm in the heart of man.[36]

Above we have drawn attention to the medieval view of nature as reflecting the spiritual world. Not only human nature but also natural things in general show a great deal of wisdom and purposiveness as well as regularity. Where there is purposiveness and regularity there is a cause which produces them.[37] In this connection the saying was coined "opus naturae est opus intelligentiae."[38] Some authors such as William of Conches and Theoderic of Chartres went so far as to place a central power in nature and to neglect nature's ties with the Creator.[39] However, for the majority of theologians in the West nature remained a mirror of a higher reality and an instrument of God.

Turning now to Aquinas's concept of nature, he makes his own Aristotle's definition and division of the senses of the term.

34  *Dialogus inter Philosophum, Iudaeum et Christianum: PL*178, 1614.
35  *Iib. Sententiarum*, d. 39, 3: *PL* 192, 747.
36  See O. Lottin, *Psychologie et morale aux XIIe et XIIIe siècles*, (8 vols), Louvain/Gembloux 1942–1960.
37  Cf. E. Gilson, *The Spirit of medieval Philosophy*, New York 1940, p. 365.
38  In His *Scriptum super libros Sententiarum* Thomas attributes the saying to Aristotle, in later works to the "philosophers." See *De veritate*, q.5, a.2 etc. The expression may have been coined early in the 13th century.
39  Cf. St. Thomas's critique of Theoderic of Chartres, in his *In II Physicorum*, lectio 1.

*Nature as the Basis of Moral Actions*

According to Aristotle in *Metaph.* V the name *nature* has first been given to signify the generation of living beings, which is called 'being begotten'. Since this kind of generation is from an intrinsic principle, the meaning of the term has been extended to denote the intrinsic principle of any movement. In this way nature is defined in *Physics* II. Since this principle is a formal or a material principle, both matter and form are commonly called nature. Now, since the essence of each thing is brought to completion by its form, the essence of each thing, expressed by its definition, is commonly called nature.[40]

This is the sense in which Aquinas uses it in the treatise on the Holy Trinity, from which we quoted. Thus there is an extension of the meaning of the term from an intrinsic principle of growth to an intrinsic principle of any movement whatever.[41]

Thomas had to face the difficulty of distinguishing between natural and enforced movements. Natural things are liable to be moved by outside agents. Water when heated by the sun, changes. Natural bodies have a natural potency to the forms proper to them and a sort of natural desire to acquire these, even if they must do so with the help of a causal influence from outside. On the other hand, things made by art do not have a *natural* potency to the forms given them by man. The distinction Aquinas makes seems razor-thin. It makes sense if we accept a preset plan of the Creator for natural beings in their mutual relationships, e.g., of water and warmth. Here we have an example which illustrates how the concept of nature Aquinas is using has a richer content, since it implicitly assumes the mutual relationship of things made by God. Thus he writes: "The work of nature presupposes the creative activity of God."[42]

40  Cf. *S.Th.* I, 29, 1 ad 4; *In II Phys.*, lectio 1.
41  Cf. *Summa theologiae* III, 2, 1.
42  *Summa contra gentiles*, III, c. 65: "Opus naturae praesupponit opus Dei creantis."

}215{

RESTORING NATURE

The term nature occurs almost 4,800 times in the *Summa theologiae* alone, quite apart from the occurrence of the adjective *naturalis*. Very frequent is the complex term *natura humana*. The term *natura* usually has the sense of the essential being of things. The specific nature of things comes from God by whom they have been created. The nature of things is a continuous participation in the divine ideas, and this explains how it is a source of the rules for our behavior according to God's will. We shall come back to this in the next section.

With regard to the further history of the term, important shifts in its meaning took place in the modern age. Scientists began to approach physical things from a mathematical point of view and paid less attention to finality as it manifests itself in the activity of natural things. The theory of the substantial forms and that of the four elements was abandoned. They were replaced by measurable physical forces and chemical properties. For Aquinas it was obvious that nature depends on God and is governed by Him, but in the modern age nature itself became the ultimate reality to many. In the 18th century nature was even the object of a quasi religious veneration. Among theologians the trend prevailed of seeing the supernatural order as an addition which leaves human nature as it is and allows man to live in his natural environment without reference to the order of grace. Nature consists of observable facts and we must follow nature, for whatever nature has made is good.[43]

With Descartes the human mind places itself outside and above nature. The dualism "mind-body" leads to that of "mind-nature."[44] Kant, for his part, let human reason take over the role of God, the supreme legislator. Nature is now surrendered to the practical intellect of man. Hegel borrows from Aristotle the concept of nature as a process which has its end in itself, sc. the identity of the starting

---

43 See J. Chevalier, *Histoire de la pensée*, II, Paris 1956, 584.
44 Using the term nature in a restricted sense is possible. Even Thomas says that "voluntas dividitur contra naturam sicut una causa contra aliam" (I-II 10, 1 ad 1), but this does not prevent him from predicating nature, in a more basic and universal sense, also of spiritual beings.

}216{

*Nature as the Basis of Moral Actions*

point and the final term. Nature as becoming is moving toward nature as being, and vice versa. According to Marx the grandeur of Hegel's *Phenomenology* lies in the understanding that the production of man by man is the result of man's own work.

In the wake of nominalism and empiricism the doctrine of things having a fixed and immutable nature was abandoned by many naturalists, especially after Darwin's theory of evolution as proposed in his *The Origin of Species* had found widespread acceptance. A group or class of apparently related and similar animals have no set nature. Instead of "the great chain of beings," Darwin believed that there is an endless multitude of variations.[45] Quite a number of physicists tend to consider the nature of things the sum of relations which they bear to the rest of the world.[46] According to the phenomenologists, human nature is continuously affected by man's existence and so exposed to constant change. Human nature received an even less sympathetic treatment from the analytical philosophers who argued that a priori statements about human nature are not verifiable and therefore meaningless.[47]

## II. Nature and Natural Law

A very outspoken denial of the traditional view of human nature is proposed in the works of Jean-Paul Sartre. Man is nothing else than that into which he makes himself.[48] Sartre needs this postulate to secure man's total freedom. According to this

---

45  In the past fifty years the animal species have made a remarkable comeback. Individuals belonging to a species have their own gene pool, and must be considered forms of life in their own right. They form an ecological unity and are discontinuous with other groups of living beings. See E. Mayr, *Animal Species and Evolution*, Cambridge Mass., 1963, 29.

46  Cf. M. Merleau-Ponty, *La structure du comportement*, p. 1. See also L. Wittgenstein, *Tractatus logico-positivus*, 1–2: the world is made up of facts, and not of objects or substances.

47  A. Ayer, *Language, Truth and Logic*, ch. 1.

48  *L'existentialisme est un humanisme*, p. 22.

RESTORING NATURE

French existentialist philosopher, a truly free decision is a *proj-ect*, that is, an act which arises spontaneously without having been influenced or determined by anything else.[49] In each free choice breaking with the past must be total. Human nature as a sort of compass to guide man simply does not exist, or one might say that it means projecting ourselves forward all the time. Sartre's theory exercised a considerable influence on the postwar generation and expressed what a good number of people in our Western societies came to think about man's actions.[50] There are also authors who reject nature as a source of moral behavior since this borrowing rules from nature would bring us down to the animal level. Did not Ulpianus say that "natural law is what nature has taught all animals"![51] But man stands far above this level. Just as he imposes his will on the course of rivers, reclaims land, builds artificial islands and tames animals, he can also give to his own life and sexuality the expression which suits him best.

Several authors argue that there is no natural law since the foundation on which it was built has now been demolished: there is no set nature to impose its rules on us, but we freely decide how to act. Norms, they assume, depend on the cultural situation. Moral relativism is the best approach to moral life. An anthropologist can point out different forms of behavior in different cultural areas, some of which may be abhorrent to peoples in another cultural area. John Locke, they claim, was a forerunner of this way of thinking. In his *Essay in Human Understanding* he observes that there is scarcely a principle of morality that has not been at some time slighted or condemned by the prevalent opinion of some society.[52] Lawmakers and judges notice considerable disagreement among the citizens and

---

49  *L'être et le néant*, p. 577 ff.
50  In his Encyclical *Veritatis splendor*, § 84 – 87, John Paul II writes that a characteristic of modern man is the desire of total freedom, a freedom which has lost its contact with truth.
51  *Liber I Institutionum. Corpus iuris civilis*, Inst. I, 1; *Dig*. 1, 1, 3.
52  *Op. cit.*, I, chapter 3.

*Nature as the Basis of Moral Actions*

leave what they consider private morality out of their proceedings, so long as no damage results to others. The distinction between the wrong in itself and the wrong because forbidden has become blurred. So they propose to tolerate the maximum amount of individual freedom consistent with the integrity of society.

This brings us to a final and most decisive factor in the rejection of human nature as a basis for moral behavior, sc. the sharply increased awareness of one's personal freedom. A good number of our contemporaries cherish the desire to be totally free from what human nature tells us. Now this position leads to serious consequences:

1) In the first place, it produces a certain disorder in the way man organizes his life and leads to a lack of consistency in what one does. Instinct governs instead of reason.

2) Our personal life has no other goal than the preoccupation to act without any inhibitions. The unity of our mental and moral life is lost. The virtues, natural law, tradition and customs are no longer held to be positive values, since they impose restrictions on the will and so reduce freedom.

3) Choosing a certain action with no other motivation than the feeling prevalent at a certain moment kills the mind. People no longer know what they are talking about or what they want to do. They want to go somewhere but do not know where this somewhere is.[53]

4) This notion of freedom causes the collapse of faithfulness. One wants constant change. The fact that the results of technology are incessantly yielding their place to new products enhances this way of thinking. Even families are no longer the rock of stability they were once. Conflicts between parents and their grown up children, promiscuity, partner swapping, divorce, refusal of stable unions, once frowned upon, are no longer the exception but a tolerated way of life.

5) Behind many of these changes modern individualism and subjectivism are at work. The sense of the common good and of

---

53  This condition found among certain youths in California has been described by Bret Easton Ellis in his novel *The Informers*.

}219{

one's duties consequent upon being citizens of a certain state is weakened. Litigation is rampant as is criticism of government and institutions. It looks as if people are becoming egoists.

6) Many reject natural law in order to claim greater freedom. When doing so they frequently appeal to their own conscience, but often the term "conscience," as used by modern man in the West, does not mean more than listening to his own desires and forming opinions in accordance with the latter. Many of our contemporaries want full autonomy in their moral life and refuse to be bound by rules or commands proposed by the Bible, the Church or tradition and custom.

The abandoning of criteria of our acts drawn from human nature has gone so far that some of the intelligentsia use the expression of a procedural democracy to suggest that the government should systematically refuse to prefer religion to non-religion, marriage to free union, protection of the unborn life to abortion, etc. Other areas where natural law norms disappear from the scene or are relegated to pockets of private groups are those of terminal patients and of human embryos, which researchers and scientists want to dispose of freely in view of their potential for providing material for medicaments able to cure certain diseases, which in this way, they hope, will yield important financial benefits.

## III. Aquinas on the Natural Law. Dissenting Views.

Natural things are good or bad depending on whether they have or do not have what agrees with and belongs to their nature. However, human nature is specified by reason. Thus St. Thomas concludes with Dionysius that "it is the good of man to be in agreement with reason, and his evil to be in conflict with it."[54] In this view the moral quality of an act is its accordance (or lack of it) with what right reason sees and establishes as useful or necessary for man. The relation of certain actions with the good of man is an objective fact. According to Aquinas, reason discovers this agreement rather than

54   I-II 94, 3.

*Nature as the Basis of Moral Actions*

constructing it. In the last analysis this relation has been placed in things by the Creator.[55] Man discovers what God wanted our actions to be and to mean; he makes his own what God intended to put in his creatures.[56] Contrary to a widespread view in his time, Aquinas points out that the natural law is not something inborn, unless in this sense that its foundation is given with human nature. The natural law is natural in so far as the intellect formulates spontaneously its first principles on the basis of our fundamental inclinations. It comprises more than the precepts formulated without further reflection by the intellect. For it extends to all moral obligations which we can deduce from these first principles.[57] Since the natural law is rooted in human nature, it is universal and eternal. However, the natural inclinations are not the natural law, but the obligations which flow forth from it. Certain acts are becoming for man, Thomas writes, since they agree with his nature.[58]

However, it is an error to think that in most cases a simple analysis of isolated objects allows us to establish a rule of conduct. The relationship between things is very complex. St. Thomas introduces the distinction between the particular nature and universal nature, and applies it to the relation between parts of the human body and the body in its entirety. The same is pertinent for human individuals and the society of which they are members. It may happen that what is against the particular nature is in agreement with universal nature. An example is the amputation of a diseased organ or member of the human body to save the life of a particular person. The death of plants and animals, which is obviously against the good of their particular nature, may benefit nature as such.[59]

---

55  I, 47, 2.

56  In man, Thomas says, the natural law is nothing else but a participation in the eternal law of God. Cf. I-II 91, 2: "Et talis participatio legis aeternae in rationale creatura lex naturalis dicitur."

57  See Ph. Delhaye, *Permanence du droit naturel*, Louvain / Lille / Montréal, 1960 (*Analecta Namurensia*, 10).

58  *Summa contra gentiles*, III, ch. 129.

59  II-II 65, 1. The principle also applies to the execution of a dangerous criminal (II-II 64, 2).

St. Thomas avoids the expressions "against nature" or "in agreement with nature." In most cases he uses "according to reason" or "against reason" (I-II 18, 5 ad 1). It is reason which knows the good of man and which formulates what agrees with it or what is opposed to it.[60] Thomas adds the following consideration: the rational soul is the substantial form of man. Therefore man has a natural inclination to act in conformity to reason.[61] What is against the order of reason is against human nature.[62] Thomas reserves the expression "against nature" mainly to signify acts against the animal nature of man.[63] Human nature becomes the source of morality of certain acts through the intermediary of man's fundamental natural inclinations.

> All those things to which man has a natural inclination, are naturally apprehended by reason as being good, and consequently as objects of pursuit, and their contraries as evil, and objects to be avoided. Therefore, the order of the precepts of natural law is according to the order of natural inclinations.[64]

These inclinations concern the basic needs and demands of human beings. The actions to which we have an inclination resulting from our nature come in under the natural law. There is in all of us an inclination to act in agreement with reason, which is acting virtuously. Therefore, acting according to the virtues in general comes in under the natural law. However, individual virtuous actions do not, since there are many virtuous acts people perform because of insights they gained in later life and to which human nature does not immediately invite. An example is the founding of a particular welfare organization.

In this way Thomas distinguishes between fundamental

60   I-II 19, 3; 94, 2.
61   I-II, 94, 3.
62   L.c., ad 2.
63   II-II 154, 9.
64   I-II 94, 2.

*Nature as the Basis of Moral Actions*

precepts and rules of conduct which are formulated later in life,[65] sometimes called secondary precepts. The former are immediately evident insights of reason about our basic duties and tasks, comparable to the first principles of the speculative intellect. From these immediately evident first principles—roughly corresponding to the Ten Commandments—other rules of conduct are derived by further reflection, reasoning and recourse to experience.[66] This opens up a wide field and leads to further developments, in particular in the field of social life. The distinction Thomas makes had been anticipated to a certain extent by some medieval theologians of the first half of the thirteenth century.[67]

As to actions which go beyond man's immediate needs reason must determine what should be done. In this respect reason has a certain margin and one may have to take into account the foreseeable results of particular actions. There are acts with a dual effect, and others are to a certain extent determined by circumstances.[68] However, with regard to acts of which the finality has been determined by nature and which are directly connected with our fundamental inclinations, man cannot invert their finality, not even to attain an honest end. He would place a contradiction in his own being and oppose himself to the intention of the Creator.[69] Man receives his nature from God. Reflecting on this gift he understands and deciphers what he must do.[70] However, while the so-called primary precepts of natural law are known to all, some of the

---

65  I-II 94, 3.
66  I-II 94, 2: "Omnia illa ad quae homo habet naturalem inclinationem ratio naturaliter apprehendit ut bona et per consequens ut opere prosequenda, et contraria eorum ut mala et vitanda. Secundum igitur ordinem inclinationum naturalium est ordo praeceptorum legis naturae."
67  William of Auxerre and Roland of Cremona. See O. Lottin, *Le droit naturel chez saint Thomas d'Aquin et ses prédécesseurs*, p. 37 ff.
68  II-II 154, 4.
69  As this reference to the Creator intimates, there is an interaction of Christian philosophical ethics and the faith.
70  Cf. *S.C.G.* I, 7 ; *S.Th.* I, 44, 3.

## RESTORING NATURE

secondary rules may escape man's knowledge because of their complexity. Here reason and arguments intervene, and certain insights may be obscured. This loss of knowledge of part of the natural law can be caused by particular situations, the influence of man's environment, and cannot always be avoided by the individual person. The development of social-political life brings with it a growth of inter-human relations and an ever more complex use of natural things and artefacts. One may think of industrialized agriculture, genetically transformed grains, etc. Views about the rights of working people have evolved considerably, as they have about the use of natural resources. The principle *"nullus peccat in hoc quod utitur aliqua re ad hoc quod est."*[71] finds an application in the growing complexities of our daily life. The right to private property is often said to be part of natural law. Aquinas, however, thinks that for the sake of usefulness and a more ordered community life land, buildings and goods, which basically are the common possession of all, came to belong to individuals.[72] While in its principles the natural law is the same for all men, the conclusions drawn from them can vary. Progress in the understanding of our fundamental obligations is also possible as can be seen in the development of the theory of human rights, of the way in which the strong and the weak are treated in our societies, etc.[73] An enormous field opens up for ethical considerations centered on human nature and the human person.

To illustrate the importance the natural law doctrine has for Thomas, one may quote several arguments. Lying is said to be sinful because speech is a sign of thought: it is unnatural and wrong to say by words something different of what one has in mind.[74] Injustice is sinful, since one wants to have more than one is entitled to and inflicts damage on others.[75] Committing suicide is totally illicit, since it is against the natural inclination to love onself and

71 II-II 64, 1.
72 I-II 95, 5 ad 4.
73 Cf. Jacques Maritain, *On the Philosophy of History*, pp. 82–83.
74 II-II 110, 3.
75 II-II 59, 4.

}224{

*Nature as the Basis of Moral Actions*

to keep oneself alive; moreover man is part of society and cannot arbitrarily withdraw oneself from it.[76] To get drunk is immoral, because one deprives oneself knowingly and willingly of the use of reason.[77] Pride is sinful for one raises oneself above what one really is and is not satisfied with what is proportionate to what one is.[78] On the positive side, religious prayer is demanded from us, since we depend on God.

Can parts of the natural law be suspended or can they change? It is impossible that the first principles be annulled, but it happens that precepts derived from them cannot be applied. A classical difficulty are some commands by God recounted in the Old Testament: Abraham had to sacrifice his son; the Jews were told to steal silver and golden vessels from the Egyptians; and the prophet Osiah had to have intercourse with a prostitute. In the *Summa theologiae* St. Thomas proposes the following solution. The natural law consists of precepts formulated by the human mind. God, the Creator of nature, can let someone know that a certain act no longer comes in under the precept as formulated, and that what holds true for man does not oblige God. To illustrate his remarks Aquinas points out that to kill an innocent person is a crime. Yet daily thousands of people die in events in which divine causality is involved. Instead of natural causes God can also use a human person to bring about the death of someone. Likewise all human possessions belong in the first place to God. Finally, God can also assign a woman to a man outside marriage.[79] At a first sight this solution seems arbitrary and unsatisfactory. On the one hand God imposes certain rules of conduct anchored in human nature, but on the other nullifies them. The answer is that, in a sense, what God does makes up the nature of things. Thomas give the example of water which according to its nature spreads itself out equally, but is raised to the height of a tidal wave under

76  II-II 64, 5.
77  II-II 150, 2.
78  II-II 162, 1.
79  I-II 194, 5.

## RESTORING NATURE

the influence of the gravitational force of the moon. This is not against the nature of water. Likewise an action caused or willed by God, on whom depends the natural activity of things, is not against their nature.[80] This solution is interesting in so far as it shows that for Aquinas physical or biological structures are not the dominant factor, but the insight which makes us see and formulate the basic moral precepts.

The ethics of St. Thomas is far removed from wanting to restrict man to blind submission to biological facts. It places human life in the light of reason and the divine ideas, inviting us to live in accordance with our true being and authentic vocation. The human person formulates his natural law, for in the changing circumstances of our existence we must determine the moral meaning of our various acts and of the use we make of things. As John Paul II writes,

> the natural law expresses and prescribes the finalities, rights and duties, based on the corporeal and spiritual nature of the human person . . . . It is the rational order according to which man is called by his Creator to direct and order his life and to use and dispose of his body.[81]

Shortly after St. Thomas Scotus and, above all, William Ockham made morality depend exclusively on the will of God. However, the natural law as based on reason made a comeback in the sixteenth century. Its study flourished in Spain but it found staunch defenders also in the Low Countries and Germany. Important authors are Vitoria, Suarez, Hugo Grotius, Samuel

---

80  I, 105, 6 ad 1: "Cum igitur naturalis ordo sit a Deo rebus indittus, si quid praeter hunc ordinem faciat, non est contra naturam. Unde Augustinus dicit, XXVI *Contra Faustum*, c. 3, quod «id est cuique rei naturalis, quod ille fecerit a quo est omni modus, numerus et ordo naturae»." Cf. *Q.d. de potentia*, q. 1, a. 3 ad 1.

81  *Donum vitæ*, § 3.

}226{

*Nature as the Basis of Moral Actions*

Pufendorf and John Locke. Suarez's view of the natural law tended to separate man's reason from nature surrounding us. This disjunction developed into a confrontation between human freedom and human nature. "The break between man's individual liberty and human nature as common to all has exercised a major influence in contemporary thought."[82] The rise of positivism, historicism and individualism undermined interest in the topic, but the appearance of totalitarian regimes led to a renewed study of ethics as based on always valid rules given with human nature.

However, many authors of the positivist and analytical schools argued that there is no passing from "is" to "ought." Even as well known and widely acclaimed moralist as Germain Grisez subscribes to this statement. Now, if the sentence is meant to say that the moral order differs from the realm of physical nature, it is quite correct. But when used to deny that the main precepts of man's moral life have their basis in their conformity with what human nature demands it is wrong. Grisez writes that "human persons are unlike other natural entities; it is not human nature as a given, but possible human fulfilment which must provide the intelligible norms for free choice." He quotes an example of what he thinks is a flaw in scholastic natural law theory, sc. the argument against contraception: contraception is said to pervert the generative faculty by frustrating its natural power to initiate new life, but then using earplugs against noise would be equally wrong, while it frustrates hearing.[83] According to Grisez the domination of the scholastic natural law theory helps to explain the negativism and minimalism of classical moral theology and its static character.[84] Surprisingly, Grisez does not offer any better

82  *Veritatis splendor,* § 51.
83  *The Way of the Lord Jesus, Volume I: Christian Moral Principles*, Chicago 1983, p. 105.
84  Father S. Pinckaers has a different and historically much better explanation: as from the sixteenth century moralists neglected to develop their explanations in the light of man's last end, happiness; instead of insisting on the virtues they reduced moral theology to a

}227{

RESTORING NATURE

arguments than this comparison. According to him the scholastic natural law theory holds that moral principles are laws of human nature. "Moral goodness and badness," Grisez writes, "can be discerned by comparing possible actions with human nature, to see whether or not they conform to the requirements nature sets." Grisez is willing to accept that nature has a certain normativity, from which a certain number of requirements follow (e.g., dietary rules), but the theory proceeds by a logically illicit step—from human nature as a given reality to what ought and ought not to be chosen, from what is in fact to what morally should be.[85] In a note he adds that for St. Thomas the first principles of the practical intellect are irreducible to those of the speculative intellect. Therefore, we should replace the "based on human nature" by "helpful to human fulfilment."[86]

A theologian will be reluctant to set aside the theory that somehow moral norms are dependent on human nature, because this doctrine has an extremely solid basis in tradition and seems to offer an excellent foundation for binding norms, while its replacement by Grisez's criterion of human fulfilment appears extensible according to people's concerns and wishes. In a country where Muslims make up the majority of the population, they may consider forceful imposition of the *chariah* on non-Muslims a way to human fulfilment, just as in the past others may have thought that the extermination of Indian tribes or recourse to slave labor would facilitate reaching fulfilment. It appears that we must look for a deeper, universal and objective basis for moral laws. It is obvious that moral law cannot be a biological structure.[87] On his point St. Albert the Great has shown the way by stressing the

careful weighing the extent of the rights of the individual person over and against the obligations of the law (*Les sources de la morale chrétienne*).

85  *Op. cit.*, 108.

86  *Op. cit.*, 105.

87  Some have read this in Ulpianus' definition of natural law as "that what nature teaches all living beings."

*Nature as the Basis of Moral Actions*

rational character of the natural law which is exclusively proper to man.[88] Aquinas argues that the natural law is not just inborn, but that its basis or starting point is given with human nature. This means that our intellect formulates spontaneously the basic principles of the moral order. These principles constitute the core of the natural law and correspond to the first principles of being in the speculative intellect. Obviously they presuppose the latter and only make sense in the context of a correct philosophical anthropology. The natural inclinations to self-preservation, intellectual development, association with others, etc. are not themselves the natural law, but the obligations which flow forth from them, as they are formulated by the intellect in view of the end of human life.[89]

An objection often raised against this position argues that in this view the natural law is static, immutable, not capable of development and adaptation to changing circumstances. Is the natural law indeed immutable? In our answer we point to the distinction between the basic precepts of moral law and further rules of conduct elaborated by human reason, which indeed show progress. With regard to the question whether regress and oblivion of the natural law are possible, Aquinas denies this with regard to its primary precepts, although it happens, he writes, that blinded by passions a certain person does not apply a general precept.[90] However, secondary precepts can be effaced by erroneous opinions or pervert customs prevalent in a society.[91] In Western countries there are erroneous opinions which, to a certain extent, obscure moral thinking, as is obvious with regard to the status of unborn human life, contraception, terminal patients, and homosexual praxis. Opinions as to what is licit differ radically from views which prevailed a century ago. Nevertheless, I do think that with regard to these forms

---

88 *De bono*, V, q. 1, a. 2: "Ius naturale est lumen morum impressum nobis secundum naturam rationis."
89 I-II 94, 2.
90 I-II 77, 2.
91 I-II 94, 6.

of behavior, those who practice them are aware that they transgress the natural order, since these acts concern the primary precepts.

The doctrine of the natural law as arising out of our basic natural inclinations as formulated by the intellect is complemented by that of the virtues having their roots in natural dispositions. Commenting a text of Aristotle[92] Aquinas explains that virtues are natural for man in a dual sense: they agree with his rational nature and may also be in accord with the particular character of some persons. The virtues are present as in their buds.[93] However, the disposition of certain persons may interfere and be the cause that the one has a disposition to certain virtuous acts, such as courageous behavior, the other to self-control or study.

## IV. Contraception and the Natural Law

It is perhaps useful to consider the application of natural law doctrine with regard to contraception, a sort of acid test to see whether it has any value in this field. When more than 30 years ago Paul VI had set up a special commission to study the morality of contraception, the majority of its members said that they could not convincingly demonstrate the intrinsic moral evil of contraception on the basis of natural law. It is worthwhile to look into the question because of its exemplary value for the understanding of the natural law.

Certain moralists such as J. Fuchs argue that the marital act as such is a pre-moral action and the intention makes it moral or immoral. However, when speaking about the marital act we mean the act as one conceives it and knows what one is doing. The act has a content related to our human nature, to the obligation one has and the ends one pursues.·When resorting to the marital act while using contraceptives one knows exactly what one is doing. There is a difference between using a tool and engaging onself in such acts as eating, drinking, thinking, loving and intercourse. The first is an open act and its morality depends on the purpose

92  *Ethica Nicomachea* 1114b6–28.
93  I-II 63, 1: " . . . secundum quandam inchoationem."

## Nature as the Basis of Moral Actions

one pursues. But acts like eating, drinking and having intercourse have a moral value by themselves. As such, and when performed in conformity with right reason, they are good. But in order to be morally good these acts must preserve their nature. This nature is not just the plain biological structure of such activities. We are dealing with acts as they are known and willed by the human agent. If this agent thwarts the natural purpose of such acts, one places a certain contradiction in them. Two partners want to unite but at the same time they prohibit what this union implies.

A source of misunderstanding in this respect is a false view of human nature. As unbelievable as it may seem to be, there are many who subscribe to a dualistic approach in anthropology. They distinguish between two layers in man, the biological and animal part on the one hand and the sphere of man's self awareness on the other. They give total priority to man as a person, to his wishes and needs, rather than to biological mechanisms and processes which in themselves, they say, never have the value of an absolute.[94] In their view we must attribute to man a greater power over his own body so that he can further determine the precise meaning of his sexual life, not unlike the way he shapes and further determines the physical world in which he lives. According to these authors it is even less natural to submit oneself to the biological structure of one's being than to intervene with one's reason in order to mold these functions and make them more suitable for the specific goods one is pursuing.

To this we answer that there is no question of a blind submission to biological structures, but to *human law*. The natural law is not a set of biological principles. It consists in the insight and command of our reason telling us that in a particular field we must act in this way or refrain from performing a particular action. Certain actions do not come in under natural law, such as—at least ordinarily—the choice of a job, but natural law is definitely concerned with the field of sexual acts, because of their essential importance in human life as well as their biological and psychological signifi-

94   A. Valsecchi, *Régulation des naissances*, Gembloux 1970.

}231{

cance. This means that people understand and formulate some of their basic duties with regard to the use of their sexual functions. For instance, they know that their sexual faculties are given them in view of securing the continued existence of mankind as well as for cementing their union; they know that they are responsible for their progeny and must take care of it. They also know that they must form a stable bond with a partner in mutual trust and esteem.

By their very nature freely chosen sexual acts are never incidental or casual nor purely biological. Because of what they are they tend to engage the entire person with his psyche and his moral responsibility. Precisely because coital union is not a mere instrument nor something irrelevant, but intrinsically human, it has its own meaning. Whosoever thwarts or neutralizes one or the other of its essential functions places a contradiction in his conduct. If it is wrong to tell a lie because this contradicts the purpose of speech and the mutual trust which must reign between men, contradicting the very structure of the coital union is much worse because a more important matter is involved, sc. profoundly human acts which concern man as a rational being as well as the survival of mankind. One cannot set aside the natural end of these acts without contradicting oneself.[95]

## V. Some Conclusions

The discussion about the existence and meaning of natural law is far from ended. Our societies are confronted with formidable difficulties when decisions have to be reached as to whether to accept or reject certain forms of behavior such as abortion, euthanasia, overt homo-

95 The Minority Report of Pope Paul's Commission argued that the sinfulness of contraception must not be derived from the fact that sexual acts are being deprived of their natural end (since this sometimes happens in nature). A reference is made to *Q.d. de malo*, q. 2, a. 1, but this reference to Aquinas is not very fortunate for the text does not concern those acts where the rule of reason is intimately connected with their natural end.

}232{

*Nature as the Basis of Moral Actions*

sexuality, refusal of military service, experiments on human embryos, death penalty, sterilization, globalization and sometimes apparently harmless issues like mendicity. Is it true that private behavior, as long as it does not overtly interfere with community life, should be of no concern to the legislator?

1) Until quite recently most of the commonly accepted moral judgments were survivals from Christian ethics, but now people may differ on basic tenets—at least a clamorous group of the intelligentsia and representatives of the media try to swing public opinion toward the acceptance of a totally neutral public life which condones any form of sexual behavior as long as no violence is done to others and even denies the right to publicly qualify such behavior as homosexual practice as unsound or as harmful to society. Behind their attitude there is a different view of human life and the human person. As long as the external shape and form of developing life is not that of a recognizable human being, the embryo/fetus is considered valuable biological material which may be used for such "noble" purposes as helping others. The idea that human life is a gift from God, to be respected and which has not been delivered to our own or other people's decisions for free disposal, has very much weakened. But that applies also to the whole of nature which in our technological age appears to have lost, in the eyes of many, its reference to the Creator.

However, the consequences of this liberalism concerning human life and the value of the human person begin to show: increasing difficulties in the field of education, the aging of the population, the disappearance of respect and of certain standards in decency, trends among certain groups to denigrate the Christian faith and Christian morals. Surprisingly, in other fields, such as that of justice, the trend goes toward a stricter application of norms of public honesty. Striking examples of applying natural law ethics are the recognition of human rights, the protection of minorities, and the total condemnation of genocide.

2) Pluralism as it prevails in most Western countries implies different views in the fields of religion, ideology, culture and

RESTORING NATURE

economy as well as the pursuit of different goals. However, it is not so certain that in the long run a strongly pluralistic state can survive.[96] Ideally, natural law ethics, agreed upon by a fair majority of the citizens, can provide a basis for the necessary spiritual unity in a country. Related to this is the question of the appointment of justices to the supreme or constitutional courts. Often nominations are politically biased since the ruling party attempts to impose its candidates. To ensure morally right judgments of the courts it is of paramount importance that the judges are in agreement with the basic principles of the natural law, even if in difficult issues they may understandably differ in the conclusions they are drawing from these principles.

3) The importance of natural law ethics for society is clearly demonstrated also by the human rights issue. Human rights are nowadays very much in the limelight, but theorizing about man's basic rights is not so new. Certain rights were recognized in the Roman Empire and, above all, in the Christian era. However, when in the 17th and 18th centuries the function of the Church as the guarantor of such rights was not perceived any more, concern with human rights as an autonomous body of rights developed.[97] It is precisely this aspect of the natural law theories of that period of history which appeals most to our contemporaries. It is perhaps useful to define first the relationship between natural law and natural rights. According to St. Thomas Aquinas, law is intrinsically a rule, an obligatory guideline, issued by the one or those in command of the society, in view of the common good. Natural law is such a guideline for man's basic conduct, formulated by man himself in accordance with his natural inclinations.

---

96 Cf. A. Schwan, "Pluralismus und Wahrheit," in *Ethos der Domokratie. Normative grundlagen des freiheitlichen Pluralismus*, Paderborn/München/Wien 1992, 105 ff.

97 See J. Punt, *Die Idee der Menschenrechte. Ihre geschichtliche Entwicklung und ihre Rezeption durch die moderne katholische Sozialverkündigung*, Zürich 1987.

}234{

*Nature as the Basis of Moral Actions*

Justice directs man in his dealing with others. It aims at a certain equality. "Right" (*iustum*) qualifies an action which is related by some kind of equality to someone else. For instance, the payment of the just salary for services rendered. "Just" is the object of the virtue of justice.[98] A thing can be adjusted to a person in two ways. First by its very nature—this is called a natural right. In a second way a thing can be adjusted to someone by agreement of common consent. Such agreement can be either private or public. There is public agreement when the whole community or the government acting in its name decrees something. Rights and duties are derived from man's nature and from positive law[99] and go together. If children have a right to be nourished and educated by their parents, the latter have the duty to do so.

Nowadays human rights are conceived as claims which individual citizens or groups of people put forward. People insist on their right to be respected, to have suitable work and job security, to shorter working hours, a right to vacation, to protection and social assistance, etc. Human nature is the foundation of the most basic claims, even if in contemporary theories about human rights this foundation is often not apparent. The advocates of human rights rather appeal to Declarations of Human Rights, proclaimed by common consent.

In this connection natural law ethics has the important task to clarify the basis of these rights, to define them more precisely, to distinguish between rights and pseudo-rights and to show which are the duties corresponding to these rights. Implementing human rights depends also on the state of development and organization of the society people are living in and on the functioning of subordinate organs. Some two hundred years ago it would not have made much sense to claim the right to a job or to adequate education from the US government. These sort of rights were generally honored by the local community.

---

98  *S. Th.* II-II, 57, 1 and 2.

99  Cf. Locke's *Second Treatise of Civil Government*, in which he derives man's natural rights from the law of nature.

}235{

RESTORING NATURE

Apparently the question of who must honor these rights is not always easy to answer. It is, for instance, not so clear whether the state itself must provide education to the young and carry out all those tasks in the social field over which it now claims to have authority. Moreover, the exercise of certain rights, such as the right to express one's own opinions or to perform certain acts is always subject to the respect of other people's rights and the requirements of the common good. In fact, living in a political society requires that one espouses a good deal of the underlying ideas and values professed by its members.

The basic human rights are characterized by the following properties:

(a) they are universal and apply to all men (this axiom is based on the fact that we all share the same human nature[100]); (b) they must be immediately evident, because they are derived from the first principles of natural law;[101] (c) they do not change and cannot be totally wiped out from our mind.[102] Certain human rights now widely accepted, at least in the Western world, were at one time not clearly recognized. For instance, the rights of working people, of women, of ethnic minorities, etc. This raises the question of the mutability of the natural law, treated by Aquinas in articles 3 to 6 of the *Summa theologiæ* I-II, q. 94. Aquinas was very much aware of the general mutability of human life. It also happens that certain conclusions are drawn from human rights which are clearly absurd or wrong. For instance, from the right to express one's views some conclude to an unhampered freedom of the media to publish whatever they want and to use any means to get access to what—in terms of profit—reporters and editors consider important. Obviously this practice should come under review from natural law principles

100 *In V Ethicorum*, lesson 12.
101 *S.Th.* I-II 100, 1.
102 *Quaestio disputata de malo*, q. 2, art. 4 ad 13. On this section see Jesús García López, *Los derechos humanos en Santo Tomás de Aquino*, Pamplona 1979, pp. 66 ff.

}236{

*Nature as the Basis of Moral Actions*

such as the right of people to their good name and privacy as well as the right not to be offended in their religious beliefs.

4) A further issue where natural law ethics has an important role to play is the relationship of the individual and the state and that between individual countries and umbrella political structures such as the European Union. In this respect natural law ethics establishes the principle that what an individual person or what particular groups or nations can do by themselves should not be regulated by the state or by other comprehensive structures. The state should not appropriate the initiatives of individual citizens, but restrict its interventions to subsidiarity, that is to those cases where help is necessary.[103] The individual person is the point of departure and the ultimate reference of social and political reality.[104] The citizen must decide what he can perform himself. The dignity of the human person demands that he conducts his own life and determines his place in society. The principle of subsidiarity protects the good of the individual.[105]

5) Natural law ethics has a major role to play in the question of the globalization of the economy and of the difficulties arising from worldwide free trade. Utilitarianism pretends to pursue the greater good of the greater number, but in a long range vision is quite helpless in defining what this greater good is and does not guarantee sufficient protection of the rights of individuals in respect of their own customs and way of life. Christian natural law ethics does not believe that the ultimate well-being of the peoples of the world is to be reached mainly by a totally unhampered freedom to trade and to develop industry. If it is true that national states have become too small for promoting the long term well-being of their citizens, the larger conglomerations and alliances are likely to be too large to secure the good of the individual citizens.[106]

---

103 *Quadragesimo anno*, § 96.
104 The encyclical speaks of the *singularis persona*.
105 A.-F. Utz, in A.-F. Utz (ed.), *Das Subsidiaritätsprinzip*, Heidelberg 1953, p. 10.
106 Cf. A. Giddens, *Konsequenzen der Moderne*, Frankfurt am Main 1995, 86.

RESTORING NATURE

6) An important question connected with the human rights issue is that of the extent to which Western nations with a high level of prosperity should admit tens of thousands of often destitute and hardly educated immigrants of a widely different cultural outlook. Natural law ethics will bring into the discussion considerations not only about the rights of people to improve their status, but also to available means and sufficient space in guest countries to settle these people, their willingness to accept the Western way of life and respect of human rights, etc. It is by no means certain that Muslim immigrants, once they become strong in numbers, will be willing to accept our values or that immigrants from very poor countries can in one or two generations become ordinary citizens, making a contribution to the common good. On the other hand, there is a duty to assist underdeveloped nations so that they can reach a higher level of well-being.

7) Finally, natural law ethics can also help determine our obligations with regard to our natural environment. While it defends the right of man to use minerals, plants and animals for his benefit, it pays increasingly more attention to a fair exploitation of natural resources, which respects the rights of the different peoples and of future generations. Economy in the use of non-renewable resources is imperative. Deliberations on the continued use of nuclear energy and the disposal of atomic waste also come in under this topic, as does the pollution of the atmosphere, rivers and oceans

These examples show the tasks lying ahead of those who accept natural law ethics as established in its principles by St. Thomas Aquinas.

# Human Nature, Poetic Narrative, and Moral Agency

Robert A. Gahl, Jr.

Pontifical University of the Holy Cross (Rome)

## 1. Introduction

My purpose in this paper is to sketch a theory according to which a full account of Thomas's understanding of human perfection requires the use of contemporary narratology. My proposal means to cut deeper than that of most proponents of a narrative moral philosophy or of narrative theology. Most of them focus on the pedagogical and therapeutic effects of stories on their readers.[1]

---

1   N. T. Wright describes the powerful capability of stories to effect profound change in convictions by referring to the famous effect of a story on its listener. "Nathan tells David a story about a rich man, a poor man, and a little lamb; David is enraged; and Nathan springs the trap. Tell someone to do something, and you change their life— for a day; tell someone a story and you change their life . . . . The subversive story comes close enough to the story already believed by the hearer for a spark to jump between them; and nothing will ever be quite the same again." *The New Testament and the People of God*, London, SPCK, 1993, p. 40. For some other fascinating studies of the pedagogical and therapeutic influence of stories see: Martha Nussbaum (e.g., *The Fragility of Goodness: Luck and Ethics in Greek Tragedy*, New York, Cambridge University Press, 1986; *Love's Knowledge: Essays on Philosophy and Literature*, Oxford, Oxford University Press, 1990; *The Therapy of Desire. Theory and Practice in Hellenistic Ethics*, Princeton, Princeton University Press, 1994) and Wayne C. Booth (e.g., *The Company We Keep: An Ethics of Fiction*, Berkeley, University of California Press, 1988; *The Rhetoric of Fiction*, London, Pen-

RESTORING NATURE

Many of them consider that communities of virtue and of faith are built upon the stories that are passed down from generation to generation, whether pagan myths and fables and family histories or sacred scripture. A smaller number of scholars more boldly claim that narrative is also somehow embedded in our very being or constitutive of ourselves as humans.[2] They propose that human rationality and volition may reach perfection only when structured around a story that each one writes, with more or less self-awareness, through the performance of each voluntary action.

Stanley Hauerwas, one of the early proponents of narrative theology, once referred to Elie Wiesel's famous declaration and complained that "one can be told once too often that 'God made man because he loves stories.'"[3] In fact, many scholars, including Thomists and orthodox theologians, now become bored when they hear talk about "narrative," especially when coupled with "theology." Surely there is some truth to Wiesel's words: "God made man because he loves stories"; but the following words, less succinct than Wiesel's, might constitute a more enlightening expression. God became man because it was only by having a human story that God could fully reveal himself to man.[4] These

guin, 1991, 2nd edition). For an insightful and creative overview of current work regarding the ethical effect of stories on their readers see Armando Fumagalli, "Etica & Narrazione," *Studi Cattolici*, 41 (1997) 585–594 and for a more extensive version see chapter 3 of the forthcoming volume edited by Gianfranco Bettetini and Armando Fumagalli, *Etica della comunicazione*, Milano, Franco Angeli, 1998.

2  The most influential of these authors is of course Alasdair MacIntyre. See especially *After Virtue*, University of Notre Dame Press, Notre Dame, IN, 1984, 2nd edition.

3  Stanley Hauerwas, "The Church as God's New Language,'" in *Scriptural Authority and Narrative Interpretation*, edited by Garret Green (Philadelphia, Fortress Press, 1987), pp. 179–98 (p. 188), where he quotes Elie Wiesel's *The Gates of the Forest*, translated by Frances Frenaye (New York, Holt, Rinehart and Winston, 1966).

4  Many Thomistic texts affirm the supreme suitability of the Incarnation so that God could perfectly reveal his salvific plan to humanity. For just one of these, see *SCG* IV.54, n. 3926: "cum beatitudo hominis

# Human Nature, Poetic Narrative, and Moral Agency

words express God's caring and purposeful love for the human being and, at once, God's providential design to save the fallen human while respecting his free and intelligent nature. The human being enjoys the spiritual faculty of intellect and yet comes to know through sensitive experience acquired in time and through the discursive reflection upon that experience. Human knowledge is therefore acquired by considering events that are causally connected and temporally dispersed. God became man in order to have a human story so that we could come to understand a bit better the ineffable nature of God.[5] A more ambitious

> perfecta in divina fruitione consistat, oportuit affectum hominis ad desiderium divinae fruitionis disponi: sicut videmus homini beatitudinis desiderium naturaliter inesse. Desiderium autem fruitionis alicuius rei ex amore illius rei causatur. Necessarium igitur fuit hominem, ad perfectam beatitudinem tendentem, ad amorem divinum induci. Nihil autem sic ad amorem alicuius nos inducit sicut experimentum illius ad nos. Amor autem Dei ad homines nullo modo efficacius homini potuit demonstrari quam per hoc quod homini uniri voluit in persona: est enim proprium amoris unire amantem cum amato, inquantum possibile est. Necessarium igitur fuit homini, ad beatitudinem perfectam tendenti, quod Deus fieret homo."
>
> 5  See Jn 1, 18: "No one has ever seen God. The only Son, God, who is at the Father's side, has revealed him." *New American Bible.* The Vulgate reads: "Deum nemo vidit umquam unigenitus Filius qui est in sinu Patris ipse enarravit." Aquinas comments on the fullness of revelation manifested by the Word Incarnate: "et haec doctrina ideo omnibus aliis doctrinis supereminet dignitate, auctoritate et utilitate, quia ab unigenito filio, qui est prima sapientia, immediate est tradita" (*In Ioannem*). For an even more detailed commentary on the human mode of revelation by the Incarnate Christ in light of Jn 1, 18, see *SCG* 4.54.4: "oportuit igitur hominem, ad perfectam certitudinem consequendam de fidei veritate, ab ipso Deo instrui homine facto, ut homo, secundum modum humanum, divinam instructionem perciperet. Et hoc est quod dicitur ioan. 1–18: Deum nemo vidit unquam: unigenitus, qui est in sinu Patris, ipse enarravit. Et ipse dominus dicit, Ioan. 18–37: 'ego ad hoc natus sum et veni in mundum, ut testimonium perhibeam veritati.' Propter quod videmus post Christi incarnationem evidentius et certius homines in divina

}241{

narrative theology proposes much more than the mere claim that stories affect our self-understanding. This more ambitious narrative theology aims to provide a deeper explanation for the importance of stories on their hearers and readers by proposing that it is because the fulfilled moral life is of the structure of a story that God became man in order to save us by his living an exemplary story. In short, we tell stories because we live stories, and not the other way around.

Likewise, an ambitious application of narratology to moral philosophy contends that human fulfillment or happiness may only be achieved by living an intelligible, coherent, unified, meaningful, and successful story. According to such a moral philosophy, we all are artists constantly engaged in the most important task possible: crafting our own selves by building the narratives of our lives around everyday actions.

Therefore, according to my proposal, aesthetics and literary studies are not entirely separate from moral philosophy. The principles of aesthetics and the tools of literary criticism must be used by moral philosophy. My proposal is based at least as much on the study of the thought of St. Thomas Aquinas as on the study of narratology. With this proposal, I contend that Aquinas's anthropology and theory of human fulfillment presuppose and entail all of the elements implicit to a narrative moral philosophy and theology. And, moreover, his theory may be best understood when examined in the light of the integrating instrument of narrative.

## 2. Human Nature: The Artist as Imago Dei

The customary density of Thomas's works reflects a brilliant mind striving to communicate as much as possible within the restricting confines of language, almost rushing to complete the task at hand. Some of the texts most dense with meaning are the

cognitione esse instructos: secundum illud Isaiae 11–9: repleta est terra scientia Domini."

# Human Nature, Poetic Narrative, and Moral Agency

prologues to major works, where Thomas sets the stage by situating all that follows within a broad context and upon a deep foundation. I would like to begin my consideration of human nature in Thomas's thought and of the human artist as *imago Dei* by commenting on what may be the least studied of those important prologues.[6] In the very beginning of his introduction to his commentary on Aristotle's *Politics*, Thomas quotes from the *Physics* (II, 2) "ars imitatur naturam" in order to explain the dependency on human nature of practical intellect's role of guiding action, especially that action which involves the exercise of the prudence proper to the prince.[7] Since nature provides the principles of every art, the activities and effects of the artist must be proportionate to nature. The human intellect, the proximate principle of art, was created in the image and likeness of the divine intellect, the artist of all created nature. It is therefore necessary that all of art imitate that which pertains to nature. Just as the apprentice artist learns from the master artist, so too the human intellect, whose intellectual light is derived from the divine intellect, learns from that which has been made in nature so as to perform in fashion similar to that of the Divine Artist.

In the prologue to his commentary on the *Politics*, Aquinas proceeds to distinguish between the speculative and practical functions of the faculty of reason. Speculative reason observes and comes to know that which is proper to nature. Practical or operative reason extends beyond the speculative by, not only knowing nature, but also making artifacts while imitating nature.

---

6    At least two reasons explain the relative neglect of Thomas's commentary on the *Politics*. First, Aristotle's political theory generates little interest among most of today's political theorists. Second, since St. Thomas never finished the work, most editions include inauthentic portions, whether from Peter d'Auvergne or Louis of Valence. See John Pierre Torrell, *Initiation à Saint Thomas d'Aquin: sa personne et son oeuvre*, Cerf, Paris, (and Editions Universitaires, Fribourg Suisse)1993, p. 502.

7    For other Thomistic uses of this Aristotelian adage see: *SCG* III, 10; *In I Post. Anal.*, proemium, 5; *SCG* II, 75.

}243{

RESTORING NATURE

The human exercises his natural vocation as *imago Dei* by imitating the Divine Artist. We imitate God insofar as our intelligence participates in His and insofar as all of our operations are guided by his creative genius. While nature proceeds from God's creative activity, art is the effect of the human's imitation of God's intelligent creative act and the effects of that divine act. By applying practical intellect, the human understands forms and their proportion so that he may order them, rearrange them, and assemble them into composites.

The medieval use of the word "ars" embraces a more extensive semantic field than covered by the modern usage.[8] Thomas uses the term "art" in various, analogous ways. In the prologue to his commentary on the *Politics* he uses the term broadly to encompass all activity (or *operationes*) that involve the ordering of things to their end. Perhaps better known are those passages where Thomas considers art more restrictively as the intellectual habit of ordering external objects towards their end and thereby excludes from this usage of the word the ordering of oneself to the due end. Thomas uses this more restricted sense of art to distinguish between the practical habits or skills required for the transitive doing or making of things and the practical habits required for the immanent action that is perfective of the agent when in accord with right appetite. Or, in simpler terms, Thomas restricts the more narrow sense of art to making as opposed to acting. According to this more narrow sense of the term, art only refers to those skills that govern "recta ratio factibilium," while prudence governs "recta ratio agibilium."[9] *Factibilia* and *agibilia*

8    See Jan Aertsen, *Nature and Creature. Thomas Aquinas's Way of Thought*, E.J. Brill, Leiden, 1988, p. 101 note36: "'Ars' may be translated by the term 'art' as long as its kept in mind that the medieval concept was much broader than the modern, aesthetically qualified concept." See also R. Assunto, *Die Theorie des Schönen in Mittelalter*, Köln, 1963, p. 12.

9    *ST*, I-II, 57.4. For parallel texts that consider art in the restricted sense of the intellectual habit of the right reason for making things, see *In VI Ethic.*, lect. 3; *In I Metaph.*, lect. 1, 34.

## Human Nature, Poetic Narrative, and Moral Agency

are both directed by practical intellect and both involve the ordering of operations to an end. But *agibilia* also include a reference to appetite and to the use made of the object by human volition. Although Aquinas borrows from Aristotle's *Ethics* this more narrow use of the term *techné* ("art") for the sake of distinguishing the intellectual and moral virtue of prudence from the skills needed for productive activities, nonetheless, his terminology also includes *agibilia* within art when used in the broad sense.[10]

In the prologue to the commentary on the *Politics*, Thomas explains how the human's artistic ordering of things to their end from the simple to the composite, and from the imperfect to the perfect, includes not only those things that are used by the human, but even human beings themselves. The highest art, whose principle is the purpose for all the others, is the governing of the city, the community that he considers perfect on account of its being self-sufficient for human life.[11] There is no higher principle that human reason can know and can constitute than the city because all other human communities are ordered to it. Therefore, the broader use of the term art includes the highest artistic endeavor: the ordering of voluntary actions towards human perfection. The human artist is image of God on account of his natural capacity to order himself to his own end and for his own sake. In the Prologue to the *Second Part* of the *Summa*, Aquinas explains why the human is an image of God with the following words: "per imaginem significatur intellectuale et arbitrio liberum et per se potestativum."[12] Although all creatures

---

10  Aristotle, *Nicomachean Ethics*, VI, 4–5.

11  See *De Regno*, I, ch. 14: "Est tamen praeconsiderandum, quod gubernare est, id quod gubernatur convenienter ad debitum finem perducere."

12  *ST*, I-II, prologue. See, for example, *De Regno*, I, ch. 1: "Nam liber est, qui sui causa est; servus autem est, qui id quod est, alterius est. Si igitur liberorum multitudo a regente ad bonum commune multitudinis ordinetur, erit regimen rectum et iustum, quale convenit liberis." See also, Aristotle, *Metaphysics*, I, 2, 982b26: "for the free man is he who acts for his own sake."

contain some trace of the Creator, among material creatures only the human being is made in the image of God.

My understanding of the architectonic order of moral and technical skill in Aquinas, and therefore of the relationship between the moral life, useful art, and fine art, is closer to that of Umberto Eco's account than that proposed by Jacques Maritain in *Art and Scholasticism* and in *The Responsibility of the Artist*.[13] Indeed, my proposal that moral action in Aquinas is an artistic ordering to the end would seem extravagant, if not outrageous, to Maritain. In *Art and Scholasticism* he claims that the art of making "remains outside the line of human conduct, with an end, rules, and values which are not those of the man, but of the work to be produced."[14] And in *The Responsibility of the Artist*, Maritain more forcefully maintains that: "Art and Morality are two autonomous worlds, with no direct and intrinsic subordination between them."[15] On account of his political concerns to defend the ordering of the state towards the common good without the slightest

13  See: Jacques Maritain, *Art and Scholasticism*, New York, Charles Scribner's Sons, 1937; *The Responsibility of the Artist*, New York, Charles Scribner's Sons, 1960; and *Creative Intuition in Art and Poetry*, New York, Pantheon, 1963; see also Umberto Eco, *Art and Beauty in the Middle Ages*, New Haven, Yale University Press, 1986 (trans. of *Sviluppo dell'estetica medievale* in *Momenti e problemi di storia dell'estetica*, vol. 1 Marzatore Editore, 1959) and *The Aesthetics of Thomas Aquinas*, Cambridge, Harvard University Press, 1988 (trans. of *Il problema estetico in San Tommaso*, Torino, Edizioni di Filosofia, 1956).
14  *Art and Scholasticism*, p. 7.
15  *The Responsibility of the Artist*, p. 22.
16  To describe the lack of overlap between the personal good and the common good of political society, in fashion similar to his defense of the autonomy of art and motivated by comparable comparisons, Jacques Maritain claims that the common good of political society is an "infravalent end," an intermediate, non-absolute end, subordinate to the absolute final end. To explain this subordination of the political to the ultimate, and therefore to create space to defend the individual from the potential threat of a suffocating regime, he uses the example of a runner who dedicates all of himself in the race, but

*Human Nature, Poetic Narrative, and Moral Agency*

risk of totalitarian consequences, Maritain defends the autonomy of the arts of production and rejects any intrinsic ordering of artistic making to the final end.[16] He only allows for there being an indirect and extrinsic subordination of the productive arts to the natural end of the human being.[17] Eco, on the other hand, in his *The Aesthetics of Thomas Aquinas,* first describes the medieval context of dogmatic recognition of the distinction between the orders of artistic making and moral doing and then goes on to show how Aquinas's artistic aesthetics are of one piece with the whole of his ordered and systematic thought. The useful arts and the fine arts are just two sets of endeavors within the broader context of ordering human life to its end. Eco describes the confusion among some students of Thomas and explains the broader picture.

> Some of the things that Aquinas has said have led some people to talk enthusiastically about the autonomy of art. But this is to misunderstand him. Indeed, autonomy

not with all of his aspects and all of his aims. The example betrays the hidden tension within Maritain's political thought, a tension which he explicitly rejected but could not avoid between the individual and the person. Maritain seems not to have noticed that, because of the limited nature of athletic competition, the runner does not apply all of his faculties to the race, whereas the citizen should apply his whole self, with all of his capabilities, to the life of his community. Even when home alone, the individual ought to responsibly exercise virtue for the sake of the community. Aquinas protects the individual from the potentially suffocating domination of the political regime by indicating that when the regime makes unjust demands upon the individual he is not obliged in conscience to satisfy them. But for Thomas, the citizen may at times be excused from satisfaction of civil law, not because he extracts himself from the community, but because his aim is to fully serve the community insofar (and only insofar) as the community is directed towards its true end. See Jacques Maritain, *True Humanism,* trans. by M. R. Adamson, London, Charles Scribner's Sons, 1938, p. 127.

17  See *The Responsibility of the Artist,* p. 22 and Jeanne M. Heffernan, "Art: A Political Good?" in *Art, Beauty, and the Polis,* ed. Alice Ramos, Washington, D.C., American Maritain Association, 2000, pp. 260–268.

RESTORING NATURE

> would be an absurd notion in a philosophical system based upon order and finality . . . . It is only within the general plan of the *Summa* that we can be clear about Aquinas's philosophy of art and beauty . . . . Aquinas's aesthetic criteria can be used to defend the autonomy of beauty, if they are employed in a different spirit from his own.[18]

Eco describes the ordering of all making to the overall end of human society with words reminiscent of Aquinas's prologue to the *Politics*. "Productive human actions are not isolated actions, but acquire value from being part of the life of the City; and the terrestrial City is an image and anticipation of the City of God."[19] The ordering of the fine arts, the useful arts, and of moral action to the Creator need not entail an absorption of the distinction, so dear to Maritain, between art and morals. Aquinas's metaphysics of order permits distinguishing strongly between the end of a crafted artwork and the end of the human. But the first must be subordinate to the second. And it is the human's task to order himself and all of creation to the Creator.[20]

For Aquinas, moral and political philosophy are those sciences dedicated to achieving wisdom regarding the principles of voluntary action in order to direct it towards its end. Respectively, they teach how to order the actions of the individual and of the whole of society towards human fulfillment. For Aquinas the artistic imitation of nature is intrinsically dynamic, voluntary, and

18  Eco, *The Aesthetics of Thomas Aquinas*, pp. 184, 186, and 187.
19  Eco, *The Aesthetics of Thomas Aquinas*, pp. 183–184. John Finnis in *Aquinas: Social, Political and Legal Theory* (Oxford, Clarendon Press, 1997) also refers to the prologue of the *Politics* to indicate that art includes voluntary action within the *polis*.
20  I owe this observation and a greater appreciation for Maritain's careful description of this distinction to Ralph McInerny and Vittorio Possenti. In another work on the topic, I hope to make more extensive use of Possenti's generous suggestions for a deeper development of the relationship between art and morals in Maritain.

}248{

## Human Nature, Poetic Narrative, and Moral Agency

intelligent, much richer than some "naturalistic" interpretations would lead one to believe. Since the artist is either the Divine Creator or his human image, artistic imitation should not be considered as either a necessary or static phenomenon, or as a pedagogical ploy implemented by Aquinas "to facilitate the analysis of what is less familiar, nature, through the analysis of what is more familiar to us."[21] Jan Aertsen, in his earlier and lesser known book *Nature and Creature: Thomas Aquinas's Way of Thought*, explains that Aquinas's understanding of the artistic imitation of nature is deeply rooted in his metaphysics of creation and nature's intrinsic dynamism. "If we would come closer to the Greek meaning of *physis* and its relation to *techné*, then we must see the imitation thesis in the first place as a manifestation of an *identical logos* in the becoming of things."[22] The highest artistic imitation therefore regards the ordering of human actions so that humans, whether individually or in communities, may reach their full perfection according to their nature.[23]

Having been made in the image of God and with the natural capacity to know Him, the human may achieve perfection only by attaining a full return to his principle and end.[24] The science

---

21  Aertsen, *Nature and Creature. Thomas Aquinas's Way of Thought*, p. 100. Aertsen here claims that A. Mansion's *Introduction à la physique aristotélicienne*, p. 229, n. 7, proposes an interpretation of the Aristotelian adage such that it would merely serve a pedagogical purpose.

22  *Nature and Creature*, p. 100.

23  See John Paul II, *Letter to Artists*, Libreria Editrice Vaticana, Vatican City, April 4, 1999, nn. 1–2.

24  See, for example, xlii. *In De Div. Nom.*, chap. 1, lect. 3, 94: "An effect is most perfect when it returns to its source; thus . . . circular motion (is) the most perfect of all motions, because in their case a return is made to the starting point. It is therefore necessary that creatures return to their principle in order that the universe of creatures may attain its ultimate perfection." I follow Jean-Pierre Torrell's description of a modified neo-Platonic exitus-reditus scheme in Thomas's thought. Thomas's view of creation combines the circular, pagan, neo-Platonic model with the linear Augustinian model. For Aquinas all creatures proceed from a free and loving God and are ordered to

}249{

of moral philosophy is a study of the principles required for this achievement of human perfection by the ordering of individual voluntary actions to the final end. Moral philosophy is therefore the scientific study of the principles to be applied by the art of directing voluntary actions towards their end. The practical wisdom required to direct human actions involves a memory of one's own identity, and of one's past experience, and the present knowledge of one's future goals or purposes. Such an artistic practical wisdom goes beyond the knowledge of universal principles and discovers the most suitable contingent particulars to achieving one's end. The suitability of those contingent particulars is highly dependent upon one's past, one's present situation, and one's future ambitions. The artistic determination of the most suitable particular action to be performed in the present is described by Thomas with the terminology of prudence, choice, and intention of the end. These Thomistic concepts could coincide with the contemporary concept of critical literary theory called emplotment, if this neologism devised to describe the artistic task of story-writing may also be applied to the authorial role of moral agency.[25]

## 3. Poetic Narrative: *Intentio Finis* as Emplotment

In this third section of my paper, I will briefly describe what I mean by "poetic narrative" in order to compare the role of "intentio finis" in Aquinas's action theory to emplotment. But first of all, I would like to briefly evoke a theme that I developed in the paper that I presented here at Notre Dame in the year 2000, "Time in Augustine and Aquinas: What Time Was It When God

Him as their end. Their *exitus* and their *reditus* are irrepeatable. See Jean-Pierre Torrell, *Saint Thomas d'Aquin — maître spirituel*, Cerf, Paris, (and Editions Universitaires, Fribourg Suisse) 1996, pp. 69–75 (L'Alpha et l'Oméga) and ch. 8, and for a more detailed analysis Inos Biffi, *Teologia, Storia e Contemplazione*, pp. 232–312, ch. 6: "Il piano della *Summa theologiae* e la teologia come scienza e come storia."

25  The earliest use I know of this term is in Paul Ricoeur's, *Time and Narrative*, vol. 1, Chicago, University of Chicago Press, 1984, 31–51.

*Human Nature, Poetic Narrative, and Moral Agency*

Created Adam?" While arguing that Augustine, although intent on developing the subjective experience of time, never rejected, and even implicitly held, Aristotle's more objective view, I referred to Augustine's description of human awareness of time as a "distentio animae." This swelling of the soul by which we remember the past, experience the present, and expect the future, causes suffering. Our desire is for eternity, even to have it all at once, now, not in little pieces. The temporal fragmentation of experience, whether cognitive, volitional, or sentimental, the fleeting character of all satisfactions, and the need to wait for completion, are an experience of the finitude that the *imago Dei* longs to overcome. In his classic study *Le Temps et l'Eternité chez Plotin et saint Augustin*, Jean Guitton comments that for Augustine the problem of time was nothing other than the larger problem of the self.[26] Augustine's struggle to clarify the moral self has very much to do with the question of poetic narrative. In Book X of the *Confessions* (10, 16:25), St. Augustine writes:

> O Lord, I am working hard in this field, and the field of my labors is my own self. I have become a problem to myself, like land which a farmer only works with difficulty and at the cost of much sweat. For I am not now investigating the tracts of the heavens, or measuring the distance of the stars, or trying to discover how the earth hangs in space. I am investigating myself, my memory, my mind.[27]

Full, personal resolution of the Augustinian quest may only be reached with final beatitude, by attaining eternal life in the Blessed Trinity. But the suffering due to "distentio animae" may

26  Jean Guitton, *Le Temps et l'Eternité chez Plotin et saint Augustin*, Vrin, Paris, 1933.
27  "Ego certe, domine, laboro hic et laboro in me ipso: factus sum mihi terra difficultatis et sudoris nimii. neque enim nunc scrutamur plagas caeli, aut siderum intervalla demetimur, vel terrae liberamenta quaerimus: ego sum, qui memini, ego animus."

RESTORING NATURE

be partially overcome in this life by unifying the discordant temporal moments of one's life around the principle and end of life.[28]

Paul Ricoeur interprets Aristotle's definition of poetry to be nothing else than the art of making plots, that is, the art of organizing events.[29] For Aristotle, poetic narrative is therefore the active imitation or representation of an action in order to teach, to uncover some heretofore hidden meaning of reality.[30] Poetic narration draws together the many elements dispersed throughout time of a single, whole action within a meaningful plot.[31] The plot gathers the beginning, middle, and end of the action into a single meaning according to the structure of a linear temporal sequence and a causal order. Each moment has its place within that order as cause or consequence.[32] Narrative poetic imitation allows for several different forms of expression: history, fiction, biography, theater, cinematog-

28  See, for instance, St. Augustine, *Confessions*, X.22.32: "ipsa est beata vita, gaudere de te, ad te, propter te: ipsa est et non est altera. Qui autem aliam putant esse, aliud sectantur gaudium. Neque ipsum verum. Ab aliqua tamen imagine gaudii voluntas eorum non avertitur." And X.28.39: "Cum inhaesero tibi ex omni me, nusquam erit mihi dolor et labor, et viva erit vita mea tota plena te."

29  See Paul Ricoeur, *Time and Narrative*, p. 33 and Aristotle, *Poetics*, 1447a2 and 1450a15.

30  See Ricoeur, *Time and Narrative*, I, 238 note 8: "For Aristotle, imitation is an activity and one that teaches us something." Ricoeur goes on to comment that with the *Poetics* Aristotle responds to Plato's anti-artistic Book X of the *Republic*, where he remarks that artistic imitation is merely concerned with that which is "thrice removed from the truth."

31  See *Poetics*, 50b23–25: "tragedy is an imitation of an action that is whole [holos] and complete in itself [teleios] and of a certain magnitude [megethos]."

32  See Aristotle, *Poetics*, "the poet should be a maker of plots more than a maker of verse, in that he is a poet by virtue of his imitation and he imitates actions. So even if on occasion he takes real events as the subject of a poem, he is none the less a poet, since nothing prevents some of the things that have actually happened from being of the sort that might probably or possibly happen, and it is in accordance with this that he is their poet." (*Poetics*, 51b27–32)

}252{

*Human Nature, Poetic Narrative, and Moral Agency*

raphy, etc. One basic distinction between the various expressions of narration is between recital and drama. Where recital is the simple telling of a story, drama is its gesticulative acting out. The narration is expressed by the actions themselves rather than by a "narrator" telling the story. Rather than having a narrator say of a character "he said," the narrator plays the role of the character and simply says. In drama the narrator becomes actor. Actors, whether of theater, or film, or simply those who perform voluntary acts, tell a story by performing the actions that constitute the plot.[33]

Today, most literary theorists object to the idea that our moral lives have the structure of narratives. They hold that stories are merely an imitation of the lives of moral characters. For instance, Louis Mink writes that "life has no beginnings, middles and ends . . . Narrative qualities are transferred from art to life."[34] Hayden White is more forceful in objecting to the hypothesis of narrative realism. "The notion that sequences of real events possess the formal attributes of the stories we tell about imaginary events could only have its origin in wishes, daydreams, reveries."[35] But the

33  Wayne Booth uses a slightly different but partially overlapping terminology. Booth distinguishes between dramatized and undramatized narrators. The dramatic narration to which I refer is even more dramatized than Booth's "dramatized" narrator. Of course, Booth allows for actions that are narrative in content. He refers, for instance, to "narrator-agents." But for his purposes he maintains a separation between narrators and protagonists. See *The Rhetoric of Fiction*, 2nd edition, Chicago, University of Chicago Press, 1983, ch. VI "Types of Narration."

34  Louis Mink, "History and Fiction as Modes of Comprehension," *New Literary History* 1 (1970), p. 557, where Mink also asserts: "Stories are not lived but told."

35  Hayden White, "The Value of Narrativity in the Representation of Reality," in *On Narrative*, ed. W.J.T. Mitchell, Chicago, 1981, p. 23. See also: Seymour Chatman's *Story and Discourse: Narrative Structure in Fiction and Film*, Ithaca, 1978, where he affirms that the beginning-middle-end structure applies only "to the narrative, to the story-events as narrated, rather than to . . . actions themselves, simply because such terms are meaningless in the real world."

Aristotelian poet, or simply any realist story teller, aims to imitate, or represent, the universal in order to disclose a deeper truth hidden in the particular and not immediately evident to the common observer. Realist literary theorists hold that we find narratives in all human cultures on account of the metaphysically prior fact that the narrative structure is constitutive of the very reality of human action.[36] Narrative is real, embedded within human action, and constitutive of the self—both individual and social. While describing tragedy, the most meaningful poetic genre of dramatic narrative in his day, Aristotle asserts that "it is the action in it, i.e., its plot, that is the end and purpose of the tragedy, and the end is everywhere the chief thing."[37] The tragedy's plot is nothing other than the end of the entire action. And by end Aristotle means much more than just the outcome. The plot is also the purpose and meaning of the individual elements that constitute the whole action or life story. The plot, therefore, is the all-encompassing form that gives meaning to the protagonist's individual moments within the dramatic poem.

The writing of history involves much more than the empirical recording of events. The columns in the morning newspaper that record the scores from yesterday's baseball games are not history. At the most, they are chronicles, or perhaps, once orderly compiled, annals. History includes human intentionality, motives, and aims. The biblical theologian N. T. Wright holds that with history

> we are trying to discover what the humans involved in the event thought they were doing, wanted to do, or

36 See, for instance, David Carr, "Narrative and the Real World: An Argument for Continuity," *History and Theory* 25 (1986) p. 117: "narrative is not merely a possibly successful way of describing events; its structure inheres in the events themselves." See also Carr's more substantial *Time, Narrative and History*, Bloomington, Indiana, Indiana University Press, 1986 and, of course, the work of Alasdair MacIntyre.

37 *Poetics*, 6a16–22.

*Human Nature, Poetic Narrative, and Moral Agency*

tried to do. The apparently obvious counter-example proves the point: when historians try to write about pre-human or non-human history they regularly invoke some idea of purpose, whether that of the cosmos, of some sort of guiding life-force, or even some sort of god.[38]

The historian's task is, therefore, a kind of poetic narration. The historian seeks to uncover the human intentions that caused the events of the past, to critically reconstruct the rational and interior ordering of past actions.

If the historian, in his effort to reconstruct the artistic ordering that was present in the actions themselves is a poet, in the Aristotelian sense of the term, why not consider the agent studied a poet? The individuals responsible for the history were also (more or less aware) of their causal agency. In the ordering of their own actions they were already performing the task of the poet, and of the historian. This is not to deny the advantages of the historian's perspective. Looking back in time allows for certainty regarding the outcome, a certainty that we can never achieve regarding the consequences of our own poetic task of ordering our lives until we have reached their mortal end. My thesis that every human exercises poetic authorship over the narrative of his moral life does not entail, and in fact excludes, that the human agent-author has complete and sole control over the narrative. Providential design, whether through accidental causes or direct divine intervention, changes the humanly anticipated events and possibilities thereby rendering the need for constant creativity on the part of the human agent-author. Plot reversal and discovery of unexpected elements makes moral life an adventure. Self-knowledge, even of the past, is always susceptible to modification and correction, even in need of such modification and correction. And, since various causal factors beyond our control and understand-

38 *The New Testament and the People of God*, London, SPCK, 1993, pp. 109–110.

RESTORING NATURE

ing deviate our lives from their anticipated path, we are constantly telling and retelling our stories.[39] It is because of our lack of full control over the successful outcome of our lives as we anticipate them that the moral life is a quest in search of more perfect self-understanding and also a greater capacity to render ourselves and our purposes intelligible to others. Despite the imperfect knowledge of the whole of one's autobiography, the poetic structure of narrative is nonetheless already present within the voluntary actions themselves. What is more, the poetic narrative structure is constitutive of the act as voluntary. For an act to be voluntary, the agent must have temporal self-awareness within the context of a story.

Thomas Aquinas's action theory, systematically developed in questions 6–21 of the *Prima Secundae*, describes voluntary action with the same governing elements found in Aristotelian poetic narrative. Aquinas's action theory entails a cascade of hylemorphic compositions: from *materia ex qua*, to *materia circa quam*, and from the direct object to the remote end. In every complete voluntary action, the human rationally applies his will to natural things in order to perform an act in view of a further end, and all this for the sake of the last end. Deliberation, choice, and use of the desired means are always for the sake of some end and always in the specific context of the accidental circumstances surrounding the chosen object. To perform a morally perfective act, the human must have self-awareness, memory of past experience, and recollection of his personal identity in view of achieving the end. Granted, morally culpable action may be defective in one of these elements, but for an action that is perfective of the human

39 See Alasdair MacIntyre's, *After Virtue*, 204: "a quest is always an education both as to the character of that which is sought and in self-knowledge." See also his "Epistemological Crisis, Dramatic Narrative, and the Philosophy of Science," *The Monist*, 60 (1977) 455: "To be unable to render oneself intelligible is to risk being taken to be mad, is, if carried far enough, to be mad. And madness or death may always be the outcomes which prevent the resolution of an epistemological crisis."

}256{

## Human Nature, Poetic Narrative, and Moral Agency

in accord with his nature all of these elements must be present. Self-awareness and previous experience are not too much to demand for moral action. St. Thomas explains the requirements needed for the first moral act performed by the pagan child. The first use of reason includes a deliberation about himself. And if he orders himself to the due end, "through grace he gains the remission of original sin."[40] Thomas further explains in his response to the third objection that the first use of reason also involves an ordering of "other things to himself as to an end, for the end is first in intention."[41] The capacity for moral agency requires self-awareness and the reflection upon other things according to their order and proportion to oneself, all for the rational purpose of achieving one's end. For Aquinas, voluntary action requires unitary self-awareness, knowledge of one's end, and the artistic design of rationally ordering, arranging, and assembling the means to the end.

At the beginning of the *Nicomachean Ethics* Aristotle uses the metaphor of the archer to show the importance of determining the end in order to guide voluntary action.[42] With this metaphor he compares archery, an art in the order of making, to moral action, the art in the order of doing, the master art that requires the

40  *ST*, I-II, 89.6: "Sed primum quod tunc homini cogitandum occurrit, est deliberare de seipso. Et si quidem seipsum ordinaverit ad debitum finem, per gratiam consequetur remissionem originalis peccati."
41  *ST*, I-II, 89.6.3: "primum enim quod occurrit homini discretionem habenti est quod de seipso cogitet, ad quem alia ordinet sicut ad finem, finis enim est prior in intentione." Emplotment is a life-long task, even *the* life-long task. As David Carr writes on p. 125 of "Narrative and the Real World: An Argument for Continuity": "we are constantly striving, with more or less success, to occupy the story-tellers' position with respect to our own lives. Lest this be thought merely a far-fetched metaphor, consider how important, in the reflective and deliberative process, is the activity of literally telling, to others and to ourselves, what we are doing . . . . narrative activity, even apart from its social role, is a constitutive part of action, and not just an embellishment, commentary, or other incidental accompaniment."
42  Book I, ch. 2, 1094a.

RESTORING NATURE

highest form of practical wisdom. Aristotle's metaphor of the archer who aims at the bullseye expresses what Aquinas calls *intentio finis* of the moral agent. The end is first in the order of intention and continuously informs all subsequent actions, whether actually or habitually, until the human modifies his determination towards the intended end, either by direct conversion from or to the due end or by choosing to perform an act whose object is incompatible with the end intended up until that moment. The intelligibility of every action is dependent upon the form given by the intended end. Since every voluntary act, insofar as it is voluntary, is informed by the end, it is chosen as an event within the whole of one's life. Therefore, since intention of the end entails the gathering together, the ordering, and the assembling of single acts into a meaningful whole extended throughout time, intention of the end is nothing other than emplotment, the poetic ordering of temporally dispersed events into one meaning, into one story.

## 4. Moral Agency: Beauty, Unity, and the Happy Ending

In Plato's famous polemic against the poets of tragedy he describes a hierarchy of artistic imitation according to the vicinity to truth of the work of art. In his conversation with Glaucon, Plato speaks of the absolute truth of the ideas in God's mind. God is the supreme craftsman who makes all that there is, even the other gods. The ideas or forms in God are that which is most real and most true. For Plato, they are God's masterpiece. Plato uses the example of a maker of beds and of a painter. The carpenter who constructs the bed only makes an imitation of the single idea of bed. The idea is real and held in the mind of God. The carpenter's bed is just a copy, an appearance of the true bed, not the true existence of a bed, but only "some semblance of existence."[43] For Plato, the bed does not have real existence. Plato compares the carpenters craft to moving a mirror so as to make the sun, the moon, and the stars appear here and there. The movement of the

43  Plato, *Republic*, trans. Benjamin Jowett, Book X.

}258{

*Human Nature, Poetic Narrative, and Moral Agency*

mirror does not make the sun, the moon, and the stars but only makes them appear in a weak semblance.

But let us continue with Plato's example. The painter paints a painting of the bed. The painting, being an imitation of an imitation, a mere appearance of appearance, is thrice removed from the truth.[44] One need not accept Plato's metaphysics of the forms to make use of his example of artistic imitation and to apply it to the moral life. The poet imitates whole actions or human lives. While performing the many voluntary actions of his personal life story, the human being also performs the imitation of poetic narrative. The human being, made in the image of the Word, imitates the Archetype by performing acts proper to his rational nature. Who then is the principal artist? The poet or the moral agent? Plato provides a possible response:

> the real artist, who knew what he was imitating, would be interested in realities and not in imitations; and would desire to leave as memorials of himself works many and fair; and, instead of being the author of en-comiums, he would prefer to be the theme of them.[45]

With rhetorical genius Plato points us to the solution. God the Creator is the principle Artist. The Father eternally begets the Divine Word through his perfect self-understanding. The Word is the perfect Image of God. We humans are the only material creatures made (through the Image) in the image of the Image.[46] As images

---

44  Plato, *Republic*, Book X.
45  Plato, *Republic*, Book X, 599b.
46  *ST*, I.35.2.3: "imago alicuius dupliciter in aliquo invenitur. Uno modo, in re eiusdem naturae secundum speciem, ut imago regis invenitur in filio suo. Alio modo, in re alterius naturae, sicut imago regis invenitur in denario. Primo autem modo, Filius est imago Patris, secundo autem modo dicitur homo imago Dei. Et ideo ad designandam in homine imperfectionem imaginis, homo non solum dicitur imago, sed ad imaginem, per quod motus quidam tendentis in perfectionem designatur. Sed de Filio Dei non potest dici quod sit ad imaginem, quia est perfecta Patris imago."

## RESTORING NATURE

of the Word, we are naturally endowed with artistic talent. The highest human artistic potency is to order all things, especially ourselves, to the end. Men and women who live their lives in such a way that they will be worthy of honor forever are the master artists deserving of the richest encomium. Only they order their lives in beautiful unity according to the demands of the principle and exemplar, the Word made flesh. *Sequela Christi* is nothing but the natural fulfillment of our imitation of the Divine Image in the principle artistic task: the accomplished ordering of voluntary acts according to the structure of poetic narrative and for the sake of the due end.

In *Saint Thomas d'Aquin—maître spirituel,* Jean-Pierre Torrell offers a splendid description of the theology of *sequela Christi* in Thomas while describing how Aquinas emphasizes that Jesus teaches us even more effectively with his actions than with his words.[47] With various formulations Thomas repeats throughout his works "plus movent exempla quam verba."[48] Like Aristotle, Aquinas perceived our need to learn how to be virtuous by observing an exemplar of virtue. But, with respect to Aristotle, Aquinas had a decided advantage. He knew the perfect exemplar, the paradigm of virtue, God Incarnate. In q. 34 of the *Prima Secundae,* Thomas explains that in the area of the moral life and the human passions, where experience is so important, example moves more than mere words ("magis movent exempla quam verba").[49] Thomas therefore repeatedly affirms throughout his work that the "action of Christ was our instruction."[50] When

---

47 *Saint Thomas d'Aquin—maître spirituel,* see for example: ch. 5, sections entitled "Imiter Dieu en imitant le Christ" (pp. 147–152) and "Je vous ai donné l'exemple . . ." (pp. 153–159) and ch. 6, "La conformité au Christ" (pp. 186–196) and ch. 14 "Le modèle de toutes les perfections" (pp. 484–489).

48 *In Ionannem* 13, 15, lect. 3, n. 1781.

49 *ST*, I-II.34.1: "in operationibus enim et passionibus humanis, in quibus experientia plurimum valet, magis movent exempla quam verba."

50 Thomas supplies various formulations of the dictum that Christ teaches by example. "Christi actio fuit nostra instructio." "Christus pro-

*Human Nature, Poetic Narrative, and Moral Agency*

commenting on the washing of feet at the Last Supper (Jn. 13.15), St. Thomas refers to Jesus' own words—"I have done this to give you an example"—to base his theology of Jesus' moral pedagogy on Jesus' divine authority.[51] Aristotle's virtuous man is, for Aquinas, the Word Incarnate.

What, then, is the literary genre of the fulfilled life? Since we all desire happiness, the genre of our moral life must be apt for achieving happiness. It must be a genre that represents a fully intelligible and therefore united life that, on account of its beauty in measure and proportion, is worthy of honor.[52] Intermediate actions incompatible or simply non-conducive to the end would distract from the mimetic splendor meant to be manifest by the plot. In her recent essay "The Dignity of Man and Human Action," Alice Ramos offers a splendid analysis of the beauty of the fulfilled moral life in Aristotle and Aquinas and a powerful suggestion. She shows that, in addition to being naturally inclined to know and to love, the human also tends to be the recipient of love, as a consequence of being considered worthy of honor. More specifically, Ramos shows how moral perfection in Aquinas involves not only glorifying God but even striving to give Him

ponebatur hominibus in exemplum omnium." And "cuncta quae Dominus fecit vel in carne passus est, documenta et exempla sunt salutaria." See Torrell, ch. 5, note 49 for bibliographical references.

51  See *In Ioannem* 13.15, lect. 3, n. 1781.

52  Contemporary moral philosophers are careful to notice that to be worthy of honor presupposes accountability and responsibility for one's actions. Accountability, a necessary feature of moral agency, requires awareness of authorship of one's actions within a causal sequence which is nothing other than narrative self-awareness. Moral responsibility also entails membership in a community such that one is aware of the duty to respond to the community, or the authoritative members of the community, regarding one's free actions. As MacIntyre wrote in *After Virtue*, p. 202: "To be the subject of a narrative that runs from one's birth to one's death is . . . to be accountable for the actions and experiences which compose a narrative life. It is . . . to be open to being asked to give a certain kind of account of what one did or what happened to one."

delight. She concludes that much as any artifact might delight its maker, by being what it is and by doing what it was meant to do, so too, the human may seek to "delight his Maker by being recognized in his life-long action as God's son and by uniting himself through his action to that Beauty that will one day approve and glorify him."[53]

So, to return to the question of the genre of life to be lived, since the fulfilled life is united around the intentional achievement of the happy end, that is, the end that fully satisfies the desires of the human agent, the genre must be comic, not tragic. To use Dante's expression, and to follow the inspiration of Calderón de la Barca's *El gran teatro del mundo*, the genre of the perfect life is the divine comedy. Divine because the end is God. Divine because the principal extrinsic efficient cause is God. Divine because the human actor represents the divine Son of God. Divine because the principal spectator is our Father God. The divine comedy, the genre of the life of moral perfection, is also divine because the actor himself is made in God's image. I would further add that the fulfilled moral life may only be of the genre of divine comedy, because the co-author along with the human co-author is none other than God. The screenwriter is God. Even the director is God.

Much more should be said in order to show the implications of the application of narratology to metaphysical anthropology, moral philosophy and theology. The role of remembrance of divine filiation in the Son ought to occupy a special place in moral and spiritual theology. Only with the memory that we are sons and daughters of the Father will we have the awareness of our identity needed to dramatically perform voluntary acts in accord

---

53 Alice Ramos, "The Dignity of Man and Human Action," *Acta Philosophica* 10.2 (2001), pp. 315–321. See also *De Ver.*, q. 1, a. 8: "ars est mensura omnium artificiatorum." I thank Lawrence Dewan, O.P., for alerting me to the fact that, surely, we cannot cause an effect in God and therefore, strictly speaking, cannot cause his delight. Nonetheless, if we glorify God by acting in accord with our nature, directing ourselves to Him, our end, then, surely, He must delight from all eternity in knowing Himself as our first Cause. See, for example, *ST*, 1.26.4.

*Human Nature, Poetic Narrative, and Moral Agency*

with a plot perfective of our nature.[54] Only a soteriology cognizant of narrative anthropology can provide a full account of the Incarnation within the economy of salvation. A theory of natural law in accord with Aquinas's treatise at the end of the *Prima Secundae* requires explicit appreciation for fulfillment of the law as imitation of the Creator and as a law entrusted not just to a species but to a community of persons who can only fulfill the law by dynamically adhering to the common story of the People of Israel and the Communion of Saints.[55] In q. 93 of the *Prima Secundae,* Aquinas explains the eternal law in terms of God's artistic creation. The eternal law is the source of natural law's participation. The eternal law is the divine design for all of creation. For the human to fulfill the natural law, he must imitate the divine artist by freely living in accord with the law intrinsic to his nature. Narrative theory is the instrument needed for developing an aesthetics of the moral life and thereby overcoming the separation of the beautiful and the good in accord with the doctrine of Thomas Aquinas. Narrative theory offers an instrument for integrating measure, order beauty, providence, and law within both moral philosophy and politics.[56]

54　The instrument of narrative could be used to integrate the many elements of Thomas's spiritual theology delineated by Torrell in his second volume on Thomas, *Saint Thomas d'Aquin — maître spirituel.* The integration of these elements within a narrative theology would allow them to illuminate one another more effectively.

55　In *A Father Who Keeps His Promises. God's Covenant Love in Scripture* (Charis Books, 1998), and in an unpublished paper, with the support of added scholarly argumentation, Scott Hahn supplies convincing argumentation to show that the Treatise on Law needs to be appreciated in its entirety. Questions 98–108 need to be read along with 90–97. The history of revelation is a story told by God through his providential actions. The divine pedagogy of the people of Israel is a history accessible to natural reason and can nourish fruitful philosophical reflection.

56　See Alice Ramos, "Aquinas and the Platonic Theme of Measure," Summer Thomistic Institute 2000, forthcoming from St. Augustine Press, and her "Beauty, Mind, and the Universe," in *Art, Beauty, and*

Please allow two additional considerations before I conclude—both of which are in self-defense. First, a preemptive defense against an hypothetical objection. "Thomas does not use the concept of narrative, so why do you feel justified in imposing this new construct upon his thought?" To respond, I would first remark that the essential characteristics of narrative present in contemporary literary theory are implicitly present in Thomas's work and firmly founded upon a solid metaphysical anthropology. All of the elements of narrative are required components of Thomas's psychology of voluntary action. All of the elements of the contemporary theory of authorship are included within his creational anthropology of the human being as *imago Dei*. To respond to the hypothetical objection, I would also add that St. Thomas *explicitly* refers to the need to use poetic artifices, such as narrative ,within *sacra doctrina*. In article 5 of the Prologue to his *Commentary on the Sentences*, Thomas asserts that "modus istius scientiae sit narrativus signorum." Thomas reports the objection that poetic artifices are wholly inappropriate within *sacra doctrina* because they contain only the minimum of truth.[57] He responds by acknowledging that poetic artifices are indeed disproportionate to human intelligence. Poetry regards that which cannot be understood by reason on account of its lack of truth ("defectum veritatis"). Poetry seduces reason through simile. But, Thomas adds, poetry is also to be used when the topic of a science is disproportionate to reason on account of its comparative excess of truth.

Finally, the second concluding consideration is to defend myself from the charge of prideful pursuit of originality. Although I opened with the proposal of a thesis and conclude with its defense, I maintained all along that what I propose is already within the texts of Thomas, although not fully developed. Moreover, many other authors, dead and alive, have nourished my research

*the Polis*, ed. Alice Ramos, Washington, D.C., American Maritain Association, 2000, pp. 70–84.

57 *In Sent.* Prol., a. 5, obj. 3: "poetica, quae minimum continet veritatis, maxime differt ab ista scientia, quae est verissima."

*Human Nature, Poetic Narrative, and Moral Agency*

with their writings. The study of Ralph McInerny's recently published Gifford Lectures[58] with Pirandellian title so apropos to my inquiry will surely profit further development of a Thomistic moral philosophy based on narrative anthropology.[59]

58 See Ralph McInerny, *Characters in Search of Their Author*, Notre Dame, University of Notre Dame Press, 2001.

59 I am indebted to many scholars who made suggestions to earlier versions of this paper and to papers that I delivered on related topics at the St. John's University and at the John Paul II Institute of the Lateran University. Especially helpful were suggestions made by Scott Hahn, Stephen Brock, David Gallagher, Alice Ramos, and Iñaki Yarza.

# The Order of Providence and the Sacrament of Order, Paralleled in St. Thomas Aquinas

Anne Barbeau Gardiner

John Jay College, City University of New York

When St. Thomas Aquinas writes about the order of Providence and the Sacrament of Order, he uses such similar phrasing and imagery that he invites, or rather compels us to see these two "orders" as parallel. In fact, Aquinas asserts that there are three parallel states of existence, one higher than the other and each with its own order—nature, the Church, and heaven. He explains that "the state of the church is between the state of nature and the state of glory," and that within each of these three states there is a similar *vertical order*: "we find order in nature, in that some things are above others, and likewise in glory, as in the angels," and so "there should be Order in the Church."[1] Note his phrase *should be*–there should be a type of *order* in the Mystical Body of Christ whereby *some things are above others,* just as there is in nature and in heaven. Although the Church is a whole new creation, certain basic structures of reality remain, at least analogously. Now what St. Thomas calls in this passage "Order in the Church" is the hierarchical priesthood, from subdeacon to pope, for in this chapter he is dealing specifically with the Sacrament of Order. As he presents it, the priesthood is not only the conduit by which Christ communicates with his Mystical Body the Church in the

---

1   "Supplement," in *Summa Theologica*, 5 vols, translated by the Fathers of the English Dominican Province (Westminster, MD: Christian Classics, 1981); rpt of 1948 ed.), Vol 5, q. 34.1. All citations to this work will be hereafter included in the text.

*The Order of Providence and the Sacrament of Order, Paralleled in Aquinas*

sacraments, but also the necessary form of government he has instituted to preserve unity in his Church.

This essay will examine the parallels St. Thomas finds between two of those three states, namely, the order of Providence and the Sacrament of Order. It will conclude by showing that these parallels shed light on the initial phase of the English Reformation. To begin, St. Thomas writes that "just as the perfections of all natural things pre-exist in God as their exemplar, so was Christ the exemplar of all ecclesiastical offices" (*ST*, Suppl, q. 40, 4). By repeating the word *exemplar* in this sentence, he points to a parallel between nature and the priesthood. Just as each creature reflects some perfection pre-existing in God from eternity, so each strata of the priesthood reflects some ministry performed by our Lord during his sojourn on earth. While nature's pattern is in God, the priesthood's is in the historical Christ. And whereas Providence directs the whole of nature, including man, Christ cares for his Church from within, since she is joined to him in one Mystical Body. She is an entirely new creation requiring a new and special providence. The 17th-Century poet John Dryden put it well when he wrote: the Church is "the same vessel which our Saviour bore, / Himself the Pilot." Once in that Ark, we can leave the known shore behind us, "And with a better guide a better world explore." While he acts as a special but hidden providence till the end of time, Christ lets his visible Church carry the scepter and the keys: "With these to bind, or set the sinner free, / With that t'assert spiritual Royalty." But this is a royalty of service.[2]

## Parallelism in the Use of Instruments

One of the striking parallels St. Thomas draws between the order of Providence and the Sacrament of Order is that divine government on both planes is carried out by "ministers," "secondary

---

2    John Dryden, *The Hind and the Panther* (1687), Part I, 131–3, in *the Poems and Fables of John Dryden*, ed. James Kinsley (Oxford: Oxford University Press,1980; pbk rpt of 1958 ed.).

}267{

RESTORING NATURE

causes," or "instruments." In nature, God's Providence has a master-plan reaching down to the smallest singular. This plan is executed by ministers or secondary causes not because of a deficiency in his power, but because of a superabundance of his goodness. As St. Thomas explains, God communicates his likeness to things first by giving them being, and then by letting some of them be the causes of other things so they can attain divine likeness not just by existing, but also by acting on others. For it is of the fullness of perfection to have the power to communicate what one has to others.[3] St. Thomas remarks that this "beauty" of ministers found in nature would surely "be lacking to the Church" if Christ had not instituted his priesthood (*ST*, Suppl, q. 34.1). And so, when he was about to withdraw his visible presence from the Church, our Lord "established Order in her," that is, appointed ministers to "dispense the sacraments to the faithful" in his place. With the phrase *even as in the natural body*, St. Thomas underscores the parallel between the natural and the Mystical Body, and with the phrase *established order*, he hints that Christ from the start left his Church with a settled, visible government. His was to be a Church in history, not out in utopia, so it needed a real structure of authority to survive. Each priest was to be "an instrument . . . moved by the agent for making something" (*SCG*, 4, ch. 74) and "like to God" not just by existing but also by "cooperating with God; even as in the natural body, some members act on others" (*ST*, Suppl, q. 34.1).

According to St. Thomas, Christ builds his Church by using priests just as a man builds a house by using tools. When a house is complete, it does not resemble the man's tools, but rather his design—"For a house is not made like the instrument which a builder uses; it is made like his art" (*SCG*, 4, ch. 77). This striking parallel suggests that when the divine architect builds his Church

---

3  *Summa Contra Gentiles*, 5 vols, translated and edited by Vernon J. Bourke (Notre Dame and London: Notre Dame Press, 1975; rpt of 1956 ed). Vol. 3, ch.77. All citations to this work will hereafter be included in the text.

}268{

*The Order of Providence and the Sacrament of Order, Paralleled in Aquinas*

by the instruments of priests, the end result is nothing like the ecclesiastical hierarchy writ large. Rather, it is a new creation, an everlasting Jerusalem raised of living stones. St. Thomas points out another intriguing parallel between nature and the Church when he remarks that just as an instrument in nature has to be "proportionate" to its agent and to share in his power, so "the ministers of Christ must be in conformity with Him." Notice his verb *must be*. St. Thomas declares that the parallel has to hold between a natural instrument and our Lord's priests. To be "proportionate" to Christ as instruments and "in conformity" with him, priests must "be men" (*SCG*, 4, ch. 74). A woman may be a saint, a doctor of the Church, or a prophet, but she may not be a priest, because she is not *proportionate* or *con-formed* to the historical Christ, the "exemplar"of priests. Evidently, form matters.

St. Thomas indicates another parallel between natural instruments and Christ's priests when he says, "even in natural things matter receives from one and the same agent both the ultimate disposition to the form, and the form itself." With the phrase *even in natural things,* he insists that the same double effect is to be expected when priests confer the sacraments. They too will bestow both the form and the disposition to form. Now Christ confers spiritual power on his priesthood chiefly for the sake of the Eucharist, the "sacrament of sacraments," by which the faithful receive the form of Christ. Consequently, the priest must dispose the faithful to receive our Lord's Body, Blood, Soul and Divinity by giving them the "proximate disposition," i.e., cleansing them from sin. It follows, then, that the priest is the proper minister of Baptism and Penance, the two sacraments that dispose the faithful for Communion (*ST*, Suppl, q. 37.4). All other sacraments flow from what is contained in the Eucharist, and so it follows that the chief reason spiritual power is conferred on the priesthood is so they may serve for this "outpouring from the Head to the members"of the Mystical Body (*ST*, Suppl, q. 36. 3).

In the order of Providence, an effect can be attributed both to a lower agent and to God, though in different ways. St. Thomas compares God's use of secondary causes to an artisan's use of a

RESTORING NATURE

tool: the effect can be "wholly attributed" to the tool and to the artisan. Now since God directly and continually preserves things in being and touches them all by the immensity of his power, his Providence controls "what, how many, and what kind of effects proceed from His power, even down to the lowest things" (SCG, 3, ch. 65–66). And so, whatever is done by secondary causes can also be attributed to him. Even defective proximate causes, which bring about bad actions, can be attributed to God in the sense that he preserves those causes in existence and gives them the power to act. Here once again a parallel can be glimpsed between the order of Providence and the Sacrament of Order. For St. Thomas declares that the work of the sacraments can be attributed both to Christ and to his instruments the priests:

> clearly Christ Himself perfects all the sacraments of the Church: it is He who baptizes; it is He who forgives sins; it is He, the true Priest, who offered Himself on the altar of the cross, and by whose power His body is daily consecrated on the altar—nevertheless, because He was not going to be with all the faithful in bodily presence, He chose ministers to dispense the things just mentioned to the faithful. (SCG , 4, ch. 76)

This parallel between Providence and our Lord's governance of his Church also holds in that some priests, by sinning, become defective proximate causes. Even so, they still receive from Christ the spiritual power to serve for an outpouring from the Head to the members of the Mystical Body. St. Thomas comments on this difficult point by saying that in nature, God's Providence rules creatures in such a way as to preserve contingency in secondary causes and free will in human beings. Neither chance nor free will are due to a deficiency in God's power, but rather to "the perfection of the order of providence" (SCG, 3, ch. 73). For a certain "beauty" would be lacking if God's design did not allow for such things. Yet nothing, not even a random event or an interior choice, escapes the rule of Providence. God wants men to act voluntarily,

*The Order of Providence and the Sacrament of Order, Paralleled in Aquinas*

not under coercion, so that the beauty of virtue can exist in his plan, but since the acts of rational creatures "are more closely ordered to God as end" than those of other creatures, their internal acts of free will, and not just the ensuing external results, "definitely fall under the order of providence." Thus, intellectual creatures are "masters of their operations through free choice of the will,"and yet, at the same time, they have their wills *inclined* by God without any violation of their freedom. This interplay of Providence and free will is a profound mystery. What St. Thomas affirms is that God alone—who by his power maintains the will in being and enables its act—causes voluntary movement in it "without violence." So while men may resist their own disposition or an angel's persuasion, they will choose "in all cases the object in accord with God's operation" within them (*SCG*, 3, ch. 88–90).

Just as God can incline our wills and yet leave room for the beauty of virtue, so in the Church our Lord's "divine liberality" provides for his priests a "divine grace," without which their spiritual power would not "suitably be exercised" (*SCG*, 4, ch. 74). But he allows this grace to be resisted and lost. On the other hand, Christ has "ordered" that the spiritual power his priests received at ordination will persist forever and not be removed, like this grace, by mortal sin. Indeed, St. Thomas declares that "even sinners and evil men, provided they have orders, are able to confer the sacraments of the Church" (*SCG* , 4, ch. 77). He finds two parallels in nature for this priestly power. Just as water cannot heat unless it receives the power from fire, so the priest's work in the sacraments exceeds the capacity of any man, "no matter how good he is." Hence, his power must be received from "some other source" (*SCG* 4, ch. 77). With the phrase *no matter how good he is*, St. Thomas insists that even if the virtue of a man is towering, it is totally incommensurate with the power needed to be a conduit between the divine Head and the mortal members of the Mystical Body. Now the parallel of water and fire holds only so far. For when water cools down, it retains nothing of the fire, but St. Thomas points out that the priest who sins still retains the power to confer sacraments. To explain this, he offers a further parallel

RESTORING NATURE

from the natural order—just as a virtue or a vice does not add or take away from a man's natural abilities, but rather causes him to use those abilities well or badly, so likewise a priest's being good or bad does not add to, or take away from the spiritual power he received from Christ, but only makes him suitable or unsuitable for using it. Now this is the heart of the matter. For if the sin of the priest could prevent the outpouring of the Head to the members, the faithful would, on receiving the sacraments, have to put their trust not in Christ but in the "goodness of a mere man" (*SCG*, 4, ch. 77). And so, when our Lord "established order" in his Church and instituted sacraments for his people's spiritual sustenance, his special providence took into account the contingencies of free will in his priests.

## The Vertical Dimension—Unity through Inequality

Yet another parallel St. Thomas finds between the order of Providence and the Sacrament of Order is that in each case, the unity of the whole results from the inequality and subordination of the parts. St. Thomas sees God's wisdom in this "orderly distinction of things both natural and spiritual" (*ST*, Suppl, q. 37.1). His phrase *both natural and spiritual* again indicates a parallelism, while *orderly distinction* suggests that there is a similar vertical order in both states of existence. Just as in the physical body there are various offices performed by various members, some higher than others, so in the Mystical Body, he explains, "each Order sets a man above the people in some degree of authority, directed to the dispensation of the sacraments" (*ST*, Suppl, q. 35.1). Inequality and subordination in the Church, as in the natural sphere, spreads duties around so that many can attain to the perfection of cooperating with God in the execution of his great design.

St. Thomas reflects that there is natural inequality in society, where "inferior arts" serve "higher" ones for the common good. If there were no subordination here, there would be no unity. For example, the woodcutter's art serves shipbuilding, and shipbuilding serves navigation, and navigation serves the art of economics

}272{

*The Order of Providence and the Sacrament of Order, Paralleled in Aquinas*

or of warfare (*SCG*, 4, ch. 75). If all these arts were on an equal plane, the perfection of the whole would suffer, for none would serve the other. (Here St. Thomas hints that there is little to be hoped for from a classless utopia or a horizontal Church.) In the natural state, then, the "order of goodness" is an "order of distinct and unequal things," with lower things ordered through higher ones, and bodily things through spiritual ones. Plants and animals are "ruled by intellectual creatures," and men who excel in the practical arts are ruled by those who "excel in intellectual power." The more a creature is able to know of the plan of Providence, then, the fitter he is to exercise government over other creatures.

According to St. Thomas, priests are parallel to such instruments in nature, for in Christ's design for his Church, they "participate more fully in divine goodness" in order to communicate it to others (*SCG*, 3, ch. 64–5). Just as natural agents have varying degrees of likeness to God, so priests have varying degrees of likeness to our Lord, the Head of the Mystical Body. St. Thomas observes that one "Order" ranks above another, insofar as its work is more nearly directed to the Eucharist, "the most exalted of the sacraments" (*ST*, Suppl, q. 37.4). Priests rank above deacons, and bishops in turn rank above priests. With regard to the consecration of Christ's body in the Eucharist, bishops do not surpass priests in power, but with regard to the Church, they do, because they dispense the Sacrament of Order by which priests receive their spiritual power to consecrate. Bishops thus have the "higher ministry" and are raised over the Mystical Body of Christ, for it is also from them that the people "seek the law" (*ST*, Suppl, q. 36.2). And so, while "each minister of the Church is, in some respect, a copy of Christ," bishops represent him more perfectly. For priests represent him fulfilling his ministry alone, while bishops represent him ordaining his ministers and founding his Church. Hence a bishop is called by the most beautiful and intimate name given to Christ as Head of the Mystical Body—"bridegroom of the Church" (*ST*, Suppl, q. 40.4).

St. Thomas remarks that between a "simple bishop" and the Pope there are "degrees of rank corresponding to the degrees of

RESTORING NATURE

union, in respect of which one congregation or community includes another." Note the word *union*: the Pope ranks above a bishop for the sake of union in the Church. From a city, to a province, to a nation, there are ever larger units until we come at last to the all-encompassing universal Church, the "community of the whole world." St. Thomas affirms that the care of this universal Bride as a single entity was conferred on St. Peter. Just as in nature kings and lawgivers rule by the decree of Providence, so likewise in the Church the Pope governs by the special mandate of Christ (*SCG*, 4, ch. 74, 76).

The role of the Pope is illuminated by still another parallel St. Thomas draws between the order of Providence and the Sacrament of Order. In both "orders," particular things are directed to the good of the whole. In nature, Providence directs particular creatures to "the good of the order of the whole universe," and so it follows that "each part is found to be for the sake of the whole." Now the Pope's relation to the universal Church is parallel to that of the "intellectual creature to the whole of the universe." As St. Thomas explains it, the intellect of man can embrace the universe as a unit and is therefore a microcosm: "intellectual natures have a closer relationship to a whole than do other natures; indeed, each intellectual substance is, in a way, all things. For it may comprehend the entirety of being through its intellect" (*SCG*, 3, ch. 112). In the same manner, the Pope oversees and embraces the Church as a unit in its entirety. Just as the "intellectual substance" embraces the whole and becomes its microcosm, so by analogy, the Pope embraces the entire Mystical Body and is a kind of microcosm of the Church.

Providence directs nature as a whole towards God as its ultimate end. In a parallel but far more intimate way, Christ directs his Bride the Church toward the divine marriage in eternity. St. Thomas speaks of the Sacrament of Matrimony as the sign that Christ's bond with his Church is permanent, a "union of one to one" that will endure forever. Since Christ is a faithful spouse, there is only "one Church" built "with His Blood" from which he has promised never to part (*SCG*, 4, ch. 78). To ensure that this

}274{

*The Order of Providence and the Sacrament of Order, Paralleled in Aquinas*

Church will remain "one," Christ has given the power of the sacraments uniquely to St. Peter, so that from him it will flow down to others by the Sacrament of Order (*ST*, Suppl, q. 34.1). This "power of the keys" descending from St. Peter to the rest of the priests preserves "unity" (*SCG*, 4, ch. 76). Thus, the Pope, at the topmost rung of the ecclesiastical hierarchy, is the instrument used by Christ, in his special providence, to ensure that the Church remain universal, rather than multi-national.

St. Thomas says that Christ appointed a single person to be governor of his universal Church because the unity of the Church requires that all members agree in matters of faith. Now since questions about belief are bound to arise that will divide the Church unless it is preserved in unity by the authority of one, it follows without "doubt," St. Thomas asserts, that Christ established the government of his Church "in the best way" when he appointed St. Peter to be the single head. The Angelic Doctor shows unusual emotion when he reiterates this warning against *doubt*: "one must not doubt that by Christ's ordering there is one who is at the head of the entire Church," for our Lord would not have "failed the Church" in her "necessities" (*SCG*, 4, ch. 74). Note his words *ordering* and *necessities*. His point is that Christ always provides exactly what the Church needs, and so we must "not doubt" that he has provided the best possible government for his Church. We have to trust that papal authority is the "best way" to guarantee that "the whole Church is one body." For the bishops have a spiritual power directed to the good of particular churches, but the Pope receives a special power directed to the common good of the Church as an entire Body (*ST*, Suppl, q. 40.6).

Regarding the unique authority of the Pope, St. Thomas makes still another memorable parallel between the order of Providence and the Sacrament of Order. Citing Aristotle's *Ethics*, he observes that in the natural state, "Whenever there are several authorities directed to one purpose, there must needs be one universal authority over the particular authorities, because in all virtues and acts, the order is according to the order of their ends." Just as there is always someone who presides with the ultimate authority in any big

RESTORING NATURE

human enterprise, so one should rightly expect to find such an ultimate authority in the Church, a court of final appeal. Bishops alone are not sufficient, he insists: "there must be a universal governing power in respect of the common good, otherwise there would be no cohesion towards one object" (*ST*, Suppl, q. 40.6). Notice his phrase *must be*. Once again, the parallel has to hold between natural and the spiritual in the ordering of government.

Although the power of bishops is of a different kind from that of priests, St. Thomas observes, the power of the Pope is of the same kind as that of bishops. In fact, "a bishop can perform every hierarchical act that the Pope can" (*ST*, Suppl, q. 40.6). Nevertheless, the Pope is still superior to bishops by "divine right." To explain this, St. Thomas cites approvingly the following passage which he attributes to St. Cyril of Alexandria, concerning the obedience due from all Christian primates to the Roman pontiff:

> *That we may remain members of our apostolic head, the throne of the Roman Pontiffs, of whom it is our duty to seek what we are to believe and what we are to hold, venerating him, beseeching him above others; for his it is to reprove, to correct, to appoint, to loose, and to bind in place of Him Who set up that very throne, and Who gave the fulness of His own to no other, but to him alone, and to whom by divine right all bow the head, and the primates of the world are obedient as to our Lord Jesus Christ Himself.* Therefore bishops are subject to someone even by divine right. (*ST*, Suppl, q. 40. 6).

Note the phrases *to no other* and *to him alone*, regarding St. Peter. In this passage, all spiritual power is said to flow down from Christ through St. Peter. The Pope not only stands highest in the vertical order of priesthood, he also stands, in a way, for the whole. He is the ultimate conduit, the first and foremost instrument of Christ, the Servant of all the other servants. The last phrase in the above citation—*even by divine right*—is St. Thomas's emphatic assertion that the papal authority comes from above, not from below, and does not depend on *vox populi*.

}276{

*The Order of Providence and the Sacrament of Order, Paralleled in Aquinas*

## An Application to the English Reformation

The last part of this essay applies what St. Thomas says about the Sacrament of Order to the first phase of the English Reformation. This is a case in point of what happens when secular men, as far as they can, take control of the Sacrament of Order. It illustrates that the form of government in the Church, with the Pope as the ultimate authority in religion, is not merely ornamental, but necessary. The undoing of the Church in England began, long before Henry VIII, with an assault on papal authority.

The English Reformation has its beginning in the 14th Century *Praemunire* Act, a law that exploded like an old landmine in the 1530s. Although the Act of 1393 was not properly passed in parliament, it was acted upon in royal council in the 1390s. The king could now appoint men to the greatest church dignities, while the Pope simply had to accept it, the law declaring that

> if any man pursue or obtain, in the court of Rome or elsewhere, such translations, excommunications, bulls, instruments, or other things, against the king's crown and regality, or kingdom, as aforesaid, or bring them into the realm, or receive, notify or execute them either within the realm or without, such person or persons, their notaries, procurators, maintainers, abettors, fautors, and counsellors, shall be out of the king's protection; their goods and chattels, lands and tenements, shall be forfeited to the king, and their persons attached wherever they may be found.[4]

---

4   This Statute of the Realm is cited and discussed in John Lingard, D.D., *The History of England*, 10 vols (London: J.C. Nimmo & Bain, 1883), 3:347. This is a Catholic history based on the documents, the first portion of which was published in 1819, before the Catholic emancipation. It stops with the revolution of 1688.

## RESTORING NATURE

Now this was the very law that Henry VIII invoked in 25 Henry 8, c. 20, at the dawn of the English Reformation.

In his magisterial history of that Reformation from the viewpoint of the Sacrament of Order published in 1687, Abraham Woodhead, the chief Catholic spokesman of his age, relates how Henry VIII began by having the English clergy condemned under the *Praemunire* Act. First he demanded from them the repayment of the money he had spent trying to get foreign universities to support his divorce. When the clergy refused, they were "condemned by the King's Bench in a Praemunire" for receiving and acknowledging Cardinal Wolsey's "Power Legantine." Although Wolsey had received the king's license to serve as papal legate in the divorce proceedings, this license had been seized with his goods. The frightened clergy next offered to ransom themselves and the Church's estates for the money the king had originally asked for, but Henry, seeing them "in these fears," now raised the stakes higher and insisted they also give him "the title of supremacy in ecclesiastical matters within his dominions." When they asked to have this title explicitly limited by the law of Christ's Church, he refused, but gave them his royal "voluntary promise" not to take more power over the clergy "than all others the Kings of England had assumed; nor that he would do anything without them, in altering, ordering, or judging, in any Spiritual matters." Of course, he was lying, but they did not realize it at first. In the "Declaration of the Bishops against the Pope," they defended the royal supremacy, thinking it meant only that spiritual causes would now be resolved in England, without any further appeal from the archbishop to Rome. But ironically, the archbishop was not to be the final determiner of England's religious causes. For it was soon enacted, in 25 Henry 8.19c, that the "ultimate and unappealable judges after the archbishop in all spiritual matters" would be certain commissioners appointed by the King! Thus, the English Church knuckled under to the State. Plainly, the alternative to a national clergy's subordination to the Pope in the Sacrament of Order is to kowtow to Leviathan—i.e., to secular men, such as

}278{

*The Order of Providence and the Sacrament of Order, Paralleled in Aquinas*

kings, lawgivers, and judges—boldly usurping their place in spiritual matters.[5]

Henry erected the entire English Reformation on this title of "royal supremacy," extorted from a clergy terrorized by *Praemunire*. The title gave him and his successors all the leverage needed to change the religion of England in two generations. Henry wielded not just the "supremacy"of a Pope in England but that of Christ himself. The proof is that no pope ever did what Henry VIII and his successors Edward VI and Elizabeth did—i.e., use "some few of the clergy" to impose innovations in religion "by his single authority, without, or contrary to, the votes of the major part of the clergy."[6] The power Henry claimed he had to combat heresies was never conceded or voted him by the clergy, "but was built, only by consequence, upon the clergy's recognizing him the Supreme Head of the Church of England."[7]

Once Henry had seized the "supremacy," he appointed as his commissioners thirty-two men, half of them laics, to act in religion as the "ultimate and unappealable judges." Sixteen laics could now reverse a judgment of the archbishop or overturn some Church doctrine, provided they had the vote of one clergyman or the king. Henry gave them all the laws of the Church to be "abrogated, corrected, reformed, as they, with his confirmation, should think meet." In 34 and 35 Henry 8. 1c, he claimed he was the "ultimate judge of heresy, without any appeal," under pain of burning after the third offence. Listed among other "heresies" was the "holding of the Pope's supremacy" in religion. Nor did Henry have any more use for councils of the Church than for

---

5   *Church Government Part V: A Relation of the English Reformation*, (Oxford, 1687), p. 25–6, 31. Woodhead died in 1678, but by a special license from the Catholic king James II, his works were being published at University College, Oxford, in 1686–1688. So much did James revere Woodhead that he had planned to erect a monument to him at Oxford before he was driven out of England by his son-in-law William of Orange.

6   Ibid., 252–3.

7   Ibid., 32. See the preface to Act 26 Henry 8.c1.

}279{

RESTORING NATURE

popes. He took for himself the "power to prohibit or reverse any ecclesiastical constitutions of councils patriarchal or general," even in things where "the temporal safety and peace of the people is not concerned."[8] Thus, he set himself not just above the papacy, but above the whole Sacrament of Order, the constitutional church government, and the entire succession of the clergy in the Catholic Church for the past 1500 years.

An egregious example of his contempt for the authority of councils is that he ordered all writings about the Christian religion contrary to the doctrine set forth in his recent book, *A Necessary Doctrine*, to be abolished, and anyone teaching the contrary, after the third offense, to be burned as a heretic. His subjects were commanded to accept his doctrine "not as appearing to him the ordinances or definitions of the Church, but as judged by him agreeable to the laws and ordinances of God," with the English clergy being only his "advisers" in the matter.[9] Thus, the *private judgment* in religion of an unstable, half-mad king became the law of the land, imposed on the consciences of his people by fire and sword.

Herbert Thorndike, a high-church apologist for Anglicanism in the 17th century, admits that the English Reformation violated the law of the "Succession of the Clergy," but he argues that there are many other laws given by our Lord that can be restored by secular men against the consent of the priesthood. He urges

> that the Secular power may restore any law, which Christ or his Apostles have ordained, not only against the major part, but all, the Clergy, and Governors of the Church: and may, for a penalty of their opposing it, suppress their power and commit it to others.[10]

8   Woodhead, *Reformation*, 30, 43.
9   Ibid., 93–94.
10  Herbert Thorndike, *Right of the Church*, ch. 5, 248, cited in Woodhead, *Reformation*, 239.

*The Order of Providence and the Sacrament of Order, Paralleled in Aquinas*

However, Woodhead answers Thorndike by pointing out that Anglicans like him are always bringing up "the good kings of Judah" in defense of their Reformation. Lancelot Andrewes did the same in his controversy with St. Robert Bellarmine. But a king is not a competent "judge" of whether something is "a Law ordained by our Lord or his Apostles." Nor is a laic to be preferred as "judge" in spiritual matters "before the whole succession of the Clergy." Besides, where did the good kings of Judah learn how to reform the people but from the priesthood? It cannot be proven, Woodhead asserts, "that the Princes of Judah ever reformed anything against the judgment of the whole body, or of the major part of the Priests."[11] Even in Old Testament times, then, the Church of God had a settled priestly government and was not under the thumb of secular men.

Woodhead sees the necessary laws of subordination and unity in the Church as having been seriously violated at the start of the English Reformation. First papal authority was spurned, and then the rest of the clergy in England was infantilized, stripped of any real authority. Indeed, it was so bad by the first year of Edward VI, that the clergy in synod, "too late perceiving that, not only the Pope, but themselves had lost their former ecclesiastical power; and that the King and Parliament ordered spiritual affairs as they pleased, without their consents," asked to be joined with [the House of] Commons as the bishops were with the Lords, "so they might have a vote also in passing Church matters." Woodhead says the "poor clergy" were trying "to obtain a joint-share at least" with the "civil state in transacting the affairs of the Church."[12]

In conclusion, St. Thomas teaches that man in the natural order cannot reach his ultimate end unaided, because Providence orders him to the love of God as his end, and this is beyond his power to attain. Hence, man must be led by divine law to the right faith. He must also submit his mind to this faith by way of

11   Ibid., 251.
12   Ibid., p. 60–62.

}281{

RESTORING NATURE

belief, or else he cannot know and love God. For God is simple, St. Thomas explains, and whoever is in error concerning him does not know or love him (*SCG*, 3, ch. 114–6). Now Christ instituted the Sacrament of Order precisely to direct man to the right faith and to sustain him with the sacraments while he strove towards God as his destiny. But at various times, such as at the start of the English Reformation, the Sacrament of Order has been made to truckle to secular men and be a branch of the civil state. Tellingly, this process starts with a repudiation of papal authority.

Just as, in the order of Providence, every creature is "confined under a certain order" and is unable to "work above that order" (*SCG*, 3, ch. 102), so in the Sacrament of Order, the "instruments" of Christ are ranked in due subordination under the Pope, the visible head who governs the universal Church as a single entity. The Pope is Christ's instrument of special providence to ensure the unity and survival of the Mystical Body. St. Thomas sees the Sacrament of Order as a vertical chain of command leading up to the Pope, who alone embraces the whole. This great order of priesthood is the virtual spine of the Mystical Body, enabling the universal Church to march steadily and safely through history towards the New Jerusalem. Without that spine, it would be horizontal all right, but crawling about aimlessly. In sum, St. Thomas is a persuasive and powerful defender of the papacy. He warns us not to "doubt" that Christ established "one Church," and "for the entire Christian people there must be one who is head of the entire Church" ( *SCG*, 4, ch. 76).

}282{

# *Nature as* Determinatio ad Unum: *The Case of Natural Virtue*

## Marie George
## St. John's University (New York)

It is a matter of common experience that there is such a thing as natural virtue, and that it is a good thing (after all, it is called "virtue"). For instance the novelist P.D. James says:

> I think there is badness in all of us. Yes. I would take the religious view that we are all in need of divine grace, but I don't think we are all capable of murder, and I do think there are people who seem to be naturally good. I've met them and they seem to be born generous, kind, stoical, self-effacing, loving, just generally rather good. Others torture animals from childhood; they take pleasure in cruelty from really quite an early age. They seem to be born with a greater propensity to evil than the rest of us.[1]

Aquinas says something very similar in a number of places, e.g., in *the Commentary on the Ethics* he notes:

> That however it is granted that there is natural virtue . . . is manifest through this that particular habits [mores] of virtue or vice appear to exist in some men naturally; for certain men immediately from birth seem to be just, or temperate, or brave on account of natural

---

1    *First Things* Feb. 2001, p. 75 (quoting a *Spectator* interview).

}283{

disposition, by which they are inclined to the works of virtue.[2]

Both James and Aquinas also mention natural vice, an inborn inclination to perform bad acts.

If natural virtue is good, it is at first sight surprising that Aquinas is critical of it, as when he says:

> For someone is able to have a natural inclination to the act of some virtue without prudence; and the greater an inclination they have without the habit of virtue, the worse it is, and the more it is able to push someone to action without prudence: as is manifest in the person who has natural courage without discretion and prudence.[3]

The reason behind this critical evaluation is elaborated on when Aquinas addresses the difference between natural virtue and true virtue:

> Whether Virtue is in Us by Nature: In both ways, however, virtue is natural to man according to a certain imperfect beginning. Certainly according to the nature of the species insofar as there are naturally in human reason certain principles that are naturally known, both of things knowable (scibilium) and of things to be done, which are certain seeds of the intellectual and moral virtues; and insofar as in the will is a certain natural appetite of the good that is according to reason. According to the nature of the individual, [virtue is natural to man]

2 *In Decem Libros Ethicorum Aristotelis ad Nicomachum Expositio*, ed. Raymundi M. Spiazzi, O.P. (Turin: Marietti, 1964), no. 1276. Hereafter cited as *NE*.

3 *Quodlibetum* 12.22 in *Opuscula Philosophica et Theologica*, vol. 2 (Castello: Tiferni Tiberini, 1886).

*Nature as* Determinatio ad Unum: *The Case of Natural Virtue*

insofar as from the disposition of the body certain are better or worse disposed to certain virtues, according as namely certain sensitive powers are the acts of certain parts of the body, from the disposition of which the powers in question are aided or impeded in their acts, and consequently the rational powers which the sensitive powers of this sort serve. And according to this, one man has a natural aptitude for science, another for courage, another for temperance. And in this manner both the intellectual virtues as well as the moral virtues are according to something in us by nature. Not, however, the completion of them. Because nature is determined to one; the completion, however, of virtues of this sort is not according to one mode of action, but in diverse modes according to the diverse matters in which the virtues operate, and according to diverse circumstances.[4]

The nature which pertains to natural virtue is not that of the species, but of the individual, i.e., his or her personal physical constitution. Indeed, natural virtue can be defined as an inborn inclination to moral virtue which follows from the physical make-up proper to the individual.

Moral virtue has to operate in regard to diverse matters and in diverse circumstances, and thus natural virtue's shortcoming is that it is an inclination that is determined to one. It is good to face danger for a worthy cause, but not just for thrills. It is good to be truthful, but not to the point of indiscretion. Natural virtue inclines one to operate in only one manner because it is a function of one's physical make-up, something which is "determined to one."

The expression "nature is determined to one" applies in the first instance to the observed limitation of the motions of the

4    *Summa Theologiae.* Ed. Instituti Studiorum Medievalium Ottaviensis. (Ottawa: Commissio Piana, 1953), I-II 63.1. Hereafter cited as *ST.*

simplest forms of natural things, those that are non-living. Iron tends to move down, and oxygen tends to move up under the conditions found on earth. They do not tend to move in the opposite directions. "Fire burns both here and in Persia;"[5] fire does not cool in Persia, but in all places burns. The very etymology of nature, "nasci" "to be born" (in Greek, "physis," "birth"), signifies something determinate, namely, like coming from like.

Non-living natural things are very limited in their activities. They are much more acted upon than acting; they show no autonomy or initiative in what they do. Thus Aquinas will often say that the forms of inanimate natural things are immersed in the matter, for things act in virtue of their form, and they undergo in virtue of their matter.

Plants move themselves by growing, etc., and thus they have a higher form than inanimate natural substances. Aquinas says that "the action of the soul transcends the action of nature operating in inanimate things; but this happens in two ways, namely as to the mode of acting and as to what is done."[6] He goes on to point out that the forms of plants only transcend those of inanimate natural things in their mode of activity. Both plants and the inanimate remain in being for some period of time. However, plants unlike inanimate things, preserve themselves in being though their own activities. Notice how Aquinas speaks of the soul in opposition to nature ("the action of the soul transcends the action of nature operating in inanimate things"). Plants manifest an incipient form of autonomy that the non-living lack. They are not entirely determined to one. In the commentary on the *De Anima* Aquinas also contrasts nature with the soul on the grounds that the soul is the principle of an activity that is not determined to one:

> It is manifest that this principle [i.e., of growth and decrease] is not nature, but the soul. For nature does not

5    Aristotle, *Nicomachean Ethics*, 1134b27 in *The Basic Works of Aristotle*, ed. Richard McKeon (New York: Random House, 1968).
6    Cf. *Quaestio Disputata de Anima* 13.

*Nature as* Determinatio ad Unum: *The Case of Natural Virtue*

move to contrary places: however, the motions of growth and decrease are according to contrary places. For all vegetables grow, and not only upwards or downwards, but it both ways. It is manifest therefore that the principle of these motions is not nature, but the soul.[7]

When plants are compared to animals, however, their activities are seen to be more natural. If one pours water in a dog's dish, it might get up to drink some, but then again it might not. Animals, while not capable of choice, do perform "voluntary"[8] actions, i.e., actions that are conscious and unforced. Plants have no indetermination of this sort. Their nutritive processes are determined by physical and chemical factors, e.g., the roots of certain plants grow naturally in the direction of water-they have no other option. In comparison to the inanimate, then, plants show activity that is not simply natural, whereas in comparison with animals, their activities are much more determinate, and therefore natural. Thus, Aquinas on the one hand says of both plants and animals that "the action of the soul transcends the action of nature operating in inanimate things," whereas on the other hand he separates plants from animals, attributing to plants (along with the inanimate natural things) only natural appetite, whereas to animals he also attributes elicited appetite.[9]

7   *In Aristotelis Librum De Anima Commentarium* (Italy: Marietti, 1959), no. 257.
8   Cf. *NE* nos. 427 and 435.
9   Cf. *ST* I 80.1: "[I]t is necessary to posit a certain appetitive power of the soul. In evidence of which a fact to be considered is that from any form whatsoever some inclination follows; as fire, from its form, is inclined to a higher place, and [is inclined] to generate what is like to itself. Form, however, in those things which share in cognition is found in a higher mode than in those which lack cognition. For in those things that lack cognition, form is only found in such a manner as determining each thing to one proper being, which is moreover natural to each thing. Therefore, natural inclination, which

}287{

RESTORING NATURE

Beings that are knowers are still less determined to one. As Aquinas puts it:

> ... there are other higher actions of the soul that transcend those of natural forms even as to what is done, namely, insofar as all things are apt to come to be in the soul according to an immaterial [mode of] being. For the soul is in a certain manner everything according as it is sensing and understanding.[10]

The sentient and rational being is not limited to being itself, but in a certain way can be all other things as well. These beings are capable of taking on the forms of other things while retaining their own form. The immaterial mode of reception of knowing beings is what underlies the indetermination of their action. As Aquinas explains:

> Certainly there is agreement [between natural things and intelligent beings] in that in natural things form is present which is the principle of action, and inclination

is called natural appetite, follows this natural form. In those things which have cognition, however, each is thus determined to its proper natural being through its natural form, which nevertheless is receptive of the forms of other things; as sense receive the forms (species) of all sensible things, and intellect of all intelligible things, and thus the soul of man knows all things in a certain manner according to sense and intellect . . . . Therefore, just as forms exist in things having cognition in a higher mode, a mode that is beyond that of natural forms, so too it is necessary that there exist in those things an inclination beyond the mode of a natural inclination which is called natural appetite. And this superior inclination pertains to the appetitive power of the soul, through which the animal is able to desire those things that it apprehends, and not only those things to which it is inclined by a natural form. Thus, therefore, it is necessary to posit some appetitive power of the soul.

10 *Quaestio Disputata de Anima* in *Quaestiones Disputatae*, vol. 2, ed. P. Bazzi et al. (Turin: Marietti, 1965), 13.

*Nature as* Determinatio ad Unum: *The Case of Natural Virtue*

following the form which is called natural appetite from which action follows: but there is a difference in that the form of a natural thing is a form individuated by matter; whence even the inclination following it is determined to one, but the understood form (forma intellecta) is universal under which many can be comprehended; whence since acts regard singulars which are in no way adequate to a universal potency, it remains that the inclination of the will stands indeterminately to many: just as if an artisan were to conceive the form of a house in the universal, under which are comprehended diverse shapes of houses, his will would be able to incline to this that he make a square house or a round house or one of some other shape.[11]

The intellect is not the act of any bodily organ, and therefore it receives the forms of things in an entirely immaterial way, abstracting both from matter and the conditions of matter. Its object is the universal truth, and the inclination or appetite arising from this knowledge has as its object the universal

---

11  *Quaestiones Disputatae de Malo* in *Quaestiones Disputatae.* vol. 2, 6.1. Cf. *Quaestiones Disputatae de Veritate,* in *Quaestiones Disputatae.* vol. 1. ed. Raymundi M. Spiazzi, O.P. (Turin: Marietti, 1964), 23.1: "Material things in which whatever is in them is as bound to and made concrete in matter do not have a free ordination to other things, but [their ordination to other things] is from the necessity of their natural disposition. Whence these material things are not themselves the causes of this ordination, as if they themselves ordered themselves to that to which they are ordered, but are ordered by someone/thing else . . . . In immaterial and knowing substances there is something that is absolutely not concretized and bound to matter; but this [varies] according to the grade of their immateriality; and therefore from this they are ordered to things by a free ordination, of which they themselves are causes, as ordering themselves to that to which they are ordered. And therefore it belongs to them to do something or desire something voluntarily and spontaneously." Hereafter cited as *DV*.

## Restoring Nature

good.[12] Since no particular good has a necessary connection with the universal good or at least in this life is known with certitude to have such a connection, the will is not determined to choosing any particular good.[13] Rather than being determined to one it is "ad utrumlibet," i.e., open to opposites.

As for knowers endowed with sense knowledge, Aquinas has the following things to say in regard to their determination. First in regard to their knowledge he points out that:

> One grade [of immateriality] is according as things are in the soul without their proper matter, but nevertheless according to their individuality (singularitatem) and individual conditions which follow upon matter. And this grade is that of sense which is receptive of the forms of individuals without matter, but nevertheless in a bodily organ.[14]

The type of receptivity that is characteristic of sense defines the determinacy of the sense appetite:

> The active principle in brute animals is intermediary between the two [i.e., nature and reason]. For the form apprehended through sense is individual, as is the form of a natural thing; and therefore from it follows an inclination to one act as in natural things, but nevertheless the same form is not always received in the sense

---

12  Note that in a sense both the intellect and the will are determined to one. Both the intellect and the will are in a certain way natures. All men desire knowledge, and all desire happiness. Cf. *DV* 22.5: "However nature and the will are ordered in this way that the will itself is a certain nature; because everything that is found in things (omne quod in rebus invenitur) is called a certain nature. And therefore it is necessary to find in the will not only that which is of the will, but even that which is of nature."

13  Cf. *ST* I 82.2: "Whether the will wants all that it wants from necessity."

14  *Quaestio Disputata de Anima* 13.

}290{

*Nature as* Determinatio ad Unum: *The Case of Natural Virtue*

as it is in natural things, for fire is always hot, but now one form, now others [are received by the sense] e.g., now a pleasurable form, now a saddening form; whence now it [the appetite] flees and now it pursues; and in this it agrees with the human active principle.[15]

Animals through sensation are able to receive the forms of other things. However, since the sense does not receive in an entirely immaterial mode, it perceives the individual as individual. The intellect not only knows things, but it knows what it means to know; and so it can think about it own act of knowing. The sensitive being knows sensible particulars. It is conscious; it knows when it is awake and sensing. However, the sense cannot go beyond the particular knowledge that it has so as to be able to understand its own act. It can make judgements, but it cannot judge its own judgements. As Aquinas puts it:

> But the judgement [that animals are capable of] is in them from natural estimation, not from some process of putting two and two together [non ex aliqua collatione], since they are ignorant of the reason for their judgement; on this account their judgement does not extend to all things as does the judgement of reason, but only to certain determinate things . . . . A consequence of the fact that their judgement is determined to one is that their appetite and action is determined to one.[16]
> . . . through appetite they [animals] are inclined to something of themselves, insofar as they desire something from the apprehension of that thing; but that they incline or not incline to the thing that they desire is not something subject to their disposal.[17]

15 *Quaestiones Disputatae de Malo* 6.1.
16 *DV* 24.2.
17 *DV* 23.1

Animals cannot say to themselves: Why am I doing this? They cannot evaluate the reasons for their actions, for they do not grasp universal principles in terms of which such evaluations are made.[18] Because their judgements are fixed by nature, they are more moved than they are movers.

Matter, then, results in a determination to one which amounts to a limit in autonomy. The more a form is immersed in matter, the less the being of which it is the form is able to act on its own. The more a form is free from matter, the more the being of which it is the form is capable of directing itself, rather than being determined to one by something other than itself.

A human being is a body, a living thing, a sensitive being, and

18  Cf. *ST* I 59.3: "there are certain things which do not act from some judgement, but as if activated and moved by others, as an arrow is moved by the archer to its end. Certain things, indeed, act with a certain judgement, but not freely, as do non-rational animals; for the sheep flees from the wolf due to a certain judgement by which it estimates that it [the wolf] is harmful to it; but this judgement is not free to it, but is put in it by nature. But only that which possesses intellect is able to act with free judgement, insofar as it knows the universal notion of the good from which it is able to judge this or that to be good. Whence wherever there is intellect, there is free will (liberum arbitrium)." Cf. *DV* 24.1: "Whence to the one considering things rightly it is apparent that it is in the same manner that judgement about what is to be done is attributed to brute animals as the manner in which motion and action is attributed to natural inanimate bodies; for as the heavy and light do not move themselves, so as to be the cause of their motion, so too brutes do not judge about their own judgement, but follow the judgement put in them by God. And thus they are not causes of their judgement, nor do they have freedom of judgement. Man, indeed, judging about what is to be done through the power of reason, is able to judge of his judgement, insofar as he knows the notion of the end and of that which is [a means] to the end, and of the relation and order of one to the other; and therefore he is not only the cause of himself in moving, but also in judging; and therefore he has free judgement (liberi arbitrii), as if to say having free judgement regarding acting or not acting.

## Nature as Determinatio ad Unum: The Case of Natural Virtue

a rational being. The substantial form of man is one, and it is immaterial in the strict sense. However, the various powers of man show the different levels of determination to one just mentioned. For the soul is not present according to its whole power in all the parts of the body because the various parts of the body are not properly disposed for every power of the soul; e.g., the eyes are not properly disposed for hearing.[19] Now, in man the potencies of matter which in non-knowing beings are actualized by lower forms do not fall directly under the control of the rational soul. However, the sensitive powers are not so immersed in matter, and thus to some extent they can be influenced by reason.

> [T]o the extent that some act is more immaterial, to that extent it is more noble, and more subject to the command of reason. Whence from the very fact that the vegetative powers of the soul do not obey reason it appears that they are the least of these powers.[20]
>
> There is found a certain gradation in forms. For there are certain forms and powers that are completely imbedded [depressae] in matter, every action of which

19 *Quaestio Disputata de Anima* 11 ad 20: "granted that one and the same soul is sensitive and vegetative, it is nevertheless not necessary that the operation of the one appears in any operation whatsoever of the other on account of the diverse disposition of the parts. From which it also happens that neither are all the operations of the sensitive soul exercised through one part; but sight through the eyes, hearing through the ears, and so forth." Cf. also ibid. 10: "If one take 'wholeness' as to virtue and power, then the whole is not in every part of the body, nor even the whole in the whole, if we speak about the human soul . . . . But as to other operations [those] which are exercised through bodily organs, the whole virtue and power of the soul is in the whole body; not however is it in any part of the body, because diverse parts of the body are proportioned to diverse operations of the souls. Whence according to that power only so much is in the bodily part which regards the operation which is exercised through that part." Cf. also *ST* I 76.8 ad 3.
20 *ST* I-II 17.8 ad 1.

RESTORING NATURE

is material; as is manifest in the forms of the elements. The intellect, however, is completely free from matter; whence even its operation is without communion with the body. The irascible and concupiscible stand in a middle mode. For the bodily change which is connected with their acts shows that they use a corporeal organ; that they are further in a certain mode elevated from matter is shown through this that they move by the command of reason and that they obey reason. And thus there is virtue in them, i.e., insofar as elevated above matter, they obey reason.[21]

One might question whether the rational faculties have no control over physical make-up or at least over certain aspects of one's physiology. Certainly one can make choices about one's diet, and diet has more or less definite ties with one's health. Although some people who eat a healthy diet become seriously ill, while others who eat a poor diet live long lives, generally the opposite is the case. At any rate, the rational faculties do not directly control health, but can command actions that have a predictable indirect effect in many cases. One can also take drugs in order to improve one's emotional state. Aquinas was not ignorant of the effects that alcohol has on feeling.[22] However, one does not directly control how one's body will react to drugs. Medicine is an art that ministers to nature. What then about different types of meditation techniques, biofeedback, etc. which allow people to gain control over their heartbeat, temperature, or other motor functions which in turn often affect the vegetative functions? These techniques also do not involve direct control. It is not

21 *De Virtutibus in Communi* 4 ad 4.
22 Cf. *ST* I-II 45.3: "And in the same place he [Aristotle] says that 'lovers of wine are more confident on account of the heat of the wine'; whence above it was said that drunkenness also contributes to the goodness of hope; for the warmth of the heart repels fear and causes hope on account of the extension and amplification of the heart."

*Nature as* Determinatio ad Unum: *The Case of Natural Virtue*

directly by thinking about heartbeat that one lowers it, but thought (or the absence of thought) affects the emotions which cause the release of certain chemicals which have an effect on the functions in question, or something of this sort occurs. Nowadays we do even have some control over our physical make-up through gene therapy, but this control is also indirect.

Granting that what control we have over our physiology is indirect, the question arises whether it is worthwhile trying to facilitate the acquisition of virtue by adjusting our physiology by various indirect means such as meditation, drugs, etc. Or should we limit ourselves to what must be done in any case if we are to acquire virtue, namely, train our sense appetites by exercising rational control over them? This is a hard question, and time does not allow us to take it up here.

Let us now consider in more detail the consequences of natural virtue being determined to one. Note that natural virtue and natural vice share this in common. The reason why natural virtue is called virtue, and often passes for genuine virtue, is because it motivates one to perform acts in accord with the extreme that is closer to the mean. The extreme closer to the mean is the one the acts of which are more similar to the acts of virtue, and it is also the one that people in general are less inclined to. If a person is timid by disposition, he will not often perform acts like to those brave people perform. Whereas if he is fearless, he will more often than not perform acts like those brave people perform. If a person had only a moderate natural disposition, he would not perform the type of acts most associated with being brave, and one would not call him naturally brave. Since natural virtue then is fixed towards an extreme, and does not adapt itself to circumstance, the person acting according to natural virtue will make frequent mistakes.[23]

23  Cf. *De Virtutibus in Communi* in *Quaestiones Disputatae.* vol. 2, 8: "There is however a certain incipient or incomplete (inchoatio) virtue which follows from the nature of the individual, according as a given person is inclined to the act of some virtue from his natural

RESTORING NATURE

Aquinas often points out that in the absence of prudence, the stronger the inclination of natural virtue, the worse it is and the more damage it can do, using comparisons such as "the more vigorously a blind person runs, the greater his injury when he strikes a wall."[24] The more naturally fearless one is, the more likely one is to engage in activities such as daredevil stunts that may lead to injury or death. The more naturally generous one is, the more quickly one is liable to end up in debt. The more naturally abstemious one is, the more likely one is to suffer the consequences of inadequate diet.

Natural virtue does not only cause problems due to its inflexibility to circumstance, it also causes problems when it comes to acts of virtues which require a motion of the appetite opposite to that to which natural virtue inclines. Here we are referring to the familiar phenomena "the virtues of our vices" and "the vices of our virtues." As Aquinas explains:

> [T]here may be a natural inclination to those things which pertain to one virtue. But there may not be an inclination by nature to those things which pertain to all the virtues; for instance, the person who is disposed by nature to courage which lies in pursuing difficult things is less disposed to meekness which consists in restraining irascible emotions. Whence we see that animals that are naturally inclined to the act of some virtue are inclined to the vice contrary to another virtue; as the lion is naturally audacious, but also naturally cruel.[25]

Examples of the virtues of one's vices and vices of one's virtues abound. There are people who are extremely truthful and

make-up or from the impression of the heavenly bodies. And this inclination is a certain incomplete (inchoatio) virtue . . . . For if someone were to follow this sort of inclination without the discretion of reason, they would frequently err."

24  *De Virtutibus in Communi* 6 ad 4. This comparison is drawn from Aristotle *NE* 1144a11. Cf. *De Virtutibus Cardinalibus* 2.
25  *De Virtutibus in Communi* 8 ad 10.

*Nature as* Determinatio ad Unum: *The Case of Natural Virtue*

honest, but then are also unduly frank. People who set high goals for themselves are often intolerant of others mistakes ("he was hard on others, and hard on himself"). Whereas people who don't set high goals for themselves are often indulgent when it comes to the failings of others. People who are diligent and conscientious can also be humorless. P.D. James mentioned people who take pleasure in cruelty from early childhood. However, the up side is that such a person would be more likely to protect a friend attacked by a gang or a pack of dogs than would the kindly natured person who was incapable of murder.[26]

That natural virtue is not virtue only reveals itself plainly when virtuous action demands that we go against the natural flow of feeling, and we consequently fail. In the meanwhile, we are seduced into thinking that we are virtuous because our actions are mostly good, when really, even when they are good, they are not virtuous in the strict sense, since they proceed more from feeling than from a habit involving reason. This illusion is at the basis of thinking that it is possible to have one virtue without having all the others. When we act chiefly according to natural virtue, we are doing mainly what we feel like doing, rather than acting out of a rational judgment that looks to the good of the person as a whole. And not only then do we fail to act in a truly virtuous manner, in addition we cultivate vice at the same time. As Aquinas puts it:

> [T]here are certain virtues which order man in those things which happen in human life such as temperance, justice, meekness, and things of this sort; and it necessary in regard to these that man, when he exercises himself in the act of a given virtue, at the same time exercise

---

26  It is arguable that the ancient equation of virtue with "virtus" or manly courage is an instance of mistaking natural virtue for moral virtue. For the natural virtue of the male is to overcome competitors and other enemies and to father offspring. Accordingly, while courage was highly regarded, chastity was not.

himself in the action of the other virtues, and then he will acquire every habit of virtue at the same time; either that or it will be the case that he does well in regard to one [virtue] and badly in regard to the others, and then he will acquire the habit contrary to another virtue, and the consequence of this is the corruption of prudence without which no disposition which is acquired through the act of some virtue has properly the notion of virtue . . . .[27]

The more one is simply yielding to a natural tendency to honesty, generosity, etc., the more one is habituating oneself to acting according to that feeling apart from the judgement of reason, and thus in other situations one is then even more liable to act according to the vices of one's virtues. So it is not just when natural virtue leads us manifestly awry that it is bad. In a more subtle way it can be just as bad and maybe even worse when it leads us to perform acts of virtue. For we are liable to think that we are truly virtuous, when in fact we are simply doing what comes naturally to us, all the while fostering other vices.

Sometimes, then, one is accidentally better off suffering from

27  *De Virtutibus Cardinalibus* in *Quaestiones Disputatae*, vol. 2, 2 ad 9. Cf. *NE* nos. 1286–87: "For we see that the same man is not inclined to every virtue, but one to liberality, another to temperance, and so forth. For it is easy for everyone to arrive at that to which they are naturally inclined. It is however difficult to attain something contrary to natural impulse. Therefore it follows that the man who is naturally disposed to one virtue and not to another knows, i.e., attains this virtue to which he is naturally disposed . . . . but he never attains the virtue to which he is not naturally disposed. What was just said is verified in regard to natural virtue, not however, in regard to moral virtue according to which someone is said to be good simply. And this therefore because no one of the virtues can be had without prudence, nor prudence without them, as has been shown. And thus when prudence, which is one virtue, is present in someone, at the same time there will be present with it all virtues, none of which would exist if prudence did not exist."

}298{

*Nature as* Determinatio ad Unum: *The Case of Natural Virtue*

natural vice than possessing natural virtue, namely, insofar as one is less likely to have illusions about one's virtuousness. Indeed others generally quickly let a person know that he is a grouch or cheapskate or chicken, etc. Thus the person suffering from natural vice is more likely to recognize that he needs to make an effort[28] to acquire virtue than is the person of natural virtue who tends to feel good about the way he is behaving and who receives

28  Cf. *In Libros Politicorum Aristotelis*, ed. Raymundi M. Spiazzi, O.P. (Italy: Marietti, 1951), nos. 1121–23: "[I]t can happen that although someone from heavenly influence or natural disposition is inclined neither to governing nor to the works of intellect or of virtue, if nevertheless through choice they set themselves to the study of wisdom and the practice of virtue, they will turn out to be people of understanding and ones that govern well. Whereas just the opposite will happen if those who are well born as to these things let themselves become lazy and give themselves over to the practice of bad works: they will become foolish and govern badly, and will become the slaves of others." Aquinas also points out that moral virtue requires an effort over and above natural virtue in regard to *synesis*: "[R]ight judgement consists in this that the cognitive power apprehend the thing according to what is in the thing. Which certainly comes from the right disposition of the cognitive virtue; just as if a mirror is well disposed, the forms of bodies are impressed in it according as they are; but if the mirror were badly disposed, then there would appear there images that were distorted and awry. However, that the cognitive power is well disposed to receiving things as they are is due radically to nature, but in its completion to practice or the gift of grace. And this in two ways. In one way directly, from the side of the cognitive virtue itself, for instance, that it is not seeped in bad conceptions, but in those that are right and true; and this pertains to *synesis* according as it is a special virtue. [I take this to mean, for instance, that one has chosen to avoid watching obscene and/or violent programs that would deaden one's natural "sensibilities."] In another way, indirectly, from the good disposition of the appetitive power, from which it follows that a man judge rightly about what things are to be desired. And thus the good judgement of virtue follows upon the habits of the moral virtues, but in regard to ends; *synesis* is concerned rather with those things that are ordered to the end." (*ST* II-II 51.3 ad 1)

}299{

RESTORING NATURE

approbation from others. People who are prone to lust generally know they have a problem. People who are naturally chaste, on the other hand, may not realize that they are not truly chaste until caught off guard the first time they experience a strong physical attraction for someone. People who are naturally cowardly generally do not think that they are brave. It is the naturally brave who sometimes fail to realize that they are not truly virtuous until faced with a difficult situation demanding courage over and above what they are naturally disposed to.

There is another reason why a person is sometimes better off possessing a natural vice rather than a natural virtue. While natural vice per se is not conducive to living a morally good life, some natural vices have better natural virtues associated with them than their counterpart vices do. For example, people who are excessively candid tend to be forthright and truthful, and people who are phony and who lie tend to be diplomatic. Truthfulness is a better virtue than diplomacy. Thus one is morally better off possessing the natural vice of excess candor than the natural virtue of diplomacy, to the extent that the former is accompanied by truthfulness, whereas the latter is accompanied by lying. The possession of a certain natural virtue, then, may end up being more detrimental than beneficial to the acquisition of true virtue when its attendant natural vice is more serious than is the vice corresponding to the absence of that virtue.

We see the importance of recognizing our natural virtues as natural. However, it might then seem that once one has recognized this, one can really do nothing about it. For to the extent that we cannot or will not try to adjust our physiology, it seems then that natural virtue is a permanent handicap to the acquisition of virtue since it sometimes results in inclinations contrary to what is rational, either due to its inflexibility to circumstance or to the "vices of one's virtues" effect. While there is some truth in the claim that inborn dispositions are a permanent source of interference with right moral action, still natural virtue is not an insuperable obstacle to the acquisition and practice of true virtue.

}300{

*Nature as* Determinatio ad Unum: *The Case of Natural Virtue*

Recall that the principal purpose of our emotions is to allow us to execute rational decisions more promptly and efficiently.[29] The deliberate activities involving emotion center around things needed for personal survival or for the continuation of the species.[30] For example, in situations of danger such as coming across an angry dog or horned cattle in a pasture the adrenaline rush that accompanies fear contributes greatly to our ability to leap the fence. We could make ourselves schedules for when we ought to eat as is done for unconscious patients, but it is much easier to remember to eat because we feel hungry. Virtue then does not involve the eradication of emotion, but rather "perfects us to following in a fitting manner the natural inclinations [i.e., the irascible and the concupiscible appetites] which pertain to natural law."[31]

Natural virtue again is the individual's inclination to moral

29  Cf. *DV* 26.7: "[W]hen the will chooses something through the judgement of reason, it more promptly and more easily does it if along with it emotion is aroused in the lower part; because the lower appetite is in closer proximity to the motion of the body. Whence Augustine says . . . 'The motion of mercy serves reason, when one in anger approves of mercy, so that justice may be preserved.' And this is what the Philosopher says in the second book of the Ethics bringing in a verse from Homer: 'Rouse courage and intense anger'; because, namely, when someone is virtuous with the virtue of courage, the emotion of anger following upon the choice of virtue makes for a greater promptness of action; if, however, it would precede, it would perturb the mode of virtue."

30  Cf. *ST* I-II 91.6: "And nevertheless if one considers the inclination of sensuality according as it is in other animals, it is thus ordered to the common good, i.e., to the conservation of nature in the species or in the individual. And this is also the case in man, according as sensuality is subject to reason. But it is called 'fomes' according as it departs from the order of reason."

31  Cf. *ST* II-II 108.2: "[T]he virtues perfect us to pursuing in a due manner the natural inclinations which pertain to natural law . . . . There is, however, a certain special inclination of nature for removing things that are harmful; whence an irascible power separate from the concupiscible power is even given to animals."

}301{

RESTORING NATURE

virtue[32] which arises chiefly from the physical make-up underlying the concupiscible and irascible appetites.[33] All humans have a concupiscible and irascible appetite naturally ordered to reason, but some individuals' appetites are better disposed to following reason than are others'. Even in those whose appetites are better disposed, however, the determination to one of their natural virtue sometimes results in emotional responses inappropriate in a given situation. Now in order to be virtuous it is not enough that untoward emotions be overcome by reason, the emotions themselves must possess some perfection according to which they readily follow reason.[34] But it seems that one cannot do anything directly about the emotions one feels due to one's physical make-up. And so it would seem that one could never become virtuous.

32  I have been focusing chiefly on moral virtue, but do not mean to discount that there are also natural virtues which dispose one to the acquisition of intellectual virtue, such as the natural virtue of *synesis* which results from the good disposition of the internal sense, particular reason.

33  A question arises how one could be naturally disposed to the virtue of justice (and the virtues annexed to justice), given that justice is in the will, which is not the act of the body. I think that different explanations may be operative in different cases. Sometimes natural virtues related to justice are emotion driven, e.g., naturally generous people often give to other because they *feel sorry* for them. And some of those who naturally shun physically harming others do so out of squeamishness; they do not like gore. In other cases, it is not that the natural virtue of justice is emotion driven, but there is a dispassionateness and objectivity present due, at least in some cases, to the lack of strong emotions which would make acting justly difficult. And perhaps there may be an element of greater natural intelligence which disposes one person to see more clearly the irrationality of unjust acts, and thus to be more repelled from performing them (cf. *ST* I 85.7).

34  Cf. *De Virtutibus in Communi* 4: "When, therefore, it is necessary that the operation of man regard those things which are the object of the sense appetite, it is required for the goodness of operation that there be in the sense appetite some disposition or perfection, by which the said appetite readily obeys reason; and this we call virtue."

}302{

*Nature as* Determinatio ad Unum: *The Case of Natural Virtue*

Aquinas raises a very similar question in an objection in the *De Veritate*:

> ... the motions of sensuality are passions of the soul to which determinate dispositions of the body are required, as Avicenna determined; hot and subtle blood is required for anger, and temperate blood for joy. But the disposition of the body is not subject to reason. Therefore neither is the motion of sensuality.[35]

Aquinas responds:

> ... the disposition of the body which pertain to the make-up of the body, is not subject to reason; but this is not required for this that the said passions exist in act, but the only thing required is that a man be capable of them. The actual transmutation of the body, e.g., the rising of blood around the heart, or something of this sort, which is concomitant with the act of passions of this sort, follow imagination, and on this account are subject to reason.[36]

Even the mildest mannered person is capable of getting angry. Even the most forthright person is capable of biting his tongue. Thus, regardless of the emotional response to which nature disposes one, one is still capable of acquiring moral virtue because one can elicit the appropriate emotions whether one is naturally prone to them or not.[37] Persons of all temperaments are capable of

35  *DV* 25.4 obj 5.
36  *DV* 25.4 ad 5.
37  Cf. *ST* I-II 17.7 ad 2: "[T]he quality belonging to the body is related to the act of the sense appetite in two ways. In one way, as preceding it, according as someone is physically disposed in some manner to this or that emotion. In another manner, as consequent to it, as when someone heats up out of anger. Therefore, the preceding quality is not subject to the command of reason because either it is from na-

RESTORING NATURE

applying the general remedy for vice, including the vices of one's virtues.[38] This remedy consists in repeatedly aiming for the other extreme, eventually habituating the appetite both not to tend so vehemently in what is generally the wrong direction, and to readily obey reason.[39] Training the sense appetite is somewhat like training a dog. The dog has its natural inclinations, e.g., to run after certain other animals. One trains it not to, pulling it back on its leash, because generally such behavior is not desirable. In some cases it may be desirable; one might want to set the dog chasing after some animal. Thus, one does not only train the dog to stay back, one also trains the dog to listen to one, so that when it is appropriate it will chase. The interaction between reason and the

    ture, or it is from some prior motion which cannot immediately calm down. But the consequent quality follows the command of reason because it follows the local motion of the heart, which is moved in diverse ways according to the diverse acts of the sense appetitite."

38  Some natural virtues are accompanied by substantial natural vices. E.g., a person who is easy to get along with may have no backbone, i.e., they may be almost lacking an irascible appetite. It will be very hard for this person to acquire the virtue of courage. And all the more so to the extent that performing the acts which natural vice inclines one to results in the formation of a bad habit. Then the person not only has the bad natural inclination to grapple with, but in addition the inclination that comes from habit.

39  Cf. *NE* nos. 375–76: "For when we strive to draw back a great deal from a sin to which we are prone, then we eventually just barely arrive at the mean. And he [Aristotle] gives a similitude with those who straighten a twisted tree; when they want to straighten it, they turn it in the opposite direction, so that it thus returns to the middle position. And it should be considered here that this is the most efficacious way of acquiring virtue; namely, that a man strive to the contrary of that to which he is inclined either from nature or custom. The way that the Stoics posited is nevertheless easier, namely, that a man little by little draw back from those things to which he is inclined .... The way that Aristotle states here is appropriate for those who desire vehemently to draw away from vice and to arrive at virtue. Whereas the Stoics' way belongs more to those who have a weak and lukewarm will."

}304{

# Nature as Determinatio ad Unum: *The Case of Natural Virtue*

sense appetite is more intimate and more complex.[40] However, the similarity is that one wants first and foremost to train the appetite to readily listen to reason, while at the same time recognizing that if this is to be the case one may need to train the appetite so that its response is no longer that which was natural to it, but in a direction that will more often be in accord with reason. The direction in which the appetite will tend, once trained, is determinate. The appetite's tendency to readily obey reason will also become determinate.[41] However, since reason does not always dictate the same

40  Cf. *DV* 25.4 and *ST* I 81.3 on reason's control over the concupiscible and irascible.

41  Moral virtue itself is a "determinatio ad unum" of a certain sort. Human beings have certain natural inclinations which are determinate: to be happy, which entails living, living in harmony with others, etc. These inclinations can only be fulfilled through virtuous acts. However, we are not determined by nature to perform virtuous acts, but are open to performing vicious acts as well. The very purpose of acquiring moral virtue is to overcome this natural indetermination so that we can live happy lives. We determine ourselves to performing virtuous acts by repeatedly performing virtuous acts, thus acquiring the habit of virtue. (Cf. *De Virtutibus in Communi* 9) Virtue is not open to opposites, unlike art which is "ad utrumlibet." E.g., the temperate person is not open to overeating, whereas the grammarian is open to intentionally making mistakes in grammar. (Cf. <u>NE</u> nos. 315, 316) Still the "determinatio ad unum" of moral virtue is not entirely the same as that of natural virtue, since moral virtue involves reason. Virtue is a habit of choosing. Such a habit is never so fixed as to entirely preclude free choice of the opposite, though such a choice may be extremely difficult. (Cf. *De Virtutibus in Communi* 1 and ad 12.) Also, moral virtue is a "determinatio ad unum" as to the end, e.g., temperance is fixed upon eating moderately. However, the means to this end are not fixed, but must be determined by reason. Thus the temperate person is not determined to always eating one specific quantity. Finally, insofar as certain moral virtues have their completion in the sense appetite, they are determined up to a point in that they have been trained to respond in a certain direction, and yet to the extent that they have been trained to listen to reason, they share the indeterminancy which comes from reason which is capable of discerning the means appropriate

## RESTORING NATURE

responses, the sense appetites, to the extent they are trained to listen to reason, share something of its indeterminacy.[42]

The general remedy for the failure of natural virtue due to circumstance is much easier. Nature has given to one person what another is only able to acquire through diligent application, namely, a tendency towards emotions that in the greater number of cases are in accord with the mean determined by reason. Now all this person has to do is get this tendency to obey reason, instead of moving unchecked. Thus, while one person after a protracted battle gets himself to the point that he desires to eat an appropriate amount, at the appropriate time (and so forth), a person with a high metabolism does so without any great effort. While one person after diligent practice finally manages to control his fears of speaking in public, a person who is outgoing by temperament has little or no problem doing so. If the latter two act with the deliberate understanding that what they are doing is appropriate, with repetition they will come to possess moral virtue, and it sure will have been a lot easier for them to come by it than it would have been for those of sensual or timid temperament.[43]

---

to the circumstances. As was noted above, "and thus virtue is in them [the sense appetites], i.e., insofar as they are raised above matter and obey reason." (*De Virtutibus in Communi* 4 ad 4) Plainly a lot more could be said about moral virtue as a "determinatio ad unum" than a note allows.

42  Again, already at the level of sense there is a certain degree of indeterminancy. A dog does not run after just any other animal, but discrimates rabbit from snake. Although, the naturally brave are often naturally lacking in meekness, most people tend both to be naturally cowardly and naturally vengeful; this shows a certain degree of indeterminacy of the irascible appetite since it tends to opposite movements when one's life is threatened and when one has been the victim of some wrong. Reason's guidance and training of the emotions imparts the sense appetites with even further flexibility, resembling the way that a trained dog chases certain specific things, and does not chase others, over and above what its instincts incline it to.

43  Cf. *NE* no. 1279: "For if someone has a strong inclination to the work

*Nature as* Determinatio ad Unum: *The Case of Natural Virtue*

The fact remains, however, that inclinations proceeding from temperament, including natural virtue, can be an obstacle to the acquisition and exercise of moral virtue.

> Every act of virtue, however, using a bodily organ, depends not only on the power of soul, but also on the disposition of the bodily organ, as sight on the power of vision and on the quality of the eye, through which it is aided or impeded. Whence also the act of the sense appetite depends not only on the appetitive power, but also on the disposition of the body. That which is on the side of the power of the soul follows apprehension. The apprehension of imagination, however, since it is particular is ruled by the apprehension of reason which is universal as particular active power by universal active power. And therefore in this regard the act of the sense appetite is subject to reason. However, the quality and disposition of the body is not subject to the command of reason. And therefore in that regard that the motion of the sense appetite be totally subject to the command of reason is impeded.[44]

Again this is not to the point that we cannot acquire moral virtue. But Aquinas is realistic as to how far human virtue can go. He does not think that the sense appetite can ever be made perfectly

> of some moral virtue and does not exercise discretion in the work of that virtue, grave harm will occur, either to his own body, as in those who are inclined to abstinence without discretion, or with respect to exterior things, if he is inclined to liberality; and similarly in the case of the other virtues. But if an inclination of this sort co-accepts understanding (intellectum) in operating so that namely it operates with discretion, then it will differ greatly according to the excellence of its goodness. And the habit, which will be like to the operation performed with discretion, will be properly and perfectly virtue, i.e., moral virtue."

44  *ST* I-II 17.7.

RESTORING NATURE

subject to reason, not even in the virtuous: "passions inclining one towards evil are not totally destroyed neither through acquired virtue nor through infused virtue, unless perhaps by a miracle."[45] Through habituation such inclinations can be made less vehement, but they cannot be entirely eradicated.[46] The fact is that if one is human, then one has to have a body and sense appetites, and the body will have its dispositions and the sense appetites will react to their proper objects, the sensed or imagined good (or difficult good), even when this is not the good according to reason.

> [F]or the integrity of human nature not only is reason required, but also the lower powers of the soul, and the body itself. And therefore it arises from the condition of human nature left on its own that something rebelling reason is in the lower powers of the soul, so long as the lower powers of the soul have their proper motions.[47]

45  *De Virtutibus in Communi* 10 ad 14.
46  Cf. ibid., 1.4 ad 7: "[T]he entire rebellion of the irascible and concupiscible cannot be destroyed through virtue; since from their very nature the irascible and concupiscible oppose reason in regard to that which is good according to sense; granted this can happen through divine power, which is able to even change natures. Nevertheless, that rebellion is diminished through virtue, to the extent that the said powers become accustomed to be subject to reason; whence it is from something extrinsic that they have what pertains to virtue, namely, from the dominion of reason over them; of themselves, however, they retain something of their proper motions, which are sometimes contrary to reason. Cf. also *NE* no. 239, *De Virtutibus Cardinalibus* 1 ad 6, and *DV* 25.7 ad 3.
47  *De Virtutibus in Communi* 4 ad 8. One might think that the perfect subjection of the sense appetite to the will was natural to man, and the loss of this was due to original sin. Aquinas maintains, however, that just as death is natural, so too conflict between the appetites is natural: "For that man in the original state was so constituted that reason completely contained the lower powers, and the soul the

*Nature as* Determinatio ad Unum: *The Case of Natural Virtue*

As we have seen, part of the reason for the rebellion of the lower appetites in some cases is rooted in the inclination that stems from the physical disposition of the organs of these appetites.

In conclusion: To the extent that matter predominates in a thing, to that extent the thing is limited in what it does. To the extent that form predominates in a thing, to that extent it is less determined and more determining of what it does. Thus, inanimate natural things whose forms are entirely material are the most determined to one, whereas animate things whose forms are less immersed in matter are less determined to one; human beings, in virtue of their immaterial souls, are least determined to one. In human beings, however, the full power of the rational soul is not realized in every part of the body, but that power is realized that accords with the disposition of the part. In human beings the vegetative powers are so much a function of the body that the rational soul has no direct control over them. The sensitive powers, since they are not so material, are apt to be directed by reason. The vegetative powers are responsible for one's bodily make-up (material coming from the parents is, of course, required). Since the rational powers lack direct control over the vegetative powers, they consequently lack direct control over one's actual physical make-up, and also over the inclinations to emotion which may follow upon one's make-up. Now, in some individuals these inclinations are in the line of true virtue. However, since these inclinations are determined to one, they lack the flexibility to circumstance requisite for true virtue, and they also bring with them vices, given there are other types of situations where the opposite movement of appetite is generally needed. Indeed, in some

> body, was not from the virtue of natural principles, but from the virtue of original justice superadded through divine liberality. When this justice was removed due to sin, man returned to the state suited to him in virtue of his natural principles . . . . Just as therefore man naturally dies, nor can be lead to immmortality except by way of miracle; so to the concupiscible naturally tend towards what is pleasurable, and the irascible to what is difficult, outside of the order of reason." (*DV* 25.7)

RESTORING NATURE

cases one is ultimately better off not possessing certain natural virtues because of the gravity of the natural vices associated with them. For natural virtue to develop into moral virtue, one must first recognize natural virtue for what it is. Doing so can be difficult since natural virtue resembles true virtue both in the acts it inclines one towards and in the pleasure that accompanies these acts.[48] Once a person has recognized natural virtue for what it is, reason must take charge so that the sense appetite becomes habituated to responding to reason, rather than simply moving in keeping with its natural disposition. Plainly, much more remains to be said on this subject and on related issues, such as: whether there is an ideal temperament;[49] how the determination to one that is characteristic of moral virtue differs from that of natural virtue; whether we should attempt to alter our physical make-up and/or physiological processes as a secondary means of acquiring virtue.[50]

48  The morally virtuous person does the right thing with pleasure, except in instances such as acts of courage where it suffices that the virtuous person perform them without pain.
49  *ST* I-II 46.5 ad 1.
50  I wish to thank Y. Gayle, S. Jensen, and W. Murray for their helpful comments.

}310{

# *Disclaimers in Aquinas's* Commentary on the Nicomachean Ethics? *A Reconsideration*

## Christopher Kaczor
## Loyola Marymount University

Thomas Aquinas's commentaries on Aristotle, in particular the *Ethics* commentary, inspire radically different evaluations. For example, according to Paul Shorey,[1] *the Sententia libri ethicorum* remains, more than 700 years after its first appearance, the most useful commentary on the *Nicomachean Ethics* ever written. For René Antoine Gauthier, the editor of the Leonine edition of *Sententia libri ethicorum,* the same work cannot be considered even the best medieval commentary on the *Ethics* and distorts Aristotle so much that it hinders rather than helps the contemporary reader.[2] Scholars have also debated the purpose for which the *Sententia libri ethiocorum* was written. Did Thomas undertake the commentary as a textbook for Dominicans studying philosophy? Was he laying a moral framework so as to introduce thirteenth century students to the more technical *Summa*? Did he write *the Commentary on the Ethics* as personal notes in preparation for

---

1   Paul Shorey, *Platonism Ancient and Modern.* (Berkeley, 1938) 90.
2   Especially harsh is the judgment of Francis Cheneval and Ruedi Imbach: "Die Aristoteleskommentare des Thomas von Aquin sind zwar für eine historish-kritische Exegese der Texte des Aristoteles bedeutungslos . . . . " Thomas von Aquin, *Prologe zu den Aristotele-skommentaren.* Herausgegeben, übersetzt und eingeleitet von Francis cheneval und Ruedi Imbach. (Frankfut am Main: Vitorrio Klostermann, 1993) XIII.

writing the moral part of the *Summa*? What does this commentary say about the relationship of faith and reason for Thomas? Is *the Sententia libri ethicorum* Thomas's moral philosophy or is it really a theological work? What is the relationship between the *Commentary on the Ethics* and Thomas's other works treating ethical matters?

Although many interesting questions face the contemporary reader when considering the *Sententia libri ethicorum*, in this article I would like to consider not the value of the commentary as a reading of Aristotle, nor even the purpose for which it was written, but rather whether the *Commentary on the Ethics* should be considered *merely* as an exposition of Thomas's understanding of Aristotle or whether the commentary reflects Thomas's own thought as well. In other words, does the *Sententia libri ethicorum* represent not only Thomas's interpretation of Aristotle, but also, with some qualifications, his own views on the topics treated? Or does the *Commentary* only present Thomas's understanding of Aristotle so that one could not responsibly cite the *Commentary* in reconstructing Aquinas's understanding of various matters?

This issue is particularly germain to the questions addressed in this Thomistic institute considering Aquinas on nature. In considering the question of how nature, in particular human nature, relates to ethics, one can perhaps find no richer resource than Thomas's commentary on Aristotle's *Nicomachean Ethics*. Indeed, the *Ethics Commentary*, in addition to Thomas's other commentaries on Aristotle, especially the commentaries on the *Physics, Metaphysics, and De anima*, constitute an indispensible treasure for understanding Aquinas on nature—or do they? For Mark D. Jordan, as well as others, these commentaries are mere summaries and expositions of Aristotle, and so it would be unhelpful, indeed irresponsible, to cite these commentaries as if they represented Thomas's own view or in order to better understand Thomas's own view about natural philosophy or indeed anything else.

In this paper, first, I will present six of the considerations given by Jordan in support of the view that Thomas's *Sententia libri ethicorum* does not represent Aquinas's own views but is

}312{

*Disclaimers in Aquinas's* Commentary on the Nicomachean Ethics?

merely an attempt to interpret Aristotle. Secondly, I will bring forward some reasons for believing that Thomas in his commentaries on Aristotle does more than mere exegesis and so it would not in fact be irresponsible to read these commentaries in order to come to a better understanding of Thomas, even though it is admitted that Aquinas's views presented in the Aristotelian commentaries might sometimes (though certainly not always) be more fully be presented elsewhere. Finally, I will answer the objections brought forward.

Jordan has argued in a series of articles that Aquinas cannot be "burdened with" the views expressed in the Aristotelian commentaries, and in particular with those in *the Commentary on the Ethics*. He argues that there are at least six distinct ways in which Thomas notifies his readers that the views of Aristotle are not his own within the text of the commentary itself. By means of these, Thomas marks his distance from the thought of Aristotle just as surely as did Albert. "Together," says Jordan,

> they show how Thomas stands as a literal expositor of Aristotle. If there are no disclaimers in Thomas after the manner of Albert's blunt reminders, there are many signs that Thomas is not to be confused with Aristotle— even with Aristotle read well.[3]

What are these signs?

According to Jordan, first, in a number of places Thomas explicitly disagrees with Aristotle. Second, Aquinas supplements Aristotle. Third, Thomas insists upon the limited scope of Aristotelian inquiry. Fourth, Aquinas notes the rhetorical limitations under which Aristotle labors. Fifth, in the *Summa theologiae*

3   Mark D. Jordan, "Thomas Aquinas's Disclaimers in the Aristotelian Commentaries" in *Philosophy and the God of Abraham: Essays in Memory of James A. Weisheipl, OP*, ed. R. James Long. Papers in Mediaeval Studies 12 (Toronto: Pontifical Institute of Medieval Studies, 1991) 99–112, at 109–110.

}313{

RESTORING NATURE

Thomas repudiates the order of exposition adopted by Aristotle in the *Ethics* indicating the limits of a pagan pedagogy. Sixth and last, the opinions expressed in any commentary cannot generally be taken to be the commentator's own. In Jordan's view, these six indications create a distance between Thomas's own judgments and the views expressed in the *Sententia libri ethicorum*.

Concerning the first category, Jordan writes: "Thomas distances himself from the Aristotelian doctrine most obviously when he disagrees with it."[4] Thomas corrects Aristotle at various points in the *Commentary on the Ethics*. For instance, Thomas indicates his disapproval at Aristotle's mention of offering sacrifices:

> Here the Philosopher speaks according to the habit of the Gentiles, which the truth having been made manifest is abrogated, hence if someone now were to make expenditures for a demonic cult, he would not be magnificent but sacrilegious.[5]

Thomas is clearly noting that the cult of worship described by Aristotle is unfit for Christians who must offer worship to God alone. Jordan notes many other examples where Thomas "corrects" Aristotle according to Christian truth:

> [Thomas] notes, against the apparent sense of the Aristotelian text, that virginity cannot be seen as an extreme beyond the virtuous mean.[6] He records that the ancients allowed marriages to be dissolved because of sterility,[7] that they posited semi-divinities known as

4   Jordan, "Disclaimers," 107.
5   Loquitur hic Philosophus secundum consuetudinem Gentilium, quae nunc manifestata veritate est abrogata, unde, si aliquis nunc circa cultum daemonum aliquid expenderet, non esset magnificus, sed sacrilegus. *Sent. Eth.* 4.7.
6   *Sent. Eth.* 2.2 (LE 47:81.124–131).
7   *Sent. Eth.* 8:12 (LE 47:488.285–288).

}314{

*Disclaimers in Aquinas's* Commentary on the Nicomachean Ethics?

daemons,[8] that they deified heroes.[9] Throughout the text, Thomas remarks that Aristotle speaks "more gentium" in calling the separate substances or planetary bodies "gods."[10]

Clearly, Thomas at times corrects what he takes to be mistakes on Aristotle's part or at least mistakes that could arise from possible readings of the text, such as the text which considers whether virginity could be a mean.

Secondly, Jordan argues that Thomas distances himself from Aristotle when he supplements the text with linguistic and doctrinal additions. Latin etymologies and technical terms are among the linguistic additions,[11] and "Thomas often enough notes a lacuna in Aristotle and then proceeds to fill it."[12] Thomas adds technical terms and Latin etymologies to help make sense of Aristotle's text and to show the insufficiency of the doctrine there advocated. According to Jordan, Thomas also shows his distance from Aristotle in this second way by the many additions which fill gaps in the text of the *Ethics*. Aristotle writes: "Whether opinion should be said to precede choice or to follow it, does not matter, for we do not intend to determine this but whether choice is identical with particular opinion."[13] Thomas notes: "Nevertheless, we must know that opinion, since it pertains to the faculty of

---

8   *Sent. Eth.* 4.7 (LE 47:222.23–26).
9   *Sent. Eth.* 7.1 (LE 47:381.88–90). As Jordan notes, Aquinas "goes on to stress that Aristotle denies deification in any literal sense. (381:118–123)." See too, Mark D. Jordan "Aquinas Reading Aristotle's *Ethics*," in *Ad Litteram: Authoritative Texts and Their Medieval Readers*. Edited by Mark D. Jordan and Kent Emery, Jr. (Notre Dame: University of Notre Dame, 1992) 229–249, at 248.
10  *Sent. Eth.* 1.14 (LE 47:50.66–76), 1.18 (47:65.78–80), 3.13 (47:157.112–113), 5.12 (47:306.158–160), 8.7 (47:465.130–131), 10.12 (47:591.126, 592.169). See too, Jordan "Aquinas on Aristotle's *Ethics*," 236.
11  Ibid., 3.22, 4.14, 6.5, and 7.7.
12  Jordan "Disclaimers," 109, see section III, 6, #456 and IV, 17, #870
13  *Nicomachean Ethics*, 1112a11–13.

}315{

RESTORING NATURE

knowledge, strictly speaking, precedes choice pertaining to the appetitive faculty, which is moved by the cognoscitive power."[14] Another place in which Thomas fills a lacuna arises from this passage in the *Nicomachean Ethics*:

> Like fear, shame is brought about by reason of danger, for people who feel ashamed blush, and those who fear death grow pale. Both qualities are in some measure modifications of the body, and so pertain rather to passion than to habit.[15]

In commenting on this passage, Thomas talks about the humors and spirits which accompany certain emotions, like honor and confusion.[16] Thomas adds to the text of Aristotle both linguistic and doctrinal additions thereby showing the inadequacy of *the Nicomachean Ethics*.

According to Jordan, "A third way in which Thomas marks his distance is the insistence upon the limited scope of an Aristotelian inquiry. . . . Thomas reiterates, for example, that the *Ethics* is concerned only with the happiness of the present life."[17] Thomas says elsewhere that Aristotle does not concern himself with the question of the operation of the mind following death. Aristotle's approach is limited by its aims and its pagan author.

Consideration of audience leads Jordan to add another way in which Thomas alerts the attentive reader not to mistake an *expositio* on Aristotle for his own views.

> A fourth way of marking distance emphasizes the particular rhetorical limitations under which Aristotle labors. As Thomas sees plainly, Aristotle needed to teach a particular audience. The audience held certain

14  *Sent. Eth.* 3.6.456.
15  *Nicomachean Ethics* 1128b12–15.
16  *Sent. Eth.* IV, 17, #870.
17  Jordan "Disclaimers," 109.

}316{

*Disclaimers in Aquinas's* Commentary on the Nicomachean Ethics?

beliefs that Aristotle appropriates for dialectical purposes, even if erroneous.[18]

Fifth, Jordan claims that the *Sententia libri ethicorum* is *merely* a commentary because he believes there are explicit contradictions between what Thomas writes in his *Ethics* commentary and what he writes in works indisputably and in every way his own, such as the *Summa*. Although several authors have argued for tensions, if not contradictions, between Aristotle's pagan ethic and Thomas's Christian ethic, I will address only one such tension. The alleged contradiction mentioned by Jordan is that in the *Summa* Aquinas rejects Aristotle's way of ordering the moral life.[19] Jordan offers a series of contrasts between the order of the *Ethics* and the *Summa theologiae*:

> First, Thomas separates the definitions of virtue and other principles or elements much more strictly from the treatment of particular virtues. Thomas insists . . . on the sufficiency of the four cardinal virtues as a comprehensive organization of all moral virtue. . . . Third, Aristotle's separate treatment of the intellectual virtues is surpressed by Thomas. . . . Thomas regards his revision of the order of the *Ethics* as an improvement in clarity and comprehensiveness.[20]

Thomas's own dissatisfaction with the lack of organization present in the summae and *Sentences* commentaries of the time extended also to the *Ethics*. For many scholars, this restructuring of the presentation of Christian wisdom constitutes one of Thomas's greatest achievements-

---

18  Jordan "Disclaimers," 109.

19  I will not treat the objection that additions indicate disagreement both because additions may be from revelation and hence outside of Aristotle's philosophical scope, and because additions may arguably be said not to contradict but to fulfill that to which they are additions.

20  Jordan "Aquinas on Aristotle's *Ethics*," 238–239.

}317{

# Restoring Nature

a scientific organization of the patristic patrimony. Aquinas certainly took the structure he found in other authors, including Biblical writers, Boethius, Ps. Dionysius, and Aristotle quite seriously, lending plausibility to the idea that we too should not ignore how Thomas structured his account of the moral life. Hence, that the organization of Thomas's account of the moral life as treated in the *Summa* differs in order of presentation from how the same elements are treated in the *Sententia libri ethicorum* indicates that the *Commentary* cannot be considered as truly representative of Thomas's own thought.

The final way of indicating the distance between Aristotle and Thomas is to note that, generally, a commentator cannot be said to appropriate as his own all of the views expressed in a commentary.

> The genre of literal exposition just by itself constitutes a kind of disclaimer. It need not suggest that the commentator disavows what is taught in the underlying text, but it does suggest that additional warrant will be required for attributing what is taught to the commentator. . . The expositor of a text cannot in general be taxed with the views being expounded.[21]

We don't, for example, suppose Stanley Rosen believes all the assertions made by the various symposiasts as explicated in his commentary on Plato's *Symposium* or that contemporary Johannine scholars themselves believe in what is found in the Gospel of John. Put another way, Thomas has adopted a genre which indicates that not his own view of the matters but only Aristotle's will be discussed.

## A Response: Literal Exposition Reconsidered

Jordan rightly locates Thomas's commentaries on Aristotle, and therefore *the Commentary on the Ethics*, within the genre of literal

21 Jordan "Disclaimers," 104, 107. See too, Mark D. Jordan, *The Alleged Aristotelianism of Thomas Aquinas.* Etienne Gilson Series 15 (Toronto: PIMS, 1990) 11.

*Disclaimers in Aquinas's* Commentary on the Nicomachean Ethics?

exposition. However, unlike contemporary philosophers or Scriptural exegetes, medieval authors did not typically differentiate exegetical, interpretative, or commentative work from creative, original, or personal work. They believed that a work of literal exposition could be *both* faithful exegetically *and* representative of the author's personal views. In fact, so widespread was this assumption in the middle ages that M.-D. Chenu argued that medieval commentaries represent the view of the commentator unless otherwise indicated.[22] In the words of Joseph Owens,

> [T]he medieval mind experienced no difficulty in seeing an author express as his own material taken nearly one hundred percent from other authors. Peter Lombard, for instance, could be regarded as the author of everything in his four books of the *Sentences*, even though practically all the material was taken from others. As long as the writer was asserting mastery over material used and was organizing and directing it to his own purpose, he was expressing it as his own.[23]

Obvious examples of such work include medieval commentaries on Scripture which sought fidelity in exegisis but did not exclude a personal adherence to that which was written in the commentary.

Of course, a fundamental difference between the Scripture commentaries and the Aristotelian commentaries is that Thomas says elsewhere that he accepts as true all that is written in Scripture,

22 M.D. Chenu, O.P., in his *Introduction a L'Étude de Saint Thomas D'Aquin*, Paris, Libraire Philosophique J. Vrin, 1950, concurs: "Ainsi, à la différence de l'exégèse moderne, qui abstient de faire sienne la pensée de son auteur, et n'a pas à dire s'il ne l'accepte pas, le commentateur médiéval fait sien implicitement le contenu de texte, et, s'il ne l'accepte pas, le dit explicitement, tandis qu'il est présumé le faire sien s'il ne dit rien" (177). As I will mention, Thomas's teacher Albert the Great does just this.
23 Joseph Owens, "Aquinas as an Aristotelian Commentator" in *St. Thomas Aquinas: Commemorative Studies.* (Toronto: PIMS, 1974) 236–37.

RESTORING NATURE

but nowhere does he say the same thing about Aristotle. In fact, he says that while Scripture is the highest and most direct authority theologically speaking, philosophical authority is only probable and indirect.[24] However, while not the highest authority in theology, philosophical authority still remains an authority. In the *Summa*, Aristotle is one of his most frequently cited sources, along with Scripture and Augustine. Amazingly, although Thomas's duties as master of theology necessitated commenting on Scripture and did not require commenting on Aristotle, more than 13% of Thomas's entire literary corpus is devoted to commentaries on Aristotle, almost the exact percentage Thomas devoted to commentaries on Scripture.[25]

That Aquinas made special time for this supererogatory task might be partially explained by the Averroist controversy, a controversy that presupposed that through commentaries one made not merely historical claims but also philosophical claims reflecting the views of both the author of the commentary and, at least allegedly, the author of the original work. Aquinas refers to commentaries by Averroes on Aristotle as if what Averroes had written in these commentaries represented Averroes's own view in addition to an Averroist understanding of Aristotle. He will write: "Averroes dicit" and then make reference to a commentary by Averroes.[26] Many scholars, including Jordan, believe that Thomas patterned his genre of Aristotelian commentary either directly or indirectly, through the Arts faculty, after the 'great commentary' style of Averroes.[27] If Thomas does truly adopt the Averroistic

24  ST I, 1, 8 ad 2.
25  In his article "Theology and Philosophy" in the *Cambridge Companion to Aquinas*, Mark Jordan rounds off the word count from the *Index Thomisticus* for the scripture commentaries at 1,170,000 or 13.5% of the Thomistic corpus and for the commentaries on Aristotle at 1,165,000 or just over 13% of the corpus.
26  See, for example, Aquinas's *Commentary on the Metaphysics*, II, 1, 286.
27  "Thomas's models in the genre would seem rather to be immediately in styles of reading learned from the Arts faculty, more remotely in the 'great commentaries' of Averroes." Mark Jordan, "The Alleged

}320{

*Disclaimers in Aquinas's* Commentary on the Nicomachean Ethics?

*sententia* style of commentary as opposed to one of the other possible genres of commentary (*paraphrasis, commentarium medium, abbreviatio, summa,* commentary with questions, *tabula, concordatia*), and if Aquinas thought that in this style of commentary Averroes put forth not just his views of Aristotle but the views of Averroes as well, then Aquinas would seem to indicate by choice of genre that his own views are to be found in the commentaries on Aristotle. A similar point could be made with respect to how Thomas handles other commentators on Aristotle. For instance, Aquinas writes as if views presented in Themistius's commentary on the *De anima* represented Themistius's own views.[28] "From the foregoing words of Themistius, it is clear that he not only holds that the possible intellect is a part of the human soul but the agent as well, and he says that Aristotle taught this."[29] It would seem that Thomas's working assumption when dealing with commentaries on Aristotle is to treat the views asserted as respresenting those of the commentators. A contemporary scholar citing Aquinas's commentaries on Aristotle as if they represented his own views would thus be imitating the very example of Thomas.

In the *Sententia de caelo et mundo,* Thomas seems to clarify that his own interest in the investigation of pagan texts is motivated primarily by the search for wisdom rather than a desire merely to understand ancient views. Certain people, Thomas notes, believe that the ancient philosophers and poets ought not to be read according to the plain sense of the text, but rather in an allegorical way since these ancient writers concealed what they were saying in fables and enigmatic sayings. Some however reject this

Aristotelianism of Thomas Aquinas," in *The Etienne Gilson Series* 15 (1990): 11. The view that Thomas's *Sententiae* imitate the commentaries of Averroes is expressed by E. Renan and criticized by René-Antoine Gauthier, "Saint Thomas et l'Éthique à Nicomaque." *Sententia libri politicorum.* Leonine XLVIII, Rome 1971, xxi.

28  Aquinas, *De unitate intellectus,* ch. 2 (51–53).

29  Aquinas, *De unitate intellectus,* ch. 2 (53); translation from Ralph McInerny, *Aquinas Against the Averroists.* (West Lafayette, IN: Purdue University Press, 1993) 73.

procedure and wish to interpret the ancients according to the more exterior sense of their words. If we adopt the first view, then Thomas argues that Aristotle does not contradict the sense of Plato and other ancient thinkers, but only their words. If we adopt Alexander's position, then Aristotle objects to both the sense and the words of these philosophers and poets. "Whatever of these is correct, we ought not to care a great deal: since the study of philosophy is not for the sake of knowing what people have said but to attain to the truth."[30] If it is supposed that the Aristotelian commentaries were meant to be part of the study of philosophy for students preparing for theology or even as personal philosophical preparation in writing the *Summa*, then it is rather implausible to claim that Thomas wrote them merely to get the sense of Aristotle's text, since a proper understanding of the text does not fulfill the "sapiential task," as Gauthier might say.

This task means that Thomas cannot be understood as operating in the *Sententia libri ethicorum* in the role of intellectual historian. Sections of the commentary are undoubtedly Thomas's own and go well beyond an interpretation of the Aristotle. For example, Thomas's lengthy preface to the *Nicomachean Ethics* suggests four ways in which reason can relate to order, namely reason contemplating order (metaphysics and natural philosophy), reason introducing order into its own reflection (logic), reason introducing order into the will (moral philosophy), and reason introducing order into exterior matter (mechanical arts). This preface contextualizes the *Ethics* within the compass of the overall

---

30  Quidquid autem horum sit, non est nobis multum curandum: quia studium philosophiae non est ad hoc quod sciatur quid homines senserint, sed qualiter se habeat veritas. *Sententia de caelo et mundo*, I, capt. X lect. 22. (LE 3.91). An objection of circular reasoning may arise from appealing to another *Sententia* since the dispute at hand is what Thomas is doing in the genre of *Sententia*. Jordan and others agree however that at least some times Aquinas speaks in his own voice in these commentaries when explicitly remarking on the truth of something or in this case where he speaks in the authorial second person plural.

}322{

*Disclaimers in Aquinas's* Commentary on the Nicomachean Ethics?

scope of philosophy. Joseph Owens notes a similar strategy in Thomas's preface to the *Commentary on the Metaphysics*.

> The assembling of so many roving tenets under the one unifying principle shows a thorough mastery of the philosophical materials, and an innate ability to organize them successfully from a new and personal viewpoint. It marks Aquinas himself as the 'author' of the work about to be undertaken, in the medieval sense of the *auctor*. He is the one who will be doing the thinking and passing the judgments and presenting the work as his own, no matter how liberally he is drawing upon someone else for material, help, and inspiration.[31]

If even material taken wholesale from others is to be regarded as the collator's own, such as Lombard's *Sentences*, from this perspective how much more is a text the author's own when much is added to the original work? One finds in the *Commentary on the Ethics* much that moves beyond the letter of the text. Topics are sometimes treated which move beyond Aristotle or treat Aristotle in surprising ways. These "additions" have caused some, most famously Harry Jaffa in his book *Thomism and Aristotelianism*, to devalue the commentary as a reading of Aristotle,[32] but they might be understood as part of an Aristotelian strategy. In the words of John Jenkins, Aquinas's principles:

> required that in order to elucidate Aristotle's text, he must both make clear Aristotle's individualistic understanding and construct, or at least suggest, the best account of the matter under discussion. In this way, Aquinas thought, he could provide expositions of Aristotle's texts which

31  Joseph Owens, "Aquinas as an Aristotelian Commentator" in *St. Thomas Aquinas: Commemorative Studies*. (Toronto: PIMS, 1974) 217.

32  H.V. Jaffa, *Thomism and Aristotelianism*. (Chicago: University of Chicago Press, 1952) 187.

would be most useful for his readers' dialectical inquiries. Although Aquinas adapted and refined Aristotle's procedures, he was, in commenting on Aristotle, following Aristotle's example. In his gloss on Aristotle's discussion on the teachings of Anaxagoras, Aquinas explains that Anaxagoras's more subtle doctrine can be found "if ... one seeks diligently [to state] clearly and manifestly what Anaxagoras 'wishes to say', i.e., what his intellect tended toward, but he was unable to express." Similarly, in the commentaries Aquinas often sought to be true to Aristotle's text by presenting not only what Aristotle understood but also what his intellect "tended toward," as Aquinas understood this by his own best lights.[33]

Whether these movements beyond the letter of Aristotle should be viewed with Jenkins as fruitful developments or with Jaffa as disasterous distortions, they do indicate that Thomas does more than merely offer an exposition of the text. The *Commentary on the Ethics* is not simply a commentary; it shows Thomas's own exploration of the issues at hand.

In this, Thomas's approach differs significantly from that of St. Albert the Great. Albert's commentary on Aristotle's *De animalibus* has this unmistakable disclaimer near its conclusion:

The entire work on natural things has been completed. In it I explicated the sayings of the Peripatetics as well as I could; nor should anyone be able to detect in this work what I myself believe in natural philosophy; but should anyone doubt, he should compare the things which are said in our books with the works of the Peripatetics, and then disagree or concur saying that I was interpreting and expositing those works; if however, having not read and compared, he will have critized,

33  John Jenkins, "Expositions of the Text: Aquinas's Aristotelian Commentaries." *Medieval Philosophy and Theology* 5 (1996): 36–62.

}324{

*Disclaimers in Aquinas's* Commentary on the Nicomachean Ethics?

> then it is agreed that he criticizes either from hatred or ignorance; and I do not trouble myself with the reproaches of such persons.[34]

Due to the standard medieval conception of commentary, Albert surmised his readers would assume his expositions of Aristotle represented his own thought and so regularly peppers the beginnings and conclusions of his expositions of Aristotle with such disclaimers. Since Albert did not assent to what was written in the commentaries, he makes it clear to his reader that the reader should consult Albert's own works to find out his personal views.

Commenting on Aristotle during a time in which the place of Aristotle's *Nicomachean Ethics* was hotly contested in the University of Paris by such an eminent *magister* as Bonaventure, Thomas makes no disclaimers of Albert's kind either at the beginning or end of his commentaries on Aristotle. If Thomas cannot be taken to agree with what is asserted in the commentaries, it would seem Aquinas was being irresponsible by not indicating his intentions more clearly to his readers, as Albert did, with explicit disclaimers at the beginning or end of the commentaries. On the contrary, Thomas concludes the *Commentary on the Metaphysics* as well as the *Commentary on the Physics* with the opposite of a disclaimer, namely an affirmation of what he has written expressed by an "Amen."[35]

---

34 *Commentaria in libros de Animalibus,* in fine (ed. Borguet, 12, 582). Expletum est totum opus naturalium, in quo sic moderamen tenui, quod dicta Peripateticorum, prout melius potui, exposui; nec aliquis in eo potest deprehendere quid ego ipse sentiam in philosophia naturali; sed quicumque dubitat, comparet haec quae in nostris libris dicta sunt, dictis Peripateticorum, et tunc reprehendat vel consentiat, me dicens scientiae ipsorum fuisse interpretem et expositorem; si autem non legens et comparans reprehenderit, tunc constat ex odio eum reprehendere vel ex ignorantia; et ego talium hominum parum curo reprehensiones.

35 I thank John O'Callaghan for bringing this to my attention.

}325{

RESTORING NATURE

## Response to Objections

If it seems then that we should read the commentaries on Aristotle as Aquinas's own views, how then shall we handle the first objection that Thomas occasionally corrects Aristotle? In this regard, two distinct matters ought not be confused, that is, possible misreadings of the text on the one hand and what Aquinas considers to be errors made by Aristotle on the other. The former poses no real difficulty for viewing the commentaries as Thomas's own work, since Scripture too, as Thomas points out, has been subject to numerous misinterpretations even by people with the best motivations.[36] Thus for Aquinas to admit that there are possible misreadings of Aristotle does not indicate that he does not assent to the text.

Jordan has identified passages in which Aquinas does not agree with Aristotle, but do these corrections of Aristotle indicate that we must not mistake Aristotle, even read well, for Thomas? Might not the same evidence lead to a different conclusion? One could read these qualifications or corrections simply as St. Thomas differentiating those erroneous aspects of Aristotle's work, which he rejects, from those true aspects of Aristotle's work (the vast majority of the text) which he adopts as his own.

Joseph Owens also noticed Aquinas occasionally correcting Aristotle in the *Commentary on the Metaphysics*, but in contradiction to Jordan Owens seems to draw the opposite conclusion from such corrections.

> Even within the strictly philosophical explanation, however, at times the judgments are made and the decisions are given on the strength of the Thomistic metaphysics of existence. These occasions are few,

36  In his *Lectura super Johannem*, Thomas notes both heretics and respected Church authorites, such has Anselm, who have in his view misinterpreted the Bible. See for example the *Lectura super Johannem* I, 2, 73; II, 2, 370; and III, 2, 467. Translated by James A. Weisheipl and Fabian R. Larcher (Albany, New York: Magi Books, 1980).

}326{

> comparatively, but they are concerned with philosoph-
> ically important issues. They are not marked off by any
> indications that they are intrusions from the outside.
> Rather they seem part of the normal flow of thought.
> Do they show that the whole thrust of the commentary
> is to propound Thomistic thought, into which the great
> body of Aristotelian philosophy is skillfully absorbed?[37]

In other words, that Aquinas would occasionally note his disagreement with what Aristotle says suggests that his commentary
is not *merely* commentary. In only seldom noting disagreement
with Aristotle, Aquinas suggests a tacit concord with the uncor-
rected views expressed. Thus, the evidence supplied by Jordan
would seem to controvert his conclusion more than support it.

Let us look for context to Thomas's commentaries on Scripture for a reply to the second objection raised, namely that the
technical additions by Thomas to Aristotle mark a distance between the two. Since both were probably written circa 1271, consider in particular the *Commentary on John* along with the
*Commentary on the Ethics*. Linguistic additions abound in the *Lectura super Johannem*. For example, Thomas considers whether the
term *cognitio* applies to the Word of God, though the term appears
nowhere in this section of the Gospel and is Thomas's technical
addition.[38] He also speaks about the many senses of the word
*principium*.[39] Further on, he treats the different senses of *de*, *a*, and
*ex* in Latin without reference to the Greek.[40] G. Geenan, O.P., notes
that Thomas: "felt duty bound to show that, as a matter of fact,
these new words [not of Biblical origin] corresponded in their
own way to the words of Scripture."[41] Thomas is well aware of

---

37   Joseph Owens, "Aquinas as an Aristotelian Commentator," 228.
38   *Lectura super Johannem*, I, 1, 26.
39   *Lectura super Johannem*, I, 1, 34.
40   *Lectura super Johannem*, 1, 6, 162.
41   G. Geenan "The Place of Tradition in the Theology of St. Thomas."
     *The Thomist* XV (1952): 133.

RESTORING NATURE

this tradition of resorting to extra-Scriptural words to clarify the meaning of Scripture and considers himself to be acting in accord with that tradition. Geenan continues:

> "Tradition" has a real place in the theology of Aquinas, since at times it is due to Tradition alone that we can arrive at an understanding of the Scriptures and that we can demonstrate that, even Scriptural texts, which at first sight and *secundum litteram* seem to affirm the contrary of revealed doctrine, express in fact this revealed doctrine such as it is taught by the Church.[42]

It would clearly be erroneous to claim that linguistic and technical additions to the Biblical word in Thomas's commentaries on Scripture and in his theology show that he was distancing himself from the Scripture. Thus, such additions of themselves would not seem to indicate a distancing from Aristotle. Rather, such additions are regularly used by Thomas to bring out the deeper sense of the text.

In answer to this second objection again we find similar strategies of interpretation in Thomas's *Lectura super Johannem*. The Johannine Gospel often poses questions that are left explicitly unanswered. For example, John 1:24–25 reads: "Now some Pharisees who had been sent questioned him, 'Why then do you baptize if you are not the Christ, nor Elijah, nor the Prophet?'" The question is not directly resolved in the text. But Thomas goes on to treat the issue himself by arguing that it is not really a question: "Their questions concerned his office of baptizing. Hence he says that they asked him, 'Why do you baptize?' Here we should note that they are asking not to learn, but to obstruct."[43] Another passage from John's Gospel reads:

> Now at the Feast the Jews were watching for him and asking, *"Where is that man?"* Among the crowds there

42  Ibid. pp.133–134.
43  *Sententia super Johannem*, I, 13, 243.

}328{

*Disclaimers in Aquinas's* Commentary on the Nicomachean Ethics?

was widespread whispering about him. Some said, "He is a good man." Others replied, "No, he deceives the people." But no one would say anything publicly about him for fear of the Jews.[44]

The emphasized sentence above is neither rhetorical nor answered directly in the text. This is similar to the cases in the Aristotelian corpus where there is no resolution to a difficulty or problem or question raised in the text. Thomas fills a 'lacuna' in the text of the Gospel by noting:

Then (v. 11), he mentions the opportunity Christ had to show the origin of his spiritual teaching. He mentions two such opportunities: one was due to the disagreement among the people; the other to their amazement (v. 15). The people disagreed in what they thought of Christ. He does three things concerning this. First, he shows what they had in common; secondly, how they differed (v. 12); and thirdly, whose opinion prevailed (v. 13). What they had in common was they "looked for him at the feast, and they asked: Where is he?" They differed . . .[45]

In his *Lectura super Johannem,* Thomas offers resolutions to the unresolved difficulty of an unanswered question by showing the question's purpose within the larger context.

We also find in his *Lectura super Johannem* Thomas describing more fully something only briefly mentioned in the text just as we do in the *Sententia libri ethicorum.* Here, Thomas is commenting on what Jesus means by telling the Samaritain woman that he can give her 'living water.'

Now water is of two kinds: living and non-living. Non-living water is water which is not connected or united

44  John 7:11–13.
45  *Sententia super Johannem,* 7, 2, 1028–1029.

}329{

RESTORING NATURE

with the source from which it springs, but is collected from the rain or in others ways into ponds and cisterns, and there it stands, separated from its source. But living water is connected with its source and flows from it. So according to this understanding, the grace of the Holy Spirit is given to man in such a way that the source itself of the grace is also given, that is, the Holy Spirit.[46]

Here Thomas does exactly the same thing that we saw him do earlier in relation to the *Nicomachean Ethics*. Thomas takes up a word or phrase and then expands on it, seeking the deeper meaning concealed, as it were, within the literal shell.

We know that Thomas accepts everything in Scripture, thus we know that he does not mean to imply by these additions that he disagrees with the authority on which he is commenting. Why, when we turn to Thomas's Aristotelian commentaries, ought we to say that these same kinds of additions indicate disagreement with Aristotle? Perhaps these additions function in a similar manner in both the *Ethics Commentary* and Scripture commentaries. Certain additions to a text can help illuminate its meaning, and so Thomas includes them in his commentaries on Aristotle and his commentaries on Scripture.

In response to the third objection that Aquinas distances himself from Aristotle by noting the limited scope of Aristotelian inquiry, it should be said that to remark on the limited scope of the inquiry is not to disclaim the truth of that inquiry. That moral philosophy has a more limited scope than moral theology indicates very little about the status of the commentary. When Thomas treats the distinctions between the sciences in *his Expositio super librum Boethii De trinitate*, he makes clear, particularly in question five, that distinct sciences treat objects that are formally distinct. But each science is a science, that is, each gives true, but perhaps not full, knowledge of reality. Jordan's objection is helpful in so far as it reminds us that Thomas believed Aristotle's inquiry to

46  *Lectura super Johannem*, 4, 2, 577.

}330{

*Disclaimers in Aquinas's Commentary on the Nicomachean Ethics?*

be limited to what can be known without revelation. However, to conclude from these remarks that Thomas therefore rejected the teachings of the *Ethics* would require that Thomas as a theologian would be required to reject the inferior sciences.

On the contrary, Thomas's remarks and strategies indicate a much more amicable attitude towards the subordinate sciences. Consider just a few examples. In his *De unitate intellectus*, Thomas remarks that: "we intend however to show that the position mentioned is not only against the principles of philosophy but also contrary to the evidence of faith."[47] The context makes clear that Thomas limits his scientific investigation soley to that which can be known by unaided reason. He seems to have a similar task, a purely philosophical task, in his *De principiis naturae*. We would not be justified, I believe, in saying that the Thomas of these philosophical works is not to be confused with the Thomas of his theological works on account of the limitations of the inquiry. We would be justified in saying that these works do not reflect *all* that he said about these matters, but not that what he said in a philosophical context he really did not hold on account of the limits of this type of inquiry. *Mutatis mutandis*, Thomas's remarks about the limits of Aristotle's inquiry do not *of themselves* indicate that the commentary is not representative of Thomas's thought.

The third objection, noting the rhetorical limitations of Aristotle, seems to prove too much, since in the Gospels Christ himself, according to Thomas's reading, often speaks in a certain way for rhetorical purposes in addressing a particular audience. The Gospel of John 6:5–6 reads: "Then when Jesus lifted his eyes and saw that a great multitude had come to him, he said to Philip, 'Where shall we buy bread that these may eat?' He said this, however, to test him, for he knew what he would do." Christ here, according to the Gospel, adopts the pose of ignorance to teach. Thomas comments as follows:

47 intendimus autem ostendere positionem predictam non minus contra philosophiae principia esse quam contra fidei documenta. *De unitate intellectus*, 2, 29–32.

}331{

RESTORING NATURE

The Lord's intention is given when he says, he said this, however, to test him. Here the Evangelist raises one difficulty in answering another. For we could wonder why our Lord asks Philip what to do, as though our Lord himself did not know. The Evangelist settles this when he says, for he knew what he would do. But it seems that the Evangelist raises another difficulty when he says, to test him. For to test is to try out; and this seems to imply ignorance.

I answer that one can test another in various ways in order to try him out. One man tests another in order to learn; the devil tests a man in order to ensnare him: "Your enemy, the devil, as a roaring lion goes about seeking whom he can devour" (1 Pt. 5:8). But Christ (and God) does not test us in order to learn, because he sees into our hearts; nor in order to ensnare us, for as we read in James (1:13): "God does not test anyone." But he does test us that others might learn something from the one tested . . . . He tests Philip . . . so that those who hear his answer might be very certain about the miracle to come.[48]

Thomas seems here to be suggesting that Christ adopted some of the same techniques as Aristotle. Jesus, in certain instances, spoke

48  intentio autem interrogantis [domini] aperitur cum dicit hoc autem dicebat tentans eum etc. ubi evangelista unam dubitationem excludens, ducit in aliam. potuisset enim dubitari quod dominus philippum quasi ignorans interrogasset; sed hoc excludit dicens ipse enim sciebat quid esset facturus. sed cum tentare videatur etiam ignorantis esse cum idem sit quod experimentum sumere, videtur quod evangelista in aliam dubitationem inducat cum dicit tentans eum. sed dicendum, quod diversimode aliquis tentat aliquem, ut experimentum de eo sumat: aliter enim tentat homo, quia ut addiscat; aliter diabolus tamquam leo rugiens circuit quaerens quem devoret. deus vero et christus tentat quidem non ut addiscat, quia ipse est qui scrutatur corada et renes . . . . ita ex hoc philippum tentat ut insinuaret aliis suam responsionem, inducens per hoc eos in certissimam futuri signi cognitionem. *Lectura super Johannem*, 6, 1, 850.

}332{

*Disclaimers in Aquinas's* Commentary on the Nicomachean Ethics?

on presupposition of others' ignorance. We find Christ asking questions in many passages of the Gospels,[49] and according to Thomas's Christology,[50] each of these instances of Christ asking questions must be subject to a similar explanation as the preceding one. In a somewhat similar way, the writers of the Gospels, though infallible by the Holy Spirit's direction, differ in what they say, often on account of their intended audience. For example, Thomas excuses what seems to be an *oratio imperfecta* in Matthew because he argues that Matthew was seeking to preserve the customary way of speaking among the Jews.[51] Later Thomas takes up the question: Why do the genealogical accounts of Christ in Luke and Matthew differ? He gives a five-part answer, the fourth of which is as follows:

> The reason for this is that Matthew wrote for the Hebrews. The Hebrews were glorified most greatly by Abraham. As it says in the Gospel of John: We are the offspring of Abraham, who was the first to believe; and therefore Matthew begins from Abraham. Luke however wrote to the Greeks, who knew nothing about Abraham save through Christ: for if Christ hadn't have been, they would have never known anything about Abraham; and therefore Luke begins from Christ, and he ended not just in Abraham but in God.[52]

49   For just a few examples, see Mark 10:5, 10:36; Matt. 9:28, 14:31, 21:25.
50   ST III, 10, 2–3.
51   *Lectura super Evangelium Matthaei,* I, 1, 12.
52   *Lectura super Evangelium Matthaei,* I, 2, 28. Cuius ratio potest sumi ex hoc quod Mathaeus scripsit Hebraeis. Hebraeis autem maxime gloriabantur de Abraham; Ioan. viii, 33: Semen Abrahae sumus, qui fuit primum credendi principium; et ideo Mattaeus ab Abraham incipit. Lucas autem scripsit Graecis, qui nihil de Abraham sciebant nisi per Christum: si enim non fuisset Christus, nihil unquam scivissent de Abraham; et ideo Lucas incepti a Christo, et terminavit non solum in Abraham, sed in Deum.

Here Luke and Matthew seek to persuade audiences having different horizons of expectation, and these presuppositions must shape their discourse, if it is to be sucessful. Of course, Thomas holds that the Holy Spirit infallibly knows the minds and hearts of all people, but Aristotle is shrewd enough to be able to surmise the presuppositions of others in a natural way through reflection. Noting rhetorical and strategic limitations does not mark a distancing of Thomas from the text of Scripture, so also noting similar limitations in the text of Aristotle poses no real difficulty for reading these commentaries as Thomas's own.

It is assumed by Jordan's fifth objection that reorganizations of the order of presentation represent, in some sense, repudiations of other ways of ordering the material. Thomas does not follow the manner of presentation of the *Ethics* in the *Summa*, but the significance of this reorganization is not self-evident. A study by Nicholas Ayo reminds us of several reorganizations of the Thomistic treatment of the creed.[53] Ayo notes that the *Collationes Credo in Deum*, the *De articulis Fidei*, and the *Summa theologiae* each present a different division of the creed, dividing the clauses of the creed into twelve articles one time, fourteen articles the other two times but even in these two cases the fourteen articles are not identically parsed. The same point could be made with the reordering of the treatment of God's characteristics that is evident in a comparison of the *Summa contra Gentiles* with the *Summa theologiae*. Although both begin with a demonstration of God's existence, the *Summa contra Gentiles* orders the discussion of God's characteristics by treating first God's eternity, and then God's simplicity, perfection, goodness, and finally infinity, while the *Summa theologiae* takes up these matters in an entirely different order beginning with God's simplicity, and moving to God's goodness, perfection, infinity, and finally eternity. Factors other than

53 Nicholas Ayo, *The Sermon-Conferences of St. Thomas Aquinas on the Apostles' Creed*. (Notre Dame: University of Notre Dame Press, 1988). See especially pp. 184–185.

*Disclaimers in Aquinas's* Commentary on the Nicomachean Ethics?

"distancing" must account for the reordering of the treatment in these cases, which lends some plausibility to the idea that these other factors may also account for the differences in the order of presentation of virtues between the *Summa theologiae* and the *Sententia libri ethicorum*. Perhaps it is not a deep dissatisfaction with prior treatments that underlies these reorderings but rather considerations of various audiences, the nature and scope of the works involved, or a desire to cast light on a topic from various angles.

We can rightly say that the *Ethics* commentary represents Thomas's own thought, as well as his understanding of Aristotle. Thomas wrote a literal commentary on Aristotle's *Nicomachean Ethics*. The literal commentary is the kind of commentary used in the middle ages for those texts of highest authority, like Holy Scripture, and it was regularly assumed that the commentator agreed with the text and assented to the truth of what is related therein, unless he explicitly said otherwise. Thomas does not have explicit disclaimers at the beginning or at the end of the text, where others usually do, although in other matters he follows the traditional form of the commentary quite precisely. The disclaimers that other scholars have brought forward as evidence of Thomas's distance from Aristotle are similar to disclaimers found in Scriptural commentaries save for those occasional corrections of Aristotle which underscore that the text is Thomas's own. In fact, if it were Thomas's intention to make disclaimers in the text, the ambiguity of the disclaimers would stand in stark contrast to the clarity exhibited throughout Thomas's corpus. Is it probable that Thomas so badly communicated his intentions about such a fundamental matter that they were not brought to light until the latter half of the twentieth century? Given the implausibility of evidence to the contrary, it seems much more likely that the commentary on the *Ethics* represents Thomas's own thought, even if not in its theological fullness, on ethical matters or issues in the philosophy of nature.

}335{

# Dignitatis Humanae, *Rights,*
*and Religious Liberty*
## Steven A. Long
## Ave Maria University

### Introduction

The problem of relating the putative natural "right" of religious liberty with the tradition of Catholic political thought has exercised many intelligences in the interval following promulgation of the document *Dignitatis Humanae* at the Second Vatican Council. This problem comprises two major issues, the first of which Maritain addressed, while the second he never expressly treated. The first issue is that of the nature or status of natural rights. The second can briefly be identified as the issue of the nature of the right of religious liberty articulated in *Dignitatis Humanae*. Any sufficient address to the second issue presupposes a high degree of clarity regarding the first.

### The Nature of Rights

Maritain articulates a philosophic account of natural rights.[1] Indeed, Maritain argues in *Man and the State* for a "secular ideology" embracing rights that can be defended from a variety of incompatible philosophic perspectives.[2] The first section of his fourth chapter concerning

---

1 Jacques Maritain, *Man and the State* (Chicago: University of Chicago Press, 1951), hereinafter cited as *MS* ; see, for instance, pp. 80–84.
2 See *MS*, p. 76, whose first section is titled "Men Mutually Opposed in Their Theoretical Conceptions Can Come to a Merely Practical Agreement Regarding A List of Human Rights."

}336{

## Dignitatis Humanae, *Rights, and Religious Liberty*

"The Rights of Man" in *Man and the State* is given the subtitle "Men Mutually Opposed In Their Theoretical Conceptions Can Come To a Merely Practical Agreement Regarding a List of Human Rights." Yet one may inquire whether theoretic divergence about rights does not render rights formulas equivocal.[3] Furthermore, the entire notion of natural "rights" suggests an independence from prudence and the common good that is only dubiously reconcilable with the Catholic Tradition. Speaking of this problem in his essay "Liberty in Catholic Tradition," Ralph McInerny argues that:

> Such efforts invite misunderstanding from friend and foe alike. Talk of human rights is of relatively recent origin and it developed in intellectual environments hostile to religious belief. The enshrinement of liberty was meant to be an act of defiance and we see all about us the problems arising from it. What cannot be overlooked is that modern talk of liberty and rights arose out of a view of the carrier of those rights which is both incompatible with Catholicism and wobbly on exclusively natural and philosophical grounds. The bearer of human rights is seen as an atom without a nature.[4]

Maritain endeavoured to justify such rights within a natural law footing, and to temper the notion of "inalienable" natural rights with prudence. Precisely where the Enlightenment-style view of rights erects them as absolute criteria universally demarcating a zone of liberty, Maritain insists that such "rights" must be limited both by the common good and by prudence. Maritain argues that this limitation bears not upon the possession of rights, but upon their exercise.[5] As he puts it:

3   See Ralph McInerny, *Art and Prudence* (Notre Dame: University of Notre Dame Press, 1988), p. 135.
4   Ralph McInerny, *Art and Prudence*, p. 100.
5   *MS*, p. 101: "Yet, even absolutely inalienable rights are liable to limitation, if not as to their possession, as least as to their exercise."

}337{

RESTORING NATURE

> If each of the human rights were by its nature absolutely unconditional and exclusive of any limitation, like a divine attribute, obviously any conflict between them would be irreconcilable. But who does not know in reality that these rights, being human, are, like everything human, subject to conditioning and limitation, at least, as we have seen, as far as their exercise is concerned.[6]

Maritain further argues that "the various rights ascribed to the human being limit each other,"[7] and that what creates "irreducible differences and antagonisms among men is the determination of the degree of such restriction"[8] combined with "the determination of the scale of values that governs the exercise and the concrete organization of these various rights."[9] This is so, Maritain argues, "Because here we are no longer dealing with the simple recognition of the diverse categories of human rights."[10]

Yet for rights to be socially significant they must be exercised, and the nature and limits of their exercise must be determined by prudence in the light of other just claims. Indeed, it is doubtful that a "right" insufficiently determinate to bind a moral agent is a genuine one. A list of putative rights whose exercise is understood in diametrically opposite ways by those called to respect these rights is practically disutile.

What can it mean to say that an inalienable "right to life" exists, but that its exercise may justly be "limited"? According to Maritain the criminal justly condemned to die "has deprived himself, let us not say of the right to live, but of the possibility of justly asserting this right."[11] Such a right is no longer serving as an absolute and universal criterion, but rather is a consideration

6   *MS*, p. 106.
7   *MS*, p. 106.
8   *MS*, p. 106.
9   *MS*, p. 106.
10  *MS*, p. 106.
11  *MS*, p. 102.

}338{

# Dignitatis Humanae, *Rights, and Religious Liberty*

subject both to higher principles and to prudence. In essence then it is the right itself and not merely its "exercise" which is limited according to Maritain's analysis. Otherwise the thief might plausibly claim that he respects one's property rights too greatly to permit one to exercise them. The inalienability of such a right takes on the aspect of a mere verbal fiction.

Despite what I have called Maritain's verbal fiction that rights are not limited in their possession but merely in their exercise, the net effect of this position is to contextualize rights in the light of prudence and the common good. Maritain criticizes rationalism for the compromise and squandering of rights, because it "led men to conceive them as rights in themselves divine, hence infinite, escaping every objective measure, denying every limitation imposed upon the claims of the ego."[12]

At the critical moment when rights vocabulary is often used to insulate issues from institutional prudence, social policy, and the whole hierarchy of ends, Maritain effectually holds that one may advert to other ends so as to limit putatively "inalienable" rights. This is to use the language of natural rights in accord with a wider view of the human good quite diverse from its normal ultra-individualist employment. In the end, such a protocol for the use of rights-talk suggests that "natural rights" are no more than just claims founded in basic *desiderata* of human nature. Such rights will no longer be presumed to demarcate spheres of liberty and duty with nearly geometric abstraction from the facts of social life, nor to be self-interpreting and axiologically independent from the essential hierarchy of natural ends.

## The Hierarchy of Ends and the Common Good

While I wish shortly to turn to the "right" to religious liberty asserted in *Dignitatis Humanae*, I would like first to clarify what I mean by "rights" as prudent claims founded in natural *desiderata*. If rights are founded in natural *desiderata*, some would suggest

12  *MS*, p. 84.

}339{

## RESTORING NATURE

that these *desiderata* be construed as incommensurable goods—as strictly incomparable. Yet truly incomparable ends can furnish no principled reasons objectively defining the relative importance and order of ends defining the nature of the good.

Further, if human ends are incomparable no objective order of subordination defines the common good. Thus principled definition of the common good—political philosophy in the Aristotelian sense—becomes impossible, for no end is deserving of greater objective honor than any other.[13] Consequently the common good is instrumentalized before individual appetite and inclination. It is this type of instrumentalization of the common good that I read Professor Finnis as propounding in *Natural Law and Natural Rights*.[14] But, to the contrary, knowledge of the objective hierarchy of ends is a necessary condition of sound moral reflection—a reflection whose sufficient condition requires the virtue of prudence. The commensuration of

13  In the Catholic philosophic tradition, especially in the works of St. Thomas Aquinas, "common goods" are ends which are by their nature more rationally diffusive and communicable to many, and which constitute the higher good of individuals—such goods are to be distinguished from individual or private goods, which are by their nature less communicable. Justice and friendship are ends higher than any material good, and indeed as I argue below, life as a good is defined as essentially ordered to these. And, as St. Thomas puts it, God is the extrinsic common good of the entire universe, or as he puts it in the *Summa contra gentiles*, 3a.17, "The particular good is directed to the common good as its end: for the being of the part is on account of the whole: wherefore the good of the nation is more godlike than the good of one man. Now the supreme good, namely God, is the common good, since the good of all things depends on him: and the good whereby each thing is good, is the particular good of that thing, and of those that depend thereon. Therefore all things are directed to one good, God to wit, as their end." See Charles De Koninck's classic work addressing St. Thomas's teaching regarding the common good, *On the Primacy of the Common Good: Against the Personalists*, ed. Ronald P. McArthur, trans. Sean Collins, *The Aquinas Review* 4, no. 1 (1997): 14–71.
14  See John Finnis, *Natural Law and Natural Rights* (Oxford: Clarendon Press, 1980), pp. 92, 156.

# Dignitatis Humanae, *Rights, and Religious Liberty*

ends here implied is neither quantitative, utilitarian, nor hedonic, but teleological. The *ratio boni*—the good life as such—is an ordered whole. As St. Thomas puts it:

> Man must, of necessity, desire all, whatsoever he desires, for the last end. This is evident for two reasons. First, because whatever man desires, he desires it under the aspect of good. And if he desire it, not as his perfect good, which is the last end, he must, of necessity, desire it as tending to the perfect good, because the beginning of anything is always ordained to its completion; as is clearly the case in effects both of nature and of art. Wherefore every beginning of perfection is ordained to complete perfection which is achieved through the last end. Secondly, because the last end stands in the same relation in moving the appetite, as the first mover in other movements. Now it is clear that secondary moving causes do not move save inasmuch as they are moved by the first mover. Therefore secondary objects of the appetite do not move the appetite, except as ordained to the first object of the appetite, which is the last end.[15]

Ends are such insofar as they are ordered to the ultimate end—all ends are "co-ordered" and "measured" in relation to the final end—and some are by nature more proximate to the end than are others. Knowledge of the order of ends is prior to right appetite, and prior to prudential consideration of the limits of circumstances and means. It follows that prudence needs to be informed both by principle—the natural ordering of ends—and by the unique and singular apprehension of circumstance.

Hence a limited natural right is a claim rooted in nature and perfected by prudence, limited both hierarchically and by circumstance. Lacking natural hierarchy among ends intelligible necessity neither adequately defines the good life nor guides

15  *S Th* I-II, q. 1, a. 6.

RESTORING NATURE

consideration of the singular, a guidance necessary to judge which putative right is morally pertinent to a situation. For example, life is desired *in* itself, but not merely *for* itself but for the other ends to which it is naturally ordered such as virtue or wisdom. This ordering of life to higher ends *defines* the moral good of life. It is such that if one may have life only at the cost of virtue or wisdom one rightly chooses to renounce earthly life—whereas one does not say that if one can have virtue or wisdom only by renouncing earthly life that one ought renounce virtue or wisdom. As Chesterton somewhere writes (I paraphrase from memory on the ground that my defect ought not impede so splendid a thought), the suicide dies because he loves life deficiently whereas the martyr loves it far too greatly to cling to a deficient imitation.

Similarly, friendship is constituted as an end in relation to the ends of virtue and wisdom. The demand that one act contrary to justice is not that of a friend, whereas a friend may insist upon acting for the sake of justice even though one will thereby be accidentally harmed. This is to say that what is *meant* by friendship must be defined in relation to the natural hierarchy of ends. Thus we can see that persevering in virtue, even when it accidentally hurts a friend, is not contrary to friendship; whereas treating friendship as superordinate to virtue is in fact contrary to the end of friendship.[16]

Hence the *ratio* under which a claim is a right derives both from the natural end to which it is appended and from the accurate apprehension of the circumstances rendering this end pertinent. Such rights are intelligible solely in terms of that wider conception of the good life whose centrality was thought by Maritain to produce "irreducible differences and antagonisms." On this analysis, contrary to Maritain's, it is the notion of rights denuded of wider context that generates incessant conflict. Divergence in understanding of the good leads to divergence in understanding of the reasonable exercise of one's "rights." Error regarding the nature of the good vitiates practical judgment. The doctrinal conclusion to be drawn—which

16  Obviously the reference here is to the higher sort of friendship, the friendship of virtue.

}342{

## Dignitatis Humanae, *Rights, and Religious Liberty*

is well-supported by historical experience—is that the language of human rights functions best within well-delineated religious and cultural consensus. Hence the unrelenting controversy stirred by "rights" in a time of widespread relativist contagion in the West.

### Does *Dignitatis Humanae* Propose Religious Liberty as an Absolute Right?

How do these considerations impinge upon the "right" of religious liberty delineated in *Dignitatis Humanae*? For purposes of argument, let us suppose that Maritain's distinction between the possession of a right and its exercise is a distinction whose whole force is the de-absolutization of rights claims. Does *Dignitatis Humanae* (DH) employ such a *limited* notion of human rights, or rather a universalist model?

It is of course well known that *DH* speaks of a "right to religious freedom":

> Freedom of this kind means that all men should be immune from coercion on the part of individuals, social groups and every human power so that, within due limits, nobody is forced to act against his convictions nor is anyone to be restrained from acting in accordance with his convictions in religious matters in private or in public, alone or in associations with others.[17]

*DH* founds this right "on the very dignity of the human person as known through the revealed word of God and by reason

---

17  *Dignitatis Humanae*, hereinafter cited as *DH*, 2: "Huiusmodi libertas in eo consistit, quod omnes homines debent immunes esse a coercitione ex parte sive singulorum sive coetuum socialium et cuiusvis potestatis humanae, et ita quidem ut in re religiosa neque aliquis cogatur ad agendum contra suam conscientiam neque impediatur, quominus iuxta suam conscientiam agat privatim et publice, vel solus vel aliis consociatus, intra debitos limites."

RESTORING NATURE

itself."[18] The document further insists that this right is founded not in the "subjective attitude of the individual" but rather "in his very nature,"[19] such that the immunity bequeathed by this right perseveres "even in those who do not live up to their obligation of seeking the truth and adhering to it."[20] Indeed, according to *DH* one may not interfere with the exercise of this right "as long as the just requirements of public order are preserved."[21]

Religious matters are said utterly to transcend the earthly and temporal order of things over which the political state presides,[22] such that if the state should presume to control or restrict religious activity "it must be said to have exceeded the limits of its power."[23] Freedom or immunity from coercion in religious matters is held to pertain to individuals both singly and "when they act in community."[24] Indeed, the right of religious liberty is said to include the right of religious groups "not to be prevented from freely demonstrating the special value of their teaching for the or-

18 *DH*, 2: "Insuper declarat ius ad libertatem religiosam esse revera fundatum in ipsa dignitate personae humanae, qualis et verbo Dei revelato et ipsa ratione cognoscitur."
19 *DH*, 2: "Non ergo in subiectiva personae dispositione, sed in ipsa eius natura ius ad libertatem religiosam fundatur."
20 *DH*, 2: "Quamobrem ius ad hanc immunitatem perseverat etiam in iis qui obligationi quaerendi veritatem eique adhaerendi non satisfaciunt."
21 *DH*, 2: "eiusque exercitum impediri nequit dummodo iustus ordo publicus servetur."
22 *DH*, 3: "Praeterea actus religiosi, quibus homines privatim et publice sese ad Deum ex animi sententia ordinant, natura sua terrestrem et temporalem rerum ordinem transcendunt."
23 *DH*, 3: "Postestas igitur civilis, cuius finis proprius est bonum commune temporale curare, religiosam quidem civium vitam agnoscere eique favere debet, sed limites suos excedere dicenda est, si actus religiosos dirigere vel impedire praesumat."
24 *DH*, 4: "Libertas seu immunitas a coercitione in re religiosa, quae singulis personis competit, etiam ipsis in communi agentibus agnoscenda est."

}344{

# Dignitatis Humanae, *Rights, and Religious Liberty*

ganization of society."[25] Religious freedom is described in the language of "inviolable rights."[26] It would seem at first blush that the language of *DH* is the language of rights purism.

But a second glance is justified. No sooner has the impressive litany of absolute religious immunities been called off the list, than one is informed that since the right to religious freedom is exercised in society "its use is subject to certain regulatory norms."[27] The nature and scope of these norms has been much discussed. But what must be noted is that the formal recognition of these regulatory norms is the recognition that there can be no absolute right of religious freedom. The two concepts—one of absolute right, the other of a "right" limited by a regulatory norm—are incompatible. And *DH* clearly teaches that the "right" to religious liberty is subject to regulatory norms.

Persons are limited in the exercise of the right of religious liberty by the moral obligation of "regard for the rights of others, their own duties to others and the common good of all."[28] Further, civil society is acknowledged to possess the authority to protect

25  *DH*, 4: "Praeterea ad libertatem religiosam spectat, quod communitates religiosae non prohibeantur libere ostendere singularem suae doctrinae virtutem in ordinanda societate ac tota vivificanda activitate humana." One is grateful that the Thugee cult members who took themselves to be worshipping the putative goddess Kali—by strangling passersby—have not been invited to further demonstrate the value of their teaching for society. Presumably, as shall be pointed out later, such instances do not meet the criteria of "religious" involved in *DH's* teaching.

26  *DH*, 6: "Inviolabilia hominis iura tueri ac promovere ad cuiusvis potestatis civilis officium essentialiter pertinet. Debet igitur potestas civilis per iustas leges et per alia media apta efficaciter sucipere tutelam libertatis religiosae omnium civium."

27  *DH*, 7: "Ius ad libertatem in re religiosa exercetur in societate humana, ideoque eius usus quibusdam normis moderantibus obnoxius est."

28  *DH*, 7: "in iuribus suis exercendis singuli homines soetusque sociales lege morali obligantur rationem habere et iurium aliorum et suorum erga alios officiorum et boni omnium communis."

RESTORING NATURE

itself against abuses perpetrated in the name of religion provided it does so in conformity with legal principles that accord with moral truth.[29] That the magisterium interprets this right as a limited one may be seen in the modulations with which it is articulated in *The Catechism of the Catholic Church*. As the catechism states:

> The right to religious liberty can of itself be neither unlimited nor limited only by a "public order" conceived in a positivist or naturalist manner. The "due limits" which are inherent in it must be determined for each social situation by political prudence, according to the requirements of the common good, and ratified by civil authority in accordance with "legal principles which are in conformity with the objective moral order."[30]

If the right of religious liberty is not unlimited, nor limited only by a lowest-common-denominator conception of "public order"; if the limits of this right are determined in each case by prudence and with a view to the common good, then clearly the right is not absolute. Yet it cannot be the case that the right of religious liberty is even a limited "right" if it is entirely an *ad hoc* effect of prudential extemporization (hence it must accord with the normative teleological order defining the common good). There must be something in the light of which one judges religious liberty a) to be a good, which b) is subordinate to higher goods, and c) subject to prudential judgment of circumstance. Granted that this "right" is subject to prudence in the light of the common good, what is it, and what can be said of its generic limits?

29  *DH*, 7: "Praterea cum societas civilis ius habet sese protegendi contra abusus qui haberi possint sub praetextu libertatis religiosae, praecipue ad potestatem civilem pertinet huiusmodi protectionem praestare; quod tamen fieri debet non modo arbitrario aut uniparti inque favendo, sed secundum normas iuridicas, ordini morali obiectivo conformes."

30  *Catechism of the Catholic Church* (New York: Catholic Book Publishing Co., 1994), Latin text Libreria Editrice Vaticana, Citta del Vaticano; #2109, p. 512.

}346{

*Dignitatis Humanae, Rights, and Religious Liberty*

## The Nature of the Putative Right to Religious Liberty

The tension internal to *DH* admittedly complicates matters. While at one moment expressly arguing that religious matters transcend the providence of the state,[31] it at the next invokes civil authority against abuses committed in the name of religion.[32] Nonetheless, in closing, I should like to suggest how one might best situate the putatively just claim to religious liberty.

First, the end of religious liberty is religious perfection. A genus is defined, not by accidental deprivation but by its *per se* ordering. And the purpose of religious liberty is the embrace of religious truth and virtue. The right of religious liberty as prudentially required by the good of religious perfection may perhaps be understood as a function of the relative independence and coherence of the natural order. For if the good of religious perfection entails rational and voluntary motion toward this end, then at the least we may see that coercion can neither supply nor substitute for such rational, voluntary motion.

Further, if by nature the internal forum of personal belief is manifested in external signs which are ontologically public even when they are designated as legally private—as, say, religious garb is ontologically public while for legal purposes (at least in the United States) it is private—then one cannot reasonably propose completely separating the internal and external *fora*. I.e., it

---

31  *DH*, 3: "Praeterea actus religiosi, qibus homines privatim et publice sese ad Deum ex animi sententia ordinant, natura sua terrestrem et temporalem rerum ordinem transcendunt." And then, again *DH*, 3: "Postestas igitur civilis, cuius finis proprius est bonum commune temporale curare, religiosam quidem civium vitam agnoscere eique favere debet, sed limites suos excedere dicenda est, si actus religiosos dirigere vel impedire praesumat."

32  *DH*, 7: "Praterea cum societas civilis ius habet sese protegendi contra abusus qui haberi possint sub praetextu libertatis religiosae, praecipue ad potestatem civilem pertinet huiusmodi protectionem praestare; quod tamen fieri debet non modo arbitrario aut uniparti inque favendo, sed secundum normas iuridicas, ordini morali obiectivo conformes."

is misleading to argue that one may believe whatsoever one wishes in the internal forum for so long as such belief does not enter into the tissue of public life, because belief by its nature implies ontologically public manifestation.

Suppression of such public manifestation of belief will essentially amount to suppression of the believer. Such suppression hence suggests an excommunication of the errant believer from civic amity and community. This does not mean that the burden of justification supporting such suppression cannot be met in any particular case: the "right" of religious freedom is limited by superior ends, and by prudence. But it suggests that there is a good that in prudential context may found a just claim to be left free of coercive penalty where religious error is concerned.

It pertains to human nature that belief be enfleshed and incarnated, and as the cockle is sown with the wheat, one cannot easily punish a person for error without reaching to the person's natural dynamism arching toward the good. Civic friendship will be jeopardized or rendered impossible with a party whose conscientious belief is judged so defective as not to merit further sustaining tolerance on the part of the community. It is concern for this dynamism toward the good itself that licenses recognition of a religious freedom extending *per accidens* to religious error and applying even to those "who do not live up to their obligation" of seeking the truth "as long as the just requirements of public order are observed."[33]

Notwithstanding the need to protect and encourage the natural dynamisms toward right religion, nothing in principle prevents penalties from being assessed when objective abuses proximately threaten the common good of a society with a positively developed religious consensus. Even latter-day American society, with its enormous *de facto* pluralism, penalized Bhagwan

---

33  *DH*, 2: "Quamobrem ius ad hanc immunitatem perseverat etiam in iis qui obligationi quaerendi veritatem eique adhaerendi non satisfaciunt; eiusque exercitium impediri nequit dummodo iustus ordo publicus servetur."

# Dignitatis Humanae, *Rights, and Religious Liberty*

Rajneesh, the drug and lust besotted religious *fakir* whose title is onamatapoetic with his reputation in the anglophone world. It may also be pointed out that the freedom identified by *DH* is described as a right "to honor the supreme Godhead."[34] Thus defined, religious liberty appears to be monotheistic and clearly falls within the genus of the morally good. Such an understanding clearly explains why it is that positivistic and naturalistic conceptions of public order are not considered to provide the sole limits for religious liberty by *The Catechism of the Catholic Church*.[35]

One cannot avoid the definitional issue whether religion is a good *per se* or *per accidens*. If the former, then one is bound to distinguish even seriously defective members of the genus from instances which are not members of the genus at all. The merely material presence of a religious element—as with a putative art work's submergence of a crucifix in urine—is in no way objectively ordered to the worship of the supreme Godhead and hence is not even a prospective beneficiary of the right to religious freedom according to *DH*.

If religion is not defined as falling within the genus of the good, then the definition of religion has been widened significantly beyond worship of the supreme Godhead, conceivably to include worship comprising the use of temple prostitutes or murder. This

---

34  *DH*, 4: "Numen supremum cultu publico honorent, membra sua in vita religiosa exercenda adiuvent et doctrina sustentent atque eas institutiones promoveant, in quibus membra cooperentur ad vitam propriam secundum sua principia religiosa ordinandam."

35  This definition in a sense permits whatever good or virtue may be found in practices which are not of themselves ordered to the worship of God—e.g., in practices found in monistic species of Buddhism or Hinduism—to be honored without either supposing a) that these practices are in themselves comparable to worship of God, or b) that the monistic explanatory matrix within which these practices often occur is necessarily correct or essential to whatever may be good in such practices. Of course, the issue of natural mystique in relation to God is an important one that cannot be treated here.

RESTORING NATURE

last does not appear to supply promising candidates for rights claims. Nor can religion be placed in every respect beyond the sphere of the state by virtue of its supernaturality, as those who composed *DH* discovered when composing its second half.[36] On at least one important analysis—that of St. Thomas Aquinas—religion is a natural virtue that falls under the heading of justice, a virtue in whose promotion the state has a legitimate interest.[37] As already has been seen, *DH* itself turns to the political state for protection against genuine harms to the common good veiled in the pretext of religion.[38]

The right application of *DH*—or of any normative social principle—can occur only with the aid of prudence. Hence the judgment that a particular sectarian movement is either antithetic or harmful to the virtue of religion and thereby harmful to the common good does not immediately establish the prudential case— or even the prudential possibility—of state sanction and regulation as medicinal remedies. But such a judgment does deny such a sect the preemptive protective shield of a "right" to promote the deformation of religion socially, i.e. it deprives it of a just claim to be free of any possible legal limit or sanction. Such limits or sanctions may not—owing to other prudential considerations—be forthcoming. But in the strict sense no "harm" has been done to one who is restrained from an act of idolatry, from sacrilege, or even from an improvident practice harmful to society.

36  *DH*, 7, see note 29 *supra* or note 34 *infra*.
37  *S Th* II-II, q. 81, a. 2, ad 3. See Leonine *S Th*: "AD TERTIUM DICEN-DUM quod de dictamine rationis naturalis est quod homo aliqua faciat ad reverentiam divinam."—"To the third it should be said that it belongs to the dictate of natural reason that man should do something through reverence for God."
38  *DH*, 7: "Praterea cum societas civilis ius habet sese protegendi contra abusus qui haberi possint sub praetextu libertatis religiosae, praecipue ad potestatem civilem pertinet huiusmodi protectionem praestare; quod tamen fieri debet non modo arbitrario aut uniparti inque favendo, sed secundum normas iuridicas, ordini morali oiectivo conformes."

}350{

# Dignitatis Humanae, *Rights, and Religious Liberty*

Such a view of religious freedom is not inconsistent with the desideratum that members of society come spontaneously through the development of conscience to the embrace of religious virtue. But as with other social goods—such as civility—that we wish to be spontaneously embraced, we may still place sanctions upon the more egregious public departures from or offenses against such goods without thereby preferring infantile conformism to adult self-possession. What is involved is not a claim that positive acts of religious worship should be coerced contrary to the consciences of those acted upon, but rather that wrongful acts and impious teachings do not escape all potential limitation by the state irrespective of the harm posed and the society concerned. *DH* does not constrain the state to be neutral toward religion as such, for indeed it is the state's lack of such neutrality which demands of it recognition for the *good* of genuinely religious liberty. Nor does the teaching of *DH* universally abandon any directive function with respect to religious virtue by the state (for harm done to the common good under the *pretext* of religion clearly requires identification of the authentic religious good, and the defense of religious liberty is important precisely in relation to this *good*). Rather, the teaching of *DH* constrains the political state to honor the natural dynamism toward religious virtue in the light of prudence and the common good.

## Conclusion

This paper has argued that Maritain's use of the notion of natural right is one prominent instance of natural right contextualized by natural law. If we embrace this way of treating rights we may well differ with certain of Maritain's judgments both prudential and theoretical, most especially with his view that the wider conception of the good life produces "irreducible differences and antagonisms." To the contrary, such differences and antagonisms seem ineluctable when rights language is deployed apart from antecedent religious and moral consensus. Nonetheless rights defined *not* along absolutist Enlightenment lines *ex more geometrico*, but rather in relation

}351{

RESTORING NATURE

to the natural hierarchy of ends and to prudence, are no longer the "utilitarian fictions" described by Alasdair MacIntyre[39] but positive points of departure for the salvage project to rescue justice from abstractionism.

*DH* affirms a limited right or just claim to religious freedom rooted in the natural teleological dynamic of man's ordering to God. This fashion of grounding a right to religious liberty must honor the natural hierarchy of ends as such. Thus understood, the right immunizes from all legal sanction neither antireligious actions nor even religious actions that are so deprived that they threaten grave harm to the common good. But because rational and volitional motion toward the end of the worship of God is a good, the degree to which persons move toward this end seems, *pari passu*, to imply a corollary just claim to be permitted so to move without unreasonable impediment. And since a defect in religious worship—as opposed to an act of idolatry or superstition—modifies what is fundamentally a just intention, such intention ought to be respected and protected.[40] While religious

39  Alasdair MacIntyre, *After Virtue* (Notre Dame: Notre Dame University Press, 1981), p. 70.
40  This tracks the theological distinction of material and formal heresy, and simply notes that inasmuch as the intention of persons in communities subject to religious error is generically good—the honor and worship of God—this intention needs to be regarded. It is also helpful here to contemplate the role and import of unified teleology in relation to the supernatural end to which it is actually further ordered in grace, as this is explained by St. Thomas in *S Th* I-II.89.6. In his response he writes: "Now the first thing that occurs to a man to think about then, is to deliberate about himself. And if he then direct himself to the due end, he will, by means of grace, receive the remission of original sin: whereas if he does not then direct himself to the due end, and as far as he is capable of discretion at that particular age, he will sin mortally, for through not doing that which is in his power to do." It is important to note that these words of Thomas refer—as does the article itself—to the unbaptized (the title of the article is "Whether venial sin can be in anyone with original sin alone?"). His teaching highlights the doctrine of unified teleology

}352{

## Dignitatis Humanae, *Rights, and Religious Liberty*

liberty is no more an absolute right—in the sense required by Enlightenment abstractionism—than is any other, nonetheless it is justly invoked in accord with the hierarchy of ends, the common good, and prudence. So limited and identified, the doctrine of *Dignitatis Humanae* does affirm a genuine good and right of religious liberty.[41]

in which the normative natural ordering of ends, as such, is understood as further ordered in grace to the beatific end which is now the *finis ultimus*, such that the unbaptized person, insofar as in his first moral act he directs himself to the due end as far as he is capable of discretion, receives the remission of original sin. I.e., insofar as the person accepts what God is giving as fully as possible, God honors this datum (the normative natural order of ends is itself now further ordered toward revelation and the life of grace and hence is not self-sufficient). Like a train line that once terminated in Boston but now goes on to New York, if one "stays on the line" one will be providentially moved to the further end, in relation to which one's will must be however more and more determinate as one moves closer (normally involving express response to the message of the Gospel, although only really culpable rejection of the end gains one's ejection from the train). Conversely, one cannot in one's action deliberately contemn the normative natural hierarchy of ends without violating the reign of grace.

41. This early work of mine pursued a natural law analysis of matters I have pursued further in the intervening years. I still would argue for principal elements of this early analysis. However, it seems clear that it needs fuller integration within the wider setting of supernatural revelation, and that its proper context is the traditional Catholic doctrine on the moral duty of men and societies toward the true religion and toward the one Church of Christ. The first section of Dignitatis Humanae affirms that religious liberty "leaves intact" this traditional doctrine—"Porro, quum libertas religiosa, quam homines in exsequendo officio Deum colendi exigunt, immunitatem a coercitione in societate civili respiciat, integram relinquit traditionalem doctrinam catholicam de morali hominum ac societatum officio erga veram religionem et unicam Christi Ecclesiam." The understanding of this traditional doctrine in the context of teleological realism and the transcendence of the common good remains part of a larger project of mine regarding the Church's social teaching.

# Is Usury a Sin Against Nature?
## Christopher Martin
## Center for Thomistic Studies
## University of St. Thomas (Texas)

I present this paper more or less as I gave it at the Thomistic Institute, after lunch on the last day. Professor McInerny was kind enough to say that he had allocated me this slot because he was confident that I would be sufficiently amusing to keep people attentive in these trying circumstances. Little has been added except footnoting. I apologize, therefore, for the frivolous and tasteless tone—it seemed right at the Institute, even if it is slightly unfitting in the proceedings.

The discussion of usury as a sin against nature may seem perverse, when I had the opportunity of discussing, for example, the reasons Aquinas alleges for why we don't assume that black swans are large, odd-shaped aquatic crows, or why the existence of mules proves the falsehood of the view that species are not fixed—a view which is, again perversely, attributed to Aquinas by some contemporary writers. But in any case perversity in the presentation is appropriate, since it's of perversity I want to speak. And I find that I cannot do this adequately without a certain clearness and crudeness in my language, for which I apologize.

There are several threads involved in this discussion, some of which I hope to follow a little without fully disentangling. One thread is the old thesis maintained by Noonan back in the 1960's, that Catholic doctrine on usury has changed, and that therefore Catholic doctrine on contraception might too.[1] The debate has

---

1    In *Contraception: a history of its treatment by the Catholic theologians and*

moved on since that time—I think mistakenly. I am as sure that Noonan's thesis is the best possible objection to the doctrine of *Humanae Vitae*, as I am sure that the objection fails. But this, I think, shows that the connection between usury and sins against the sixth commandment, though perhaps a contingent one, is not one I have invented.

To begin with, some simple conceptual clarifications and delimitations of the notion of "sin against nature" or "unnatural vice" in this context: every sin is against the natural law, and thus in some sense "anti-natural," but not all are "against nature" or "unnatural" in a strong sense. Simple (non-contraceptive) fornication is not in this sense "against nature," but sodomy is. When I say sodomy, I use the word in the old sense, in which it was used, for example, in the legislation of my own and other countries, meaning anal sexual penetration, typically of a male by a male. I am sorry to have to be so explicit, but the Scripture commentators are to blame. They have a tendency to tell us nowadays that the sin of the men of Sodom was that of inhospitableness. Now, I grant that you might call what they wanted to do to Lot's guests "inhospitable," in the same way that you might want to call wanton murder or maiming "unkind"—though exactly why you should want to do so is beyond me. And I grant that inhospitableness, in a primitive state of society, was pretty much as destructive of society as willful murder, or oppressing the widow and the orphan are, or as defrauding labourers of their wages is in a more developed society. It is certainly true that it is these sins, which are clearly destructive of society, which are stigmatized in Scripture, together with the sin of Sodom, as crying out to heaven for vengeance. But is it maintained that sodomy, as traditionally understood, is not destructive of society, and therefore cannot be what is thus stigmatized in *Genesis*? Such a view can certainly be held, and indeed is held, but I don't think we ought to accept it without argument merely because it's politically correct.

*canonists*, John T. Noonan, Cambridge: Belknap Press of Harvard University Press, 1965.

## RESTORING NATURE

Also, I think, the drama and urgency involved in the notion of "a sin crying out to heaven for vengeance" is rather lost if we interpret the sin of the men of Sodom as mere inhospitableness. Nowadays, in a more complex society, I expect to pay for my lodging, but my hosts may still be inhospitable. On my journey down from Mamre to Sodom I might stop one night at a bed and breakfast in Gomorrah, perhaps, be charged the full 30 shekels or whatever, and be lodged in the basement, next to the furnace, with dirty sheets on the bed, and no towel. Bad, enough, I grant you. But if the following night I stay at the Sodom Suites, and am charged 30 shekels for a pleasant quiet room with full facilities and clean linen, only to find that the bell-boy tries forcibly to join me in the shower, am I really likely to exclaim "You guys are as bad as the place down the road! The inhospitableness of both will call down God's vengeance!" I think not. So much for exegesis.

Crying out to heaven or not, it makes very clear sense to call sodomy unnatural or "against nature," and it was called such even by some pagans.[2] First, the words *physis* in Greek and *natura* in Latin are often used to mean in general what would nowadays be called sexuality, as right down into the modern period the word *kind* was used in English. This fact makes all sins against the sixth commandment to be, more strictly, offences against nature than, for example, is dishonesty in business dealings. But there is still a strong sense of "sin against nature" according to which sodomy is a sin against nature, while not all sins of unchastity are.

Sodomy goes against the natural teleology of sexuality, and while this fact is not, I would judge, enough on its own to prove that sodomy is bad, it does help to mark out clearly in precisely what way sodomy is being said to be bad. Not all sins against the sixth commandment (Catholic enumeration, by the way) are in this sense sins against nature, as I have already said. Straightforward

---

2   Aristotle (*Nicomachean Ethics*, VII, around 1148b29–30) appears to call homosexual activity a bestial vice. A bestial vice is *pro tanto* inhuman, and thus unnatural for human beings.

## Is Usury a Sin Against Nature?

non-contraceptive fornication is not: it is, as the song says, "doing what comes naturally" in wrong circumstances, with the wrong partner, at the wrong time, what have you. Masturbation, on the other hand, is as reasonably called "against nature" as sodomy is—and for the same reason, that the natural teleology of sexual activity is frustrated. What about a more thorny issue, that of contraceptive sex?

There was a strong tendency in the early part of the twentieth century for moral theologians to assimilate contraceptive sexual activity to unnatural acts, to masturbation or sodomy, or even to identify it with them. The expression frequently used to classify it, by e.g. Prümmer, "onanismus conjugalis" shows this.[3] This

---

3    D.M. Prümmer, O.P., *Manuale theologiae moralis*, Herder, Freiburg-im-Breisgau, 5th edition, 1961, Vol. III paras. 699 - 704. For a more serious authority, see Pius XI, *Casti Connubii*, 559–60, Dz 3716–7 (I allow myself the decent obscurity of a learned language): "At nulla profecto ratio, ne gravissima quidem, efficere potest, ut quod intrinsice est contra naturam, id cum natura congruens et honestum fiat. Cum autem actus conjugii suapte natura proli generandae sit destinatus, qui, in eo exercendo, naturali hac eum vi atque virtute de industria destituunt, contra naturam agunt et turpe quid atque intrinsice inhonestum operantur. Quare mirum non est, ipsas quoque s. Litteras testari, divinam Maiestatem summo prosequi odio hoc nefandum facinus illudque interdum morte punisse, ut memorat S. Augustinus (*de adulteriis conjugiis ad Pollentium*, Lib. II c.12): 'Illicite namque et turpiter etiam cum legitima uxore concubitur, ubi prolis conceptio devitatur. Quod faciebat Onan, filius Iudae, et occidit illum propter hoc Deus' . . . [Q]uemlibet matrimonii usum in quo exercendo, actus, de industria hominum, naturali sua vitae procreandae vi destitutatur Dei at naturae legem infringere." It is my thesis here that to treat contraception as a sin against nature in the strict sense, in a theoretical context, is a mistake, and that to hold that it is a mistake, since the time of *Humanae Vitae*, clearly expresses the mind of the Church. This does not mean that it was a mistake, even theoretically, for Prümmer or Pius XI to *assimilate* contraception, particularly in the forms in which it was chiefly practiced in that day, to unnatural vice. Moreover, what is theoretically an error may be a valid rhetorical, pastoral or catechetical move, as I shall

# RESTORING NATURE

assimilation was reasonable given the methods of contraception available up to the 1960's—principally *coitus interruptus* and various barriers. The use of these methods has a clear and strong physical analogy to unnatural vice—broadly speaking, that of emitting semen in the wrong place, where its natural teleology is or is meant to be frustrated.

This assimilation was reasonable, as I say. It had the unforeseen but problematic consequence that when pharmaceutical methods of contraception became available, it seemed to many an open question whether the older teaching was still valid, since the old objection—the physical similarity of contraception to unnatural vice, which justified condemning contraception as if it *were* unnatural vice—no longer held.

Well, I take it that *Humanae Vitae,* by reasserting the traditional teaching on other grounds, fairly authoritatively invalidated the idea that contraception is wrong because it is or resembles unnatural vice. A much-mocked authoritative decision from Rome in the late 1980's or early 1990's clarified this.[4] It was then stated that in order for a married couple to collect samples of semen for analysis (typically for help with sterility, though perhaps for other health reasons) it was legitimate for them to use a condom during intercourse, provided that the condom was so treated—typically, holed—so that it was useless for contraceptive purposes. This

argue below. Lastly, the fact that "natura" may mean "sexuality" implies that all sexual sins, though not offences against nature in the sense that sodomy is, are offences against nature in a stronger sense than other sins might be, though even they may be offences against the natural law. A recognition, even within the same period, that contraceptive sex, even when physically similar to unnatural vice, is not to be identified with it, is the 1916 decision of the Sacred Penitentiary cited at Dz 3634, according to which the passive co-operation of a woman in her husband"s "onanismus conjugalis" may not be a sin, while passive co-operation in the "usus Sodomitarum" very definitely is.

4    Unbelievably, the resources of this Catholic university, and those of the EWTN website seem insufficient to provide me with a reference for this. Perhaps I made it up.

}358{

*Is Usury a Sin Against Nature?*

decision, if correct—and it hasn't been seriously challenged, just laughed at—shows, I think, that the mind of the Church is now that what is wrong with the use of a condom is not the physical barrier it sets up, as such, not the creation of another, unfitting, unnatural place for the deposit of semen, but its use precisely as a contraceptive. (It is worth saying this clearly—though perhaps it is scarcely necessary in this forum—since I have the impression that many people outside the Church think the Catholic objection to condoms is in some way an objection to a magically evil object. I am not sure there are any intrinsically evil physical objects, magically so or otherwise, though I know that the case has been made with regard to abortifacients and nuclear weapons. Could one set aside considerations of propriety, scandal, co-operation in evil, etc., I can see no difficulty in using condoms as handy emergency water-containers, or as party decorations. Certainly I cannot conceive that there is any objection to the use of condoms in anal intercourse, homosexual or heterosexual, in order to provide some protection against fatal disease. What the couple are about in such a case is already frustrated of its natural teleology, and no number of condoms, worn how or where they like, is going to make this any worse or any better. In such a context considerations of propriety, scandal, co-operation in evil, etc. scarcely arise as serious objections, and in any case might be considered to be outweighed by the consideration of not callously or carelessly risking one's own or another's life. While I'm on the subject and being so outspoken, I think it worth while drawing attention to the astonishing silence in the media on the dangers of heterosexual anal intercourse, with regard to the spread of AIDS. I gather that quite a lot of men are very keen on this practice—and I know that the danger it involves to the female partner is hugely greater than that of ordinary intercourse. But no one seems to be willing to speak clearly enough to encourage women to protect themselves from this danger. Perhaps the media are afraid the practice might die out, which would be, in their view, a sad step back towards traditional ethics.)

The time has come, at last, to approach the other half of my

RESTORING NATURE

proposed topic: that of usury. It is a *topos* among those opposed to traditional Catholic teaching on usury that it is tied in with a view of usury as unnatural, in fact an unnatural vice. Calvin is the first author I have found who ridicules traditional teaching on these grounds,[5] but something of the same attitude is found in Smith.[6] It is true that the notion of the unnaturalness of usury

5   Calvin's view is discussed fully by Noonan in *The Scholastic analysis of usury*, Cambridge: Harvard University Press, 1957, pp. 365–7. I cannot forbear to quote a delightful piece of unconscious humour found on the Internet, an article from *Progressive Calvinism*, February, 1957; "John Calvin On Interest" by Frederick Nymeyer (Copyright 8 1957 Progressive Calvinism League).

   John Calvin (1509–1564) has about the best record of any ancient theologian on this question of interest and usury . . . . Calvin had a logical mind. He was quite the opposite of being naive. He apparently did not like absurdities or inconsistencies. He must have looked around and said to himself that the ancient interpretation of the Mosaic law on interest must be wrong. He must have asked himself what the logical situation was on interest, and then decided that he would interpret Scripture in a sensible sense.
   What did Calvin write on the subject of interest? Eugen von Bohm-Bawerk, the famous Austrian economist, in his classic *History And Critique Of Interest Theories* (the German title is *Kapital und Kapitalzins*) wrote: "At the outset [of a letter to Oecolampadius] he rejects the usual scriptural foundation for the prohibition, seeking to show that, of the writings customarily adduced in its support, some are to be differently interpreted, and some have lost their validity because of the entirely changed circumstances. The scriptural authority for the prohibition being thus disposed of, Calvin turns to the rational arguments usually given to support it. Its strongest argument, that of the barrenness of money (pecunia non parit pecuniam), he finds of "little weight." It is with money as it is with a house or a field."

   The use of bald assertion of modern views as self-evidently true, in the place of argument, is naively charming.
6   Smith is more subtle than Calvin or his modern friends, and seems

}360{

# Is Usury a Sin Against Nature?

is to be found in a number of traditional authors—indeed, even in Aristotle.[7] In its developed form, as for example in the *locus classicus* of *The Merchant of Venice*, we find it said that usury takes "a breed of barren metal."[8] The suggestion is that money is by nature sterile, but usury makes it breed, contrary to nature. The parallel to sodomy, which makes human sexuality—which is by nature fruitful—to be sterile, is clear. According to Noonan, we find the same idea of the unnaturalness of usury in Giles of Rome and Bernardine of Siena.[9] It is also to be found in the sixteenth century English author Thomas Wilson.[10] As late as the twentieth century, Dr Prümmer, whose attitude to taking interest on loans is fairly relaxed, in practice, nevertheless feels obliged to make a distinction between loans of a *res infructuosa in se* and loans of a

to confine himself to the suggestion that gaining money by lending money at interest is itself "natural." Adam Smith, *An inquiry into the nature and cause of the wealth of nations*, London, Dent: 1973, ed. D.D. Raphael (Everyman's Library), Book I, Chapter IX, "Of the Profits of Stock" and Book II, Chapter IV, "Of Stock Lent at Interest." Scanning through these chapters on interest with an eye to how often the words "natural" and "naturally" occur is enlightening.

7    *Politics*, I, 10, 1258b 5–10. "There are two sorts of wealth-getting, as I have said; one is a part of household management, the other is retail trade: the former necessary and honorable, while that which consists in exchange is justly censured; for it is unnatural, and a mode by which men gain from one another. The most hated sort, and with the greatest reason, is usury, which makes a gain out of money itself, and not from the natural object of it. For money was intended to be used in exchange, but not to increase at interest. And this term interest, which means the birth of money from money, is applied to the breeding of money because the offspring resembles the parent. Wherefore of all modes of getting wealth this is the most unnatural."

8    William Shakespeare, *The Merchant of Venice*, Act I scene 3, line 116.

9    *The Scholastic analysis of usury*, pp. 59, 71.

10   Thomas Wilson, *A Discourse upon usury*, ed. R.H. Tawney, New York: Kelley, 1965. Wilson goes so far in pushing the association between usury and unnatural vice as to say that "The Sodomites were wholly destroyed for their covetous and filthy lives," p. 221.

*res fructifera*—distinguishing further between a *res fructifera naturaliter* (e.g., a fruit-tree), a *res fructifera artificialiter* (something sold at a profit) and a *res fructifera civiliter* (a house let out to rent). Also he speaks in the same context of a "res sterilis."[11] This notion is surprisingly seldom found in papal and conciliar documents, but it is to be found nonetheless: the fifth Lateran Council (1515) defines usury as "quando videlicet ex usu rei quae non germinat, nullo labore, nullo sumptu nullove periculo lucrum fetusque conquiri studetur."[12] Benedict XIV, in *Vix pervenit* (1745), speaks of gain "ex ipsomet mutuo, quod *suapte natura* tantundem dumtaxat reddi postulat."[13] An earlier and less authoritative, but far better-known allusion to this idea is found in Dante, who takes the trouble to associate usurers with sodomites by putting them in the same burning desert region of the Inferno.[14]

It is easy to see the rhetorical, catechetical, or pastoral justification of this association of usury with sodomy. Sodomy, in many societies, is regarded as supremely shameful (even ancient Athenians of good class, much addicted to this practice, regarded passive sodomy as shameful[15]). To associate one's audience's darling vices with others which they would despise is good pulpit technique. Plato himself does it in the *Gorgias*, when he manages to associate Callicles's theory of the good with the shameful practice of scratching one's genitals and with the arts of the bathhouse boy, and political skill and success with the despised arts of the

11  Dominic M. Prümmer, O.P., *Manuale theologiae moralis*, Herder, Freiburg-im-Breisgau, 5th edition, 1961, Vol. II paras. 285, 288.
12  *Dz* 1442, Lat V sess. x, "Inter multiplices"
13  *Dz* 2546. Italics mine.
14  Dante Alighieri, *The Divine Comedy*, Inferno, canto XI, 49–54; 113–116; canto XV, XVI, XVII, esp. 44–74.
15  K.J. Dover, *Greek popular morality in the age of Plato and Aristotle*, Berkeley: University of California Press, 1974, pp. 215–6. Ref. A passing acquaintance with e.g. prison or navy folklore will show that passive sodomy is more shameful than active precisely because of its passivity—active sodomy can rejoice in the glory of aggression, perhaps.

}362{

*Is Usury a Sin Against Nature?*

pastry-cook and vintner.[16] What evokes most shame is not necessarily that which is in itself most bad—but the motivation, especially among the young, to avoid what is shameful, is far stronger than the motivation to avoid what is bad. I take this to be evident. Plato here, and constant preachers since, tried to instill shame by association, and thus provide a strong motivation for avoiding evil, a motivation which cool philosophical or theological reflection might not provide, even supposing the hearers to be capable of following it.[17] I have often thought that the popularity of the moral schema of the Seven Capital (or Deadly) Sins in the Middle Ages rests on its power to associate sins together, and to make people ashamed (by association) of what they were not previously ashamed of. Certainly the popularity of the Seven Deadly Sins cannot be explained by their conceptual or analytic power,

16  *Gorgias* 494e 1–5.
17  The matter is not trivial. Nineteenth century British visitors to the United States—Mrs Trollope, Captain Marryat, Dickens—were amazed and shocked to find that while people of both nations professed the same moral views, in the United States no shame seemed to be attached to any kind of financial sharp practice. The moral theory was present in the United States as in Britain, but since the motivation of shame was lacking, practice was (in this matter at least) far worse in America. Even in our own time I have come across a Catholic institution which refused to grant an employee his legitimate claims for expenses for his first year of employment, on the grounds that he had missed a deadline—a deadline which they had not bothered to communicate to him. I am not, I hope, indulging in a mere prejudice in favour of my own country if I say that this action would be unthinkable in a British institution. This is not because the administrators of a British institution would more likely to keep before their minds the fact that depriving labourers of their wages is a sin crying out to heaven for vengeance (like, indeed, the sin of Sodom). On the contrary, administrators of a Catholic institution anywhere are more likely to remember this than the administrators of any typical British secular institution. It is just that in the more snobbish and less egalitarian culture of Britain *shame* attaches to an employer who is seen to treat his servants shabbily, as it does not seem to in America.

}363{

RESTORING NATURE

since they seem to lack any justification in ethical theory, in Scripture, or even in moral psychology.

But though the association between usury and sodomy is rhetorically justified, there are difficulties in making the association theoretically strong. Some might cavil at the idea that money has a nature. After all, as Aristotle points out, the very etymology of the Greek word for money, *nomisma*, indicates that it is something that exists by law and convention (*nomos*).[18] The contrast between that which exists by nature and that which exists by convention is strong, at least from the period of the Sophists down. Money, then, is almost by definition something that exists by convention, not by nature.

I don't think we need make very heavy weather of this. If Aristotelian purists prefer not to speak of the "nature" of what is artificial, then let them speak of its "art" or "design" or "quasi-nature"—so long as they recognize that Aristotle himself, in explaining the principles of nature (the four causes), often uses artificial examples.[19] Let them also recognize that it is hard to explain or illustrate final causes in nature without using artificial examples or without drawing parallels, as Aristotle does, between what exists by nature and what exists by art. It is also surely relevant that when Kripke sought, in 1970, to re-introduce Aristotelian concepts of nature and essence into contemporary English-speaking philosophical discourse, he started with the essence or nature of the table and reading-desk in front of him, before going on to the essences of natural objects such as alligators, politicians, and lumps of gold.

Whether or not we agree to speak of "the nature of artifacts" (as I intend to), we certainly have to admit that artifacts and artificial kinds, perhaps even more clearly than many natural kinds, have clear sets of necessary characteristics associated with them,

18 *Nicomachean Ethics*, V, 5 1133a 30–31: "This is why it has the name 'money' (*nomisma*)—because it exists not by nature but by law (*nomos*) and it is in our power to change it and make it useless."
19 *Metaphysics* 1042b 10–15.

}364{

*Is Usury a Sin Against Nature?*

necessary characteristics which include their teleology. It is thus not absurd to talk of the nature of money, and of the fulfillment or frustration of its natural teleology. The parallel between usury and sodomy is not undermined by the artificiality of money.

What is undermined—and this is not trivial—is Noonan's thesis. Since the nature of money is an artificial nature, it depends on human will, and on the human society in which it finds its function, role and teleology. There is no doubt that society, while remaining a society—that is, not losing any of the characteristics of a society that a society has by nature—can change, perhaps quite radically. There is no oddness, then, in supposing that the nature of money within a society may change, or indeed cease to exist, without radically altering its own nature or even that of the society in which it exists, in other respects. Thus even if lending at interest was seen by medieval thinkers as contrary to the nature of money in the then state of society, there is nothing absurd in the view that in the changed society of our day, money has so changed that the lending of money at interest does not go against its nature, and might not even be wrong at all, except in special circumstances. (I do not myself affirm this, but I think that it is the view of most non-specialist Catholic moral theologians of today. Noonan himself, I guess, thinks that this is so.)

What Noonan or the supporters of his thesis now need to show is that the nature and teleology of human sexuality, and its function in society, have or may have undergone similar changes, as society has changed. This has not been made out. It seems obvious that artificial natures, if I am to be permitted the phrase, whose very existence, let alone characteristics, depend on human will, may change quite radically. It is not so obvious that human sexuality, whose existence and characteristics are not in the same way subject to the human will, can change radically, or indeed at all, in more than accidental relations.

I don't mean by this to deny what I have just maintained, that there are indeed artificial natures. What is conventional—such as the institution of money, or of a natural language—is not *ipso facto* necessarily arbitrary. Natural languages are quite as conventional as money is, but they are clearly not arbitrary—no language has a word that can mean equally and in all contexts both "Yes" and "No," for example. But it would be as foolish to deny that the (conventional) nature of a natural language can change, as to maintain that all features of a natural language are purely arbitrary. An artificial or conventional nature is a reality, but it need not be a wholly static reality. Given what St. Thomas says about mules (I knew I'd be able to get it in somewhere), it would appear that he thinks that even natural kinds are not static—how much the less need conventional or artificial kinds be so! But this does not mean that artificial or conventional kinds are merely arbitrary or fictional.

St. Thomas, however (now that we have returned to him), though speaking of the unnaturalness of usury, has no truck with the preacher's attempt to equate it or assimilate it to sodomy. For him, usury is straightforwardly a sin against the seventh commandment (Catholic enumeration): a species of theft—or perhaps a sin against the eighth commandment, a sin against honesty or truthfulness. Either way, it is irreducibly a sin against justice, not against nature. (Incidentally, it's not a sin against charity either, according to St. Thomas, except in so far as a sin against justice is in some way *a fortiori* a sin against charity. That usury was a sin against charity seems to have been the predominant view among the Church fathers and among Catholic writers in the modern period, up to the time of the Thomist revival.)

Usury, for St. Thomas, is not only a sin against justice: it belongs in the same genus as other well-known sins against justice, and bears a strong resemblance to them. Odd Langholm, in his magisterial work on usury in the Middle Ages,[20] remarks how medieval thinkers in general (in scientific theological work, if not always in preaching and exhortation) assimilate the vice of usury to other familiar frauds in buying and selling. This is particularly clear in St. Thomas.

20  See, for example, his *The Aristotelian analysis of usury*, Oxford: O.U.P., 1985.

## Is Usury a Sin Against Nature?

What is interesting in St. Thomas is that we can see him, in different passages, trying out parallels with other forms of fraud in buying and selling, for size, as it were, against usury, rejecting several, and only at length coming to his mature doctrine, which sets usury firmly in its place as a species of selling what does not exist.

For example, in *Commentary on the Sentences* III, 37, 1, 6, we find him wondering whether usury is not a kind of tampering with the measure. A man lends 100 crowns and demands 110 back: is this not similar to the man who sells with a fourteen-ounce pound weight, and buys with an eighteen ounce pound? Similar indeed; very like; close, St. Thomas judges, but no cigar.[21]

In *Summa theologiae* II q.77 a.1 and in *De Malo* q. 13 a.4 (and perhaps in *De Emptione et Venditione ad Tempus*) St. Thomas toys with idea of assimilating usury to simony: as the simoniac sells the power of the sacrament, which is not his own, but Christ's, so the usurer sells time, which is not his own, but God's.[22] I don't know how common simony is these days, but this kind of sin is still proverbially at least current today for anyone who has ever been told of the purchase of the Brooklyn Bridge.

Again, in *Summa theologiae* II-II q. 78 a.1 St. Thomas first suggests the idea that usury sells the same object twice over (another unspectacular and quite common form of fraud in buying and selling) before he decides on his mature answer. St. Thomas's mature answer, which he gives at that place and sticks to elsewhere, is that the usurer sells (or at least exacts a price for) the use of

---

21  "Another reason can be given. Every other kind of thing has a usefulness of its own. Money doesn't: it is the measure of the usefulness of other things. This is clear from what the Philosopher says in the fifth book of the *Ethics*. For this reason the use of money—its measuring of usefulness—does not derive from itself but from the things it measures, according to the difference of the one who changes money for things. Hence to take more money in exchange for less seems to be using one measure in getting and another in giving out. This is obviously unfair."

22  Cf. *Summa theologiae* II-II q.100, on simony.

RESTORING NATURE

money as contrasted with the consumption of money. But the use of money is identical with its consumption: therefore the usurer is exacting a price for, or "selling" in a loose sense, something that does not exist at all. This is not selling the Brooklyn Bridge, which does after all exist, and has pretty much the characteristics desired by the purchaser, and merely does not belong to the purported seller. This is selling a silver mine, a gold brick, or (excuse the phrase) land lots in Texas.

This is a world away from the assimilation of what usurers do to what goes on in smoky backrooms and bathhouses in Greenwich Village or Montrose. Usury is as bad as, and no more shameful than, selling a gold brick. Pulpit rhetoric—trying to talk sinners into shame by association—has no place in St. Thomas's account of usury. This is not to say that pulpit rhetoric is ineffective or dishonest: but understanding can only be helped by seeing usury as a simple piece of financial fraud, akin to selling a silver mine, rather than as in some way akin to sodomy, just as the Catholic understanding of sexuality took a step forward when it was seen that the badness of contraceptive sex lay in its being contraceptive as such, not in its supposed or real similarities to the sins of Sodom or of Onan.

# Distinguer pour Unir:
# Putnam vs. Aquinas on the Unity of Nature
## John O'Callaghan
## University of Portland

In this paper I argue against a recent objection that Hilary Putnam directs at the Aristotelian account of essential or substantial form. The objection is that while the Aristotelian assumes a single essential form for any particular natural kind of thing, the plurality of contemporary sciences shows that there are many essences for any such natural kind. The setting for this objection comes from within Putnam's worries about how language or the mind "hooks up with the world." He had long argued that no system of representations, mental or linguistic, could have an intrinsic or built-in relationship to the world. To that extent I will call his former objections episte-mological, insofar as they were directed at the intentional features of representation in various different accounts. More recently he has granted that the Aristotelian notion of form, and its application to the identity of concepts may avoid those objections. He has in mind the Thomistic-Aristotelian thesis that the mind's concepts are formally identical to and determined by the objects in the world that fall under those concepts, the Concept Identity Thesis. He confines himself to the discussion of essential concepts and substantial form. Consequently, the types of discourse he focuses upon are the scientific discourses within which the Aristotelian presumably thinks the essences of natural kinds are revealed.

In scientific discourse when we use a term like 'dog', it succeeds in referring to dogs because the concept we have in mind is in some fashion formally identical to dogs. But Putnam objects that the various different sciences of today reveal a multitude of essences for

}369{

any particular natural kind. The application to the Aristotelian account of representation is straightforward. The advance of the sciences has shown us that there are too many substantial forms in any particular kind of thing to provide the unity of conceptual identity required by the Aristotelian account. To put it plainly, Putnam denies, or at least doubts that "substances have a unique essence."[1]

Notice the genre of Putnam's objection. It is a somewhat familiar story about the dependence of Aristotle's metaphysics upon the rudimentary state of the natural sciences known to the Greeks. Insofar as modern science has advanced and even replaced the various Aristotelian sciences, it has at the same time shown Aristotelian metaphysics to be outdated and implausible. And so Putnam has himself written of his desire to revive Aristotelian commonsense about the world around us, without the "excesses" and "fantasies" of Aristotelian metaphysics.[2]

I will proceed by briefly describing Putnam's argument. My subsequent approach to it will have three parts. First I will point out certain of its presuppositions. Second, I will provide what I take to be my own good but ultimately inadequate response to the argument. Third, I will provide what I take to be a good and adequate response taken directly from St. Thomas.

## Putnam's Argument for the Multiplicity of Substantial Forms

The greatest difficulty facing someone who wishes to hold an Aristotelian view is that the central intuition behind that view, that is, the intuition that a natural kind *has* a single determinate form (or "nature" or "essence") has become problematical.[3]

1   "Aristotle After Wittgenstein," in *Words and Life*. Hilary Putnam. Ed. James Conant. Cambridge: Harvard University Press, 1995. p. 74.
2   Cf. Putnam's Dewey Lectures in *The Threefold Cord: Mind, Body, and World*. New York: Columbia University Press, 2000.
3   "Aristotle After Wittgenstein," p. 74.

}370{

*Distinguer pour Unir: Putnam vs. Aquinas on the Unity of Nature*

In order to help us understand how this Aristotelian intuition has become problematical, Putnam puts forward his objection to the multiplicity of essential forms with the example of his dog Shlomit. Take the several theoretical sciences that may investigate the nature or essence of dogs, for example, evolutionary theory, genetic theory, and anatomy.[4] Each of these discourses will claim to be telling us what is "essential" to being a dog. The evolutionary biologist will say that it consists in a certain history of descent shared by the members of a certain population that is the natural kind, and will discount genetic structure and morphology. The geneticist will say that it consists of a certain genetic structure shared by the members of the set of dogs constitutive of the natural kind, and will discount evolutionary descent and morphology. And the anatomist will say that it consists of a certain morphological structure shared by those dogs, and discount genes and evolutionary descent. *Prima facie*, the conceptual contents of these essential descriptions are not identical one to another. To the extent that any particular science, anatomy for instance, does not contain within itself the principles of the other science, genetics for instance, it cannot include genetic information within its essential description. So what counts for it as "essential" excludes elements included by other sciences. One description involves historical events, another genes, and the third bones and the like. But each is supposed in its content to be identical to a substantial form in the world. Consequently, as we have three non-identical essential descriptions of the same natural kind, the natural kind must have at least three types of essence determined by multiple substantial forms, the evolutionary, the genetic, and the morphological. Thus, there is no unique essence to determine the identity of the concept *dog*, and subsequently to determine the identity of the term 'dog'. Putnam's Shlomit is the cousin (on the evolutionary scale!) of Quine's unfortunate cycling mathematician who is and is not essentially bipedal.

4    Putnam does not consider the anatomist. But what he says would apply *mutatis mutandis*. I am adding the anatomist to set up a certain parallel in the discussion of Aquinas.

# Restoring Nature

Putnam simply provides this example, but I think it fair and useful to construe his general argument as follows:

1) Sciences give essential descriptions of X's (where X refers to a natural kind, e.g. dogs).
2) The essential descriptions of X's given by the different sciences are manifestly diverse.
3) Therefore, the essential forms that constitute the identity of the descriptions are diverse.
4) But the essential forms that constitute the identity of the descriptions are identical to essential forms of *res extra animam*, according to the Thomistic-Aristotelian.
5) But then from 3) and 4) the essential forms *in res extra animam* must be diverse since identical to diverse essential forms *in anima*.
6) Therefore, X's, insofar as they fall under different sciences do not have unique essences.
7) Therefore, the uniqueness of the natural kind concept X employed in the different scientific descriptions of X's is not determined by a unique essence of X.
8) Therefore the Thomistic-Aristotelian view is false, since the Thomistic-Aristotelian assumes the contradictory opposite of 7).

Putnam's objection is not unrelated to his problems with different conceptual schemes and what he calls *Metaphysical Realism*. Putnam objects to *Metaphysical Realists* that there are no essences "out there" awaiting discovery; instead the conceptual scheme of a particular science determines for itself what counts as essential for it. To be fair, Putnam thinks that once the science has made unto itself an essence in view of some interest of the scientist, everything else falls into place; it's not just anything goes.[5] Still, the distinct conceptual schemes of the sciences determine distinct essences. However, the objection is supposed to be directed at the Aristotelian, and so cannot simply assume this "conceptual

5    Cf. "Aristotle After Wittgenstein," p. 78.

}372{

*Distinguer pour Unir: Putnam vs. Aquinas on the Unity of Nature*

scheme" analysis. Consequently the task for the Thomistic-Aristotelian in replying to Putnam's argument is to argue that the *prima facie* diversity of intensional form does not entail a diversity of extensional form, even as he holds on to the *formal identity thesis*.

## The Presuppositions

I want to begin by considering three presuppositions of Putnams' argument, the first two of which I think are fairly straightforward and almost obvious. First, he presupposes that natural kind terms like 'dog' are used univocally across the diverse sciences that he mentions, or, in other words, that the concept *dog* remains the same. His objection attempts to drive a wedge between two terms, the subject term and the predicate term of an essential description—in our example, 'dog' and whatever for a particular science would fill in the predicate space of a definitional statement like 'a dog is essentially _____'. While the subject term retains a certain conceptual identity across the sciences, the predicate term does not.

This identity of subject term is presupposed, since otherwise Putnam's argument is a straightforward fallacy of equivocation. Change the example. Jill the geneticist says, "a bat is essentially an animal of such and such genetic structure," while Jack the manager says, "a bat is essentially a wooden structure of such and such geometric structure." The essential descriptions are *prima facie* diverse. But why are none of us troubled in the least by the incipient "argument" between them? Simply because 'bat' does not have sufficient conceptual identity in the two different discourses. Thus, Putnam is not arguing that substance terms do not have identity conditions, but rather that substantial forms do not constitute those identity conditions.

This presupposition remains, whether one is an Aristotelian or a "conceptual schemer." Even if Putnam is right that the conceptual schemes of the different sciences determine for themselves what counts as an essential description, he must recognize

}373{

the larger discourses within which the sciences take place, and which predetermine the conceptual unity of many of the terms used within the sub-discourses. Indeed Putnam is committed to this unity because he thinks the objection he is posing to the Aristotelian is not an internal Aristotelian objection, but an external one. The plurality of essences position is supposed to be a coalescing consensus coming from *outside* of Aristotelianism as a fundamental objection to it; Aristotelian natural science is outmoded, and so consequently is Aristotelian metaphysics. He writes that

> the greatest difficulty facing someone who wishes to hold an Aristotelian view is that the central intuition behind that view, that is, the intuition that a natural kind has a *single* determinate form (or "nature" or "essence") has become problematical.[6]

There can be no such problem, however, if the conceptual identity conditions of the natural kind *term* is itself conceptually determined within each separate area of discourse. So the question raised by this first presupposition is what the larger discourse is within which these scientists are arguing, and how it determines the conceptual identity of the terms they take for granted as common.

This brings me to the second presupposition of Putnam's argument, namely, that there are natural kinds. Putnam is not an idealist about things in the world and their features. He writes "not just anything can be called the nature of dogs. On the other hand, it does seem that more than *one thing* can be called knowing the nature of dogs." What he means by this is that objects in the world have their properties or features. The various combinatorial possibilities of the features will determine different sets within which an object falls. For Putnam, the entire set of actual and possible combinations of features is Wittgenstein's Tractarian form, and it is the "metaphysical" form that he believes was presupposed by

6    "Aristotle After Wittgenstein," p. 74.

*Distinguer pour Unir: Putnam vs. Aquinas on the Unity of Nature*

his earlier objections to representationalism.[7] His point would be that no particular subset of this set is in itself privileged over another, as far as we can tell. Thus we are thrown back upon our interests in pursuing various sciences, and how we focus upon different features as "essential." Once a science has determined for itself what it will focus in upon, from then on the results it achieves are in effect determined by those features. Consequently, Putnam believes that any claim about the "essence" of some kind of being is interest dependent. In a pragmatic vein, and quoting James, he writes "the trail of the human serpent is over all."

Still he must presuppose that the natural kind with its features is "out there." What is to be counted as essential is interest dependent, but the result of the counting is foreordained by the natural kind and its features once the interest is in place. By analogy, think of the candy store. I am interested in how many bags of M&M peanuts I can purchase there, while you are interested in the Bit O' Honey. Once we've sorted out what we are interested in, there will be right and wrong answers to the questions, how much does a pound bag of M&M peanuts cost, and do they have enough on hand to meet my needs? If it's the case that the candy store doesn't happen to sell Bun Bars, then if that is your interest, you're out of luck. Nothing you can do or say will make true the statement that Bun Bars are an essential feature of this candy store, just as nothing you can do or say will make true the statement that it is essential to Labrador retrievers that they breathe through gills. But the crucial thing for Putnam with regard to those features the candy store or the natural kind does have is that there is no way to find order among the features, no way of arranging or ordering them that is not simply a reflection of our interests in doing so. Thus the metaphysical key to Putnam's argument consists in driving a wedge between the natural kind and its essence(s), much as at the semantic level the key was to drive a wedge between the subject and predicate in a definition. But driving this wedge is not so easy, as one of his examples unwittingly shows. He asks us to consider the

7   See "Aristotle after Wittgenstein," p. 63.

}375{

# RESTORING NATURE

possibility of a "synthetic dog," that is, a dog, not cloned, but synthesized from the appropriate organic chemicals to have, from the point of view of the genetic biologist, the essential DNA. The geneticist is wont to count the being as a member of the natural kind. But Putnam argues that the "evolutionary biologists would not regard a 'synthetic' dog as a dog at all. From their point of view, such a thing would simply be an artifact of no interest,"[8] since it does not have the history of descent necessary or essential to the population that makes up the natural kind. Conversely, if a geneticist finds in a population of common descent an individual with a significantly different genetic structure, he will exclude it from the natural kind.

So even for Putnam kind membership seems upon reflection to depend upon what the scientists take to be essential to the natural kind, and he cannot so easily drive this wedge between natural kinds and essences. If the identity of natural kinds is determined solely by extension, upon reflection it appears that short of a larger setting within which the sciences operate, the diverse sciences that Putnam has in mind cannot assume a single natural kind about which they can argue. Here Putnam's Lockean inheritance of real and nominal essences comes to the fore. "We are making unto ourselves the species of things." An essence for Putnam is not an intrinsic principle of being in an object that is studied by the sciences. It is rather an element of discourse. It is part of a classificatory scheme of abstract properties chosen by an interested party. The nominal essence thus chosen constructs the natural kind or species.

If Jack and Jill aren't talking about the *same kind of thing* when they give their respective accounts of the essence(s) of bats, Putnam's objection is once again based upon a straightforward fallacy of equivocation on 'bats'. The Aristotelian *expects* to find a plurality of essences among a plurality of *different kinds of things*. The trouble, if there is one, is with a plurality of essences for *one kind of thing*. So, we are entitled to ask Putnam, if it is neither the members, nor

8    "Aristotle After Wittgenstein," p. 77.

}376{

*Distinguer pour Unir: Putnam vs. Aquinas on the Unity of Nature*

a putative single essence that determines the identity of the natural kind presupposed in his argument, just what does?

The final, and perhaps most difficult presupposition to notice is Putnam's procedure of reading off the identity of the forms involved from the descriptions. We are supposed to be able to tell from simple inspection of the descriptions alone that they are diverse, and that the forms involved, from the Aristotelian point of view, must therefore be diverse. We have difficulty in knowing the natural kind and its features. But our descriptive resources are clear and distinct to us. This prior clarity of our linguistic resources is implicit in Putnam's thesis that it is our interests that are determining what counts as essential for us; I surely know what I want, even if I can't find it. And it is explicit in the transition from step (2) to step (3) in Putnam's argument. Putnam then makes the transition from step (3) to step (4), from the more and better known to the less, when he argues from the diversity of the descriptions to the diversity of things described.

Continuing to interpret present day Aristotelians as trying answer the question how our language "hooks up with the world," Putnam explicitly attributes this method to the Aristotelian. He writes:

> One might say (if one is a latter-day Aristotelian who has taken account of the linguistic turn), that, in a certain sense, the metaphysical form of our descriptions needs to be isomorphic to the metaphysical form of the object represented, for reference to succeed .... Speaking phenomenologically, we see propositions as imposing a certain kind of order on the world . . . . The metaphysical structure that our propositions project onto the world is what the world would copy in the best case, the case of the most successful and most complete reference, or so my "latter-day Aristotelian" would think.[9]

9    "Aristotle After Wittgenstein," p. 72.

Notice the emphasis upon the logical notion of "isomorphism." Isomorphism in set theory requires that a function mapping one set to another be *one to one and onto*, that is, that any element of the range is the value of only one element of the domain, and that there be no element of the range that is not the value of the mapping function. The set theoretic structure of the domain and all its internal logical relations are perfectly mirrored in the range, and vice versa. So the use of isomorphism in this context is telling. But even isomorphism does not seem to be enough to capture the portrait of the neo-Aristotelian that Putnam would like to paint.

> [T]he strongest line for the neo-Aristotelian to take is to say that what enables reference to take place is a matching (mere isomorphism doesn't seem to be enough), some kind of a matching between the metaphysical structure our propositions project onto the objects and the metaphysical structure those objects actually have.[10]

In Putnam's portrait of the Aristotelian who has taken the linguistic turn, we are to think of the elements of sentences, subjects and predicates, as the domain, the world as the range, and formal identity as the mapping function. For his Aristotelian, the reference of our words is most successful and the truth of our statements guaranteed when they find their exact mirror image in reality. And if there is logical complexity in the description it must find its exact isomorphic or mirror image in some complexity in the thing described. The Aristotelian proposes to read a metaphysical structure off of his propositions and project it onto a world where it finds its perfect match.

But in this movement Putnam displays his Cartesian inheritance. To be fair, in his work he has wanted to move us past the sort of skeptical questions bequeathed to us by modern epistemology. Advocates of the linguistic turn in philosophy, Putnam included, objected to the instrospective, and infallible, but

10  Ibid., p. 73.

*Distinguer pour Unir: Putnam vs. Aquinas on the Unity of Nature*

particularly the private character of the Cartesian picture of the mind. They countered it with the public character of language. However, it can be argued that the linguistic turn was for many, if not all, simply a projection of the Cartesian mind into a public and social space.[11] The social mind is as introspectively clear and infallible to *us*, the linguistic community, as Descartes' mind was to him, the private individual. This is why Putnam's discussion of Aristotelianism is animated by the typically Cartesian question, *mutatis mutandis*, how it is that language hooks up with the world. The question presupposes for its intelligibility an independent purchase upon language apart from the world, just as Descartes' question about the relationship of his ideas to the world required an independent purchase on his ideas provided to him by his methodical doubt, and the criteria of clarity and distinctness for determining which ideas were true to the world.[12]

Still, both Putnam's description of the neo-Aristotelian and his objection show how difficult it is to escape the Cartesian. In both, we begin with an idea (Descartes) or a word (Putnam) and try to discern the world through it. While Putnam wishes to declare his own independence from Descartes, he is unwilling to read the neo-Aristotelian in any fashion other than as just another modern philosopher trying to answer Descartes' question with Aristotelian tools—how does the neo-Aristotelian projection form

---

11  Cf. Richard Rorty's Introductions, particularly the second, to the various editions of *The Linguistic Turn*. Chicago: The University of Chicago Press, 1992. See as well, *Why Does Language Matter to Philosophy?* Ian Hacking. Cambridge: Cambridge University Press, 1975.

12  Anyone familiar with Putnam's Brain in the Vat thought experiment should be able to recognize the parallel between the role of the mad scientist and Descartes' evil demon. In our discussion Putnam's scientist, determining for himself the essences of things, is playing the role of Descartes' God. Again it is only fair to point out that by pragmatically distancing us from "essences," Putnam is trying to move us away from the scientism he thinks is so destructive of our culture.

}379{

RESTORING NATURE

word or idea to world succeed where all else have failed? But if we look closely at the form of Putnam's objection it is clear that he has not escaped the Cartesian picture as much as he would like. Just consider how similar his argument for the diversity of essences is to Descartes' argument for the essential diversity of mind and body. Descartes argued from the diversity of his ideas of *res cogitans* and *res extensa* to their diversity *in res*; Putnam argues from the diversity of essential descriptions provided by the sciences to the diversity of the things described. In what follows, I will show that on the contrary the Thomistic-Aristotelian is not proceeding from language to world, but from world to language.

## A Good but Inadequate Response

My response to Putnam will proceed in reverse order through these presuppositions. Let me begin with my good but inadequate response. The movement from the diversity of our scientific descriptions to a diversity of things described is a straightforward fallacy. It is not the fallacy of equivocation I have been pointing at thus far. Rather it is the intension/extension fallacy. Consider these two descriptive phrases, 'the morning star' and the 'evening star'. One describes an astronomical body that is typically observed in certain predictable locations in the morning sky. The other describes an astronomical body that is typically observed in certain predictable locations in the evening sky. Notice also that the descriptions are *prima facie* diverse. Does this diversity of descriptions entail that the evening star is not the morning star? No. In fact, the evening star is the same astronomical body as the morning star, namely, the planet Venus. The fallacy involved in arguing otherwise moves from a diversity of intensional content in descriptions to a diversity of extension.

Now Putnam could claim that the example is inappropriate because the terms, and the subsequent judgment, come from within the same conceptual scheme, Astronomy, where his example concerning dogs involves multiple conceptual schemes, Evolutionary Theory, Genetics, and Anatomy. But he has no such easy out. As

}380{

*Distinguer pour Unir: Putnam vs. Aquinas on the Unity of Nature*

I've argued, Putnam's objection requires that the diverse descriptions cannot be understood to be coming from entirely diverse conceptual schemes; otherwise he escapes the Scylla of the intension/extension fallacy only to fall into the Charybdis of equivocation. In addition, his objection to the Aristotelian is not supposed to presuppose a commitment to the "conceptual scheme" view. Finally, and in any case, we could simply change the example—the number of planets (Astronomy) is the cube root of 729 (Mathematics). Thus Putnam has no easy out from this fallacy.

Oddly enough, Putnam is well aware of the fallacy in other contexts, as it plays a large part in the argument of his famous and widely commented upon paper "The Meaning of 'Meaning'." That paper is the *ur*-paper in Putnam's argument against the supposed built-in, world involving identity of mental representations. The details of that argument are not of immediate concern. What is important is Putnam's recognition of the fallacy, and the ground for recognizing that it is a fallacy. As he puts it there, "the timeworn example of the two terms 'creature with a kidney' and 'creature with a heart' does show that two terms can have the same extension and yet differ in intension."[13] Indeed, Putnam even points out indirectly the danger of the fallacy earlier in the very paper in which he brings up his multiplicity of essences objection, "Aristote After Wittgenstein." He writes:

If we say that any pair of different sentences describe *different* events, then events themselves begin to look suspiciously like ghostly counterparts of sentences. That is, events become things to which, on the one hand, we give exactly the same structure as sentences, but which, on the other hand, we put out into the world. The inventions of such intermediaries is a piece of philosophical legerdemain.[14]

13  "The Meaning of 'Meaning'," Hilary Putnam. In *Mind, Language, and Reality*. Cambridge: Cambridge University Press, 1975. p. 218.
14  "Aristotle After Wittgenstein," p. 66.

So avoiding this intension/extension fallacy implies that one cannot simply argue from the diversity of evolutionary, genetic, and morphological descriptions and definitions that their extensions are diverse.

I think this response, though good, is inadequate for two reasons. First, it is damnation with faint praise to be able to say nothing of one's view, other than that it answers all fallacious objections. Second, I think Putnam could make a plausible defense against the charge of committing the fallacy *in this case*. He may grant that in general it is a fallacy to proceed from a diversity of intension to a diversity of extension. So he would have to give up the claim that it is by a reflection upon the diverse essential descriptions of the different sciences that we have come to the consensus view that natural kinds do not have unique essences. But he might add that it is the Aristotelian commitment to the Concept Identity Thesis that avoids the fallacy, and at the same time makes the Aristotelian subject to his objection. By contrast, in the ordinary case of the fallacy there is no claim present that there is an identity between the description and the thing described. The diversity of intensions *in conjunction with* the Identity Thesis entails the diversity of extensions. That is, after all, the crucial stage of his argument in steps (2), (3), and (4). Consequently, in this special case there is no fallacy involved, and his argument goes through.

I say that Putnam could respond in this fashion, but it would require that he abandon the general force of his argument. His Diversity of Essences Thesis is supposed to be a position coming from outside of Aristotelianism. Putnam wants to grant the internal consistency of the Aristotelian account, and defeat it as inadequate to the way things are now agreed upon to be. But adding the Concept Identity Thesis to avoid the fallacy and defeat the Aristotelian places the objection within Aristotelianism as a matter of consistency. It is no longer the case that the problem is with the Unity of Essence position as such, but rather with the joint satisfiability of the two theses, Unity of Essence and Identity of Concepts. Thus Putnam faces a dilemma. Either his objection

}382{

*Distinguer pour Unir: Putnam vs. Aquinas on the Unity of Nature*

comes from outside of Aristotelianism, in which case it is fallacious, or it comes from within Arisotelianism, and it is subject to an Aristotelian response that makes clear what the position is, and why the two theses are consistent.

The Aristotelian side of this dilemma brings me to what I think is the good and adequate response to Putnam's objection, a response shamelessly taken almost whole and entire from Aquinas, *mutatis mutandis*. First, in the transition from (2) to (3) the argument requires that we be able to read off by simple inspection the diverse identity of the forms involved in the diverse linguistic expressions. But this movement from a grasp of the identity of our concepts in linguistic expression to the world, presumably justified by the Conceptual Identity Thesis, is in stark contrast to St. Thomas's Aristotelianism. Commenting on Aristotle's *De interpretatione* he writes:

> the intention of Aristotle is not to assign identity of the concept of the soul through a comparison to articulated sound, as namely of one articulated sound there should be one concept . . . but he intends to assign the identity of concepts of the soul through a comparison to things.

The first thing to recognize from this passage is that the Aristotelian guided by St. Thomas is not at all interested in answering the skeptical question about how our language manages to hook up with the world, since he can't get the question off the ground. We have no purchase on our words apart from their worldly involvement. It is a mistake when we try to answer that question, rather than ask how it is that our opponent manages to identify the diversity of his linguistic descriptions.

Putnam could bandage his argument by recognizing that the Thomistic-Aristotelian is not going from concepts to things but from things to concepts, and yet still charge that since it is a metaphysical identity thesis, the asymmetry of the epistemological movement does not matter. The diversity of the things themselves, genes, bones, and historical events,

RESTORING NATURE

must lead to a diversity of essential concepts. Recast the argument as follows:

1) If the formal identity of things determines the formal identity of the concepts under which they fall, then essentially diverse things determine diverse concepts.
2) But the formal identity of things does determine the formal identity of the concepts that fall under them. (Concept Identity Thesis)
3) Therefore, essentially diverse things determine diverse concepts. (MP on 1&2)
4) But the objects studied in the diverse sciences are essentially diverse.
5) Therefore the objects studied in the diverse sciences determine diverse concepts, including essential descriptions and definitions. (3&4)
6) Therefore, the essential definitions of some natural kind supplied by the diverse sciences are diverse. (5)

This possible rescuing of the argument is all well and good, except for the minor problem that it also involves a fallacy. It straightforwardly begs the question in step 4, when it simply asserts the contradictory opposite of what the Aristotelian denies. We've already seen that Putnam cannot argue non-fallaciously for 4) simply on the basis of the diversity of the descriptions given by the sciences for the same natural kind. Perhaps there is a non-fallacious argument for 4), but Putnam has not given one.

But couldn't Putnam just rest content with common sense, the Aristotelian's own ace in the hole, the Aristotelian commonsense that Putnam hopes to revise without the fantasies of essentialism? Forget all the rhetoric about the developing and coalescing consensus that the Aristotelian must face. Bones just ain't the same thing as genes, and neither is identical to historical events and populations. Any fool, including the Aristotelian fool, can tell.

Well, no. In taking this tack, Putnam would be relying upon a vagueness in his initial example, a vagueness to be found in

}384{

*Distinguer pour Unir: Putnam vs. Aquinas on the Unity of Nature*

step 4) of the recast argument. *Prima facie*, it speaks of historical events, genes, and morphology. But no anatomist simply studies bones. No evolutionary biologist simply studies events. And no geneticist simply studies genes. In each case they study kinds, the history of kinds of events, the bones of kinds, and the genes of kinds. Here we see the importance attached to Putnam's presupposition that there are natural kinds. Without reflecting upon it, Putnam is relying upon a deeper unity in the objects of study than is immediately evident when they are simply described as bones, genes, and events. Which bones? Whose genes? Looking back at my outline of his original objection, it turns out that step 2) is false when it claims that the essential descriptions of X's (dogs) given by the different sciences are manifestly diverse. The formal identity and unity of the linguistic expressions involved is to be found in the formal identity and unity of the kind considered in its evolution, genetics, or morphology. That is, incidentally, one of the points behind the gruesome Aristotelian insight that the anatomist's hand is only called a human hand analogously. It must always be considered with respect to the living whole of which it is an anatomical part.

It would be good at this point to remember that no Aristotelian thinks that the form of X is read off of X by simple inspection. One comes to understand the form through analysis, and then synthesis. The diverse sciences are themselves part of this complex process of analysis and synthesis. As Maritain put it, "we distinguish in order to unite." If this is true of *res extra animam, a fortiori* it is true of *res in anima,* since the Thomistic-Aristotelian identifies the form of expressions in the soul from the form of things beyond the soul. Despite the *prima facie* diversity in the expressions provided by the different sciences and their sub-disciplines, in any particular case of a natural kind they are formally identical because they express in different ways what is not diverse in things beyond the soul.

Indeed, on a Thomistic theory of truth, that is what the truth of such expressions consists in, that what is understood

}385{

RESTORING NATURE

separately or diversely by the mind is predicated to be one in things. The unity of subject and predicate adequately captures the unity of the thing defined, and is thus true. Contrary to Putnam's first presupposition, no wedge is to be driven between subject and predicate. When we engage in the act of defining some scientific object, we are in pursuit of definitions that more and more adequately express the formal unity of the thing defined.

## A Good and Adequate Response

Of course at this point I am subject to the charge of begging the question that I just directed at Putnam. As he simply asserts the essential diversity of a kind, I am simply asserting the essential unity of a kind. We are at a standoff. But, is there no argument for my position? Here I turn for aid and comfort to St. Thomas, though the careful listener will have seen the trail of the Angelic Doctor over all. It was disingenuous of me to claim that my good but inadequate response earlier was my own. It was also shamelessly taken from Aquinas, from precisely the same place where I will now look for the good and adequate response.

While Putnam thinks his objection is new, and a product of reflection upon the advances of modern science, like the words of the song, "everything old is new again." The fact is, Aquinas dealt with Putnam's very objection, *mutatis mutandis*, when he addressed the medieval plurality of forms argument, in question 76, article 3, of the first part of the *Summa*. Consider the terms of the medieval debate. The objectors argue that there must be a plurality of substantial forms in a human being because of the diversity of "scientific" descriptions under which a human being falls, vegetative, sentient, and rational. Consider this particular objection that Aquinas cites:

> The Philosopher says in *Metaph.*, viii., that the genus is taken from the matter, and the difference from the form. But *rational*, which is the difference constitutive of man, is taken from the intellectual soul; while he is called

}386{

*Distinguer pour Unir: Putnam vs. Aquinas on the Unity of Nature*

> *animal* from the fact of having a body animated as form
> to matter by a sensitive soul. Therefore the intellectual
> soul is not essentially the same as the sensitive soul in
> man . . .[15]

Notice that the objection begins with a diversity in how man is "called," *rational*, or *animal*, when an essential definition is put forward. The reason given to explain the diversity of "calling" is the diversity of substantial forms in man; presumably each term is mapped to a distinct reality in the world. Thus the manifest linguistic duality of the definition *rational animal* is taken to be an argument for a real duality in the thing defined.

The background for the argument, not surprisingly, presupposes two streams of thought. The Aristotelian stream of the objection is unmistakable from the language of definition, genus, species and difference, as well as the analysis in terms of form and matter. But the other is the Augustinian insight into the great diversity between animate life as we see it in animals, and the rational life we know ourselves to possess when we turn within and reflect upon ourselves. In the *De trinitate*, Augustine had distinguished the mind, the inner man, as the major part of the soul, and as consisting of memory, intellect, and will. But he had also written of the "outer man" that:

> anything in our consciousness that we have in common
> with animals is rightly said to be still part of the outer
> man. It is not just the body alone that is to be reckoned
> as the outer man, but the body with its own kind of life
> attached, which quickens the body's structure and all
> the senses it is equipped with in order to sense things
> outside.[16]

15  Aquinas, St. Thomas. *Summa Theologiae*. Ottawa: Garden City Press, 1941. I.76.3 obj.4.
16  Augustine. *The Trinity*. Brooklyn: New City press, 1991. Trans. Edmund Hill, O.P. p. 322.

Augustine's reference to the principle that "quickens the body's structure and all the senses" is enigmatic, as it is not clear in him whether it should be taken to be a part of the soul, or another soul entirely. It is, after all, the body's "own kind of life attached." But it is clear that Augustine thinks it is to be wholly distinguished from the life of the mind, even if the mind and the quickening principle of the body are two parts of the soul.

Now in his *Disputed Questions on Truth*, Aquinas manages to preserve this special character of mind in the Aristotelian language of powers, when he held that the mind was a special "general power" consisting of the particular powers of memory, intellect, and will. This general power had its own special unity over and above the unity it has in the soul with all the powers of the soul, vegetative and sentient, and should thus be clearly distinguished from the "sensitive" part of the soul. It is rarely noted, however, that Aquinas abandons this "special" character and unity of the Augustinian mind in the *Summa*. No longer are memory, intellect, and will given pride of place as a single general power within the soul; no longer do they have their own unity apart from and mediating their unity with the other powers in the soul; rather, all of the powers, sensitive, vegetative, and rational are hierarchically ordered and united in the soul itself.

In the *De veritate* Aquinas was not at all concerned with the plurality of souls discussion. But in the *Summa* he is. His 13th century Augustinian opponents could very easily use his Aristotelianism against him, and argue that if the mind has the special unity and life that Aquinas grants to it in the *De veritate*, then on Aristotelian grounds it is not sufficient to hold that it is a general power of the soul; it must be another soul entirely. A distinctive form of life requires a distinctive principle of life, a distinctive soul. This argument is precisely what is taking place in the objection that Aquinas considers here in the *Summa*, an Augustinian objection posed in Aristotelian terms. To resist that move and retain the special character of the mind in the soul could only be *ad hoc* on Aquinas' part; and to his credit he abandons the grounds for the objection. He

}388{

*Distinguer pour Unir: Putnam vs. Aquinas on the Unity of Nature*

abandons throughout the discussion his earlier position that the mind has a special unity within the soul that distinguishes it from the unity it shares with all the other powers of the soul.

What concerns me here are the reasons Aquinas' gives for rejecting the plurality of souls. Aquinas' first response is my own inadequate response. Often calling it "the error of the Platonists," he diagnoses in his opponents what I have called the Intension/Extension fallacy, to confuse the features of our manner of knowing with the features of the thing known.

> From diverse intelligible characteristics or logical intentions, which follow upon the mode of understanding, it is not necessary to posit a diversity in the natures of things, since reason is able to apprehend one and the same thing in diverse ways.[17]

Notice the generality of the point. It is not simply about the plurality of souls debate confined to human nature. It concerns any movement from the plurality of ways we understand to a plurality of things understood.

My reason for saying that this is a good but inadequate response is that Aquinas himself treats it that way. Yes indeed, the plurality view is fallacious if it rests merely on the diversity of descriptions involved. But Aquinas recognizes that with an additional thesis no fallacy is involved. He writes, "the opinion [could be] maintained if, as [Plato] held, the soul were united to the body, not as its form, but as its mover." This Platonic possibility focuses upon the metaphysical function of the soul, rather than on how it is described in diverse discourses.

So Aquinas turns to offer positive arguments for the unity of the soul, and not simply dialectical defenses against the plurality position. He offers three arguments, two of which bear directly on Putnam's objection. The arguments focus upon the formal character of the soul, which Aquinas has just stressed in mention-

17  *S.T.*, I.76.3 ad 4.

}389{

RESTORING NATURE

ing what he takes to be the Platonic position as a contrast. The first argument considers the unity of the object under consideration. The metaphysical function of form is to provide the unity of being present in some object. Aquinas writes:

> Nothing is simply one except through one form, through which the thing has being; for a thing is a being and is one from the same principle; and so those things which are named from a diversity of forms are not one thing simply, as for example a white man.[18]

St. Thomas argues that if something is described through a diversity of forms, it is because it is not absolutely one. But notice the difference between saying that and saying, on the other hand, that any diversity of descriptions involves a fundamental diversity of forms; the latter is what St. Thomas flatly denies as fallacious, as the "error of the Platonists." So here he cannot be taking the diversity of linguistic descriptions at face value as providing evidence for their formal diversity. Rather, the diversity or identity of forms in a description is judged on the basis of a judgment of the diversity or identity of those forms in *res extra animam*. Consider the examples 'a man' and 'a white man'. According to his initial good but inadequate response, we cannot simply read off the manifest complexity of the phrase 'a white man' that it involves a plurality of forms in *res extra animam*. On the contrary, we judge that the description 'a white man' involves a diversity of forms because we already presuppose that *white* is a diverse form from *man* in *res extra animam*.[19] Apart from our knowledge of the diversity of *white* and *man* in *res extra animam*, we cannot judge the description 'white man' to involve any more forms than does 'man' alone, or for that matter 'white' alone.[20]

18  *S.T.*, I.76.3 respondeo.
19  It is not necessary to take 'already' here as a temporal adverb.
20  See the discussion of this topic in the *Metaphysics* and St. Thomas' commentary on it. The example 'white man' is a common one for

}390{

*Distinguer pour Unir: Putnam vs. Aquinas on the Unity of Nature*

Now consider the manifest complexity of the phrase 'a rational animal'. Aquinas argues, "an animal with many souls would not be simply one." But the unity he has in mind here is the unity of the natural kind that Putnam presupposes. He writes, " . . . in things composed from matter and form, something is one through the form, and derives both its unity and species (natural kind) from it."[21] In the life of a species or natural kind of animal, when we recognize a unity in its form of life, we recognize a unity

Aquinas as he simply takes it over from Aristotle, and it appears in almost every discussion of definition and essential unity. It is for him the paradigmatic case of a linguistic phrase that has no definition. This is how Aquinas understands Aristotle's discussion of the "garment" and the "white man" in Book VII of Aristotle's *Metaphysics*. The imaginative suggestion is made that we substitute a single term, for instance 'garment', for the complex phrase 'white man' in order to signify the unity that a white man is. Clearly we are to understand 'garment' here to be nothing more than a sound or inscription, and not with its ordinary meaning. They might as well have used 'jabberwok', or even better 'whiteman'. The basic idea is to give a single name to what is otherwise referred to by two. Then just as the single term 'man' has a definition because it signifies the unity that is a rational animal, 'garment' as used here is supposed then to have a definition, as it is a single term signifying the unity that is a white man. And since it is a single term that is taken to be synonymous with the phrase, 'white man', it seems to follow that 'white man' must itself have a definition. And yet, following Aristotle, Aquinas denies this line of argument. Whether we use 'garment', 'jabberwok', or 'whiteman', there is no definition because the unity signified is an accidental one of diverse forms; and it doesn't matter whether we signify that accidental unity with one sound as in 'whiteman' or with two as in 'white man'. In short, we do not judge the number of distinct forms from the number of distinct words, but the number of distinct words from the number of distinct forms. So not every single word has a definition, since the unity it signifies may be better captured by two or more words.

21  " . . . in rebus compositis ex materia et forma, per formam est aliquid unum, et unitatem et speciem sortitur." Aquinas, St. Thomas. *In Metaphysicam Aristotelis Commentaria*. Turin: Marietti, 1926. L. VIII, lc. 3, #1725.

RESTORING NATURE

that cannot be adequately accounted for on the supposition that there are many essences present in the natural kind. Thus, Aquinas accounts for the unity of the natural kind that Putnam presupposes in his objection. But we saw that it was precisely the unity of the natural kind that Putnam had difficulty maintaining with his example of the synthetic dog, once he had denied the essential unity of the natural kind. And, however much charitable interpretation we apply to the objection, without the unity of the natural kind, Putnam simply doesn't have a valid objection.

Aquinas' first argument for essential unity then sets the stage for his second argument that focuses directly upon what is involved in providing an essential definition; as he puts it "from the manner in which one thing is predicated of another." The key contrast is with accidental predication. The example is *rational animal*. Man is a rational animal. Think of the contrast he has just mentioned with "a white man," or "man is a white animal." Aquinas writes, "those things that are derived from different forms are predicated of one another accidentally." A definition by contrast is true to the extent that its parts, *genus* and *difference*, are united by the definition in a way that reflects the simple unity of the form in the thing defined. Thus a man is said to be an animal through some form, a sentient one. Now suppose the man were said to be rational through another form, and vegetative through yet another form. Then the relations of rational life to sensitive life to vegetative life in man would be accidental, no more related one to another than is the relation of being white to being vegetative, sentient, and so on.

On the contrary, man is rational, sentient, and vegetative through "one and the same" form. That is why the definition *man is a rational animal* is both true and *necessary*. It is not as if we have two or more forms tied together by some metaphysical glue called necessity. We have but one form, and the necessity involved is the necessity of self-identity for forms, that is, the transcendental character of being called *unity*.[22] It is impossible for there to be

22  Cf. Aquinas, St. Thomas. *Quaestiones Disputatae De Veritate*. Turin: Marietti, 1948. I.5 ad 16.

}392{

*Distinguer pour Unir: Putnam vs. Aquinas on the Unity of Nature*

a man who, lacking the form of animality, retains the form of rationality, or lacking the form of rationality retains the form of animality, precisely because it is one and the same form by which a man is an animal and is rational. Recall that the setting of the plurality of souls argument holds that a being is a man through the rational form. So Aquinas writes "it is necessary for something to be an animal and to be a man through *the same form*; otherwise no man could truly be an animal in such a way that animal could be essentially predicated of the man." The other direction of analysis is equally true, namely, that no animal could be truly called rational in such a way that rational could be essentially predicated of the animal.

This analysis is confirmed throughout Aristotle's and Aquinas' works. Most obvious is the movement of the *De anima* from vegetative to sensitive to rational form, as the higher type of form is not joined to the lower by "metaphysical glue," but rather includes the powers of the lower form within its own unity. The argument is based upon recognizing in human action that reason does not add on something additional to animate acts that are the same in other animals; rather rational is the form that animate acts take in human beings that renders them specifically different from the animate acts of other animals. And it is not that this animal who grows, moves, eats, and reproduces also happens to think. It is rather that the form of this animal's growth, movement, eating, and reproduction is rational, or ought to be, given *what it is* for this animal to be.

Finally, this account is confirmed by Aquinas' analysis of what it is to be *rational* in question 79.8. Aquinas argues that rational means movement from one thing known to another. But the reason why human beings move from one thing know to another is because their mode of knowing is propositional. Propositions are formed from the partial, inadequate and simple grasp we have of things by means of our intellect. So Aquinas argues that truth is only found in a judgment, since only there do we find an act of intellect that is adequate to its object in asserting that what is understood diversely is one in reality. We then *reason* in argument

RESTORING NATURE

when we relate these judgments one to another. But our intellect has these partial and inadequate grasps of things because of its abstractive character, that is, because of the way in which it engages its object through the sensitive acts of the body.[23] Thus rationality is the distinctive form that intellect takes in an animal. It is because the formal principle of intellect in man is the very same form by which he is an animal that he is essentially rational. Consequently, while it is comparatively easy to see that in man being an animal is not adequately understood until it is understood to be rational, it is often more difficult to see that being rational is not adequately understood until it is understood to be animate or incarnate, the act of an animal. Intellect apart from animality is not rational. By that account neither angels nor God are or can be rational. The only regulative ideal of reason that Aristotle and Aquinas would recognize is the good man.

Definition brings about an enrichment of the form of the subject by the form of the predicate because subject and predicate are different expressions of the same form. Here Aquinas' remarks on the transition from the "vague" universal to the distinct are appropriate.[24] Putnam thinks of the Concept Identity Thesis along the lines of a synchronic judgment that two trees, for instance, have the same form. Since the linguistic expressions appear different they must not have the same form, just as in observing these two trees we may judge that they do not have the same form. The better analogy is the diachronic recognition that the acorn and the oak are the same being, and have the same form,

23  S.T., I.85.3, 85.4, and particularly 85.5.
24  The human intellect in the first apprehension does not seize on the spot (*statim*) a perfect cognition of a thing, but in the first place apprehends something of it, namely the quiddity of the thing itself, which is the first and proper object of the intellect, and then it understands the properties, accidents, and encompassing essential relations of the thing. And according to this it is necessary that it compose or divide one apprehension with another, and from one composition or division proceed to another, which is to reason. (*S.T.*, I.85.5 respondeo.)

*Distinguer pour Unir: Putnam vs. Aquinas on the Unity of Nature*

one rudimentary, the other flourishing. Simple observation at any particular moment will not tell us this. Rather, we must attend to the genesis of the one from the other to recognize that they are really one thing after all, despite the appearance of being one thing and then another thing. Just as one cannot drive a wedge between the acorn and the oak, neither can one drive a wedge between the subject and the predicate in a definition. Consequently, the fundamental unity among diverse essential descriptions to be found in diverse sciences is based upon their joint unity in the form of the natural kind that they all claim to describe.

Recall that Putnam had granted that "not just anything can be called the nature of a dog." Aquinas would ask, why not, if Putnam is right about the multiplicity of essences? Applying Putnam's point to Aquinas' example, presumably Putnam does not want to grant such claims as that being white is part of human nature, that is, that the description *white man* is a legitimate essential description of the natural kind, however much racists might want it to be.[25] But why not? Recall that he cannot appeal to the fact that *white* is not a feature of all members of the natural kind. We saw with his example of the *synthetic dog* that membership in the natural kind depends upon what is taken by the interested party to be essential to the natural kind; so the fact that all members of a set might not possess some feature doesn't tell us anything other than that we were not interested in that very feature when, prompted by our interests, we gathered together the members of that set and called it a natural kind. The unity of essence position rests, among other things, upon the insight that in man being rational has a lot more to do with movement, reproduction, and eating than does being white; indeed that in man

---

25  Here it is on point that Putnam's various different lecture series on these topics of language, world, and essentialism, often enough end with lectures on the pragmatic implications for ethical and political themes current in philosophy. With many pragmatists, Putnam often indicates that he believes metaphysical commitments are ethically and politically dangerous.

RESTORING NATURE

being rational, mobile, gustatory, and reproductive are fundamentally the same thing, the same form of life, while being white is not.

Now with the resources from Aquinas' discussion at hand, let us return to Putnam's position. Notice, if a genetic biologist happens to *presuppose* that evolutionary descent is not essential to *his* discourse within the genetic study of a natural kind, he may still carry on with his scientific investigations. But we could ask whether that presupposition is required by his science, or immaterial to it. Does it actually change what he does internal to the practice of genetics? Or we could argue that he should concern himself with evolutionary descent, at least to the extent of showing how his genetics sheds light upon evolution, and so on. But when he begins to respond to these latter concerns, and *argues* rather than presupposes that evolutionary descent is not essential to the natural kind itself, and not just his genetic study of the natural kind, he is no longer engaged in his science as such. Presumably it is not a well confirmed hypothesis of any particular natural science under which some natural kind falls that there may be a multiplicity of natures for that kind of being, a multiplicity required by the multiplicity of sciences other than that particular one. What exactly would the experiment be that might falsify or confirm that hypothesis? Experiments take place within and are evaluated by a particular science, not outside of and across many. How does such a hypothesis exhibit within a particular science the theoretical virtues of simplicity, predictive power, and fruitfulness for further research programs? It is clear that such a thesis is not part of any particular science, but is rather an extra-scientific *philosophical position* that one takes about the sciences, and that requires argument. And it is not simply *read off of* the descriptions and success of contemporary sciences, as if it were a clear and distinct idea.

Now, is it or is it not the case that the different scientists presuppose a fundamental unity in the natural kind that bears upon the diversity of their essential descriptions? Of course it is. What is the fundamental evidence that the evolutionary biologist points

}396{

*Distinguer pour Unir: Putnam vs. Aquinas on the Unity of Nature*

to as supporting his theory? The fossil record, the fossilized remains of the morphology of the species he studies. What is the Holy Grail of geneticists and evolutionary biologists when they get together? We've all seen the fantastic account provided by Steven Spielberg, but the mundane goal is to find genetic material the structure of which shows how the genetics of life coalesces with the evolutionary chain observed in the fossil record. Doesn't the geneticist think that the genetic structures he studies find, among other things, differential expression in the morphology of the animals he studies, and differences that either promote or undermine their survivability in the evolutionary story? I am not even an amateur in Biology, so I make these remarks from the outside. My own field of undergraduate study was Physics, and there the examples of unity in diversity are legion. Perhaps the most famous example is the fundamental unity behind the Ideal Gas Law in Thermodynamics and Statistical Mechanics applied to the Kinetic Theory of Matter. One "conceptual scheme" trades in molar quantities of elements, pressures, volumes, and temperatures, while the other trades in the kinetic energy of vast ensembles of atoms and molecules, momenta, and elastic collisions. The random walk phenomena of Brownian motion in Fluid Dynamics and the Kinetic Theory of Matter is another. The Quantum Theory of Radiation applied to both Black Body Radiation in Thermodynamics and the photoelectric effect in Electromagnetism, and so on. These advances are now so taken for granted that it is hard for us any longer to "conceptually" separate them. But it was not always so.

Those who are being educated in the sciences are taught that finding this unity in diverse theories is a theoretical virtue in the sciences that goes beyond simple experimental confirmation or falsification; it is certainly not a curse. Indeed does anyone really expect the sort of argument that Putnam imagines? What little I know of Biology suggests to me that the scientists in question will greet each other's results with excitement to the extent that they shed light upon their own theories, and dread to the extent that they undermine them. Yes dread, precisely because they know

}397{

RESTORING NATURE

that the results of other sciences do bear upon what they take the nature or essence of their object of study to be, even when those results are not internally necessary for the conduct of their science. They don't want to engage in a science that is fundamentally different from and possibly even inconsistent with everything else we know about the world; no one any longer is *interested* in caloric, spontaneous generation, or phlogiston. In *Physics*, through complicated mathematical manipulations you can still probably hold on to the *ether* of the 19th century, if you are *uninterested* in just about everything else in Physics.

From the reformulated argument I provided for his objection, it is clear that Putnam's commitment to the multiplicity of essences is logically prior to his understanding of the diversity of sciences, and does not follow from it. But then Putnam must face the bar, and recognize that the price of *his* metaphysical commitment is the loss of the unity amidst diversity that is found in the sciences of today, as well as their complex and sometimes troubling union with the "commonsense" world he would defend. Our interests do play a part in how we conduct our lives, including our lives as "scientists." But one of the things we are interested in is understanding better the unity amidst diversity that we recognize in the world and among ourselves. And it is for that reason that we should try to understand better the need for the Thomistic-Aristotelian commitment to the unity of essence. Contrary to the story line of the history and philosophy of science in the modern period that Putnam gives us, the marvelous development of the sciences should not be the occasion of our singing dirges, but rather songs of the vindication of Aristotelian metaphysics with its commitment to the unity of nature. *Distinguer pour unir.*

# Aquinas: Nature, Life and Teleology
## Vittorio Possenti
## University of Venice

One observation forces itself upon us at the outset. It is just as hard to think about the problem of life today as it was a hundred or a thousand years ago. If we observe the state of the sciences, we are led to the conviction that an important issue still remains open: to develop a philosophy of life and the organism which is adequate to the level of biological discoveries. Our most urgent need in the dialogue between science, philosophy and theology does not arise, as it has happened for centuries, from physics and cosmology but from the life sciences, notably biology and genetics. This is a necessity on which thinkers of different schools, such as H. Jonas and J. Polkinghorne,[1] are agreed. Physics is no longer the guiding science, or the sole guiding science: its place has been taken by biology and it is high time that philosophy and theology turned to address the issues it raises, without entrusting the realm of nature and life solely to the sciences. While there is still a rich crop of studies about Big Bang theory and scientific cosmology in general, little has been written on philosophical biology, where the presence of the theologians has been exiguous. One may wonder why this should be so: perhaps because Big Bang theory seems allusively to evoke the truth of creation, though a more

---

1    The latter observes: "Down to the present the debate [between science and theology] has been too much under the control of scientists trained as physicists . . . We urgently need the participation of more biologists, more experts in the human sciences, and naturally more theologians," *Credere in Dio nell'età della scienza*, Raffaello Cortina, Milan 2000, p. 93.

}399{

RESTORING NATURE

careful consideration of this scientific theory, rather controversial and highly 'speculative', shows that it has nothing to do with the theme of creation, as it deals only with cosmic becoming: as such it is unable to formulate statements on what transcends becoming and then on creation, understood as the total position in being of all things. But one may also conjecture that this insufficient interest in biology stems from the difficult problem of teleology and, more generally, from the reductionist attitude frequently displayed by scientists when they pass beyond their own field of research and formulate hypotheses and theories with universal implications, prompted by an unbridled enthusiasm which has proved ill-advised on other occasions in the past.

Perhaps we can reconstruct a parallel between the post-Newtonians' enthusiasm for mechanicalism and the passion of biologists today for biology and genetics. The former, intoxicated by the spectacular conquests of Newtonian physics, claimed that man was no more than a machine, no doubt highly complex and delicate, but a machine all the same. A similar intellectual euphoria now seems to have infected certain biologists, over-eager to think of man as merely a biological machine equipped for survival.

The difficulties of thinking about life are aggravated by the profound shift in perspective brought about by modern scientific cosmology, which has since merely become more acute. This phenomenon could be described as a "regression of life due to the enlargement of the universe." Once nearly everything was life; today nearly nothing is: in our universe, enlarged out of all proportion, almost everything is mass, energy, inanimate force. We have passed from the ancient panvitalism to the current situation in which life is rare and improbable in the universe, when precisely it is not fundamentally reduced to non-life, to mechanically and chemically ordered matter (pan-mechanicalism). One might suppose that this attitude is connected with the immense enlargement of the cosmos due to the doctrine of an expanding universe, unknown to the ancients: as the dimensions of the cosmos have grown, the biosphere has shrunk proportionately, and it represents

*Aquinas: Nature, Life and Teleology*

a much smaller percentage of the cosmos. Though it has some foundation, this position is not the whole truth, since it is also the fruit of the modern tendency to reduce the organic to the inorganic. All this creates a dialectical situation in biology: on the one hand it is a marginal science, since the biosphere forms no more than a tiny party of the universe; on the other it is central, because it deals with what counts most: life, including human life.

However, the cultural change from ancient to modern times is clear. The problem for the ancients was life and organism, and so their works contain numerous manifestations of animism and hylozoism. (By animism I mean the idea that attributes a soul to all things, including those that we consider inert; and by hylozoism the assumption that the principle of life is originally intrinsic to matter). This evokes the obvious reference to Plato, who saw the whole cosmos as a living being endowed with perfection and beauty (cf. *Timaeus*, 30 b-d). So the ancients saw matter not as *res extensa* but as *res vitalis*, so to speak. Though they possessed very few and shaky notions of biology, their culture was biological, vitalistic, organicist.

If this was the problem of the ancients, that of the moderns has been the problem of spirit and with it *res extensa-res cogitans* dualism. The hegemony of this dualism—completely unsuited to understanding the phenomenon of life, which cannot be reduced either to extension or to thought—entailed either the expulsion of the problem of life from research or else the project to reduce life to a mechanical element, starting from the assumption that the fundamental phenomenon is not action but the movement of that which is inanimate, studied in mechanics. Parallel with these developments, the concept of nature *as the inner principle of movement and life* was inevitably rejected. "Nature" as *res extensa* was abandoned to science, while philosophy from Descartes to Husserl has confined itself to the realm of spirit/thought. The authentic concept of nature is not understood either by the naturalists-nominalists, who reduce it to a classificatory idea, nor by the spiritualists, who see it as something deleterious, an obstacle or a limit to the spontaneity and freedom of the self.

}401{

## Restoring Nature

The greater awareness that now exists about the nature of life should finally lead us to reject this dualism, which causes an almost endless series of misunderstandings. If one still wants to speak of "dualism," it remains possible in relation to the "body-soul" nexus, which has little connection with the concept of *res extensa-res cogitans*, unless we presuppose the Cartesian mechanicalism, namely the idea of the body-automaton, which entails a complete rejection if the concept of life: the automaton is in fact an inanimate mechanism. Cartesian mechanicalism, contrary to all evidence and all common sense, has been abandoned even in reductionist theories of life, as is shown by various contemporary positions in which the vital is reduced to physico-chemical and thermodynamic reactions, never to mere extension.[2]

## Nature and Life

A reasonably well-informed observer will perceive that the question of nature is extremely delicate and gives rise to numerous controversies. This is due to its marked semantic multiplicity and ubiquity, which tend to foster ambiguity rather than clarity. The difficulties inherent in the conception of nature are hardly new, since over three centuries ago Pascal, in his scintillating style, had already framed a weighty objection to it in just two lines: "J'ai grand peur que cette nature ne soit elle même qu'une première coutume."[3] Not far from Pascal's position is that expressed by the contemporary historicist school, which sees the concept of nature as always historical, cultural, and hence variable, relative to a period and its specific culture. We all know the important moral

2   The hope that Cartesian dualism may be superseded does not imply the end of all forms of dualism. The discovery of the two spheres of matter and spirit which took the place of primitive panvitalism and hylozoism—an achievement of Greek thought—introduced a new theoretical situation which had once again to be reckoned with. Some form of dualism is a better solution than panvitalism alone or panmaterialism alone.
3   n. 93, ed. Brunschvicg.

*Aquinas: Nature, Life and Teleology*

implications of these positions in the debates over the environment, sexuality, family, and bioethics: what is natural and what not? we often ask ourselves. Is the concept of nature morally relevant? Are some things unnatural and contrary to nature?

Pascal's observation implies a criticism. If nature is a habit or a custom, then like all habits it will be liable to change and so cannot provide a solid basis for normative judgments. The changes implied by Pascal's idea of nature will be both diachronic and synchronic, that is affected by differences in both time and place, and vary according to the different cultures present on the planet. This concept, which various phases of Greek thought, including stoicism, presented as making for universality, a bridge between different cultures, and which gave rise to the influential and enduring concept of *kata physin*, is now understood as a relative and cultural concept, hence incapable of constituting a universal and transcultural ambit.

There remains the question whether Pascal's objection helps us to think about the problems inherent in a philosophy of nature and the organism, to which we shall now turn. A denial, which I feel is inevitable, depends on the perspective in which Pascal is placed: that of a moral point of view, not the perspective of life and of philosophy of nature. This suggests we should look in a different direction for an idea of nature more suitable for the phenomenon of life. Here the trail has been blazed by Aristotle, notably in the *Physics* and *Metaphysics*, and continued by various authors, including Thomas Aquinas in his commentaries on these works as well as in other places.

As a preliminary step in understanding Aquinas's treatment of the concept of nature, it is worth introducing the way he defines and comments on it. Pietro da Bergamo's *Tabula aurea* lists fifty positions or items containing the term "nature," and twenty-five containing "natural," without counting the fact that the *Tabula* almost always lists numerous references to Aquinas's works for each single position. The considerable frequency of occurrences of the term "nature" (fewer, however, than others such as anima, deus, gratia, christus, fides—though this should hardly be

RESTORING NATURE

surprising given that Aquinas is a theologian) provides extrinsic but significant testimony to its importance.

Taking my cue from some of these citations, I should like to enter the epistemological ambit of "natural philosophy," a term not free from ambiguities yet significant, charged with echoes and a persistent fascination—even Monod in his essay *L'Hasard et la Necessité* (*Chance and necessity*) uses it in his subtitle ("Essay on the natural philosophy of contemporary biology"), despite the risks it entails, of which the author is lucidly aware. The immense development of the modern sciences has not extinguished—in fact it has at times made even more acute—the desire for a philosophical understanding of the cosmos and life, though in the face of their relentless advance both philosophy and theology have preferred to occupy themselves with history and left nature to the sciences. Hence the almost chronic weakness of the philosophy of nature, the risks of an accentuated concordism between faith/theology and science, and the turning of theology towards hermeneutics.

I have gathered three sentences on nature in Aquinas' works:

1) Naturalia sunt quorum principium est natura; natura autem est principium motus et quietis in eo in quo est. (*In Phys*, L. I, lectio 1, n. 3)
2) Natura nihil aliud est quam principium motus et quietis in eo in quo est primo et per se et non secundum accidens. (L. II, lectio 1, n. 145; cf. *Physics*, l. II, 192b20 ff.)
3) Nomen naturae primo impositum est ad significandam generationem viventium, quae dicitur nativitas. Et quia huiusmodi generatio est a principio intrinseco, extensum est hoc nomen ad significandum principium intrinsecum cuiuscumque motus (*S. Th.*, I, q. 29, a. 1, ad 4m).[4]

---

4   In *Metaphysics* (1014 b 16ss) Aristotle reviews the various meanings of nature (cf. also the comment of Aquinas on n. 808). In Aquinas cf. also on the various meanings of nature: *S. Th.*, III, q. 2, a. 1; and *Contra Gentiles*, L. IV, c. 35, n. 3: "The term nature was originally

}404{

## Aquinas: Nature, Life and Teleology

From these definitions it appears that nature, an intrinsically analogous concept, far from being a hypostatized entity or an extrinsic principle, exists with and in natural beings.[5] Its central character

used to indicate the generation of creatures that are born." Cf. also the study by G. Cottier "Le concept de nature chez saint Thomas," offprint from: Collana 'Dialogo di filosofia', n. 10, Herder-Università Lateranense, Rome 1993, pp. 37–64.

Note in passing—without giving the topic all the emphasis it merits—that on the basis of the concept of nature and life in Aquinas, it is life that is natural, not death. This seems to contrast with the contemporary spiritual climate, in which death is so strongly connected to life that it is death that is natural rather than life. Once men asked themselves about the meaning of death; now they ask the same question about life.

5    If life and biological-organic life are not equivalent concepts this means that the concept of life is in itself analogous: there exist different embodiments or levels of life, and a single term is used to denote very different forms of life. The problem is made more acute by the poverty of terms available in Italian and English: we say life to indicate animal life, human life, and ultra-human life: and in man to denote bodily life, psychic life, and spiritual life. In Greek, by contrast, there are three terms that indicate the broad differences in the phenomenon of life: *zoé, bios, psyché. Zoé* indicates the life manifested in all organic beings; in a certain way it is the principle of life, whose contrary is not death but non-life, since those that die are single living organic entities, but not the principle of life itself. It is significant that the Greek of the N.T. uses the term *zoé* also to indicate eternal life (cf. Jn 12, 25). *Bios* alludes to the modes or conditions of life: if *zoé* is the life by which we live (*qua vivimus*), *bios* is the life we live (*quam vivimus*). We know that the different modes or conditions of life, such as the political, the theoretical or the contemplative life, are rendered into Greek using *bios* accompanied by the relevant adjective. *Psyche* is the vital breath, the soul, and hence also life (also in this regard the reference to Jn 12, 25 may be relevant: "He that loves his life loses it, he that hates his life . . . ," where life is *psyché*). It remains doubtful whether "biology" is the most suitable term to indicate the object of this science; perhaps it has paid the price of the meaning previously acquired by the term "zoology." All things considered, if I may express a well-grounded preference, the neologism *zoelogy* seems more appropriate than biology. However the common usage has its force and it is convenient to follow it.

}405{

# RESTORING NATURE

is of being a principle of automovement and change *from within*: its inwardness or immanence is expressed by the term *in quo est*, which marks the difference between natural and artificial, in the sense that artificial objects receive change from without. This action which emanates from within comes out more deeply the higher and more perfect the nature from which it proceeds. For a correct understanding of the Latin wording, we have to remember that *motus*, being understood in its broad sense—as local movement, growth, diminution, alteration—signifies change or mutation. As nature establishes the existence of an inside, it proves to be a principle of inwardness. In Aquinas's works there are numerous passages in which he follows Aristotle by distinguishing between transitive action and immanent action: the latter being peculiar only to living beings.[6] The concept of immanent action, whose source and term lie within the active subject, is the immediate explanation of the idea of nature denoted by *"in quo est"*: where there is nature, there is immanent action. Both aspects of self-movement and change from within point towards the phenomenon of life, to which we shall return.

Since the concept of nature defined in this way refers to *nasci*, to *nativitas*, and hence to the generation of living things, we are directed towards the reality of life and led to explore the concept of life. The link connecting the concepts of nature and life is attested by the fact that self-movement is peculiar to life: "Movere se ipsum pertinet ad rationem vitae, et est proprie animatorum."[7] And again: "Primo autem dicimus animal vivere, quando incipit ex se motum habere . . . . Vitae nomen sumitur ex quodam exterius apparenti circa rem, quod est movere seipsum." The continuation of this period includes in *movere se ipsum* also *agere ad operationem*.[8] Life consists in the fact that a certain substance moves itself in such a way that its action proceeds from itself and remains within itself, that it be beginning and end of its action.

---

6   "Actio immanens est tantum viventium," *De potentia*, q. 10, a. 1.
7   *In Phys.*, L. VIII, l. 7, n. 1026.
8   *S. Th.*, I, q. 18, a. 1 and a. 2. Cf. also *Contra Gentiles*, l. I, c. 97.

}406{

*Aquinas: Nature, Life and Teleology*

The concept of nature as the inward principle of movement and of quiet in a being, and that of life as manifesting itself as self-movement, are so closely interwoven as to form almost a single concept. In the wake of these observations one can understand the distance that separates the concepts of nature as employed by the scientist and the philosopher: for the former, Nature (with a capital N) is almost always synonymous with the cosmos, the universe, where life is very rare, while the philosopher sees "nature" as the principle within every living thing. In this sense physical, inanimate Nature, which represents the great bulk of the cosmos, does not possess "nature."

The subject endowed with life appears as an individual being which has its own center within itself, in opposition or diversity to the rest of the world, and possessing an essential boundary between inner and outer.[9] This situation can be explained by resorting to the idea of form, as Jonas does, emphasizing its partial independence from matter. In the metabolism as a dynamic function of exchange with the environment, the organism remains identical to itself, not in terms of matter, which alters through this exchange, but in terms of its form, which persists. In reflecting on life we are led to discover the concept of form in two versions: an inanimate version where form results from the aggregation of particles of matter; and a vitalistic version, where form is the cause of the unity of the living being.

"Natura est principium motus et quietis in eo in quo est." Confronted with this definition of nature that refers to change and rest, to concepts that we are accustomed to understand in rigorously mechanical terms, we are strongly tempted to suppose that it is superseded and of little relevance to the bioethical and philosophical problems that so often arise in the field of scientific-biological and genetic discoveries.

But it is wise to suspend judgment until we can see more clearly and grasp what lies unsaid, what the formula does not say

9    Cf. H. Jonas, *Organismo e libertà*, edited by P. Becchi, Einaudi, Turin 1999, p. 110 and 113.

## RESTORING NATURE

openly to our ears, which have been accustomed for centuries to a different music. To this end we need to undertake a further exploration, actually a fairly extensive one, since after three centuries of Newtonian physics and the like we tend to believe, on the whole, that motion with its laws is *always induced from without, not from within*. One of the major postulates of Newtonian physics, whose privileged locus lies in its application to inanimate objects and which is suited to mechanicalism, is that every movement is induced from without, never from within: a force is exerted between bodies (gravity); one body strikes another and sets it in motion. That there can exist an inner principle of movement is extraneous to Newtonian physics: it was not conceived for the phenomenon of life, but focused solely upon the inanimate. Newtonian mechanics is an essay on the outside world, in the sense that inwardness is unknown and the actions and reactions it deals with concern only the outside. If, on the contrary, the definition advanced by Aristotle and Aquinas refers to nature as the principle of the movement and the quiet that reside in the subject itself, for the sake of symmetry we could say that their natural philosophy is an essay also on the inside world, on immanence, on that which is intrinsic and lies within the subject. It might be objected that after Newton much progress has been made by the sciences and biology, which have enlarged the picture from mechanics to take in the exchange of heat, chemical and molecular reactions, electromagnetism, etc. Nothing could be truer, and yet the phenomenon of life can only be understood by resorting to an inner principle of self-construction.

## Two Problems

Now, in the light of the ideas of nature and life I have introduced, I shall try to meditate on two problems: A) the question of teleology; B) whether in Aquinas there is some principle or criterion that provides a basis for a philosophy of the evolution of life. This will be a preliminary survey of topics whose extreme complexity hardly needs to be stressed.

*Aquinas: Nature, Life and Teleology*

## A) The Question of Teleology

When one begins to reflect on teleology / finality, he immediately comes up against a well-known objection: teleology is out of court because modern science refuses to recognize it and rejects it as useless. Science has, in fact, been constructed on a lengthy battle against Aristotelianism under the aegis of the exclusion of all final causes. However, their exclusion is an a priori proscription of modern science, in the sense that it is not the outcome of reasoning and verification, but it is a postulate imposed right from the start: "As for final causes it is evident that their rejection [by modern science] was a methodological principle that guided the inquiry and not the conclusion of results obtained by inquiry."[10] On the problem of teleology, the Cartesian dualism accepted as a gentle metaphysic in the service of science long proved useful for the needs of scientists and theists, since it enabled both to manage the vast zone of the *res extensa* mathematically, omitting from it a zone for the spirit, for consciousness, where teleology alone was valid.

The solution of excluding final causes from nature (which was understood as pure *res extensa*) and conveniently marginalizing them in the minimum area of the *res cogitans*, while exploiting to the utmost the advantages of thought-matter dualism, functioned for a certain period. But when this dualism failed and was transformed in the nineteenth century into materialistic monism, in which both organism and thought were reduced to matter alone, it then offered no advantages at all: if man and his consciousness, in which finality is undeniable, are a part of nature, how can one seriously maintain that final causes ought to be excluded from nature? In this regard materialistic monism is playing on two contradictory tables, because it makes man, in whom it recognizes the category of finality, a part of nature, to which it denies all teleology.

Since final causes are causes, finality turns out to be an integral part of the great question of causality, which has remained

10  *Organismo e libertà*, cit., p. 47.

}409{

substantially unresolved in the course of modern philosophy after Hume and Kant, in the sense that it appears as a form that places phenomena in a temporal sequence, instead of as an event with many facets but nevertheless real, one which produces something in being. To understand the universal presence and nature of causality, we need to abandon the categories of the intellect (Kant), to descend into concrete bodily and biological life, and from there to begin again to understand the many ways of real causation, which cannot be reduced to efficient causes alone and still less to mechanical causes.

The idea of finality is not related to any form of change whatsoever, but to those changes directed to an end, and in a more meaningful and strong way to those movements which proceed from less perfect to more perfect and which can be grasped by intellectual analysis. In development of an organism, teleology represents exactly such a movement from the less to the more. Now it happens that if we have recourse to mathematical laws and methods in the analysis of movement, the very idea of a more and of a less perfect loses meaning as mathematics does not know that idea. In principle, sciences which heavily use mathematical methods in the realm of life necessarily neglect teleology right from the start.

The problem of final causes can be embodied in a number of questions that are periodically reproposed: do purposes exist even where they are not projected by man? Is the concept of purpose valid and present only where there is a thinking consciousness that raises and chooses them? For the supporters of final causes the solution lies in showing that finality is not just a concept projected by man onto things, nor a concept that can be employed only in the sphere of consciousness, but that final causes exist in the whole sphere of living things, not only those endowed with subjectivity and will. On the contrary, the modern exclusion of purpose concerns both ontogenesis and phylogenesis. On the basis of this exclusion, ontogenesis is understood as the necessary effect of efficient causes that stem from the determinations contained in the seed; and phylogenesis is the result of random

## Aquinas: Nature, Life and Teleology

mutations and natural selection. Once final causes are excluded from ontogenesis and phylogenesis, it seems that they remain applicable only to conscious subjects, or rather to that part of their actions that are dependent on consciousness. So there would be finality in walking, since the subject decides where he is heading for, but not in breathing or digesting, which are involuntary functions. However, the exclusion of final causes from ontogenesis is not self-evident (think of the teleology immanent in the embryo), so that today rejection of final causes seems much more common within the ambit of evolution (phylogenesis).

The purpose of renewing discussion about final causes entails taking up the subject again from its most difficult side, that of the difficulties we meet in dealing with the question of purpose in *artificial* objects, in *inanimate* objects, and in the life of *organisms not endowed with consciousness*. We are, in fact, disposed to concede by direct introspective experience that subjects endowed with consciousness form representations of their purposes and act on the basis of those purposes. There is nothing more natural, it seems, than to raise a wall between the two classes and decide that while conscious subjects conceive the idea of a purpose, inanimate objects, artificial objects, and living beings lacking consciousness are devoid of any purpose, and that applying the idea of a purpose to them is no more than an anthropomorphic projection. However, the question is by no means so simple.

Artificial objects (a term I intend to use in a broad sense) are those made by man and can be subdivided into *inanimate* objects, like a knife, and *animate* objects made up of people like a parliament. In both cases, that is in man-made objects, the purpose—attributed always by man himself—is the cause of their production, of their coming into existence; but this happens in different ways. In inanimate things the aim is external; it does not reside in the things themselves but in the mind of their designer. The knife is made to cut and this teleology stems form the mind of the craftsman; it is not immanent in the knife, which is devoid of any purposes of its own and possesses those that the craftsman assigns to it, so that here there is a divide separating purpose and

}411{

object. By contrast, in "animate objects," such as social institutions, the purpose is immanent. If we take the example of a parliament, its existence is inseparable from its purpose: if the purpose ceases, the parliament as such is dissolved. An external observer who examined its activities without knowing anything about its purpose could only conclude that it is a meaningless gathering of people: he sees individuals who will acquire meaning only if their purpose is known and they are not intelligible without it. Moreover the individuals who make up the parliament share the same purpose as the institution, which is not external, as in the previous example. Both in the case of inanimate objects and that of animate objects, *the idea of an artificial object cannot be conceived without that of its purpose*, which is precisely the cause of its coming into existence.

A further problem is posed by organisms not endowed with consciousness or by those parts of the human body whose functioning is involuntary, such as the digestive apparatus in the example given above, and in both cases it seems difficult to deny the existence of an immanent teleology intrinsic to the very operation of the organism or of the single organ. It should not be forgotten that finality is not only external, i.e. of the whole that is directed towards some end, but it is also and firstly within the organism, even where there exist purposes without intentions. The final causes have to be retrieved within every organism endowed with life, however small and insignificant it is. Undoubtedly one has to avoid any kind of anthropomorphism in considering the purpose, as would happen if we held that an arrow shot by an archer at a target was a sufficient proof of final causes. In reality it is an incorrect and anthropomorphic example of final causes. The notion of final causes, far from being first established on the level of conscious beings and then extrapolated out of them, should be ascertained from the primordial viewpoint of the being qua agent, within the nexus between the agent and its action, by which the risk of anthropomorphism is avoided.

To sum up this point: in Aquinas we meet with a voluntary finality through which the agent moves freely or by choice

*Aquinas: Nature, Life and Teleology*

towards a known end and a "physical" finality by which the agent moves either towards an end known instinctively (as in the case of animals) or else in an executive way towards an end not known in any way (as in plants).[11] The ontological and gnoseological thematization of these aspects of the question takes the form of what it later came to be called the "principle of finality," of which I shall provide two formulations: a) *potentia dicitur ad actum* (potency refers to act); b) *omne agens agit propter finem* (every agent acts in view of an end / purpose).[12]

In the first case the final cause is understood as an intrinsic ordering of the potency to act, and its question is related to the primordial nexus between potency and act that is valid in every subject liable to change. Finality as immanent ordering of potency to act is present in all beings subject to change. Consequently this formulation of the principle of finality does not possess transcendental range, as it does not apply to God where potency is absent. In the second formulation of the principle, there appears the decisive term

11  "Proprium est naturae rationalis ut tendat in finem quasi se agens vel ducens ad finem: naturae vero irrationalis, quasi ab alio acta vel ducta, sive in finem apprehensum, sicut bruta animalia, sive in finem non apprehensum, sicut ea quae omnino cognitione carent," *S. Th.*, I II, q. 1, a. 2.

12  The formula "omne agens agit propter finem" can be found, for instance, in *S. Th.*, I, q. 44, a. 4; I II, q. 1, a. 2; q. 6, a. 1; q. 9, a. 1; q. 12, a. 1.

    In the *Critique of Judgment* Kant recovers finality, but stops short at the antithesis by which an end is either real, but then is present in the consciousness as a principle of intentional action, or is attributed to the technique of nature, but then is only a subjective rule of the reflecting judgment. For Aristotle even a non-intentional end can exist and have an objective reality. On the concept of intrinsic finality cf. *Physics*, l. II, c. 8.

    Hegel insists upon finality with particular vigor and revalues Aristotle's position, especially in the *Encyclopaedia*: cf. nn. 55, 204, 360. "The definition Aristotle gives of life already contains inner finality; and it is thus infinitely higher than the concept of modern teleology, which has before it only the *finite* finality, *external* finality" (n. 204).

}413{

# Restoring Nature

"agent," which *possesses far more general implications and range than the term "efficient cause."* Reflection on the principle of finality involves a reflection on the concept of agent and action (immanent, transitive, with or without consciousness), and indirectly on that of nature as a principle of becoming. Unlike the first, the second formulation of the principle of finality possesses transcendental range and it applies also to divine action.

To introduce the theme of final causes we have to relaunch a philosophy of action (in an ontological sense even before a moral sense). If we turn our attention to the efficient cause, we come up against the disadvantage of placing ourselves on the side of transitive action alone, forgetting immanent action, where nothing is produced but one's own being is perfected. Newtonian physics, like Monod's biology, in which only efficient causes are considered, is a tributary of an impoverished idea of action and of agent, in the sense that the only action considered is that which works from the outside, so that immanent action and the inner finality of the organism are cancelled.[13]

A philosophy of action and nature can be found in H. Jonas, especially in two well-known works, *Das Prinzip Verantwortung* (*Il principio responsabilità*) and *Organismus und Freiheit* (*Organismo e libertà*), which seek to explore multiple forms of action without postulating a priori the non-existence of a final cause. Jonas's careful analysis, which it is not possible to reconstruct here, reaches an important conclusion:

13  Monod invokes both external forces, which have produced and forged *artificial* objects, and internal forces or "internal morphogenetic interactions" (cf. p. 22) that operate in the living being. By this term, on the one hand he approaches the idea of nature, since the organization of the living thing is not imposed on it from outside but from inside, on the other he interprets internal forces as efficient causes and this fails to escape from mechanicalism. We know, moreover, that for Monod the scientific method consists in a systematic refusal to consider final causes, understood as a project (cf. p. 29). It is symptomatic that Monod understands finality only as project, not as an inner nexus between agent and end.

*Aquinas: Nature, Life and Teleology*

It therefore makes sense (and is not just a metaphor borrowed from our subjectivity) to speak of the immanent purpose, even though wholly unconscious and involuntary, of digestion and the digestive tract of a living body, and to speak of life as the purpose in itself of this body . . . The 'aim', apart from all consciousness, whether animal or human, has in this way been extended to the physical world as its originating principle.[14]

And in the second of the works cited above: "There is no organism without teleology, there is no teleology without inwardness, and besides life can be known only by life."[15]

This means—to repeat another statement by Jonas—that God is never a pure mathematician. One notes the similarity between Jonas's ideas and the philosophy of nature of a vital and teleological stamp to which we are referring, a similarity that stems from the theme of *appetitus* (appetition), which is found throughout living nature, to which Jonas devotes adequate space. Appetition constitutes an important form of action.[16] In substance, the concept of nature signifies not just an operation from within but also an operation in conformity with a purpose: nature is auto-activity towards ends, and even a non-deliberate or non-intentional purpose is real. Think of instinct, which does not know and yet functions towards an end. The mechanistic dualism of the *res extensa*, by which Descartes equated animals with machines and automata, stripped them of all inwardness. They possess no inside, they include no nature as an inner principle of movement. Cartesianism renders the phenomenon of life unintelligible and transforms the concept of soul, which is altered from the principle and form of life into a locus of pure subjectivity (*res cogitans*).

---

14  *Il principio responsabilità,* Einaudi, Turin 1993, p. 94.
15  *Organismo e libertà,* cit., p. 127.
16  On appetition/*appetitus* cf. *S. Th.* I, q. 6, a. 1, ad 2m; q. 59, a. 1; q. 80, a. 1; III, q. 29, a. 1.

Teleology thus seems to appear or disappear depending on whether one adopts a philosophical or scientific approach. The latter adopts a completely disontologized method, which may be useful on its plane, that of purely scientific explanations, and which generally entails an a priori exclusion of all purpose. However, it is essential not to confuse the methodological utility of disregarding finality in sciences and ontological judgment directed to the real being, as Jonas suggests.[17] This position is similar to Maritain's: both observe that natural science fails to tell us everything about nature and that a different (ontological) approach is called for, one that seeks to integrate final causes into the explanation of life. On the plane of scientific method, several scholars consider that the idea of understanding life scientifically (i.e., through physics and chemistry) means assimilating it to that which is not life; it means equating organic with inorganic, setting aside teleology: this is the mechanistic version of the philosophy of nature. For those who adopt a philosophical method, life is understood as a peculiar and original phenomenon; they avoid undue reductionism and hence remain open to the possibility of teleology. It is not rash to add that since scientific method fails to consider either the intrinsic potency-act nexus or the concept of action/agent but only efficient causes, science seems unequipped to recognize teleology.

Attempts to cancel final causes and move towards a "new mechanicalism" applied to life include that accomplished by J. Monod in *L'Hasard et la Necessité* (*Il caso e la necessità*). Monod seeks to explain embryogenesis and ontogenesis only by means of physical and chemical laws, embracing an explicitly reductionist project: "Living beings are chemical machines."[18] The organism, though understood as a machine *sui generis*, which is constructed by itself—i.e., that is not constructed like ordinary machines through the action of external forces and instruments acting on particles of matter (cf. p.48)—is assimilated to a ma-

17  *Il principio responsabilità*, cit., p. 88.
18  *Il caso e la necessità*, Mondadori, Milan 1970, p. 47.

*Aquinas: Nature, Life and Teleology*

chine. The reduction of the living organism to a machine cancels nature as a principle of activity from within and distances the idea that there exist multiple degrees of immanent activity. Another grave limitation of this position is that it marginalizes the ambit of appetition, of the "inclination towards," which cannot be explained in mechanistic terms or reduced to an efficient cause. Monod's perspectives are a consequence of the markedly reductionist premises he adopts, among them the exclusion of all final causes. According to the author the fundamental postulate of scientific method is that nature is objective and not projective,[19] and so the only purpose we can speak of is that within a human subject and his conscious activity.

Monod recognizes three characteristics of living things: teleonomy, autonomous morphogenesis, and reproductive invariability. The third element is easy to understand as it means the unchanging transmission of species' characteristics; teleonomy hints at the fact that all living things are endowed with a project; autonomous morphogenesis alludes to self-construction: living things construct themselves by themselves. However, his systematic refusal to resort to final causes leads firstly to an epistemological contradiction between the postulate of objectivity of nature and teleonomy (the former excludes the teleology which the latter invokes) and secondly to "reducing" teleonomy, which becomes a secondary property derived from invariability, the only one that is valid as a primitive property (the fundamental biological invariability is the DNA: the gene is the unvarying bearer of hereditary characters). This is defended as the only position consistent with the postulate of the objectivity of science, which denies final causes: *the exclusion of teleology is not, however, a result but an a priori prohibition raised by modern science.*[20]

If the philosophical biology advanced by Monod does away with the idea of nature as the inner principle of movement, it places a heavy burden on the sphere of liberty, which meets with

19   Ibid., p. 17.
20   Cf. ibid., p. 32.

}417{

its first attestation and its first (though minimal) condition in the idea of nature as it is presented here: it is nature that, not being reduced to receive forces and messages from without but acting as self-movement and self-construction, conveys the first stirrings of freedom. By contrast, in a universe where everything is determined from outside, it is impossible for freedom to exist, since one condition for its existence is, in fact, immanent action, capable of development starting from within.

### B) Evolution

In hinting at the difficult problem of evolution, we will mention two problems: a) the relationship between creation and becoming; b) the possibility that the hylemorphic doctrines of Aquinas are able to justify the evolution of life better than other recent theories such as that of Monod. We will be concerned solely with evolution of life, putting aside theories on the evolution of the universe, presently fashionable in relation to the subtle Big Bang theory. However, it is wise not to undervalue the mutual support that this theory and that on evolution offer, though the physical becoming of the universe and the evolution of life stay as two very different processes.

a) *Creation and becoming.* The principle *creatio non est mutatio*, of very high importance in Thomas Aquinas and in Christian theology, clarifies the impassable difference between creation understood as the total and absolute position of all things in *being* (*creatio ex nihilo*) and change or transformation (*mutatio*), which supposes existence of that which is/will be subject to becoming and transformation. Now, the realm of becoming and cosmic evolution entirely belongs to *mutatio* and is wholly separate and without influence on *creatio*. As creating does not mean to be the cause of becoming, creation accounts for the existence of things, not for their becoming, which sets a different field of research.[21] The very

---

21 In a thorough study by William Carroll we read: "To use Big Bang cosmology either to affirm creation or to deny it is an example of misunderstandings of both cosmology and creation ... The Big bang

# Aquinas: Nature, Life and Teleology

activity of divine causality operates differently in creation and becoming. In the former, He is not only prime cause but unique and total cause of all being; while in the latter, He operates as prime but not unique cause, because we have to consider also secondary causes endowed with the ability of action and causality.

Philosophy and theology will address themselves to the doctrine of creation, which according to Aquinas is accessible to the knowledge of reason.[22] On the contrary, the realm of change, becoming, cosmic evolution is doubly accessible: to the consideration of philosophy through the analysis of becoming (dialectics of act and potency) and of hylemorphic doctrine, and to the analysis of different sciences. The field of philosophy of nature is exactly the realm of *mutatio* of every degree and order. Consequently there is no possibility of proving or disproving scientifically the philosophical and theological doctrine of creation, as science is concerned only with laws of universal becoming. The idea that scientific fallibilist theories such as the Big Bang can confirm the truth of creation rests on impossible harmonies.

I add that the Big Bang hypothesis stimulates the mind, since it seems to contradict a generally accepted rational postulate that more cannot come from less. On the basis of this postulate, how can we suppose that in an initial, extremely concentrated, mechanical, energy-rich and thermodynamic nucleus pre-contained the whole future development of the cosmos in its almost infinite forms, and life in all its endless richness? How can we exclude that there exists another guiding, transforming, elevating causality? Jonas similarly observes that in the Big Bang model the effect is greatly superior to the cause:

> described by modern cosmologists is a change; it is not creation. The natural sciences cannot themselves provide an ultimate account for the existence of all things. It does not follow, however, that reason remains silent about the origin of the universe. Reason embraces more than the categories of the natural sciences . . . ," "Thomas Aquinas and Big Bang Cosmology," *Sapientia*, n. 53, 1998, p. 81 and p. 93.

22 Cf. *De potentia*, q. 3, a. 5.

In this new sense of "origins" we observe a total reversal of the most ancient idea of the superiority of the creative cause to its effect. It was always supposed that the cause must have contained not just more force but also greater perfection than the effect. The producer must have greater "reality" than that which it produces: it has to be superior even in its formal essence, so as to explain the degree of form enjoyed by the things deduced from it.[23]

The model of genetic deduction introduced by the moderns inverts this order and considers the less as the origin of the *more*.

b) *Aquinas and evolution of life.* Evolution can mean simply change, but it also means oriented change, "change towards." At once the question arises whether it moves towards more complex and perfect forms of life, so that the assumption *id verius quod posterius* (that which comes after, this is truer) is valid. This way of understanding evolution does not exhibit, at first sight, a character of unreality or unreasonableness. Hence a second question: if evolution is directed towards a growing complexity, what ontological metaphysics presents itself as best suited to offer a foundation and an explanation of this event?

In evolution the principal problem to consider is not so much ontogenesis as phylogenesis, the passage or transformation from species to species. Anyone who desires to take the subject of evolution seriously is unlikely to conceive of it in any way except as an event that produces a change of being, i.e., a substantial transformation from which emerges a new living being that previously did not exist. This approach is different from that in which evolution is presented as a simple unfolding of what was given originally, in which—as Bergson seems to maintain—no substantial transformations take place but the unfolding of a single flow of life and *élan vital* which never ends and leads we know not where.

Our aim here must necessarily be somewhat limited: to show that Aquinas's hylemorphic and "vitalistic" ontology includes

23  H. Jonas, *Organismo e libertà*, cit., p. 54.

certain intriguing doctrines which can be used in formulating an evolutionary conception. We shall take as our starting point a passage in the *Summa Contra Gentiles* which deals with the ascending perfection of forms (and substances) in the process of generation and the related substantial transformations, and so opens a path towards a philosophy of evolution of life:

> And so, the more posterior and more perfect an act is, the more fundamentally is the inclination of matter directed toward it. Hence, in regard to the last and most perfect act that matter can attain, the inclination of matter whereby it desires form must be inclined as toward the ultimate end of generation. Now, among the acts pertaining to forms, certain gradations are found. Thus, prime matter is in potency, first of all, to the form of an element. When it is existing under the form of an element it is in potency to the form of a mixed body; that is why the elements are matter for the mixed body. Considered under the form of a mixed body, it is in potency to a vegetative soul, for this sort of soul is the act of a body. In turn, the vegetative soul is in potency to a sensitive soul, and a sensitive one to an intellectual one. This the process of generation shows: at the start of generation there is the embryo living with plant life, later with animal life, and finally with human life. After this last type of form, no later and more noble form is found in the order of generable and corruptible things. Therefore, the ultimate end of the whole process of generation is the human soul, and the matter tends toward it as toward an ultimate form. So, elements exist for the sake of mixed bodies; these latter exist for the sake of living bodies, among which plants exist for animals, and animals for men. Therefore, man is the end of the whole order of generation.[24]

24  *Summa Contra Gentiles*, l. III, c. 22, trans. by V.J. Bourke, University of Notre Dame Press, Notre Dame 1975, pp. 86–87.

RESTORING NATURE

Shortly before this we find another noteworthy passage:

> Prime matter tends to perfection in acquiring in act a form that before it possessed only potentially, though it ceases in this way from having in act what it previously possessed: for in this way matter receives all the forms to which it is in potency, so that its potentiality *is brought to act by stages,* since it is unable to do so simultaneously (my stress).

Aquinas' doctrine transmitted in the above quotations, and in general hylemorphic doctrine about the matter-form relationship, should be understood in its scope. It is a philosophical doctrine which can support and clarify those scientific theories according to which the evolution of life is really passed from vegetable to animal stage and then to a human one. Supposing that sufficient empirical evidence is available for the 'fact' of the evolution of life, then Aquinas' position can be used in order to give an account of how the evolution of life occurred.

His position seems to suggest that the evolution of life has terminated in man. J. Maritain understood it in these terms, in a study in which he advanced the hypothesis that evolution is essentially completed by the appearance of the human species.[25] Evolution has been ascendant and went from the vegetable to the animal, then passed to the world of the spirit with the advent of man, and here it seems to have stopped. This presents the fascinating hypothesis that while the physical evolution of the cosmos may continue endlessly, that of life has already completed its fundamental stages and from now on little is to be expected of it. However, the idea that ascending evolution has ended with man does not imply that every other level of evolution is over; it is not unlikely that the evolution of vegetable and animal species can go on. Naturally there remain all the great questions about how

25 Cf. "Vers une idée thomiste de l'évolution" in *Approches sans entraves,* Fayard, Paris 1973, pp. 105–162.

*Aquinas: Nature, Life and Teleology*

life appeared and then how the spirit developed from it, but in a certain sense they appear to be questions about the past.

Now, if we pay attention to some positions of the new epistemology of physics, for instance that developed by I. Prigogine—very attentive to the phenomenon of irreversibility, to the so-called 'arrow of physical time'—are not we obliged to recognize that Aquinas' treatment seems too linear and simple, too little open to surprise and novelty? An adherent of the position according to which we find in Nature bifurcations, instabilities, surprises, Prigogine explains his view as follows: "Everywhere we direct our observation, we find evolutions, diversifications, instabilities . . . The vision of nature has been subjected to a radical change in respect of the multiple, of the temporal, of the complex."[26] Anyway, as the arrow of time means that the cosmos has an history, this perspective is analogous and perhaps homogeneous with Aquinas' idea of a becoming of life due to really new compositions of prime matter and an unlimited multiplicity of forms. Should Aquinas have conceived this idea in a frame of fixity, this outcome is not essential to the argumentation, which can be placed in a dynamic horizon: we can hardly conceive how many beings can proceed from ever new compositions of matter and form, in a position open to ontological pluralism. This also implies that for philosophy of being the evolution of life is natural, while for Monod it is to some extent pathological, a deviation from normal status. The respective philosophies of evolution differ in keeping with differing conceptions of the becoming of being and of the invariance or stability of being: the first one according to Aquinas, the latter according to Monod.

In fact, his framework is quite different: evolution is not explained as a process within becoming, in the nexus between matter and gradually changing forms, but as an event due to chance and to defects in the mechanism of invariance. In opposition to Aquinas, where we find a natural idea of the evolution of life, he holds that "evolution is not a property of living beings, since its roots lie in the imperfections themselves of the conservative mechanism which, by

26  I. Prigogine, I. Stengers, *La nuova alleanza*, Einaudi, Turin 1981, p. 274.

}423{

contrast, represents their only privilege."[27] Monod is a supporter of stability, of the "prodigious stability of certain species that have succeeded in reproducing without appreciable variations for hundreds of millions of years" (p. 94). Here evolution emerges paradoxically from a stable context and emerges not through an intrinsic disposition of "prime matter" to change of form, but on the basis of chance.[28]

When related to chance, evolution is not "natural," it is an exception. Necessity, invariance, stability are the rule, to such an extent that teleonomy is related to invariance: "The essential teleonomic project consists in the transmission, from one generation to another, of the content of invariancy characteristic of the species." When writing these words, Monod, though fiercely hostile to final causes, is forced to admit them: *the purpose is the transmission of invariance.*[29] Another decisive step is taken by observing that in living things "spontaneous structuring must be considered as a mechanism" (p. 26). Removing "nature" as an activity and as self-construction from within, omitting the link between agent, action and purpose, reducing autonomous morphogenesis to a mechanism, to a stable structure supported by invariance (as happens in the case of lifeless crystalline structures), creates the necessary and sufficient premises to reduce life to non-life.

The variation that gives rise to evolution is random and hence unpredictable. Random mutations are seized on by invariance and transformed into necessity: "Chance alone gives rise to all change, all creation in the biosphere."[30] Chance and necessity also signify contingency plus necessity, a mixture difficult to handle. Evolution thus emerges as almost a pathology of the normal and the previously existing, or one might say that Monod has a conception of evolution

27  *Il caso e la necessità*, cit., p.98.
28  "The only mechanism through which the structure and performance of a protein could be modified and these modifications transmitted, even in part, to its offspring is that which derives from an alteration of the instructions contained in a segment of its DNA sequence." (Ibid., p. 94).
29  Ibid., p. 25.
30  Ibid., p. 95.

*Aquinas: Nature, Life and Teleology*

as an exception.[31] These theories, in which man emerges by chance from the random working of evolutionary mechanisms, help to eliminate from science and culture the idea of natural theology, of a universe created by a wise mind, in which man is the image of God.

The important objections which weaken Monod's position should not lead us to refuse it totally. In my opinion it should be necessary to correlate two lines of argumentation which do not contradict each other: the line of ontology and philosophy of nature, which through hylemorphic doctrine can provide an account of accidental and substantial transformations and of the causes required for this, and the line of empirical sciences, which, according to Monod, tries to explain evolution as a combination of chance and necessity. That a series of unrelated causes can produce a random mutation in an organism and that this can be incorporated through invariance, well, all this can be explained with a different conceptual framework which points to the idea of substantial transformations and of causes required for this output. It is wise to coordinate Monod with Aquinas, but giving direction to the latter. Stripped of its absoluteness, Monod's position on chance and evolution can be partially recuperated, as an element capable of giving rise to different versions of the matter-form relationship.

## Conclusion

The definition of the concepts of nature, of life and of finality that emerges from the positions we have described appears to be of a

---

31  In Monod's scheme invariance is both affirmed to provide a place for stability and also denied to find a place for mutations, which are the contrary of invariance. Invariance seems to be a sort of revolving door that now blocks mutation and now accepts and fixes it. It is denied to find a place for mutation and then straight after affirmed to find a place for the transmission of the mutation. If we wanted to translate Monod's scientific language into the philosophical language of hylemorphism, we would have to say that the formal cause in Monod is invariance, i.e., the DNA that controls the invariance of the species.

}425{

type that is not a priori but ontological-real. They start from the following methodological approach: to study and understand *life* means devoting oneself to studying and understanding *living beings*: in them form is not imposed from the outside, as happens in objects produced by technology, but the living process is the activity itself of the form. By contrast, for some time now, matter devoid of life has become the knowable *par excellence*, that in relation to which we seek to explain life. For materialistic monism the most natural and original state of things is not to be alive. It follows that it is the existence of life in a mechanical universe that requires an explanation, and the explanation has to be advanced in terms of that which is devoid of life. By contrast Aquinas's ontological and epistemological paradigm as embodied in his philosophy of nature and of life offers a different way of understanding this subject.[32] While it can accept within narrow limits the evolutionary model based upon chance and necessity, it is similar to that based on organism and freedom (Jonas). The latter does justice to the commonsense insight that sees life as an open, self-organizing evolutionary phenomenon.

32  Interesting points concerning the theme of life are found in the volume AA. VV., *La vita*, edited by M. Sanchez Sorondo, PUL-Mursia, Rome 1998. Also note the essay "La realtà ontologica dell'evoluzione: dall'universo ordinato alla terra da costruire," by L. Galleni, in AA. VV., *Prismi di verità*, edited by M. Malaguti, Città Nuova, Rome 1997, pp. 141–166. This study insists on the fact that "no reflection of God and hence of God the creator can forego the description of nature and hence of the creation that comes to us from science" (p. 141). Three different theories of evolution are also presented: gene-centered evolution, close to Darwin and Monod (random genic mutations and ordering through natural selection); organism-centered evolution, or evolution of self-organization, in which the appearance of ordered structures in living things is due to phenomena of self-organization; biosphere-centered evolution, which assumes as its scientific object the whole biosphere and the relationships of living things to one another and to the non-living; and which seeks to identify a preferential direction in evolution towards forms of greater complexity (this is the case of Teilhard de Chardin and the assumption of the evolutionary movement towards the noosphere).

# The Primary End of Marriage
### Anthony Rizzi
### California Institute of Technology
### and Louisiana State University

Man is the crown of material nature. No physical being exceeds him in worth, dignity or glory. After the gift of the intellect and will, the next most striking thing about man is that he is *two*. God created him male *and* female. Man was alone and radically incomplete before his helpmate was made. She is bone of his bone, flesh of his flesh. They are one in species, yet they are different; they are complementary. Man is head, she is heart. As with all aspects of man, his sexuality is both in his physical and his spiritual sides. The best place to begin understanding this sexual nature is in the union of marriage. If we can understand here we can begin to understand his nature more completely.

Not too long ago I was involved in a mail conversation with a bishop about the primary end of marriage. I held, with the magisterium of the Church,[1] that the primary end of marriage is procreation; his position was quite ambiguous and in fact implied that the unity[2] of husband and wife *and* procreation were *both* the primary end of marriage. It is from this and similar experiences

---

1 St. Thomas, St. Augustine and Pius XI in his encyclical "*On Christian Marriage*" (the latter makes the matter one of virtual certainty) are among the teachers of the Catholic Church that manifest this position. Pius XII also made statements about the importance of remembering the primary end of marriage: procreation (cf. D2295).

2 By unity, one means not a vague ambiance, but the oneness—note that "unity" contains the word "unit," meaning one—that comes through a commitment that matures into a habit of fidelity and trust.

# RESTORING NATURE

that I came to know the state of the culture[3] on this question and to conclude that special emphasis must be put on the question: what is the primary end of marriage? This is fitting also because one must know what something is for and where it tends before one can really understand it. In fact, following Aristotle, one would like to know what marriage is made from, what it is made into, what causes the transition and what it's for. The final cause will implicitly contain the first three.

Many of us have been blessed with parents who are living demonstrations of the essence of marriage, the real love between a man and woman. Those who do not have such parents also know because of what was/is missing in their life and, most manifestly, by the resulting pain. Members of both groups know, by presence and by absence respectively, how important offspring are to the marriage of their parents, for they are the fruit of their union, the very personification of their love. Yet, which comes first: does the love between the man and the woman, in principle, precede procreation or is it the other way around? More precisely, is marriage constituted[4] such that its primary end is the procreation of children or is its primary aim the unity of the spouses?[5]

3   Both the secular culture and the Catholic subculture share a lack of commitment to the proposition that procreation is the primary end of marriage. Since culture shapes us in hidden ways, it is particularly important to raise the flag of danger at the potholes in current thought and habit that lead to the erroneous positions.

4   Of course, this constitution of marriage entails a respective constitution in the nature of mankind so that this marital relationship is native to the relationship between man and woman.

5   One might of course argue for other candidates for primary aims, but these certainly are the most obvious candidates; indeed, one would have to strain beyond comprehension at any that did not reduce in the end to something essential to one or both of these. There are lower level (third and beyond) ends that may be discussed; since the fall of man, for example, St. Paul says that marriage can be a remedy to concupiscence (i.e., disordered desire—ordered desire and pleasure are part of God's design). This end should not be looked down on, given our current state, which still is under the effects of

}428{

*The Primary End of Marriage*

Let's dispose of the most obvious solution quickly. One might say, as the bishop mentioned above, that they are both the primary end. To do this one must forget the logical law of the excluded middle, or the ontological form of it: something cannot be and not be at the same time and in the same manner. Logically, either the primary end[6] of marriage is procreation or it is unity; it cannot be both.[7] The only way that both could be the primary end is if they were really the same thing. It may be argued that in the Trinity that is the case.[8] In the case of mankind, however, it is clear that two really distinct things are involved: one involves little people coming into being, the other does not. In fact, modern culture is a window shop of examples of how these distinct things can be separated. Indeed, much of modern moral discourse, within and without the Church, shows that these ends are so far from being the same thing that many fall into the error of saying

the fall. Yet, to understand a thing, it is best to recall its natural state, not its state after its partial corruption. Its corrupted state can then be put into a proper perspective.

6    Here, as throughout this paper, I use the word "end" in its full philosophical meaning—i.e., the reason for existence or final cause.

7    Of course, there is no question that different things can have different primary ends. However, recall that we focus on one entity: the thing called marriage. For it to be one, for it to have its own unity, it must not be divided against itself. Also, one must note that immaterial aspects, such as the primary end, can only be distinguished by *what they are*, not by *where they are*, since they have no *"where."* This distinction is a particularly difficult one for the modern mind, immersed as it is in the pictorial (imagination) and the material. Here, one can have, in some sense, two winners of a race. The winner of the race is the guy who crosses the finish line first; because one man is here and the other there, they can cross the line at the same time. This, in turn, can happen because of the quantitative separation that obtains in material things. In a non-material thing, like justice, one cannot have two parallel instances, two parallel justices; one would be justice, the other injustice. There is no "place," no *"where,"* to separate them; hence they must be separated in their *what.*

8    One must, of course, use an analogical meaning for procreation.

## RESTORING NATURE

that they are completely separable—whence, we get the not-so-long-ago academic fad of deriding *Humane Vitae*.

Two things, however, can be such that one contains the other as the soul contains the body or as the mold contains the form of the object that will be cast. As we know, man is not a soul with a body added but a soul whose very nature is to be united with a body. Without the body it's not really a man. In the same way, procreation could imply unity or vice-versa. So, which of these two *apparent* possibilities is the truth?

Well, one cannot argue that unity is the primary end of marriage and that procreation is thereby required by the unity. Saints and others unite with family and friends in the most intimate ways; no children result. In case you say "but these are not as intimate," consider that most of us attempt and, in various degrees, are united with God, and that does not procreate babies[9] and never has, even with the greatest of saints. Further, we are told that procreation does not exist in heaven; if unity requires procreation in its conception then obviously none will be united in heaven. So, the reasonable person must conclude that unity among men doesn't require openness to procreating children with each other.[10]

9   Recall that we are talking about procreation of children concretely—not the spiritual, analogous thing, but the actual physical procreation of children; otherwise we have left our subject and are talking about something else.

10   Because unity does not necessarily include procreation, making unity the primary end of marriage deprives marriage of any truly unique character and makes it indistinguishable, say, from the relationship of two life long friends. Unity, thus, is more generic, and marriage is a specification of the type of unity; the predicate "procreation" demands the subject "marriage." All unity among men, including marriage, has as its ultimate goal bringing men to their final end, God. For marriage as marriage, the primary end is procreation. As part of the generic category "unity," *not* as marriage *per se*, one can say that marriage is primarily directed towards unity of the spouses with God—just as one might say a clock is for primarily for telling time, but all telling time is for ordering one's activity so as to get done what one should.

*The Primary End of Marriage*

Now there is only one option left if one is to be able to say, as common sense does, that unity and procreation are inextricably linked in marriage. One must say that procreation includes the concept of unity between the man and a woman. How is this so?

Let's look at procreation in general. In the lowest of animals procreation does not even demand two individuals of the species. This is because the creature under consideration is so low on the scale of life, so close to inanimate objects, that its reproduction does not demand much more than it would to change one stone into two by simply breaking it in half. The goal in this case, which is preservation of the species, requires no more. As one rises to higher animals, the needs of the species rise and the mode of procreation eventually moves to reproduction involving a female and a male. Here nature's goal is still preservation of the species, but the individuals, in particular the offspring (which indeed every individual is), demand more and more. The higher one ascends, the higher the demand. The highest non-human primates require not only the biological advantages of male and female parents, but they also require specific training (like hunting) as well as general training of the sensory intelligence and emotive powers. In other words, the most advanced animals require the analog of a human upbringing, but only an analog—not the thing itself.

When one reaches man, a threshold is crossed: he has an intellect and will; he is a person. The goal is no longer preservation of the species, but is now the good of the individual. The aforementioned spiritual nature of the man gives man a dignity infinitely far above the purely material world of the animals. He is not made to be used, but to be loved. He can never be a mere means to an end, like an artifact with no essential nature. He is a self, a knower, so has his *own* end (an end *for* himself, as self), Truth Himself.[11]

In short, procreation has a meaning *dependent* on what is being procreated. If the procreation[12] under consideration is that of

11  Such dignity was raised to unspeakable higher levels by adoption into the life of the Godhead at Baptism.

12  Here I am employing an analogical use of the word procreation.

RESTORING NATURE

animals, then the union that produces the offspring must be consonant with the needs and goals of the animal species. In fact, it may not even demand a union. However, the procreation of a man is the procreation of something that demands of its nature to be loved. By necessity of his nature, a dignity in body and spirit must attend his coming to being. It would not befit a man to be grown in a garden like a vegetable or to be brought into existence in a human factory. No, the nature of man calls for—indeed demands—coming into being from love. In like manner, man is only happy in loving; so the progenitors would violate their own specific nature, as well as that of their offspring, if they did not bring the offspring into the world through love. The most profound level of this love is the love between two[13] that is so effective and real that it demands to be incarnate in some way. That is, it "produces" and then naturally overflows toward a third. Again, if a man is not the product of a real commitment, a real love,[14] he is not receiving his need as man. His nature is being suppressed, even undone in some way. In fact, the complementarities of man and woman call in a special way for this unity.

Hence, when one says that the primary end of marriage is procreation, one presupposes that a real living growing love

Univocally speaking, someone may argue that the word only applies to the joint action of God and man in creating another man. God alone creates the soul of man, but man acts as a necessary agent by God's design.

13   This seems especially true in a limited creature like man.
14   Recall that love demands a second person and a whole love requires reciprocation. Further, one may *not* say that the child could be the object of the love and thereby obviate the need for two spouses, because, among many other things, the child does not exist before the act of love brings him into being. Such a love for the non-existent child that attempts to separate out one of the parents is not a true love for it is, at best, love of an abstraction, not the love of a person. It is a love that rejected the opportunity of loving an already existent person as well as the need of the offspring to be the center of an already existing mutual love. In short, to attempt to love outside the boundaries of one's nature and the nature of those to be loved is no love at all.

}432{

*The Primary End of Marriage*

between a man and woman must exist. In no other way could the procreation under question be the one proper to man. Procreative love is the primary end of marriage. Said in another way, human procreation is the predicate that implies its proper subject: marriage. It is perseity in the second sense of St. Thomas.

The Christian can better understand this love that is fecund, this love that overflows outside of itself. God created marriage for the purpose of procreation and procreation was to be in analogy[15] with His own inner life. That is, God created man in His image.[16] He, in His desire to share His goodness, crafted such a splendid nature for that image of Himself which is us that according to His design it would include an echo of His own nature; man would be given the power to procreate.[17] He would be made two *so that* a third could come forth. He would be made male and female so that *by* their profound love a child would be conceived under God's loving Providence. God thereby would create a triangle of triangles, resounding echoes of His awesome nature. He, being Trinitarian, would create man with an analogical trinitarian nature. The Christian knows that God is Trinity, that man, woman and child are an analogous trinity, and, though *the world says it takes two* to make a child, *the Christian knows it takes three.*

Marriage, then, exists so that man may procreate and in this way have a unique expression of love—a love so deep it "generates" another, thereby multiplying opportunity for love. In this fashion, man shares by analogy in God's inner nature. Like the Father, the human father must watch over, guide and educate his

---

15  Unity and "procreation" won't be strictly identical as they are in the Trinity.
16  Each individual man is created in the image of God by reason of his intellect. This discourse shows that the image of God imparted to man exists at more than one level. However, the second level "image" (procreation) is on a much lower plane of analogy than the first.
17  Keep in mind that in man this means procreation of persons. So, for example, the trinitarian image is not present in animals in this profound way, but in a much weaker analogical way.

}433{

RESTORING NATURE

children. But, before (in time) this, he must love his wife as his own body, just as before creating us the Father loved the Son.[18] One could go on, but it is clear that procreation properly understood demands unity of love of the husband and wife and more.

So we are now ready to state the full array of facts about marriage. In answering Aristotle's four questions, one may say the following about marriage:

**Material cause**—that out of which something is made: *a man and a woman.*

**Formal cause**—that into which something is made: *a uniquely ordered (specified by the final cause) unity of life and love.*

**Efficient cause**—that which causes something to be made: *the express consent of the spouses.*

**Final cause**—the reason for existence: *procreation (properly understood) of children (which includes the formal cause as said above).*

Several objections may arise to the final cause as stated above. An objection may arise that a man meets and, in the proper order, loves a woman before he marries her and has children. This question springs from confusion between order in principle and order in time. The order in which the events related to marriage happen *in time* is first to meet, court and propose to a woman. If the woman accepts, the marriage can be formed. However, even in the order of time the principle shows itself early on. For the young man, when he asks the woman to marry him, is really saying "I love you so much that I would like you to bear our children." And the woman in response is saying "I love you so much that I would like to bear our children." Procreation, properly understood, is at the heart of marriage. Indeed, the sexual act is the clear statement of this procreative love. This, then, underlines the fact that the primary reason for the existence of marriage is procreation, what happens when notwithstanding.

A more difficult objection asks "if procreation is the primary end of marriage, what about couples who have not been able to

18   The love of the Father and the Son is the Holy Spirit, but we are children by adoption.

}434{

*The Primary End of Marriage*

have children?" It seems that in this description of marriage, the couple is not married and this contradicts Church teaching. To answer this point, further clarifications and important distinctions must be made.

We begin by restating the definition of marriage, including concepts only implicit before, in an explicit manner. The essence of marriage is the commitment of a man and a woman to love each other for life; included in that love is commitment to give to each other the gift of being united spiritually and the right[19] of uniting physically. If a child is impossible for reasons that are not deliberate on the part of the man and woman, the act itself remains a valid, good and indeed holy act. Recall that procreation in man necessarily implies love.[20] The marital act is the instrument of this procreation and thus must include in its nature an expression of the love between the man and the woman. St. Thomas says, as the Church does, that this is an instrument of grace. In this way, this act of love, which can bring a man into the world, becomes the act of bringing God into the love of the man and the woman. In the case where a child is not possible, the act is deprived of its ultimate power, yet it still has its aspects of expression of love and unity that are built into the act so as to make it the fitting setting when it calls the hand of God to create a child.

It may be helpful to use some analogies. If by some impossibility the sacrament of the sick were to be rendered inactive as a sacrament, it would nonetheless be a good way to prepare oneself for whatever graces God might send near death. This analogy is

---

19 In fact, marriage only depends on the giving of the right to the goods of marriage—not on the actual fact of exercising the right. Take, for example, a couple who is not impotent (but may be sterile) and who, after their marriage ceremony and before their wedding night, were killed in a car wreck. Would their marriage be invalid by reason of not being consummated? No, because they were capable of sexual intercourse and they freely gave that right to each other.

20 Not to say the act forces love, but that it must have love to be what it naturally expresses and is meant to be, not a perversion.

}435{

RESTORING NATURE

imperfect in that what remains in the case of a couple unable to have children is more profound than what remains in the analogy.[21] In the analogy, the grace of the sacrament is lost, and in the marriage the special fruit of the union is lost. In absolute terms, the loss is an unfathomable loss. The marriage suffers a true evil—the inability to procreate. It does not serve compassion to deny that a man who loses an arm suffers an evil. Saying it is not bad only serves to convince the person undergoing the loss that the speaker has no real understanding of his suffering. However, in the same way that a man would still be a man if he lost an arm or even if he lost everything but some small and tenuous hold on his bodily life, i.e., some small connection keeping body and soul together, a marriage is possible as long as the couple has at least some last vestige of that inextricable connection between procreation and unity. In such a marriage, conjugal love itself is the last vestige of the procreative life.[22] The drama of procreation, sexual intercourse, an act of mutual giving, of expressing love of each other, can still occur even though there is no earthly[23] hope of its completion—i.e., a child.

The childless couple can make their marriage fruitful through adoption of children or through becoming special protectors of unborn children or in an infinite number of other ways. But, an especially powerful path of grace in such a marriage must be their love expressed in the conjugal act. All this obtains because the primary end of marriage is procreation.[24]

21 We have already mentioned that the act can be the source of marital graces.
22 Hence, in the case of permanent impotence no marriage is possible, because the primary end would not even be rescued by its link with the secondary end of love and unity between the man and wife.
23 One never knows, for St. Elizabeth, thought to be sterile, gave birth to St. John the Baptist.
24 Mediating on procreation, properly understood, as the primary end of marriage bears out, in a more complete way, the truth of the thoughts and arguments of Pope Paul VI and Pope John Paul II on the subject of marriage and the conjugal act.

*The Primary End of Marriage*

Man's sexual nature is not completely elucidated by studying marriage alone, but much of that nature is revealed and entry points to the rest are uncovered by understanding it.

# From Nature to God:
## The Physical Character of Saint Thomas Aquinas' First Way
### Mario Enrique Sacchi
### School of War of the Argentine Navy
### (Buenos Aires)

Many philosophers think that all the famous Thomistic five ways are demonstrations of a metaphysical character, so much so, that they only deal with these demonstrations when they must approach the question about if there is a God in their analysis on the subject of first philosophy. Contrary to this opinion, in this paper we will try to prove that Saint Thomas Aquinas' first way is not a metaphysical demonstration, but an argument which belongs to philosophy of nature properly.

It is also important to notice that it was not St. Thomas who propounded for the first time the five ways. In 1932 René Arnou, S. J., former professor at the Pontifical Gregorian University, edited an anthology where he transcribed the main demonstrations offered by several philosophers who developed those proofs before Aquinas.[1] Let us restrict our considerations only to the first way. Arnou's anthology shows that Plato,[2]

---

1 Cf. *De quinque viis Sancti Thomae ad demonstrandum Dei exsistentiam apud antiquos Graecos et Arabes et Iudaeos praeformatis vel adumbratis: Textus selectos*, collegit et notis illustravit Renatus Arnou, S. J. (Romae: Apud Aedes Pontificiae Universitatis Gregorianae, 1932).
2 Cf. Plato, *Leges* X 893b-896b. See *De quinque viis Sancti Thomae...*, pp. 11–15.

*From Nature to God*

Aristotle,[3] and Maimonides[4] expounded this proof prior to St. Thomas. But, although Aquinas admitted Plato's original authorship of the first way, he affirmed that Aristotle's explanation follows in the steps of his master with only the exception of some linguistic differences in the way's formulation.[5]

St. Thomas drew up the first way by synthesizing and making deeper Aristotle's sentences such as they were stated in Books VII and VIII of his *Physics*. Aquinas summarized the Aristotelian theory as follows:

> The first and more manifest way is the argument from motion. It is certain, and evident to our senses, that in the world some things are in motion. Now whatever is in motion is put in motion by another, for nothing can be in motion except it is potentially that towards which it is in motion; whereas a thing moves inasmuch as it is in act. For motion is nothing else than the reduction of something from potentiality to actuality. But nothing can be reduced from potentiality to actuality, except by something in a state of actuality. Thus that which is actually hot, as fire, makes wood, which is potentially hot, to be actually hot, and thereby moves and changes it. Now it is not possible that the same thing should be at once in actuality and potentiality in the same respect, but only in different respects. For what is actually hot cannot simultaneously be potentially hot; but it is

3  Cf. Aristotle, *Phys.* Bk. VII, ch. 1: 241b-243a2; Bk. VIII, ch. 5: 257a33–258b9; *Metaphys.* Bk. IV, ch. 6: 1071b3–22; Bk. XII, ch. 7: 1072b14–30; Bk. XII, ch. 8: 1073a14–b1; 1074a10–17, and a38–b14. See *De quinque viis Sancti Thomae...*, pp. 21–41.

4  Cf. Maimonides, *Dux Perplexorum*, Bk. II, ch. 2. See *De quinque viis Sancti Thomae...*, pp. 73–79.

5  "Aristoteles, ponens omne quod movetur ab alio moveri, a Platone qui posuit aliqua moveri seipsa non dissentit in sententia sed solum in verbis" (St. Thomas Aquinas, *In VIII Phys.*, lect. 1, n. 7). Cf. *Summ. c. Gent.* I, 13. See *De quinque viis Sancti Thomae...*, p. 13, footnote 1.

}439{

## RESTORING NATURE

simultaneously potentially cold. It is therefore impossible that in the same respect and in the same way a thing should be both mover and moved, i.e. that it should move itself. Therefore, whatever is in motion must be put in motion by another. If that by which it is put in motion be itself put in motion, then this also must needs be put in motion by another, and that by another again. But this cannot go on to infinity, because then there would be no first mover, and consequently, no other mover; seeing that subsequent movers move only inasmuch as they are put in motion by the first mover; as the staff moves only because it is put in motion by the hand. Therefore it is necessary to arrive at a first mover, put in motion by no other; and this everyone understands to be *God*.[6]

It is clear that St. Thomas respected strictly Aristotle's physical argument. The reasoning of the Thomistic first way belongs to the discourse of philosophy of nature. We find in this proof no resort to metaphysical apodictics, to such an extent that Aquinas limited his statements to speculation on the subject of philosophy of movable being. That is why the first way begins with the explicit declaration "The first and more manifest way is the argument from motion." The starting point of this demonstration confirms its physical character: "It is certain, and evident to our senses, that in the world some things are in motion." Moreover, before St. Thomas, Aristotle was convinced of the absolute priority of motion as the act first known by man's senses and intellect.[7] Aquinas

6 St. Thomas Aquinas, *Summ. theol.* I, q. 2, a. 3c, trans. by the Fathers of the English Dominican Province, 2nd ed., Online Edition 2000 by Kevin Knight. Cf. *Comp. theol.* I, 4; *In VII Phys.*, lect. 1, n. 4.

7 "The word 'actuality', which we connect with 'complete realit', has, in the main, been extended from movements to other things; for actuality in the strict sense is thought to be identical with movement. And so people do not assign movement to non-existent things, though they do asssign some other predicates" (Aristotle, *Metaphys.*

*From Nature to God*

echoed the Philosopher's doctrine. St. Thomas say that motion, among all the acts, is maximally evident and patent to us for we know it by sense perception. That is why motion is the first thing men call *act*, and from motion many other things are called *acts* as well.[8]

The physical study of movable beings shows that the existence of motion requires both the potential state of a movable subject capable of moving in order to reach some perfection absent from its own nature, and an extrinsic cause, or a mover, which puts that subject in motion. Potentiality is a *conditio sine qua non* of motion because everything in motion seeks perfections of which it finds itself bereft. Otherwise, it would seek nothing, for the possession of perfections implies necessarily an actual, not potential, state of accomplishment. Furthermore, an extrinsic mover is also necessary to put a movable thing in motion because, as Aquinas points out, " . . . it is not possible that the same thing should be at once in actuality and potentiality in the same respect," in such a way that it is impossible that " . . . it should move itself." As we can see, this Thomistic statement also discloses the physical foundations of St. Thomas' firm rejection of any absurd *causa sui*.

Now, provided that "whatever is in motion must be put in motion by another," there are no reasons for going on to infinity

---

Bk. IX, ch. 3: 1047a30–34, trans. by W. D. Ross, in *The Works of Aristotle*, 2nd ed., 7th rpt. [Oxford: Clarendon Press, 1972], *ad locum*).

8   "[Aristoteles] dicit quod hos nomen actus, quod ponitur ad significandum entelechiam et perfectionem, scilicet formam, et alia huiusmodi, sicut sunt quaecumque operationes, veniunt maxime ex motibus quantum ad originem vocabuli. Cum enim nomina sunt signa intelligibilium conceptionum, illis primo imponimus nomina, quae primo intelligimus, licet sint posteriora secundum ordinem naturae. Inter alios autem actus, maxime est nobis notus et apparens motus, qui sensibiliter a nobis videtur. Et ideo ei primo impositum fuit nomen actus, et a motu ad alia derivatum est" (St. Thomas Aquinas, *In IX Metaphys.*, lect. 3, n. 1805, editio iam a M.-R. Cathala, O. P, exarata retractatur cura et studio Raymundi M. Spiazzi, O. P. [Taurini & Romae: Marietti, 1950], p. 432a).

}441{

# Restoring Nature

or in an endless series of causes. All causes caused by another are effects of a preceding cause from which they receive their moving power. However, if there were not a first cause of motion, from which all effects in motion receive their moving power, there would be no second causes of motion, which stands in contradiction to both common experience and the principle of causality. It is thus that human reasoning comes to the conclusion that the causality of a first mover, "put in motion by no other," as St. Thomas says, is absolutely necessary for moved movers to exercise their own moving causality inasmuch as they are second causes of every subsequent motion.

St. Thomas' first way has been misinterpreted by many authors who thought that his loyalty to Aristotle's philosophy of nature would be an insurmountable obstacle because it could not be adapted to the modern scientific understanding of the world. For instance, Étienne Gilson was of the opinion that the Aristotelian *Weltanschauung*, which is at the base of Aquinas' first way, would be the main impediment for accepting it nowadays:

> The first way is presented by Thomas Aquinas as more 'manifest' because the fact of motion from which it starts is particularly evident to sense. Nevertheless, its language is disconcerting to modern readers because it is borrowed from a scientific view of the world that has ceased to be considered scientifically valid.[9]

According to Gilson, St. Thomas' first way depends on Aristotle's physical conception of the material universe. Both Aristotle and Aquinas accepted an old-fashioned universe in which

> .. directions in space are physically real; the is a 'high' and there is a 'low'. The world is made up of four elements, with the heaviest one, earth, at the center of

9   Étienne Gilson, *Elements of Christian Philosophy* (New York: The American Library, 1963), p. 64.

}442{

*From Nature to God*

things. All heavenly bodies are satellites circling around the earth, each of them moved by its own mover, and the demonstration consists in showing that the number of these separate Movers must need be finite. Less strongly marked, even there, than it was in Maimonides, the presence of the Aristotelian cosmography in this [Thomistic] formulation of the proof cannot be overlooked.[10]

It is well known that Gilson's criticism of Aristotle's and Aquinas' cosmology increased more and more throughout the literary career of the French historian and philosopher. Nevertheless, one does not find in his criticism the strict distinction between, on the one hand, Aristotle's and St. Thomas' philosophical conception of the material world and, on the other, their prudential respect for the theories of the ancient astronomers, cosmographers, and biologists whose opinions, given that they had no philosophical scope, were notwithstanding useful just for "keeping up appearances," so much so that neither Aristotle nor Aquinas considered those opinions as if they were apodictical inferences. On the contrary, they resulted from the investigations of a certain kind of epistemic knowledge which Aristotle attributed to what he called *mixed sciences* and St. Thomas *scientiae mediae*, i.e., that kind of science today comprised within the range of mathematical physics.[11]

Gilson insisted constantly that Aristotle's cosmology is unsuitable for upholding St. Thomas' first way:

> . . . we today are so far removed from the universe of the Greeks that to start from the physical framework of

---

10  Ibid.

11  Cf. Juan Alfredo Casaubon, "Sobre las relaciones entre la filosofía y las ciencias positivas": *Universitas* (Buenos Aires) 1 / 1 (1967) 48–53; Id., "Las relaciones entre la ciencia y la filosofía": *Sapientia* 24 (1969) 89–122; and Gustavo Eloy Ponferrada, "Ciencia y filosofía en el tomismo": Ibid. 47 (1992) 18–19. See also Mario Enrique Sacchi, *Elucidaciones epistemológicas* (Buenos Aires: Basileia, 1997), pp. 139–227.

RESTORING NATURE

such a universe in order to prove anything is to disqualify the whole argument [viz., Aquinas' first way] at the
very outset . . .[12]

It is very difficult for us to know why Gilson interpreted the Aristotelian-Thomistic argument from motion just by contrasting this
philosophical demonstration with the modern development of
mathematical physics. At least to some extent, Gilson's position,
such as we can deduce it from his own words, seemed to leave
aside the philosophical nature of the *ex motu* proof:

That which is moving continues to move in virtue of
the same property of matter by which it remains at rest
unless acted upon by some external force. At the level
of purely scientific explanation, which was that of Aristotle, given that bodies are already in motion, no
prime mover is required in order to account for this motion.[13]

If one considers these statements verbatim, it would seem necessary to infer that Gilson rejected the first way outright because he
denied the truth of its very starting point: *Omne quod movetur ab
alio movetur*—Whatever is in motion is put in motion by another.
To say "That which is moving continues to move in virtue of the
same property of matter by which it remains at rest unless acted
upon by some external force," as Gilson did, implies falling into
the old mechanicist error of those thinkers who ignored the capital Scholastic distinction between the pure potentiality of first
matter and the degrees of potentiality existing in every sensible
body, that which is the reason why mediaeval philosophers called
it *materia secunda*. Furthermore, in saying that " . . . given that bodies are already in motion, no prime mover is required in order to
account for this motion," Gilson neglected plainly the principle

12 Étienne Gilson, *Elements of Christian Philosophy*, p. 65.
13 Ibid.

}444{

*From Nature to God*

of causality, for both Aristotle and St. Thomas proved that a first unmoved mover is absolutely necessary to put in motion every moved mover and every moved thing as well. It is surprising to hear from a Thomist philosopher, as Gilson was, such a grave denial of the principle of causality as was stated in his last assertion.

Another defect perceived in Gilson's interpretation of the first way lies in his unfitting comparison of the philosophical status of this proof with the mechanics of modern mathematical physics. The Aristotelian-Thomistic first way arises from a process carried out according to the demonstrative method of philosophy of nature. Inversely, Gilson's objection to this proof starts from a vast prejudice against Aristotle's philosophy of nature, which St. Thomas echoed almost entirely, for Gilson thought that the Greek-Scholastic philosophy of nature would have been overcome as a whole by modern mathematical physics. In the last analysis, Gilson lessened the first way because he misunderstood the very philosophical signification of this proof.

Three conclusions can be extracted from this brief assessment of Aquinas' first way. Firstly, it is evident that the *ex motu* proof demonstrates apodictically the absolute necessity of a prime unmoved mover whereas all the other ones are invariably moved movers, and, at the same time, all these movers in motion receive their own causal power by participating in the causality of that first unmoved mover. Such as it has been included in his *Summa theologiae*, I, q. 2, a. 3c, St. Thomas developed the first way as a syllogism whose logical form shows the rigorous deduction of its inference from its premises. Moreover, Aquinas saw no difficulty in assigning a divine nature to the first unmoved mover—which "everyone understands to be *God*"— because it is patent that being such a cause of every motion is not predicated of any wordly mover. Consequently, the supra-mundane essence of the prime unmoved mover makes clear that its entity transcends entirely all wordly beings, at least implicitly.

We can also deduce a second conclusion from Aquinas' first way, i.e., that, in addition to His supra-mundane transcendence, another four attributes are predicated of God's quiddity, namely

}445{

RESTORING NATURE

immovability, immutability, eternity, and the greatest perfection. Immovability is predicated of God's nature because it is included in the first way's inference: God is understood as the prime mover which is never in motion. The same must be said of the divine immutability since a being which is never in motion cannot change, for the first unmoved mover has no passive potency to obtain any further actuality. Eternity also predicates of the prime unmoved mover because every movable thing, stricly speaking, is a sensible body which moves itself in time; but given that God is essentially the first unmoved mover, time is not an adequate measure of His duration. Finally, the prime unmoved mover's perfection is the greatest one because its immovability implies that it needs nothing, for motion is always an operation of a being in potency in order to reach perfections absent from its own essence.

Let us clarify the scope of these physical deductions of the above-mentioned divine attributes. Philosophy of nature deduces them within the range of its own scientific method, for they are deduced inmmediately from the very conclusion of the first way. However, the physical deduction of these attributes does not mean that the philosophy of movable being is itself a theorization on God's nature. Philosophy of nature includes no theological speculation within its epistemic range. In a noteworthy passage of his commentary on Boethius' book *On the Trinity*, St. Thomas declared explicitly that the philosopher of nature deals only with sensible things because the subject of his research is limited to movable wordly entities, so that a being absolutely unmoved, as God Himself is, cannot be studied within the subject of this philosophical knowledge. Aquinas said that natural science does not deal with the prime mover as though it were its own subject or a part of this subject. Philosophy of nature deals with the first mover just as the *terminus ad quem* of its investigation, but the *terminus ad quem* does not belong to the quiddity of things which the philosopher of sensible being studies, even though it is in a certain way related to such things. For instance, the term of a line is not a line, but its term keeps a certain relation to the line. So,

}446{

*From Nature to God*

even though the prime mover's nature is really different from the nature of movable things, it is related to them inasmuch as it is the principle of their movements. Therefore, philosophy of nature deals with the first unmoved mover in the measure that it is the cause of every motion which movable beings exercise, which is to say that such a science does not investigate the prime mover's essence, but only takes into consideration the first mover's moving condition.[14] In consequence, the physical deduction of some divine attributes does not mean that philosophy of nature is concerned with a speculation on God's nature. Philosophy of nature deduces them without getting involved expressly in an inquiry into God's quiddity, but the analysis of those divine attributes in themselves is a concern of another science.

The third conclusion reads as follows: it is presupposed in the very starting point of metaphysicians' philosophical theology that there is a prime unmoved mover which possesses certain attributes, but the consideration of these divine attributes cannot be carried out by the philosopher of nature himself, for this investigation belongs to the subject whose subject is being as such. In fact, philosophy of nature cannot advance on the content of many inferences gotten from its own scientific reasoning. Let us take for example two physical deductions. *A)* One of them is concerned with the demonstration of the subsistence and immortality of human soul. Philosophy of nature proves both these attributes

---

14 "De primo motore non agitur in scienti naturali tamquam de subiecto vel de parte subiecti, sed tamquam de termino ad quem scientia naturalis perducit. Terminus autem non est de natura rei, cuius est terminus, sed habet aliquam habitudinem ad rem illam, sicut terminus lineae non est linea, sed habet ad eam aliquam habitudinem ita etiam et primus motor est alterius naturae a rebus naturalibus, habet tamen ad eas aliquam habitudinem, in quantum influit eis motum, et sic cadit in consideratione naturalis, scilicet non secundum ipsum, sed in quantum est motor" (St. Thomas Aquinas, *Expositio super librum Boethii De Trinitate*, q. 5, a. 2, ad 3, recensuit Bruno Decker, editio photomechanice iterata [Leiden: E.J. Brill, 1965], pp. 177–178).

of man's substantial form by means of its own scientific method, but it cannot find out how our soul subsists and lives in a state of separation from the body. *B)* The same happens with Aristotle's and Aquinas's first way, for it demonstrates physically that there is a prime mover absolutely immovable and immutable, but philosophy of nature cannot develop a further argument to prove why both its immovability and immutability lead us to deduce that God lives a completely quiet life which is the best and the happiest one. In Books VII and VIII of his *Physics* Aristotle proves that there is a prime mover absolutely unmoved and immutable, but he demonstrates that God's life is the best and happiest one only in Book Lambda of the *Metaphysics*:

> We say therefore that God is a living being, eternal, most good, so that life and duration continuous and eternal belong to God; for this *is* God.[15]

St. Thomas' first way does not resort to metaphysical reasoning because he was persuaded that philosophy of nature proves efficaciously and sufficiently that there is a prime unmoved mover. It is true that some Scholastic interpreters of this way present it as though it were able to demonstrate God's universal efficient causality, or as if the proof for a prime unmoved mover would demonstrate that it is the first uncaused cause of everything. But this is a wrong interpretation of the first Thomistic way, for such an assumption would render the second one—the *via causalitatis primi agentis*—completely superfluous. In short, we find no reasons for seeing in Aquinas' first way a metaphysical demonstration of God because he developed his argument from motion by respecting strictly the scientific method of the philosophy of movable being.

Finally, St. Thomas' *ex motu* way is the very best crystallization of the Christian doctrine concerning the power of man's

---

15 Aristotle, *Metaphys.* Bk. XII, ch. 7: 1027b28–30, W.D. Ross' translation, *ad locum.*

*From Nature to God*

natural reason to understand God starting from the knowledge of nature itself. Due to the fact that He is the first unmoved mover of every natural movement, the principle of causality allows men to rise to the knowledge of such a mover through philosophical speculation on natural moving things.

# Natural Theology
## in St. Thomas's Early Doctrine of Truth
### Michael M. Waddell
### Augustana College (South Dakota)

## I. Introduction: A New Instance of an Old Problem

One of Thomas Aquinas's great legacies is the clarity of his teaching about the relationships between theology and philosophy, faith and reason, and grace and nature in general. Of course, that clarity has not prevented the occasional dispute over the philosophical or theological status of any number of particular doctrines. And, in fact, a new controversy has recently begun to form around the status of Thomas's doctrine of truth.

The dispute turns on whether or not Thomas's doctrine of truth is fundamentally theological. In his book *Medieval Philosophy and the Transcendentals: The Case of Thomas Aquinas*, Jan Aertsen contends that Thomas's doctrine of the transcendentals is a philosophical teaching. Inasmuch as Thomas takes truth to be one of the transcendentals, Aertsen must, of course, (re)construct Thomas's doctrine of transcendental truth on philosophical grounds—or, as he describes it, without a "theological foundation."[1] It is worth noting that Aertsen's use of the term "theology" (here) includes *natural* theology; thus, in his effort to claim Thomas's doctrine for philosophy, Aertsen goes so far as to eschew even any natural theological underpinnings. On the other

---

1 Jan Aertsen, *Medieval Philosophy and the Transcendentals: The Case of Thomas Aquinas* (New York: Brill, 1996). See pp. 105, 107. Hereafter, *MPT*.

side of the dispute, in their recent book *Truth in Aquinas*, John Milbank and Catherine Pickstock argue that Thomas's doctrine of truth is "inherently theological."[2] It is striking that Pickstock and Milbank also use the term "theology" in such a way as to include not only *sacra doctrina* but also tenets that most scholars would recognize as "natural theology." They contend, however, that there can be no "natural" knowledge of God, which means that Thomas's doctrine of truth must be primarily a matter of *sacra doctrina*. Thus, while these parties disagree about whether or not Thomas's doctrine of truth is "theological," they seem to agree, if only tacitly, that any reference to God is to be avoided in a properly philosophical account of truth. (It is this assumption, I think, that leads Aertsen to attempt to (re)construct transcendental truth without reference even to natural theology. The same assumption leads Pickstock and Milbank, who recognize that Thomas's early doctrine of truth does entail reference to God, to construe his teaching as inherently theological [i.e., a matter of *sacra doctrina*].)

In this paper, I propose to examine Thomas's early teaching on truth in order to assess whether this doctrine is adequately described as "theological" (as Milbank and Pickstock claim) or as lacking "theological foundation" (as Aertsen claims). I will conduct this examination with an eye toward supporting two theses. First, I take it that Thomas's early doctrine of truth rests upon a *philosophical* grasp of God and can therefore be construed as a matter of natural theology. I would take this first point to be entirely uncontroversial, except that Aertsen, Pickstock and Milbank have all controverted it. Second, I will argue that both parties in our interpretive dispute have misconstrued Thomas's teaching on truth because of their own misgivings about the category of natural theology—misgivings that reveal more about contemporary polemics than about Thomas's thought.

2    John Milbank and Catherine Pickstock, *Truth in Aquinas* (New York: Routledge, 2001): 19. See also pp. xiii, 1, 4, 6.

## RESTORING NATURE

## II. The Foundation of Thomas's Early Doctrine of Truth

St. Thomas renders his first independent discussion of truth in the *Quaestiones disputatae de veritate* (*DV*), a work produced during his first Parisian regency of 1256–59.[3] It is the teaching propounded in this text that I here refer to as Thomas's "early" doctrine of truth and that I would like to examine in this essay. The *Disputed Questions on Truth* take their title from the topic announced in the first question (*quaestio est de veritate*), and indeed the majority of Thomas's account of truth can be gleaned from this first question.[4] For the purposes of this paper, I would like to focus on one of the most salient features of this account: the transcendentality of truth.[5]

3  I say "independent" discussion because Thomas does in fact treat the topic of truth in his *Commentary on the Sentences* (*In I SN* 19.5 ). The *De veritate* is, however, the first treatment of truth wherein Thomas was at complete liberty to determine both the order and the topics to be examined.

4  As I argue elsewhere, though, Thomas's early doctrine of truth cannot really be understood apart from the larger context of the entire *Disputed Questions on Truth*. See my article "Truth or Transcendentals: What *Was* Thomas's Intention at *De Veritate* 1.1?" (forthcoming), and my dissertation *Truth Beloved: Thomas Aquinas and the Relational Transcendentals* (University of Notre Dame, 2000).

5  Properly speaking, the transcendentality of truth is an ontological topic and thus primarily a concern for metaphysics. One might also consider elements of Thomas's doctrine of truth that are more proper to epistemology. And, indeed, it seems to me that Aertsen, Pickstock and Milbank are all interested in the epistemological aspects of Thomas's doctrine as well as its ontological components. For example, Aertsen contends that one of the central motifs of Thomas's doctrine of the transcendentals—a motif that is often overlooked—is that the transcendentals are the *primae conceptiones* of the human intellect (see, e.g., *MPT*, 20 and especially 427). And one of Milbank and Pickstock's aspirations is to depict Thomas's theory of truth as a "correspondence theory" that is both theological in nature and a useful corrective of many twentieth century theories of truth (see, e.g., *Truth in Aquinas*, xiii and 1). Without straying too far from

}452{

*Natural Theology in St. Thomas's Early Doctrine of Truth*

Thomas's early doctrine of truth is perhaps best known for its claim that truth is transcendental.[6] In point of fact, though,

the topic at hand, let me note that the same aversion to natural theology that I think detracts from these interpreters' accounts of ontological truth in Thomas's early doctrine is also an obstacle to their accounts of his more epistemological concerns. First, before Aertsen can claim that truth is one of the *primae conceptiones* of the intellect, he must be able to make the case that truth is a *modus entis generaliter consequens omne ens* (a general mode of being, or a "transcendental"); to do this, he must have recourse to natural theological knowledge about the Divine Intellect (as I will argue in this paper). Second, if Pickstock and Milbank wish to extract from Thomas's writings a "correspondence theory" of truth, wherein the "correspondence" that grounds truth is a conformity of Divine Intellect and created thing, then either 1) this correspondence spans a relation between created thing and the Divine intellect as naturally knowable, or 2) it spans a relation between created thing and the Divine Intellect as it is not accessible to the human intellect operating according to its natural powers. If the first condition holds, then the correspondence theory of truth is accessible to natural theology. If the second condition holds, then either 2.1) we cannot know the correspondence between Divine Intellect and creature (i.e., we cannot know the "*quid est*" of the relation, perhaps because we cannot know the content of the Divine Intellect and thus cannot grasp the intellectual term of the relation), or 2.2) we can only know the truth relation through revelation. If 2.1 obtains, then this theory is not of much use as an epistemological account of how things are "true." If 2.2 obtains, then we can only have true knowledge when God reveals the content of the Divine Intellect to us. But, of course, until we arrive at the beatific vision, we cannot know the Divine Intellect (for it is identical with the Divine Essence), and all revelation that we are capable of receiving is in fact created (albeit a special "infusion" of grace for the faithful who receive it). Thus, it follows from 2.2 that either we cannot know the truth (the same consequence that follows from 2.1) or we can only know the truth as a correspondence between created things and created—although divinely inspired—revelation. If the latter is the case, then we are faced with the problem of how to bridge the gap between (created) revelation and the Divine Intellect. For it would seem that the only way to know that revelation is a "true" presentation of the content of the Divine Intellect

}453{

RESTORING NATURE

the text often cited as Thomas's more or less systematic discussion of the transcendentals, and truth's place within them, is really devoted to ascertaining the definition of truth.[7] Thus, Thomas begins the first article of the *De veritate* by announcing: "*quaestio est de veritate, et primo quaeritur quid est veritas.*"[8] The familiar "*quid est*" formulation suggests that Thomas will be seeking the *quiddity* of truth,[9] and in fact the article culminates with

is either to know the Divine Intellect immediately or to receive yet another revelation. The first is not possible in this life, and the second leads to an infinite regress of revelations attempting to verify revelations. In the end, then, if we assume that epistemological truth consists in a correspondence between created thing and Divine Intellect, then we seem to be left with only two options: either the truth relation is naturally knowable or truth consists in a relation that is inaccessible to the human intellect in this life. In the case of the former, epistemological truth is a matter of natural theology. In the case of the latter, Milbank and Pickstock's attempt to extract from Thomas a "correspondence theory of truth" that is "inherently theological" has also begotten a theory that is inherently useless in this life.

6  Most commentators acknowledge that Thomas held truth to be transcendental throughout his career. See, however, Lawrence Dewan, O.P., "St. Thomas's Successive Discussions of the Nature of Truth," in *Sanctus Thomas de Aquino Doctor Hodiernae Humanitatis*, Studi Thomistici 58 (Citta del Vaticano: Libreria Editrice Vaticana), 153–168.

7  Properly speaking, of course, it is not possible to "define" truth since truth transcends the bounds of all genera. But this is only a lesson learned after the question has been asked in *De veritate* 1.1, and the question is still framed in terms that would normally demand a defintion: *quid est veritate?*

8  All Latin quotations from the *Quaestiones disputatae de veritate* in this paper are taken from *Quaestiones Disputatae*, Vol. I (Romae: Marietti, 1949). English translations of the text are my own.

9  This suggestion becomes problematic, though, almost as soon as the article is under way: for the topic actually disputed in the objections and the objections contra is whether "true" adds anything to "being." The polemic of the objections is, I suspect, one reason why commentators have often been distracted from recognizing the central endeavor of this article. Another reason is that the discussion of

}454{

*Natural Theology in St. Thomas's Early Doctrine of Truth*

Thomas's assertion that truth consists in the *adaequatio rei et intellectus*.[10]

The route to this "definition" is by no means easy, though, for the body of the article is complicated by the problem of "adding to being." As becomes clear in the corpus, Thomas thinks that truth is a *modus entis generaliter consequens omne ens*—a general mode of being, or what we now refer to as a "transcendental." But there is a difficulty with trying to define any transcendental. Definitions are comprised of a genus and a specific difference, which difference must be outside the essence of the genus itself. Now, transcendentals, as general modes of being, run through all of the categories of substance and accidents, and cannot be contained within any single genus. Thus, the only category—and here I use the word in the non-technical sense—sufficiently broad to contain a transcendental is being itself. However, as Aristotle noted, being cannot be a genus, for there is nothing outside the nature of being that can be added to it in the manner of a specific

the general modes of being is really quite intriguing. In the end, though, both the problem of adding to being and the discussion of the general modes of being are subordinate to the task of defining truth.

10    To be precise, the article culminates in St. Thomas's harmonization of several authoritative definitions of truth according to the logic of analogy. Thomas's states that truth has been defined in three ways: the first is according to that which precedes the *ratio* of truth (namely, being); the second is according to that which formally completes the *ratio* of truth (namely, the conformity of thing and intellect); and the third is according to the effects following from truth (namely, judgments and statements). Notice, though, that Thomas is only able to maintain a place for the first and third sorts of definition by connecting them analogically to the second, focal definition. I take it to be an open question whether the need for a young theologian, like Thomas, to present a doctrine that was consistent with authoritative statements might have influenced his judgment that the formal notion of truth consists in the conformity of intellect and thing.

}455{

difference.[11] This, in a nutshell, is the problem of adding to being: one cannot add anything to being in the manner of something extrinsic to it, as, for example, specific differences add to genera. And yet truth (like all transcendentals) cannot be contained by any genus less broad than being itself.

Before he can "define" truth, then, Thomas must articulate a solution to the problem of adding to being. He spends approximately the first twenty-percent of the corpus describing the problem itself and gesturing toward a solution, namely, that some things are said to add to being inasmuch as they express a mode of being that the name "being" itself does not express.[12] He then devotes about forty-five percent of the corpus to sketching a taxonomy of the ways in which these various modes of being might be articulated. First there are the "special" modes of being (*specialis modus entis*), which constitute the various genera of substance and the accidents. Then there are the "general" modes of being (*modus generalis consequens omne ens*). These general modes can be formed in two ways: either according to every being in itself (*in se*) or according to every being in relation to another (*in ordine ad aliud*). In the first way, one can posit something about every being both positively (producing the terms "*ens*" and "*res*") and negatively (producing the term "*unum*"). In the second way, one can also posit something of every being both positively and negatively. Here Thomas reverses his order of exposition to note that one can either speak (negatively) of beings as they are divided from others (producing the term "*aliquid*") or speak (positively) of beings *in relation to* others. But in order for there to exist some relation that is predicable of every being, there must be some thing that is capable of being related to every being (*aliquid quod natum sit convenire cum omni ente*). As Aristotle notes in book

11  On the impossibility of being's being a genus, see Thomas's *Commentary on Aristotle's Metaphysics* b. III, l. 8 (par. 433); see also Aristotle's *Topics* 122b20 and 127a25.
12  Thomas's solution to the problem of adding to being is worked out in greater detail in *DV* 21.1, where he treats the related question "whether 'good' adds anything to being" / "*utrum bonum aliquid addat supra ens.*"

*Natural Theology in St. Thomas's Early Doctrine of Truth*

III of *De anima*, the soul is just such a thing.[13] Now, the soul (*anima*) has two faculties through which it can relate to all being, namely, the appetite and the intellect.[14] Thus, the name "good" (*bonum*) is said of being in relation to appetite (*ad appetitum*), and the name "true" (*verum*) is said of being in relation to intellect (*ad intellectum*).

With all of this happening as propadeutic to Thomas's discussion of the definition(s) of truth—which discussion is the focus of the last thirty-five percent of the corpus—it is easy to see why some interpreters have lost sight of the centrality of Thomas's attempt to define truth and concentrated instead on his comments about the transcendentals. However, Thomas's discussion of the problem of adding to being and his sketch of the modes of being in article 1.1 are primarily intended to prepare for the definition of truth as a general mode of being in relation to the intellect, an *adaequatio rei et intellectus*.

Isn't it intriguing, then, that while Thomas obviously assumes truth to be a transcendental, he proposes a definition of truth that cannot sustain its transcendentality? Notice that the two terms of the truth relation Thomas has proposed in article 1.1 are "thing" (or *res*) and the intellectual faculty of the soul (*anima*). By "soul," one presumes that he means the human soul;[15] but not every

---

13  *De anima* III.8 (431b21).

14  Thomas's provocative statement is actually better rendered: 'In the soul, however, there is a power cognitive and appetitive' / "*In anima autem est vis cognitiva et appetitiva.*" While the letter of Thomas's text actually suggests that we are dealing with just one faculty dually described as cognitive and appetitive, it is sufficient for our purposes to use the traditional description of intellect and appetite as separate faculties of the soul.

15  Pickstock seems to think that the term "soul" (or, as she pens it, "Soul") applies both to the human form and to God (see *Truth in Aquinas*, 8–9). This strikes me as odd, particularly since Thomas makes explicit reference to the Aristotelian theory of soul in this passage. For Aristotle, the term "soul" (*anima*) denotes the form of a living thing, which makes it proper to plants and animals (see *De anima* 402a6, 412a28, 414a13). Inasmuch as Thomas's account demands a soul with both appetitive and intellectual faculties, he ob-

## RESTORING NATURE

instance of being is actually related to a human intellect. For example, somewhere deep within the earth, there are surely rocks that no human has ever known. (The example is Augustine's, not mine.[16]) And yet, because these rocks exist, the transcendentality of truth would demand that they be conformed to some intellect.

At this point, it would seem that Thomas has several logical options. First, he could maintain that truth consists in the *adaequatio rei et intellectus*, but reject the notion that it is transcendental. Let's call this the "non-transcendental" option. Second, he could continue to hold to the transcendentality of truth but alter his definition so that things are called "true" merely by virtue of their conform-ability to the human intellect, not necessarily their actually being so conformed.[17] Let's call this the "anthropological" option (because truth is grounded in a potential relation to the human intellect). Finally, Thomas could maintain his commitment to the transcendentality of truth and insist on the *adaequatio* formulation of the *ratio* of truth, but modify his description of the intellect that must actually be related to the individual thing in order for that thing to be "true." Let's call this the "theological" option. Perhaps we should consider each of these options in turn.

## Option #1: Truth is Non-Transcendental

It seems apparent that Thomas is committed to the transcendentality of truth in his early doctrine.[18] First, as we have seen in

---

viously has in mind the soul of the human animal. It is striking, however, that Thomas does not simply construe truth and goodness in relation to intellect and appetite, since these faculties are (analogically) common to humans, angels and God. The philosophical advantage of this alternative approach will become apparent when we consider the foundation of Thomas's theory of truth.

16 See *Soliloquies*, bk. II, ch. 5.

17 In other words, things could be called "true" in virtue of their *potential* to be known rather than their actually being known.

18 Lawrence Dewan, O.P., has argued, however, that Thomas no longer presents truth as transcendental in his (later) *Summa* account. See

article 1.1, he classifies truth as one of the general modes of being. Second, in the responses to the objections of article 1.1, Thomas also describes the relationship between truth and being in terms classically associated with the transcendentals: truth and being differ *in ratione* but are the same *in re*.[19]

## Option #2: The Anthropological Foundation

There is, however, evidence that Thomas considered the possibility that transcendental truth might better be described as the conform-ability of being and intellect rather than the actual conformity of the two. On multiple occasions, Thomas actually describes the truth of things (i.e., extra-mental truth) in terms that would suggest truth to be precisely being's potential to be known rather than its actually being known. For example, at *DV* 1.1 ad 5, Thomas states that "inasmuch as something has being, it is capable of being equated to intellect / *ex hoc quod aliquid habet de entitate, secundum hoc natum est aequari intellectui*." And at *DV* 21.1 co., Thomas claims:

> any thing whatsoever is said to be "true" just insofar as it is conformed **or conformable** to intellect; and therefore all who rightly define "true" place intellect [or understanding] in its definition / *unumquodque ens in tantum dicitur verum, in quantum conformatum est **vel** **conformabile** intellectui; et ideo omnes recte definientes verum, ponunt in eius definitione intellectum.*

Inasmuch as every being is knowable by the human soul, this gambit of reducing the truth of things to their potential to be

Father Dewan's "St. Thomas's Successive Discussions of the Nature of Truth" (reference above).

19 Thomas suggests that truth and being differ *in ratione* in *DV* 1.1 ad 5. In *DV* 1.1 ad sc 1, he also suggests that truth and being differ *in nomine* but do not differ *in re*.

## RESTORING NATURE

known would surely enable the anthropological foundation to preserve the transcendentality of truth.

## Option #3: The Theological Foundation

In spite of the fact that Thomas occasionally describes extra-mental truth in terms of the potential to be known, and in spite of the fact that this description preserves Thomas's commitment to the transcendentality of truth, it appears that this was not Thomas's preferred solution. Notice: the definition of truth that Thomas posits in article 1.1 is "*adaequatio rei et intellectus.*" This formulation does not describe truth as an ability to be equated with intellect, say, an "*adaequabilitas rei et intellectus*"; it posits an actual relation between thing and intellect. Now, no less an authority than Augustine himself chaffed at the suggestion that such a relation could be built into the definition of truth precisely because there are many things that are not known by the human intellect and that would therefore not be "true." And, indeed, Thomas confronts this argument in the fourth objection of *De veritate* 1.2. His response is worth noting:

> To the fourth, it should be said that Augustine is speaking about the vision of the human intellect, upon which the truth of the thing does not depend. For there are many things that are not known by our intellect(s); but there is no thing that the Divine Intellect does not know in actuality and the human intellect in potentiality . . . Therefore, in the definition of the true thing can be placed the vision of the Divine Intellect in act, but not the vision of the human intellect, save in potency. / *Ad quartum dicendum, quod Augustinus loquitur de visione intellectus humani, a qua rei veritas non dependet. Sunt enim multae res quae intellectu nostro non cognoscuntur; nulla tamen res est quam intellectus divinus in actu non cognoscat, et intellectus humanus in potentia . . . Et ideo in definitione rei verae potest poni visio in actu intellectus divini, non autem visio intellectus humani nisi in potentia.*

Thomas here recognizes that a relation to human intellect could not be built into a definition of truth that allowed for it to be transcendental, unless it be qualified that this relation need merely be *in potentia*. While Thomas's diction does occasionally suggest that extra-mental truth might consist in such a potential relation, his definition of truth as *"adaequatio rei et intellectus"* does not seem to posit a merely potential relation.[20] An *adaequatio* is an actuality, not a potentiality. Thus, if Thomas intends to maintain the transcendentality of truth, and if he intends to maintain the definition of truth as an *adaequatio rei et intellectus*, then the intellectual term of the truth relation must actually be found in the Divine Intellect.

And this is precisely where Thomas grounds ontological truth in *De veritate* 1.2. Thomas's main concern in this text is to explain how truth is primarily in the intellect but secondarily in things (*res*); however, in order to explain how truth is in things, Thomas is obliged to note that things are related differently to the practical intellect and the speculative intellect. The practical intellect is the measure of the things it makes, whereas the speculative intellect is measured by the things it knows. Thus, Thomas states, real things (*res*) are the measure of the

20  One might object that perhaps Thomas abandoned the *adaequatio* definition of truth after realizing that it made it impossible for transcendental truth to be grounded in a relation to the human intellect. And, in fact, the description of truth as *"conformatum vel conformabile intellectui"* in *DV* 21.1 might even be taken as evidence that Thomas's definition of truth developed from 1256 to 1259 (the years when the disputations behind *DV* 1 and 21 likely occurred). However, in Thomas's most mature treatment of truth (*Summa Theologiae* [*ST*] 1.16.1), he still gives the *adaequatio* definition a privileged place and does not describe truth in terms of a conformability. Moreover, he insists that the relation to intellect that is essential to the truth of things is the relation to the Divine Intellect (*ST* 1.16.1, co.) and he supports the exclusion of the human intellect from the *ratio* of truth on the grounds that this relation is accidental to extra-mental truth (*ST* 1.16.1 ad 1). Thus, I see no reason to maintain that Thomas ever abandoned the *adaequatio rei et intellectus* formulation in favor of one that would make transcendental truth consist primarily in the potential relation between things and human intellects.

}461{

## RESTORING NATURE

human speculative intellects that know them; but they are measured by the *Divine* Practical Intellect that makes them. Because natural things (*res naturales*) stand between these two intellects, they can be called "true" either in relation to the human intellect (inasmuch as they are apt to produce knowledge of themselves) or in relation to the Divine Practical Intellect (inasmuch as they fulfill that to which they have been ordained by the Divine Intellect).[21] But Thomas is careful to point out that the relation between thing and Divine Intellect is prior to the relation between human intellect and thing. And while it might look as though even the posterior *ratio* of truth in terms of the relation to human intellect could sustain a transcendental theory of truth, we should recall that just a few lines later (in the response to the fourth objection) Thomas will state that the human intellect cannot be introduced into a definition of extra-mental truth unless it be qualified that the relation between thing and intellect need only be potential. Thomas's definition, of course, does not make this qualification; so it appears that Thomas means to ground transcendental truth in the Divine Practical Intellect. This is likely why, after apparently beginning to ground truth on an anthropological foundation in article 1.1, Thomas so quickly turns to delineate the relations between natural things and the Divine Practical Intellect in article 1.2. To be sure, he does maintain that things can also be called "true" in relation to the speculative human intellects that know them. This complicates his account of truth and runs the risk of distracting readers from the fact that things are *essentially* called "true" in relation to the Divine Practical Intellect that creates them.[22] At the same time, by maintaining space for the anthropological account of transcendental truth

---

21  See *DV* 1.2, co: "*Res ergo naturalis inter duos intellectus constituta, secundum adaequationem ad utrumque vera dicitur; secundum enim adaequationem ad intellectum divinum dicitur vera, in quantum implet hoc ad quod est ordinata per intellectum divinum . . . Secundum autem adaequationem ad intellectum humanum dicitur res vera, in quantum nata est de se formare veram aestimationem . . . *"

22  For the notion that things are "essentially" true in relation to the Divine Intellect but only accidentally true in relation to the human intellect, see *ST* 1.16.1 co. and ad 1.

}462{

*Natural Theology in St. Thomas's Early Doctrine of Truth*

within the theological account, Thomas does greater justice to the fact that we do indeed call things "true" in relation to human intellects. Put slightly differently, Thomas's account of transcendental truth preserves the domain of the "natural" while acknowledging its dependence on the divine—dare I say the "supernatural." We should not lose site of the fact, however, that the primary ontological foundation of truth is the Divine Intellect. Nor should we overlook the fact that the knowledge of God required for this doctrine—viz., that He exists, that He is intelligent, and that He creates the world—is accessible to natural reason.[23]

## III. Natural Theology Shunned

As I mentioned at the beginning of his paper, there has recently been controversy about the status of Thomas's doctrine of truth. Jan Aertsen maintains that Thomas's theory of truth does not have a "theological foundation," while John Milbank and Catherine Pickstock insist that it is "inherently theological." It should be clear from the preceding discussion of *De veritate* that Thomas grounds transcendental truth in the Divine Intellect, which can be known by natural theology. Interestingly, though, neither Aertsen nor Pickstock nor Milbank is keen on acknowledging the natural theological foundation of this teaching.

## IIIA. Aertsen's Philosophical Rendering

In his *Medieval Philosophy and the Transcendentals*, Aertsen argues that Thomas's entire doctrine of the transcendentals is mustered

23 I suspect most Thomists would take it for granted that these are tenets of natural theology. However, one could muster abundant textual evidence that Thomas holds the relevant propositions to be accessible to natural reason: that God exists (see *ST* 1.2.3 and *ScG* 1.13); that God is intelligent (see *ScG* 1.44); and that God creates the world (see *In II Sent.* 1.1.2 and *ScG* 2.15–16). For a more general discussion of philosophy's ability to know God, see *In De Trinitate Boetii* (*In DT*) 5.4.

}463{

on philosophical grounds and without "theological foundation."[24] Presumably, inasmuch as Aertsen takes Thomas's doctrine of transcendental truth to be part of his larger doctrine of the transcendentals, his thesis about the non-theological nature of the transcendentals should pertain to Thomas's theory of transcendental truth as well. Let us, then, consider whether Aertsen's thesis holds with respect to Thomas's teaching on truth.

One of the most puzzling claims in Aertsen's book is that "Thomas follows Albert in his view of the relational character of *verum* and *bonum*, but not in his theological foundation."[25] Now, I do not find this claim puzzling because I think Thomas's theory of transcendental truth is fundamentally theological, i.e. a matter of *sacra doctrina*. On the contrary, Thomas grounds transcendental truth in the relations of things to the Divine Intellect; and inasmuch as one can know philosophically that the Divine Intellect exists and that every created being is related to It through the act of creation, it seems clear that Thomas's theory of transcendental truth could be constructed on philosophical grounds. My puzzlement arises from the fact that Albert grounds his own theory of transcendental truth and goodness in the same kind of naturally knowable relations between creatures and God.[26] Aertsen even states that one might call the foundations of transcendental truth and goodness in Albert's construction "theological," "as long as the term is not understood in opposition to 'philosophical,' but as a further qualification of it."[27] Thus, Aertsen is knowingly using the term "theological" to describe a philosophical enterprise, viz., natural theology. So, when Aertsen says that Thomas does not follow Albert in his "theological" foundation of the transcendentals, he does not mean to assert that Thomas's theory is philosophically

---

24  See *MPT*, 1, 2, 19–20, 23. See also *MPT*, 105, 107, 377–78.
25  *MPT*, 105. See also *MPT*, 107, 377–78.
26  See Albert's *Comentarii in I Sententiarum* d. 46, N, art. 13–14.
27  *MPT*, 55. See also *MPT*, 60, 64. Aertsen also uses the term "theological" in this way to describe the causal foundations of the transcendentals in the thought of Philip the Chancellor (*MPT*, 39) and Alexander of Hales (*MPT*, 46).

*Natural Theology in St. Thomas's Early Doctrine of Truth*

established whereas Albert's is a matter of *sacra doctrina*. Rather, he means to suggest that Thomas's theory is grounded in the "anthropological" foundation Thomas initially appeared to be constructing in *De veritate* 1.1.

Now, as we have already noted, Thomas himself recognized that the attempt to ground transcendental truth in a relation to the human intellect is fraught with difficulty. Most notably, it is quite unlikely that every instance of being is actually known by some human intellect. Thus, if one wants to preserve truth as a transcendental and determine it in relation to the anthropological foundation, one would have to tinker with Thomas's definition of truth as an *adaequatio rei et intellectus*. And, in fact, this is precisely what Aertsen does. In several texts, he suggests that truth consists in the "conformability" or "knowability" of being rather than its actually being conformed to intellect or its actually being known.[28] While Thomas's diction does sometimes lend itself to constructing truth in this way, his definition of truth is not easily squared with the notion that the truth of things consists in a potentiality rather than an actuality.[29] Moreover, the progression of Thomas's own texts suggests that transcendental truth is not securely founded in an accidental relation to the human intellect: for just as soon as he has described truth in terms of the relation between being and the human intellect, Thomas quickly seeks to delineate the prior and essential relation that exists between the thing and the Divine Intellect.[30] I suspect that even Aertsen himself recognizes that Thomas really did intend for transcendental truth to be founded primarily in the relation to the Divine Intellect, for he eventually admits as much, stating that "The relation to the divine Logos is essential for the truth of things. Ontological truth

---

28  See *MPT*, 254, 271, 398.

29  This description of truth as an *adaequatio intellectus et rei* continues to be, as far as I can tell, Thomas's preferred definition throughout the rest of his career. See *ST* 1.16.1, co.

30  See *DV* 1.2, co.

}465{

RESTORING NATURE

has a divine ground."[31] And again, "In Thomas's account of 'True as a relational transcendental' . . . the ultimate meaning of the definition of truth in terms of adaequation is the conformity of the thing with the divine intellect."[32] What is even more odd, after stating explicitly that "Thomas follows Albert in his view of the relational character of *verum* and *bonum*, but not in his theological foundation," Aertsen admits in the final chapter of his book that "The theological foundation of the transcendentals is common to Thomas and his predecessors."[33] Now, perhaps Aertsen means to situate the theological foundation of truth alongside the anthropological foundation, so that ontological truth would be grounded in both relations simultaneously; perhaps he might even acknowledge the ontological priority of the theological foundation while still insisting that Thomas's theory of transcendental truth could stand on the anthropological foundation alone.[34] However, even this qualified account would seem to fall short, for the anthropological foundation, as we have already noted, simply cannot support transcendental truth as long as one defines truth in terms of an actual *adaequatio*. Thus, as long as Thomas holds to the

31  *MPT*, 273.
32  *MPT*, 370.
33  *MPT*, 377–78. The quotation continues: "Characteristic of medieval thought is that it inquires into the origin of being, into the ultimate ground of truth and goodness. Yet there are differences too. The theological foundation is not for Thomas the first thing to be said in explanation of the transcendentality and convertibility of the primary notions but the final conclusion of his metaphysical analysis. The theological foundation is absent in his basic texts about the transcendentals."
34  Thus, Aertsen's statement that "The theological foundation is not for Thomas the first thing to be said in explanation of the transcendentality and convertibility of the primary notions but the final conclusion of his metaphysical analysis" might be taken as an indication that the theological foundation exists but that the anthropological foundation is the first ground of ontological truth. See *MPT*, 377–78.

*Natural Theology in St. Thomas's Early Doctrine of Truth*

description of (transcendental) truth as *adaequatio rei et intellectus*, he would seem to be bound to the theological foundation.

Given that the "theological" solution is more readily harmonized with Thomas's definition of truth and his commitment to its transcendentality, and given that even Aertsen must eventually admit that it is Thomas's fundamental approach, one wonders what could have motivated Aertsen to deny that Thomas's doctrine of transcendental truth has a "theological" foundation in the first place. At this point, I can only psychologize, for Aertsen's motives are never made explicit. However, Aertsen does state that he intends his *Medieval Philosophy and the Transcendentals* to contribute to discussion of the question "what is philosophy in the Middle Ages?" Aertsen's thesis is that 1) "there is a philosophy in the Middle Ages" and 2) "philosophy in the Middle Ages expresses itself as a way of thought that can be called 'transcendental.'"[35] It becomes clear, moreover, that Aertsen intends the category "medieval philosophy" to be quite distinct from "medieval theology."[36] Accordingly, Aertsen must present an account of the transcendentals that is completely devoid of

35  See *MPT*, 1: "The title of this book speaks of 'Medieval Philosophy' and 'the Transcendentals.' It can be read as affirming that there is a philosophy in the Middle Ages *and* that this philosophy encompasses a doctrine of the transcendentals alongside many others. But our aims in this work are more ambitious. Our title means to suggest a more intrinsic relation between the terms 'Philosophy' and 'Transcendentals' than mere juxtaposition. We want to show that philosophy in the Middle Ages expresses itself as a way of thought which can be called 'transcendental'. The present book may therefore be seen as a contribution to the discussion of the question: what is philosophy in the Middle Ages?"

36  See *MPT* sections 0.1 and 0.3, where Aertsen discusses Gilson's conception of medieval philosophy as "Christian philosophy" and Alain de Libera's conception of medieval philosophy as the intellectual's "experience of thought." Aertsen is critical of both accounts because of their insufficiently distinguishing philosophy from theology. Presumably, Aertsen means for his own theory to avoid this shortcoming. See especially *MPT*, 8–10 and 17.

}467{

RESTORING NATURE

theology.[37] Now, inasmuch as Thomas's doctrine of the transcendentals provides the case study for Aertsen's thesis, Aertsen has an obvious interest in presenting Thomas's account of transcendental truth in terms that are decidedly not theological.[38] If Thomas's theory is constructed on theological grounds, Aertsen's thesis fails—at least with respect to the very case he chose to illustrate it.[39] It seems to me, thus, that Aertsen might well be a man in the grip of a theory. While attempting to separate the transcendentals—and thus medieval philosophy—from theology, it appears that Aertsen might have become over zealous and tried to keep God out of the picture altogether. If this diagnosis is correct, the unfortunate irony of the situation is that Aertsen

37 Thus Aertsen's insistence that there is no theological grounding of the transcendentals. See, for example, *MPT*, 107.

38 In fact, Thomas's account of truth plays an especially important role in Aertsen's understanding of Thomas's doctrine of the transcendentals. First, the text that Aertsen takes to be Thomas's most complete exposition of the transcendentals (*DV* 1.1) actually comprises a discussion of the quiddity of truth (see *MPT*, 243). Second, Aertsen thinks that Thomas's attempt to define truth in terms of a relation between *res* and the *human* intellect is an innovative moment in the history of the transcendentals (see *MPT*, 105 and especially 257).

39 Now, it seems to me that when Aertsen is performing careful exegesis of the texts, as he does for example in his sixth and ninth chapters, he is more apt to acknowledge that transcendental truth has a divine ground (e.g., 377). However, when he is arguing for his thesis about the nature of medieval philosophy (or when he is trying to distinguish Thomas from his predecessors), he is prone to claim that Thomas's doctrine of the transcendentals is not theologically founded and thus to alter the description of truth to make it consist in a potentiality to be known by the human intellect rather than an actual relation between intellect and thing. For examples of Aertsen's claiming that the transcendentals (or transcendental truth) do not have a divine ground within the context of arguing about the nature of medieval philosophy in general, see *MPT*, 20 and especially 378. For examples of Aertsen's making the same claim within the context of trying to distinguish Thomas's doctrine from his predecessors', see *MPT*, 105.

}468{

*Natural Theology in St. Thomas's Early Doctrine of Truth*

could have argued for Thomas's doctrine of the transcendentals having a "theological" foundation and still being thoroughly philosophical. Instead, for reasons he does not make clear, he chooses to distance his account from even the natural theological foundation of truth. Whatever his motives, it seems apparent that inasmuch as Aertsen denies the natural theological foundation of truth, he departs from Thomas's own dominant conception.

## IIIB. Pickstock and Milbank's Theological Rendering

Like Aertsen, Catherine Pickstock and John Milbank also use the term "theology" (or "theological") to refer to matters that most Thomists would recognize as pertaining to natural theology (e.g., God's existence and the doctrine of creation).[40] Given that Thomas's account of (transcendental) truth depends on ontological participation in the Divine truth, it should, then, not be surprising that one of the primary tenets of their recent book *Truth in Aquinas* is that "for Aquinas, truth is theological without remainder."[41] What is surprising is that Pickstock and Milbank deny that there is any such thing as "natural" knowledge of God, and therefore take Thomas's doctrine of truth to be (primarily) a matter of *sacra doctrina*.[42]

Whereas Aertsen's motives for trying to remove the natural theological underpinnings of Thomas's early doctrine of truth are

40  See *Truth in Aquinas*, 23, 26, 43. See also, for example, pp. 20–21, 39, 51–52. My point here is not so much that they actually describe these individual doctrines as matters of *sacra doctrina* ("theological"), although they sometimes do; rather, I mean to suggest that by holding Thomas's doctrine of truth to be a matter of *sacra doctrina*, they also imply that God's existence, God's intelligence, and creation—which points comprise the premises essential for deducing Thomas's doctrine of truth—are not accessible to natural reason. And, in fact, Milbank and Pickstock make some of these (entailed) claims more or less explicitly. See, for example, pp. xiii and 39.

41  *Truth in Aquinas*, 6. See also pp. xiii, 1, 4, 19.

42  See, for example, *Truth in Aquinas*, xiii and 39.

}469{

RESTORING NATURE

(at best) opaque, at least Pickstock and Milbank provide some hints as to why they construe Thomas's doctrine of truth as properly theological. In keeping with the agenda of the "Radical Orthodoxy" movement, they aspire to eradicate the distinction between the natural and the supernatural.[43] One of the consequences of this goal is that Pickstock and Milbank want to erase the distinction between natural theology and *sacra doctrina*, thereby destroying the category of *natural* theology altogether.[44] After all, if there is no such thing as the "natural," there can be no such thing as natural knowledge and *a fortiori* no natural knowledge of God. Their deconstruction of the category of natural theology seems to rest primarily on the argument that all rationality, as a participation in the Truth of the Divine Intellect, is a consequence of grace and, thus, grounded in faith.[45] Accordingly, in their interpretation, "It follows that reason and faith are . . . construed by Aquinas as successive phases of a single extension always qualitatively the same."[46] Sometimes Milbank will go so far as to argue that reason and faith are not even distinct "phases."[47] Logically, of course, even if one grants Milbank and Pickstock their claim about faith and reason not being distinct, the resulting "extension" could be either philosophy or theology. To preclude the possibility of an autonomous philosophy, Milbank asserts that we should not conceive of philosophy as naturalizing the supernatural, but rather as being legitimated only in the supernatural knowledge of *sacra doctrina* received by faith through grace.[48] Thus, for

43  Or, at least, to render the notion of an autonomous natural realm nihilistic. See *Truth in Aquinas*, 21.
44  *Truth in Aquinas*, xiii, 19, 30, 35, 36, 51, 52, 55, 56; see, however, 20, 32.
45  For a general form of this argument, see *Truth in Aquinas*, xiii. On rationality as participation in the divine light, see 10, 11, 12, 13, 14, 16, 17–18, 22, 23, 24. For the further notion that this participation comes through grace, see 39, 43, 51–52.
46  *Truth in Aquinas*, 24.
47  See, for example, *Truth in Aquinas*, 39, 43.
48  See, for example, *Truth in Aquinas*, 55.

}470{

*Natural Theology in St. Thomas's Early Doctrine of Truth*

Milbank and Pickstock, there is no autonomous philosophical knowledge of God,[49] save perhaps the barest glimmer that He exists[50]—and even this carries with it a glimpse of the Divine Essence, which can only be had by grace.[51]

Now, while it might indeed be the case that all understanding—like created existence itself—is ultimately participation in the Divine Truth and is therefore an effect of grace, it seems to me decidedly un-Thomistic to construe this as an indication that all truth is grounded in faith and is, thus, inherently theological. In fact, such a conclusion would only follow if 1) it were impossible for the natural realm to exist as dependent upon God while simultaneously being "natural," or 2) it were impossible for natural reason to know that God exists as cause of the world.[52] But, of course, Thomas's doctrine of creation is evidence that neither of these conditions holds—at least not in Thomas's mind. The first thing to be said here is that Thomas takes creation to be a philosophical doctrine: from our natural knowledge of the world, we can understand that the world is a contingent being and that it depends upon a God who necessarily exists.[53] Thus, we can have natural knowledge of God as cause of the world. Moreover, if we can have *natural* knowledge of anything, which natural knowledge is itself created by God (according to the assumption we have granted Milbank and Pickstock), then it must not be impossible for natural things to exist as dependent upon God while remaining "natural." Indeed, one would not even suspect such a

49  See, for example, *Truth in Aquinas*, xiii, 39, 55.
50  See, for example, *Truth in Aquinas*, 25, 30; see, however, 32.
51  See, for example, *Truth in Aquinas*, 32 and especially 39.
52  The force of the first disjunct is as follows: if it is impossible for something natural to depend on God, then there is no such thing as natural knowledge precisely because all knowledge is ultimately participation in God's knowledge. I take this point to address the ontological conditions that must hold before the epistemological possibility of natural knowledge of God (as addressed in the second disjunct) can be realized.
53  See, for example, *In II Sent.* 1.1.2 co.

}471{

RESTORING NATURE

thing unless one already believed that the natural must necessarily be separated from the divine, which, of course, Thomas does not. Accordingly, the fact that all truth ultimately derives from God's creative agency does not necessarily imply that the doctrine of truth falls within *sacra doctrina* nor that all rationality is grounded in faith.[54] (Indeed, the very suggestion reeks of fideism!)

Obviously, the status of Thomas's doctrine of truth is determined largely by the status of his doctrine of creation. Milbank seems to understand this, and it is worth nothing that he does argue against Thomas's having a purely philosophical doctrine of creation. His argument amounts to this: Thomas never sets forth such a doctrine in a text that is both 1) an independent work, and 2) completely free of properly theological elements.[55] To the first point, one might acknowledge that it is important to distinguish between what Thomas says in the voice of commentator and what he says in his own voice. But, while one should not assume that the two voices are identical, they do, in fact, often concur. Milbank's second qualification is more germane to our

54  A complete account of this matter would, of course, entail more detailed explanation of the differences between faith and reason, including the role of revelation as source of propositions accepted on faith and the role of the will in eliciting the intellect's assent to these propositions. For purposes of this paper, it suffices to note that the gift of faith, through an infusion of grace beyond the natural, operative and cooperative grace offered to all people, grasps truths not accessible to the natural reason. It might also be helpful to bear in mind here Thomas's general theory of the relationship between grace and nature: grace does not destroy nature, but perfects it. It follows, then, that faith neither destroys reason nor exists entirely separate from it; rather, through the grace that begets and proceeds from faith, the natural power of reason is elevated to grasp truths it otherwise could not. For St. Thomas's account of faith, see *ST* 2–2.1–15.

55  See *Truth in Aquinas*, 26. By "independent work," I mean a text in which Thomas is not commenting upon another authoritative text, such as a work of Aristotle or the *Sentences* of Peter Lombard.

}472{

*Natural Theology in St. Thomas's Early Doctrine of Truth*

concerns, though. To this second point, let us acknowledge that Thomas was a theologian by trade. Most of his writings were, accordingly, theological in nature. But that does not mean that there are not distinctly philosophical moments within his teaching, nor does it mean that those philosophical moments are not attainable by natural reason.[56] This is especially true of a doctrine like creation, which Thomas explicitly describes as being demonstrable by reason (even though this description occurs in a theological commentary).[57] Inasmuch as Thomas's doctrine of truth can be extracted from his doctrine of creation, I take it to be equally the case that truth is something that exists "naturally" and is naturally knowable to the philosopher.

## IV. Conclusion: Despoiling Nature in Thomas's Early Doctrine of Truth

In spite of their fundamental disagreement about whether or not Thomas's doctrine of truth is theological, Jan Aertsen, Catherine Pickstock and John Milbank all seem to share the same attitude toward the role of natural theology in Aquinas's doctrine. Aertsen, who expressly states that natural theology can be construed as a subset of philosophy, nevertheless makes incredible concessions

---

56  Nor, indeed, does it mean that Thomas did not write *any* philosophical works. A thorough defense of the claim that Thomas did leave a philosophical teaching embedded in his more properly theological texts would, of course, entail discussion of Thomas's various statements about the relationship between philosophy and theology, including *ST* 1.1.1, *Summa Contra Gentiles* (*ScG*) 1.7–9, and *In DT* 5.4.

57  It is beyond the scope of this paper to argue that creation is actually a philosophically demonstrable doctrine. However, it is clear enough that Thomas thinks it to be such. See, for example, *In II Sent.* 1.1.2 co.: "*Respondeo quod creationem esse, non tantum fides tenet, sed etiam ratio demonstrat.*" See also *ScG* 2.15–16; *In Phys.* bk. VIII, l. 3 (par. 996) and l. 21 (par. 1154); *De substantiis separatiis.* For a good introduction to the topic of creation in Aquinas's thought, see Baldner and Carroll, *Aquinas on Creation* (Toronto: PIMS, 1997).

}473{

RESTORING NATURE

in order to remove Thomas's doctrine of transcendental truth from its natural theological foundation. I can see no good philosophical reason for him to do this; in fact, it makes better philosophical and exegetical sense to reject the anthropological foundation of transcendental truth in favor of the theological foundation. However, I suspect that Aertsen's desires 1) to produce a medieval philosophy that is separate from theology and then 2) to identify this philosophy with the doctrine of the transcendentals (especially Thomas's doctrine of the transcendentals) has led him to reject even the hint of theological commitment that might be associated with the natural theological foundations of Thomas's early theory of truth. Thus, in his rush to claim Thomas's doctrine of truth for philosophy, Aertsen seems needlessly to have jettisoned natural theology. Milbank and Pickstock, on the other hand, rightly note that Thomas's theory of truth depends upon the Divine Intellect. However, because they reject the notion that natural reason can know God's existence and His activity as Creator, Pickstock and Milbank have attempted to claim for *sacra doctrina* teachings that most Thomists would recognize as natural theology. In the end, both parties seem to be trying to remove natural theology from Thomas's doctrine of truth, more likely because of their own contemporary agendas than because of any textual or systematic concerns emerging from Thomas's own statements. The shame is that in doing so, they conspire to rob the natural world of the divine—which is something it can scarcely afford to lose.

# Intellectus Agens:
# Why Does Thomas Trust De Anima III.5?
## Héctor Zagal
## Universidad Panamericana (Mexico City)

### 1. Introduction

This paper points out five problems within the argumentation used by Saint Thomas in his *Commentary on Aristotle's De anima* III, 5, lesson X. This argumentation deals with the following issues: (1) *intellectus agens* is like an artist; (2) *intellectus agens* is like light; (3) *intellectus agens* is not a habit; (4) *intellectus agens* is more noble (*nobilior*) than *intellectus possibilis*; (5) human knowledge and error.

The role of separated substances in human knowledge is basic in order to understand Thomas' position against Latin Averroism. According to Saint Thomas, *intellectus agens* is a certain light deriving from such separated substance.

Why does Aquinas introduce this metaphysical light in natural human knowledge?

Why does Aquinas try to synthesize Saint Augustine and Aristotle?

Would it not be easier to reject Aristotle's *De anima* in order to avoid Latin Averroism?

As a conclusion I will propose three reasons to explain why Thomas is interested in preventing readers of Aristotle's *De Anima* from Alexander's and Averroes' interpretations.

### 2. Light and Art: Two Ways of Explanation

*De anima* III, 5, 430a10 is well known as a problematic locus. What does Aristotle really think concerning the existence of the

RESTORING NATURE

intellect? For instance, During and Tricot[1] have pointed out that Aristotle never uses the expression *ho poietikós noûs* and that he uses only on one *occasion ho pathetikos nous.*

However, Aristotle does introduce the distinction of the understandings.[2] The distinction is in concordance with the principle of priority of *to energeia.*

The *intellectus agens* is the efficient cause of knowledge. It is impossible that the *intellectus possibilis* should begin to know without the intervention of an agent. Aristotle uses two analogies in order to explain the necessity of the agent intellect: "the art paradigm"[3] and "the light paradigm."[4]

## 2.1. Finality and Artifacts: the Model of Art

Let us concentrate on the first one, the art paradigm. Artificial beings are different from "natural" beings. However, in both there is one material cause and one principle of operation. In artifacts the principle is external. A hammer is an artificial being. The artisan uses tools as exterior instruments. On the contrary, a plant seeks the sun because its nature (*anima*) moves it to obtain its end: to live. *Intellectus* is no exception. There must be an active principle in the rational soul. This principle is called *intellectus agens.*

This is the first argument of *In De anima* III, 5, lesson X.

## 2.2. Act and Knowledge: the Model of Light

I will concentrate now on the model of light. I quote the main passage:

---

1   J. Tricot, *Aristote, De L'âme,* Vrin, Paris, 1969, p. 181. n.1.
2   See Victor Caston, "Aristotle's Two Intellects: a Modest Proposal," *Phonesis,* XLIV-3, 1999, p. 198.
3   *De an.* III, 5, 430a10–14.
4   This small book has been of great help to me: Antonio Robles Ortega: *La teoría del conocimiento en la tradición aristotélica (siglos IV a.C.-XIII d.C.),* Universidad de Granada, Granada (Spain), 1997.

}476{

## Intellectus Agens: Why Does Thomas Trust De Anima III.5?

> There is one intellect, which is able to become everything; and there is another one which acts upon everything, as a sort of state, as light; for light too, in a way, makes potential colors actual.[5]

*Intellectus agens* does not know. It is a necessary, but insufficient, condition of human knowledge. In this sense the analogy of light is appropriate. Light illuminates, makes things turn visible, but "light does not see." The analogy is also fortunate inasmuch as the source of light is usually exterior to the illuminated object.

Saint Thomas comments on this passage in a surprising manner. This light of the understanding is a participated light of the separated substances.

> And because this active force is a certain participation in the intellectual light of separated substances, the Philosopher compares it to a state and to light; which would not be an appropriate way of describing it if it were itself a separated substance.[6]

Thomas is audacious in making this interpretation if one takes into account the history of heresies. For instance, Valentin suggested that Jesus took his nature from another spiritual substance.

The passage just quoted does not admit many readings. The separated substances explain the efficiency of *intellectus agens*. Separated substances produce the *vis activa* of human intelligence.

Aquinas' references to separated substance become somewhat problematic for many reasons. Thomas presupposes the notion of "participation," which has been reviled by Aristotle himself in *Metaphysics* I, 8, and VIII, 6. Participation is assumed within the model of the light, but the model itself is metaphorical. Human action is in a manner an effect of separated substances. I am not sure if Saint Thomas is referring here to the angels (separated

5    *De an.* III, 5, 430a14–16.
6    *In De anima* III, 5, lesson X, n. 739.

}477{

RESTORING NATURE

metaphysical substances) or to celestial bodies. Found in favor of this second thesis is *De Veritate* ("About Prophesy"). Thomas affirms that foretelling is a natural action thanks to the intervention of the stars. Aquinas quotes Aristotle *On Dreams* in order to sustain such a thesis. If Thomas is thinking about angels when he speaks about separated substances, why does he introduce a revealed premise in a philosophical work? Saint Thomas does not read the passage following Saint Augustine. The doctrine of Illumination of Saint Augustine would have perhaps been able to explain the topic. But the price would have implied sacrificing human nature. On the contrary, Aquinas' theory of *intellectus agens* stresses the natural power of human beings.

As it appears, the argument based upon the light paradigm implies many problems. However, one of the merits of Thomas' commentary is to highlight the *quodammodo* in this famous metaphor and to make a beneficial use of the analogy. Colors, as much as the *intelligibilia*, are already present in matter.[7] Light and *intellectus agens* make the act of knowing them possible. Aquinas is here hindering Averroistic interpretations. Thomas underlines the limits of the *intellectus agens*. Light allows colors to be seen, but light itself does not see. Therefore *intellectus agens* could not be an acting substance.

### 3. Is *Intellectus Agens* a Habit?

After proving that human knowledge implies *intellectus agens*, Aquinas deals with an enigmatic sentence. Aristotle affirms that *intellectus agens* is a habit. According to Thomas, *intellectus agens* could not be the habit *primorum principiorum*. This intellectual virtue presupposes the actual presence in the mind of certain intelligible and understood objects. We are not able to apprehend the truth of first principles if we do not previously understand the meanings of the words. Therefore, the habit of *primorum principiorum* is different from the *intellectus agens*. Thomas is thinking of *Posterior Analytics* I, 1.

7   Cf. *In De an.* II, lesson. XIV, n. 400 and *In De an.* III, Lect. VIII, n. 717.

This argument is not enough in order to avoid Latin Averroism. Thus, Thomas introduces a corollary. *Intellectus agens* is denominated *hexis* by Aristotle in order to distinguish it as act. Aquinas plays with the Latin etymology. *"Habitum"* comes from *"habere."* *Habitum* is opposed to *privatio*. According to Thomas, Aristotle writes that *intellectus agens* is a habit because it is *energeia*. My objection is naïve: not all *energeia* is *hexis*.

## 4. Proving the Immateriality of *Intellectus Agens*

The tour de force of Aquinas' analysis is to be found in *In De anima* III, 5, lesson X, n. 733. Saint Thomas obliges himself to prove the four properties of *intellectus agens*: separation from matter, impassibility, purity (*sit immixtus*), and essentially in act. Following Thomas, I will concentrate in the fourth property. Thomas demonstrates that *intellectus agens* is essentially in act in three ways.

### 4.1. A Strange Proof: Agens Est Nobilior

These are the propositions which are central to the first argument:

(a) "Agens est honorabilius patiente."
(b) "Agens est principium activum materiae."
(c) "Intellectus agens comparatur ad possibilem sicut agens ad materiam."
(d) "Ergo, intellectus agens est nobilior possibili."
(e) "Sed intellectus possibilis est separatus, impassibilis et immixtus."
(f) "Ergo, multo magis intellectus agens."

Thus Aquinas announces the conclusion:

(g) "Ex hoc etiam patet, quod sit secundum substantiam in actu."

In order to reinforce (g), Saint Thomas expresses the proposition as the conclusion of the demonstration *quia* (*to hoti*): "quia agens est nobilus patiente, non nisi secundum quod est in actu."

}479{

RESTORING NATURE

The reasoning presupposes previous proofs and is hard hitting. Of course, attributing the property of "nobility" to the *intellectus* is a metaphorical statement. This turn of phrase is not an originality of Saint Thomas. Aristotle speaks of axioms, a term which comes from the Greek word *to axioma*, and which means in ordinary language "dignity, honor, category." The problem is that in this passage Saint Thomas speaks of grades of nobility and, parting from this gradation, infers that *intellectus agens* in essentially in act.

The nobility to which Saint Thomas refers is the "property" or "stage" of actuality. "P is nobler than Q, if P is in act and Q is not." The obliged question, therefore, is how to measure actuality? What is the index of *dynamis* and *energeia*? Luckily, Aristotle answers this question in *Metaphysics*: we should not seek a definition (*horos*) for everything. It is enough to capture the analogy by *epagoge*. Aristotle explicitly refers to the relationship between *dynamis* and *energeia*.[8] We should grasp the *horos* of *dynamis* by looking at nature. The tree trunk is a statue of Hermes in potency.

Let us be tough. Would a materialist accept the argument of the agent's nobility? Would he agree with our inductions? I guess not.

A materialist could object, for instance, against the premise (c): intellectus agens comparatur ad possibilem sicut agens ad materiam. The former "premise" is an analogy. In a way it is not a statement but a reasoning. In *Rhetoric* Aristotle studies the so-called rhetorical induction or reasoning by *paradeigma*.[9] Its structure is: A/B::C/?. This type of reasoning and explanation is fundamental in Catholic Theology, for instance, in this passage from the *Summa contra gentiles*:

> Sicut vita naturae corporis (a) est per animam (b), ita vita iustitiae ipsius animae (c) est per Deum (d).[10]

8   *Met. IX*, 6, 1048a35ff.
9   *Ret.* I, 2, 11357b72ff. I have referred to this in several places, for instance, "Metáfora y analogía en Santo Tomás," *Medievalia*, 29–30, 1999, p. 109ff.
10  *CG IV*, 17.

}480{

The force of such argument (a/b/c/d) rests on the *ratio* or proportion between both pairs of terms. This *ratio* allows the inference of (d), as when we reason: "If two ties cost ten dollars, then one tie costs five dollars." If the ratio is merely arithmetical, the conclusion is impeccable. It could be enunciated as a simple equation with one unknown. But our reasoning fails if the seller is proposing discounts. In the streets of Mexico, the cry "Two ties for ten pesos, one for six" can be often heard. The *ratio*, which is behind the analogy, is not a number. Aristotle warns that the *ratio* of the analogy cannot always be expressed by definitions or numbers. It appears at times ineffable. These considerations affect the argument brandished in *De anima* III, 5 by Aristotle and Thomas in order to sustain that the "intellectus agens sit secundum substantiam in actu" (g).

As it may be seen, we could easily take the analogy further than its strict terms. "Intellectus agens comparatur ad possibilem sicut agens ad materiam" is not a univocal statement.

## 4.2. The Treatise on Error: Sense and Understanding

According to Saint Thomas, *De anima* III, 4 deals with the immaterial nature of *intellectus possibilis*. Aristotle and Thomas develop the argument upon the analogy between perception and intellect. Saint Thomas's commentary develops the idea that in the way sense-perception is immaterial, so too, by analogy, is understanding.

The resemblance between sense and intellect implies some risks. Even though it is correct, Aristotle will have to distance himself more from this analogy inasmuch as the comparison may imply the pure passivity of intellect.

The analogy between sense and intellect has limits, which could compromise the spirituality of the human being. I want to emphasize this point. Saint Thomas is unusually obliged to correct Aristotle in *Metaphysics* II. In this book, Aristotle uses the celebrated comparison: our intellect is to the maximally intelligible what the eyes of a bat are to the sun. Here we transcribe Thomas' correction:

RESTORING NATURE

> Sed videtur haec similitudo non esse conveniens. Sensus enim quia est potentia organi corporalis, corrumpitur ex vehementia sensibilis. Intellectus autem, cum non sit potentia alicuius organi corporeri, non corrumpitur ex excellenti intelligibili. Unde post apprehensionem alicuius magni intelligibilis, non minus intelligibilia, sed magis, ut dicitur in tertio De Anima.[11]

Because of the insufficiency of the argument based on the analogy perception/understanding, Thomas resorts to a new argument in *In De anima* III, 5, lesson X.

Aristotle links the "spirituality" of intellect to the theory of error. Aristotle's strategy is fascinating:

> All these suppose the intellect to be something corporeal, like sensation, and that both sensing and judging are of 'like by like', as we explained at the beginning of his treatise. But they ought at the same time to have treated of error, ¾which is a state more natural to animals [than truth], and in which the soul spends the greater part of its time. So it must follow, either that all that seems to be really is (as some maintain) or that error is a contact with what is unlike ¾this being the contrary of knowing like by like.[12]

According to Thomas, Aristotle puts the argument in a very detailed way:

> He [Aristotle] shows the difference between understanding and sensation; and this in two ways; the first as follows. Understanding may be 'correct' or 'incorrect'. (n. 620)

11  *In Met.* II, lesson. I, 283.
12  *De an.* III 427a26ff.

}482{

*Intellectus Agens: Why Does Thomas Trust De Anima III.5?*

The possibility of being mistaken is a sign that the *intellectus* is not a corporal faculty.

As Aristotle introduces a problematic mention of the animals in *De anima* III, 3, Saint Thomas feels obliged to add a not very convincing precision. Why does Thomas accept that animals do have mistakes? Would it not be easier to correct Aristotle? Instead of this easy solution Aquinas explains:

> And since it might be objected that 'correct' understanding, at least, is the same as sensation, he adds that sensation is found in 'all animals' whilst understanding is found only in rational animals, that is, in men. For it is proper to man to come to an understanding of intelligible truth by way of rational enquiry; whereas the immaterial substances (*substantiae separatae*), which are in a higher degree intellectual, apprehend truth immediately without having to reason about it. Therefore 'correct' understanding is not the same as sensation. (n. 631)

The recourse to the separated substances in no way contributes to the explanation of our matter. Separate substances are more knowable *quoad se*, but not more knowable *quoad nos*. Thus, I wonder if the reference to such substances is a useful instrument against materialism.

The argument of error is problematic in the same extent as animals and human beings commit errors in knowledge. The strategy of Saint Thomas is to refer to separated substances, which, in this case, cannot but be angels.[13]

The distinction between sensibility and intellectual knowledge is not sharp. Further on, we read in *De anima* III, 3 (427b27ff):

> Concerning understanding (*noein*), since it is one thing and sensation another, while imagination seems to

---

13 See the diatribe against Averroes in Thomas's *Commentary on Aristotle's Physics* (VII) about the form of the celestial bodies.

RESTORING NATURE

differ from both of these and from opinion also (*hypolep-sis*), let us settle first what imagination is, and then speak of the other matter [opinion]. If, then, imagination is that by which we say that some phantasm arises within us, it follows (if we are not speaking metaphorically) that it is one of the faculties or a disposition in virtue of which we perceive and pronounce either falsely or truly. Such faculties are sensation, opinion, knowledge, understanding . . . But belief (*pistis*) follows immediately on opinion, for one never finds a man not believing the opinion that seems to him to be true. But there is no such thing as a belief (*pistis*) amongst animals, although there is imagination in many.

Aristotle has proportioned a valuable argument in order to distinguish between *intellectus* and perception. On this occasion, psychological attitudes become entangled. *Doxa* and *pistis* are not psychological states of animals. The proposition "beasts lack beliefs" is highly plausible. *Pistis* is a propositional attitude which supposes *doxa*. Opinion and belief suppose the possibility of reflection. That is to say, he who "opines" judges his own mental state.

The sentence:

(P) "I consider that Pericles was a good governor,"

is different from:

(Pᵃ) "Pericles was a good governor."

In sentence (P) there is a consciousness of the true and of error, of the possibility that we might be wrong regarding our evaluation of Pericles' government.

Saint Thomas' commentary does not contribute to blurring the distinction between *intellectus* and sense.

*Intellectus Agens: Why Does Thomas Trust De Anima III.5?*

For it seems that, as imagining is to the senses, so is opinion to the intellect. When we sense any sensible object we affirm that it is such and such, but when we imagine anything we make no such affirmation, we merely state that such and such seems or appears to us. The word 'imagination' [*phantasia*][14] itself is taken from seeing or appearing. Similarly, when we understand an intelligible object we affirm that it is such and such; but when we form opinions, we say that such and such seem or appear to us. For, as understanding depends upon sensing, so opinion depends on imagining. (n. 632)

In Saint Thomas' argument, the analogy between understanding/sense and opinion/*phantasia* contributes to the underlining of the reflexive aspect of knowledge. Thomas plays with the word *phantasia*. Opinion reflects upon the appearances. For example, "My girlfriend deceives me" as I found her drinking a martini with another man, is an opinion. When one admits that we are dealing with an opinion and not with an absolute judgment, one is reflecting. The *intellectus* implies a reflection upon the sense of perception. In this way, if we see a table levitating, we think that it is an "illusion" or a trick of some other kind. We are reflecting. Pure human perceptions are rare.

It should not be forgotten that the aim of Saint Thomas is to prove that the *intellectus* has no organ. Thomas considers that Aristotle "probat quod non sit idem opinio et phantasia, duabus rationibus." To guess, to estimate is an intellectual action, not a corporeal one.

The argument of the error is the best argument used in *De anima* III to defend the spirituality of intellect.

---

14  See n.668.

RESTORING NATURE

## 5. Aquinas Surrenders to Aristotle

Maritain is ironic with that well-known style of writing lectures. The scholar analyzes a specific argument or question in a classical author and then he criticizes it, just as I did.

What is my purpose? I will be sincere. I do think that Aquinas' *In De Anima* III, lesson X involves many complications. The reason is clear: Thomas surrenders faithfully to Aristotle's text.

I guess Thomas has three reasons for commenting on Aristotle in this way instead of simply rejecting him.

### 5.1. A Guide for Students

Aquinas wrote his commentaries on Aristotle in order to guide students and prevent them from Latin Averroism. Students had an urge to read Aristotle. It was better to guide than to forbid. Thomas succeeded because he commented on Aristotle using Aristotelian principles. This is why some scholars considered that Saint Thomas was an Averroist.

### 5.2. An Aristotelian Imperative

Aquinas notices that a separated *intellectus agens*, even though it is an Aristotelian-like statement, is incompatible with Aristotle's principles. Saint Thomas' argument against Alexander is brief and is in perfect consonance with the Aristotelian gist:

> for human nature would be a deficient nature if it lacked any one of the principles that it needs for its naturally appropriate activity of understanding; and this requires both potential and agent intellect. Hence, complete human nature requires that both of these be intrinsic to man. (n. 734)

Once again we find ourselves with a dialectical argument based on the principle of Nicomachus' *Ethics*: our natural desires

}486{

could not be vain.[15] This principle is inferred from another—more general—of physics: nature does nothing in vain. A human being who wishes to understand and who must resort to an exterior power in order to do so is a "naturally" incomplete human being. Natural desires without the natural sustenance to execute them *are contradictio in terminis*.[16]

## 5.3. The Hypostatic Union

I guess that Thomas ventures on Aristotle, against a certain Platonic tradition, because the Aristotelian concept of *physis* allows a clearer expression of the Trinitarian and Christological Mysteries. My thesis is that in the way that Aristotle conceives *physis*, it is feasible to adapt it as an instrument of the Catholic dogma. I am now referring to the hypostatic union.

The Incarnation of the Word implies that both natures united in the Second Person of the Blessed Trinity should preserve their own activity. In Jesus exists a divine *energeia* and another human *energeia*. It should be remembered that monophysitism had been recurrently condemned, as had monotelism. Monotelism (one *telos*) is a variation of monophysitism. Monotelism arose based on the doctrine of Sergio, Patriarch of Constantinople (610–619 A.D.) and Cyril of Alexandria (circa 631 A.D.). Cyril postulated the mono-ergestism in Christ. Jesus has one unique *energeia* in the Incarnate Word. Pope Martin I condemned this heresy (circa 649 A.D.). Obviously Saint Thomas was also familiar with these condemnations.

The Aristotelian *physis* is characterized by emphasizing that the principle of natural operations has its roots in each living being. The living being is the efficient cause of its own operations. The efficiency is proportional to the grade of being. In consequence, *energeia* is a manifestation of the particular nature.

15  Cf. *NE* I, 1094a21ff.
16  This response is implicit in the *Q. De anima* III, *corpus*: *Whether the possible intellect or the intellective soul is one for all human beings*.

RESTORING NATURE

Operatur sequitur esse, et modus operando sequitur modus essendi.

The Aristotelian *physis* referred to the hypostatic union is a guarantee against Docetism. If Christ acts as man, then he is man. There must be a proportion between the human *energeia* of Jesus and his *physis*. Only human beings can act humanly. The relationship between the human *agere* and the human nature is one to one. Human actions necessarily proceed from a human *physis*. I guess Thomas observes that the Aristotelian *physis* prevents us against Docetism. *Mutatis mutandi*, we can say the same of divine nature, called into question by Arianism. If Jesus executes divine actions, such as forgiving sins in his own name, then he is God.

The risk of Platonism is to put the final and the efficient cause outside of natural beings. This is the well-known objection of Aristotle against Plato. If species are causes, then corporeal beings will lack causality. Species exist "separated" from the singular and corporeal beings.

The separated existence of the *intellectus agens* may be the tribute that Aristotle pays to Plato. Aristotle does not surpass his master when separating the intellect.

## 6. Conclusion

Saint Thomas—judging by the arguments of *Contra gentiles*, *De Unitate Intellectus* and *In De Anima* III, X—recognizes that the doctrine of the separation of the *intellectus agens* attempts against a fundamental Aristotelian principle: that each being has in its own *ousia* the necessary powers to exercise natural operations.

This principle is crucial in the Christian doctrine of responsibility, and even more so in Christological studies. I believe that in this way the efforts of Saint Thomas to 'save' Aristotle are explained. Without hylemorphism, Docetism is a risk for Christianity. The separation of *intellectus agens* is in fact incompatible with the hylemorphic union of human body.

The resort to separated substances is an emergency solution that has some advantages: